Yellowstone & Grand Teton National Parks and Jackson Hole

A COMPLETE GUIDE

1ST EDITION

Yellowstone & Grand Teton National Parks and Jackson Hole

Jeff Welsch &
Sherry L. Moore

The Countryman Press
Woodstock, Vermont

Frontispiece: Credit: National Park Service

ISBN 978-1-58157-078-6

Cover photo by Tomas Kaspar Photography
Interior photos courtesy of the National Park Service unless otherwise specified
Book design by Bodenweber Design
Composition by PerfecType, Nashville, TN
Maps by Mapping Specialists Ltd., Madison, WI © The Countryman Press

Published by The Countryman Press, P.O. Box 748, Woodstock, Vermont 05091

Distributed by W. W. Norton & Company, Inc., 500 Fifth Avenue, New York, NY 10110

Manufactured in the United States of America

10 9 8 7 6 5 4 3 2 1

GREAT DESTINATIONS TRAVEL GUIDEBOOK SERIES

Recommended by *National Geographic Traveler* and *Travel + Leisure* magazines.

[A] CRISP AND CRITICAL APPROACH, FOR TRAVELERS WHO WANT TO LIVE LIKE LOCALS.
— *USA Today*

Great Destinations™ guidebooks are known for their comprehensive, critical coverage of regions of extraordinary cultural interest and natural beauty. The authors in this series are professional travel writers who have lived for many years in the regions they describe. Each title in this series is continuously updated with each printing to ensure accurate and timely information. All the books contain more than one hundred photographs and maps.

Current titles available:

THE ADIRONDACK BOOK

ATLANTA

AUSTIN, SAN ANTONIO
& THE TEXAS HILL COUNTRY

THE BERKSHIRE BOOK

BERMUDA

BIG SUR, MONTEREY BAY
& GOLD COAST WINE COUNTRY

CAPE CANAVERAL, COCOA BEACH
& FLORIDA'S SPACE COAST

THE CHARLESTON, SAVANNAH
& COASTAL ISLANDS BOOK

THE CHESAPEAKE BAY BOOK

THE COAST OF MAINE BOOK

COLORADO'S CLASSIC MOUNTAIN TOWNS:
GREAT DESTINATIONS

THE FINGER LAKES BOOK

THE FOUR CORNERS REGION

GALVESTON, SOUTH PADRE ISLAND
& THE TEXAS GULF COAST

THE HAMPTONS BOOK

HONOLULU & OAHU:
GREAT DESTINATIONS HAWAII

THE HUDSON VALLEY BOOK

THE JERSEY SHORE: ATLANTIC CITY TO
CAPE MAY (INCLUDES THE WILDWOODS)

LAS VEGAS

LOS CABOS & BAJA CALIFORNIA SUR:
GREAT DESTINATIONS MEXICO

MICHIGAN'S UPPER PENINSULA

MONTREAL & QUEBEC CITY:
GREAT DESTINATIONS CANADA

THE NANTUCKET BOOK

THE NAPA & SONOMA BOOK

NORTH CAROLINA'S OUTER BANKS
& THE CRYSTAL COAST

PALM BEACH, MIAMI & THE FLORIDA KEYS

PHOENIX, SCOTTSDALE, SEDONA
& CENTRAL ARIZONA

PLAYA DEL CARMEN, TULUM & THE RIVIERA
MAYA: GREAT DESTINATIONS MEXICO

SALT LAKE CITY, PARK CITY, PROVO
& UTAH'S HIGH COUNTRY RESORTS

SAN DIEGO & TIJUANA

SAN JUAN, VIEQUES & CULEBRA:
GREAT DESTINATIONS PUERTO RICO

THE SANTA FE & TAOS BOOK

THE SARASOTA, SANIBEL ISLAND
& NAPLES BOOK

THE SEATTLE & VANCOUVER BOOK: INCLUDES
THE OLYMPIC PENINSULA, VICTORIA & MORE

THE SHENANDOAH VALLEY BOOK

TOURING EAST COAST WINE COUNTRY

WASHINGTON D.C., AND NORTHERN VIRGINIA

YELLOWSTONE & GRAND TETON NATIONAL PARKS
AND JACKSON HOLE

YOSEMITE & THE SOUTHERN SIERRA NEVADA

If you are traveling to, moving to, residing in, or just interested in any (or all!) of these enchanting regions, a Great Destinations guidebook is a superior companion. Honest and painstakingly critical, full of information only a local can provide, Great Destinations guidebooks give you all the practical knowledge you need to enjoy the best of each region. Why not own them all?

ACKNOWLEDGMENTS

The authors would like to thank the many residents and visitors who shared their special insights into this magnificent region. A special thanks to Denny and Sally Becker of the Teton Treehouse Bed & Breakfast in Wilson, Wyoming, for pointing us in all the right directions in Jackson. Our gratitude also goes out to Pete and Jinny Coombs of the Diamond J Ranch in Ennis, the epitome of true Montana hospitality and spirit.

We'd also like to thank our family and friends for hanging in there with us during the research and writing of this book. Now that we're available again, you're all invited to come see us so we can share with you the abundant wonders of Yellowstone, Grand Teton and Jackson Hole.

From afar, we have long treasured the Greater Yellowstone ecosystem as one of the most extraordinary places the world. After three years of living in Yellowstone's backyard and a year immersed in research for this book, the depth of our appreciation, admiration and respect for this wild country has increased immeasurably. We are truly fortunate to be witnesses and have access to one of the planet's last great naturally functioning ecosystems.

Jeff Welsch and Sherry L. Moore
Belgrade, Montana
August 2007

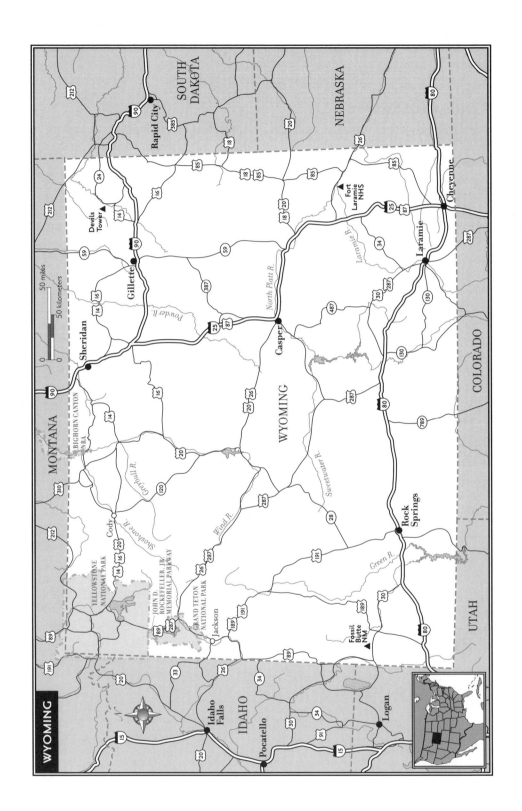

Contents

Hikers navigate one of the two trails to the summit of Mount Washburn in Yellowstone

Introduction

If wondrous scenery, incomparable wildlife viewing, riveting geology and the chance to witness a natural environment at work aren't enough incentive to put the Greater Yellowstone Ecosystem at the top of your vacation list, then how about this:

It could all be gone tomorrow, vanquished in a cataclysmic instant.

We're not talking about global warming. Or the encroaching masses of humanity that threaten to love Yellowstone National Park, Grand Teton National Park and Jackson Hole to death. Or a pen stroke from a presidential administration that, until a dramatic and unexpected reversal in June 2006, appeared to favor recreational desires over intrinsic values in our national parks.

We're not even talking about a recurrence of the dramatic 1988 fires that scorched one-third of Yellowstone's 2.2 million acres, from which the park has made an astonishing recovery.

It's far more ominous than that.

It's megatons of pent-up geothermal fury, poised to unleash its ire on the planet much the way it did about 640,000 years ago . . . and about 700,000 years before that . . . and about 700,000 years before that.

Detect a trend?

Maybe. Or maybe not. Scientists can't say for sure when, or if, the molten rock just beneath Yellowstone's 1,500-square-mile caldera will erupt in such a violent manner as to make Mount St. Helen's seem like a hiccup.

Of course, such natural shock and awe wouldn't bode well for those of us living downstream—downstream being everywhere from West Yellowstone to West Philadelphia. But truth be known, this uneasy alliance between man and nature is part of the allure of the world's first national park and its majestic younger sibling 8 miles to the south.

For as you marvel at the jagged fault-blocked Grand Tetons rising abruptly above Jackson Lake to a cloudless sky, you'll contemplate the silent rumblings underfoot and realize that Mother Nature sets the ground rules here. As you admire the belching, hissing and spewing of Yellowstone's 10,000 geothermal features, you'll respect just how alive and unpredictable this planet truly is.

As you perhaps glimpse a pack of wolves hunting down an aging elk, or coyotes herding a frightened pronghorn or a young bison suffocating in a bog, you'll begin to understand that the beauty of this extraordinary ecosystem lies partly in its cruelty.

And that's just the point.

Yellowstone and Teton are not drive-thru zoos.

You'd never guess it by the summer "bear jams" and the occasional tales of camera-toting tourists gored by elk, charged by bison or warned with an irritated snort by protective mother bears.

Many among the 3 million who visit each year forget this axiom, and often pay a price, sometimes with their lives. Every year, people who treat this deceptively tranquil island of wilderness with cavalier hubris or carelessness tumble over cliffs, drown in swift rivers, fall into boiling geysers or meet some other tragic fate.

It's understandable why some might disregard nature's laws.

When the world's first national park was created in 1872, the idea was to preserve a place of natural beauty, yes, but purely for human benefit. Predators deemed contrary to this vision were eradicated, most notably wolves, mountains lions and grizzlies. Hunting was allowed and poaching was common. At one time, federal officials slaughtered thousands of elk because they overgrazed the park. Bison were pushed perilously close to extinction. Until the 1960s, bears routinely congregated at the parks' entrances for food handouts from giddy tourists, a petting-zoo image perpetuated on Saturday mornings by Yogi, Boo Boo and Jellystone Park.

For the past three decades, efforts have been made to inch Yellowstone and the adjoining 310,000 acres of Grand Teton as close as humanly possible to their natural states. Hunting is now prohibited. Fishing is strictly regulated. Animals within the parks are protected. Sensitive areas are off-limits to human traffic. Snowmobile use is limited, for now.

The crowning moment of this earth-first philosophy came in 1995, when 31 gray wolves from Canada were introduced into Yellowstone's northern range. The controversial transplant brought the park's ecology full circle seven decades after a government-sponsored slaughter ended with the shooting of the last wolf.

Many scientists credit the thriving packs with restoring the health of the ailing Lamar River Valley ecosystem. This so-called "trophic cascade" starts with the fear *Canis lupus* has re-instilled in elk, their favorite cuisine. No longer able to casually browse, the elk have become more nomadic, allowing cottonwood, willow and aspen to regenerate after 70 years of futility. The new plant growth in the Lamar has led to the return of songbirds and beavers, whose dams have created improved habitat for the struggling Yellowstone cutthroat trout. In turn, newly sprouted streamside berry bushes are providing forage for the endangered grizzly bear, whose existence has been threatened partly by beetle and fungus decimation of whitebark pines.

Remarkably, much of this grand ecological experiment has taken place right in front of our eyes. Nowhere on the planet are wolves more readily visible to the public. Thus, the return of a creature still vilified in the ranching community as a frothing livestock predator has been a year-round economic boon to gateway towns. An estimated 250,000 people have seen wolves in Yellowstone's wilds nearly every day since 2000.

It's true that visitors must tread lightly in Yellowstone and Grand Teton, but lest anyone find the regulations too limiting, there is a rich assortment of outdoor and man-made indoor pleasures on the fringes of the two parks and in the sage valley known as Jackson Hole.

River runners ply the Snake River's Class III rapids south of Jackson. West Yellowstone touts itself as the snowmobile capital of the world, with Cody and Cooke City not far behind. The rivers cascading out of Yellowstone and Grand Teton offer the finest trout fishing on earth, with hundreds of guides eager to share their second-favorite holes. Five downhill ski resorts are within 50 miles of either park. Jackson Hole is a mountain biker's mecca worthy of mention in the same breath as Moab. Snowmobilers miffed at tightening regulations in Yellowstone have found rich playgrounds in the surrounding national forests. And nearby federal wilderness areas provide adventure for visitors wishing to see the land much the way Jim Bridger and John Colter saw it in the early 19th century.

The burgeoning surrounding communities of Jackson, Dubois and Cody in Wyoming; Ennis, Gardiner, Red Lodge, Livingston, Bozeman and West Yellowstone in Montana; and Driggs, Ashton and Idaho Falls in Idaho offer diverse restaurant fare and comfortable lodging ranging from the provincially rustic to cowboy-lux guest ranches. As for culture, you can attend a rodeo or fish fry one night and catch the symphony or a minor-league baseball game the next.

For those wanting the full park experience, rustic lodging and basic dining are available inside both parks, from frontier luxury at historic Old Faithful Inn and Jenny Lake Lodge to no-frills rooms at Mammoth Hot Springs and bare-bones cabins at Tower Junction. Campgrounds are plentiful. And there's always the certainty of solitude in the backcountry.

Some 98 percent of Yellowstone's visitors traverse less than 2 percent of the park. For that, the flora, fauna and natural splendor of Yellowstone, Grand Teton and Jackson Hole are grateful. After all, despite the millions of acres of wild country, these parks are still mere islands in a sea of humanity rapidly squeezing in from all sides. Their futures are by no means secure, even as current management practices nudge them toward more naturally functioning ecosystems where humans are expected to leave only footprints and dollars.

Today, those who put Yellowstone and Grand Teton at the top of their vacation lists can still discover that Mother Nature has reserved some of her finest handiwork for northwest Wyoming and narrow slices of Montana and Idaho. That's true whether your tastes lean toward the towering backdrop of the snowcapped Tetons or the intricate web of life spun in front of your eyes in vast Yellowstone.

And part of this allure is in the understanding that what Mother Nature gives she can also take away in a cataclysmic instant.

—Jeff Welsch

An artist has a young audience while painting on a Firehole River bridge.

THE WAY THIS BOOK WORKS

Unlike most travel guides on Yellowstone National Park, Grand Teton National Park and Jackson Hole, which treat the three areas as distinct entities, we're combining them as if they're the one large ecosystem—and vacation destination—that they are. Our book's eight chapters are delineated by specific interests or informational needs because most likely your visit will include lodging, dining, attractions and recreation in all three places.

The regions are distinguished within each chapter so that if, for example, you plan to stay in Yellowstone two nights, Grand Teton two nights and Jackson three nights, all of your choices will be conveniently located a few pages apart. When you're ready to contemplate meals, options are similarly within the same chapter. If you're looking for a specific restaurant or hotel, check the indexes at the back of the book for the page number. In addition, services available in the parks are separated from services available in the surrounding gateway communities, where most commercial activity takes place.

In each chapter, entries are listed alphabetically, with a few exceptions where the sheer volume of one particular listing begs for it to be first. For example, in Chapter 7, which covers shopping, Jackson's art galleries are listed first.

Every attempt has been made to organize important information so that it is easily found and understood, but changes do occur regularly in tourist areas. What might have been true last week might not be so during your visit. Many businesses, including lodging and restaurants, will change their hours and rates or even close altogether at the whim of the weather, which can be fickle in these parts. The good news for visitors to Yellowstone and Grand Teton is that the apparent global warming trend has meant longer seasons. Rates tend to be lower in the spring and fall, between busy seasons.

Because of the dramatic differences in lodging prices between seasons, we've listed a range, showing the summer and winter rates where possible. For dining, we've used price codes as follows:

Inexpensive: Up to $15
Moderate: $15–30
Expensive: $30–65
Very Expensive: Over $65
Credit Cards are abbreviated as follows:

AE—American Express	CB—Carte Blanche	D—Discover Card
DC—Diner's Club	MC—Master Card	V—Visa

The area code for Yellowstone, Grand Teton and the Jackson Hole region is 307. Montana is 406 and Idaho 208.

NEARBY CITIES

Except for Jackson, which at 8,650 is no metropolis, the gateway communities neighboring Yellowstone and Grand Teton are small and thus offer limited amenities, most geared toward tourist needs—quick meals, cameras, outdoor gear, etc. If you need a broader range of goods, stop on the way in Billings, Bozeman, Butte, Idaho Falls, Pocatello or Salt Lake City. Even though some of these towns are small in their own right, they serve as regional hubs and have all the usual big-box suspects. They have many of the chain restaurants and motels that are sparse in the park gateway communities.

Big Sky, Montana

It's incomprehensible now, but less than four decades ago the West Fork was just another picturesque creek tumbling eastward through a forested canyon toward the Gallatin River. In the late 1960s, *NBC Nightly News* anchor Chet Huntley rode on horseback into what is now known as Mountain Meadows, initially envisioning a golf course. Once he saw towering Lone Mountain to the west, his thoughts shifted to skiing. In 1973, Big Sky Resort opened and quickly became a destination resort on par with Sun Valley, Aspen and Whistler. Today, homes are sprouting, huge hotels rise from the mountainsides and two ski areas cover thousands of acres of deep-powder terrain blessed with sunny skies. For the most part, Big Sky doesn't have the pretentiousness of some resorts, with the exception of the gated Yellowstone Club. The 'Y' Club, with mansions scattered among the lodgepoles, is pretentiousness defined: The most expensive home in world history, a 53,000-square-foot palace on 160 acres offered for $155 million, was to be completed in 2007 (it surpasses a $139 million castle in England). Don't let that scare you away. Even if Big Sky often looks as if construction was done willy-nilly with little thought to environmental impacts, there is actually some affordable lodging, great fishing on the Gallatin and reasonably priced skiing—and you're within an hour of Yellowstone's West Entrance.

Bozeman, Montana   120 miles to Old Faithful (2 hrs 30 min)

Few Intermountain West communities have undergone a more dramatic metamorphosis than Bozeman. Once a cowboy town known mostly for the agriculture school at Montana State University, this town of 38,000 in a broad valley surrounded by towering mountains has become so trendy that many locals deride it as "Boz-Angeles." Art galleries, boutiques and a wine bar share a red-brick Main Street with an Army-Navy outlet and burger joints, and MSU is known now more for filmmaking and engineering. Perhaps it was inevitable, given the access to unparalleled trout fishing, deep snow for powder hounds and proximity to Yellowstone. But there's no doubt that the dramatic evolution was hastened by what locals refer to simply as "The Movie." Robert Redford's beautifully filmed version of Norman Maclean's novella *A River Runs Through It* called attention to the area's natural qualities. Flocks of fly fishermen descended on the Madison, Gallatin and Yellowstone Rivers, many staying and building the trophy homes that dot the landscape. Legend has it that Redford was so chagrined by the impact on the Gallatin Valley that when he returned to film *The Horse Whisperer* in the nearby Boulder River Valley, he wouldn't reveal on screen the movie's location. Unabashed sprawl and the loss of small-town charm aren't without benefits. Downtown is alive at night and there is ample entertainment, dining and lodging. The Museum of the Rockies offers a captivating look into the planet's distant past. And the trout fishing is still the best in America.

Ennis, Montana   102 miles to Old Faithful (2 hrs 8 min)

It started as an outpost to supply feverish gold miners at nearby Virginia City and grew into a cattle town, but now two words define this quaint western community of 1,000: fly fishing. The world-renowned Madison River flows past the eastern edge of Ennis, in the heart of the Madison Valley, luring fly anglers for much of the summer and into the fall. A number of dude ranches are in a wide valley sandwiched by the Madison Range to the east and Gravellys to the west, helping the area to retain much of an unspoiled, Old West feel. There's just enough to cover your basic vacation needs, which makes it an ideal base for visiting Yellowstone if you like to avoid crowds. For pure western Americana, make a point of attending the Fourth of July parade and rodeo. Ennis is especially quiet in the winter and spring, when the winds blow. The serenity could disappear if the private gravel road from Ennis to the Moonlight Basin Resort at Big Sky is ever opened to the public, as has been rumored for years. Currently, a manned gate greets travelers who drive up dusty Jacks Creek, and generally only employees are allowed passage. A public thoroughfare would likely turn Ennis into a destination stop for Big Sky visitors weary of the gorgeous but winding and dangerous US191 drive up the Gallatin Canyon from Bozeman.

Idaho Falls, Idaho *143 miles to Yellowstone (2hrs 47min)*

Like so many of the towns in this region, Idaho Falls began as an outpost along the Snake River to serve miners. Later, when the mines played out, Mormon pioneers moved into the area, giving eastern Idaho the highest concentration of LDS members outside of Utah. Today, even as Idaho Falls has evolved into a jumping-off point for Yellowstone and Grand Teton National Parks, the Mormon presence is still felt. It isn't easy finding stores open on Sundays in Idaho Falls (population 50,000) and surrounding small towns. This is the potato country for which Idaho is renowned, though in the colder, higher-altitude climes of the northeastern part of the state, seed potatoes are the prime crop. The largest irrigation canal in the world was built here to provide sustenance for potatoes, sugar beets and other crops. In the past few decades, the town has become more diverse, with folks moving in from elsewhere looking for a simpler life. In addition, many employees of the Idaho National Laboratories live in the city and commute via bus to the nuclear facility in the stark Craters of the Moon country 30 miles to the west. Idaho Falls is a good place to gear up before heading toward the parks because it has many of the chain stores, lodges and restaurants.

Lander, Wyoming *196 miles (3hrs 54min)*

For many tourists making the Yellowstone-Teton pilgrimage from the Midwest or East, Lander provides that first hint that they're getting close to outdoor nirvana. This charming community of 7,000, which sits in a broad, sunny valley at the base of the southern end of the majestic Wind Rivers, has made the classic Intermountain West evolution. Once a resource-extraction center, its natural beauty and slower pace have lured outdoor enthusiasts, 1960s throwbacks and folks with a creative bent, especially telecommuting writers, artists and photographers. They seem to blend seamlessly with Fremont County's prolific cattle and sheep ranchers. The National Outdoor Leadership School is headquartered here, and this decidedly western town along the Popo Agie River is a fine base for rock climbing adventures in the rugged Wind Rivers or Sinks Canyon State Park, where the river disappears into a cave. One reason Lander has been able to retain much of its small-town persona is that residents need only travel 25 miles to the northeast, to Riverton on the Wind River Indian Reservation, for big-box and other work-a-day amenities. Lander isn't as well-known as such similarly blessed mountain communities as Livingston and Telluride, but it came as no surprise to the town's residents that *Outside* magazine once ranked it as one of America's "Dream Towns."

Livingston, Montana *111 miles to Old Faithful (2hrs 44min)*

This is a classic example of a town reinventing itself. In the mid-1980s, the Burlington Northern Railroad pulled out of Livingston. Other communities might've folded, but Livingston had a hole card that other industrial towns don't: a stunningly beautiful setting. It sits at the foot of the Absaroka Mountains where the Yellowstone River emerges from Paradise Valley and turns east for its journey across the plains. A raw exterior remains, thanks to the brick remnants of the railroad plant, where locomotives are still repaired, but a closer inspection reveals a low-key, intimate vibrancy that makes residents feel as if they're living in the best-kept secret in America. It isn't uncommon to see such celebrities as movie stars, authors and artists walking amid the townsfolk wearing jeans and sweatshirts, earning little more than a passing nod as they wander between the 13 art galleries, eclectic restaurants and fly-fishing businesses. The lure is Paradise Valley, which is framed by the Absarokas and Gallatins between Livingston and Yellowstone National Park. Livingston's denizens spend much of their summers in the valley, floating the serpentine river as it winds gently amid the cottonwoods. Living here does require some toughness: The winter winds are so ferocious that empty railroad cars are known to topple over. The local joke is that you can tell when the wind has stopped . . . everyone falls down. Then again, the wind scours the valley, keeping it clear of snow much of the winter, a historical phenomenon that made it a mecca for wildlife and the Crow Indians. Hence the name Paradise Valley.

Pinedale, Wyoming *174 miles to Old Faithful (3hrs 57min)*

There are few better places to witness a contentious clash of cultures than Pinedale (pop. 1,500), on the western base of the majestic Wind River Range. Its proximity to the Wind Rivers, the Wyoming Range, the parks, numerous lakes and prolific big game make it an outdoor shrine. The town also clings to its mountain-man roots; the Museum of the Mountain Man is here. Like much of southwest Wyoming, it also sits atop vast reserves of a natural gas called coal-bed methane. Thousands of wells have been drilled in Wyoming's Powder River basin in the state's northeast corner, and thousands more could spring up on the stark high-desert landscape south of Pinedale to slake a nation's appetite for natural gas. Thing is, many of these remote areas are the strongholds of such wildlife as elk and pronghorn. Aside from fears that the wells and roads will interrupt migratory routes, coalbed methane extraction requires extensive amounts of groundwater in drought-stricken, barren country. The controversy has split rural communities like Pinedale, which like the money drilling has brought but also recognize the value of tourism and a pristine environment. Coal-bed methane has poured money into schools and other infrastructure throughout the state. On the other hand, Pinedale's setting in the upper Green River basin is as picturesque as any, and it's not unusual to see a moose or bear wandering into the city limits. Other Intermountain West states are proceeding with a much more cautionary approach toward coal-bed methane than Wyoming, which has always been the first to queue up for an energy boom and the first to pay the price during the inevitable bust. Stay tuned.

Pocatello, Idaho *189 miles (3hrs 25min)*

"Poky" has the undeserved reputation as the "Armpit of Idaho," thanks to the steam-belching phosphate plant just off Interstate 86—the first sight for many tourists. Truth is, Pocatello's setting in the Portneuf River Valley between rounded, juniper-covered hills is more picturesque than that of Idaho Falls, which sits in a broad plain. Furthermore, the town of 50,000 is the home of Idaho State University, giving it a cultural edge over neighboring communities. Another unique feature of Pocatello: It is an island of diversity in a sea of Mormon towns. Its founding as an important railroad town in the late 1800s brought a diversity of families, including some of the first African Americans to live in Idaho. At one time, Pocatello had more black people than the rest of the state combined. The town is a testament to forward thinking. ISU's Holt Arena is the oldest enclosed football stadium on a college campus and the second oldest of any kind in the nation, behind only the Houston Astrodome. Pocatello has put some effort into selling itself as a gateway to the parks, with mixed success. It does share an airport with Idaho Falls, but most visitors arriving there are heading toward the parks, meaning they're veering away from Pocatello.

Red Lodge, Montana 180 miles (4hrs 9min)

This appealing town of 2,000 at the foot of the mighty Beartooth Mountains is the largest community on the last relatively undeveloped corridor to Yellowstone. Originally a coal-mining town, Red Lodge was best known for years as the starting point for the breath taking drive on the "Highway to the Sky" into the Beartooths. As the town is proud of noting, former CBS newsman Charles Kuralt dubbed it "the most beautiful roadway in America." The highway, built from 1931 to 1936 to help Red Lodge escape the claws of the Great Depression, reaches 10,000 feet en route to Cooke City and Yellowstone's Northeast Entrance. The influx of tourists helped offset the shutting down of the coal industry and eased the sting of the worst mining disaster (73 died) in Montana history. More and more, Red Lodge is moving away from its grimy roots and capitalizing on all the outdoor possibilities, the arts and the Beartooth Highway. Skiing, mountain biking, golfing, fishing and the brewery are favored activities, and the town offers numerous entertaining events. The Pollard Hotel meshes frontier history with contemporary amenities. On the Fourth of July, Red Lodge can get as wild and woolly as it did in its days of yore.

HISTORY

GEOLOGY

Yellowstone National Park

Relax. You're not going to be vaporized by a sudden rumbling from the Earth's most schizo-phrenic subsurface. When the time comes, scientists believe the fury beneath the greater Yellowstone ecosystem will provide plenty of warning, in which case you'll want to book the first flight to Mars because the third rock from the sun quite likely will need some major restoration before humans can inhabit it again.

It's all because the earth under Yellowstone is tossing, turning, pushing, pulling, hiss-ing, snorting and heaving unlike anywhere else on the planet so accessible to humans. Some 40 such super-volcano "hot spots" exist worldwide, but most are deep beneath the oceans—though Hawaii's Kilauea volcano and Iceland reveal similar geological unrest on a much smaller scale.

Yellowstone's 10,000-plus geysers, hot springs, fumaroles, travertine terraces, mud pots and paint pots comprise more geothermal activity than the rest of the globe com-bined. Some 1,000 to 3,000 earthquakes are measured annually, and there have been 30 quakes rated 5.5 or higher on the Richter scale since 1900. And this activity offers a mere glimpse of the underground roiling that's stretched from northwest Wyoming to northern Nevada since the first of three major eruptions 2.1 million years ago. The numbers from that initial blast are staggering. More than 600 cubic miles of ash rode air currents to the Pacific Ocean, Midwest, Gulf of Mexico and Canada, covering thousands of square miles in minutes. Compare that to Mount St. Helen's minuscule .026 cubic miles of ash covering 11 states. And it surely wasn't the first major eruption. Specimen Ridge, which features 27 fossilized forests stacked on top of one another, including the preserved remnants of red-woods, oaks, mangrove and breadfruit, has petrified trees dated to 50 million years old.

The simple explanation for all this hyper-terra activity is that Yellowstone is mostly a giant caldera sitting atop a combustible fire pit where molten rock, otherwise known as magma, is a mere 3 to 5 miles below the surface. In that initial blast, mountains were blown to smithereens and the land collapsed, creating a gaping 1,300-square-mile hole. By comparison, Oregon's Crater Lake, another volcanic mountain that collapsed when it erupted, is 37 times smaller. While Crater Lake filled with water after the collapse of Mount Mazama, Yellowstone's caldera was carpeted by lodgepole pine, rock, streams, plains, steamy vents and large lakes.

What remains in Wyoming's far northwest corner is a circular thin and delicate crust stretching roughly from Lewis Lake on the south and Lake Butte on the east to Norris/Canyon Village on the north and the Montana-Idaho border on the west. The gaps and fissures in the Earth's surface, combined with the magma's shallow depth, ensured the meeting of fire and water. The result is hot spots ranging from the Old Faithful geyser's dramatic eruptions every 90 minutes and the hissing of steamy fumaroles at Roaring Mountain to gurgling mud pots scattered throughout Geyser Basin and the graceful travertine terraces of Mammoth Hot Springs—all different in appearance and definition.

Here's a brief look at the four thermal features for which Yellowstone is famed:

* **Geysers**: The best-known of Yellowstone's thermal attractions are the least common: about 3 percent. Still, the park's 250 geysers (Icelandic for "gush forth") represent more than half of the world's total, and except perhaps for Mammoth Hot Springs, no type of thermal feature draws more tourists. Geysers are formed when water and snow seep into the hot rock. As the heated water rises above the cold water and races to the surface, it expands and becomes trapped by steam bubbles in a chamber of resistant rhyolite rock. ("Rhyolite" comes from the Greek word for stream and is named for its many striking colorful flow bands, including obsidian and quartz.) The pressure eventually forces it skyward violently. Think of your kitchen pressure cooker. Even geysers are distinct: Fountain geysers spray water widely, while cone geysers, like Old Faithful, are more like an uncorked fire hydrant. Most of Yellowstone's geysers are distributed throughout nine basins, about half in Upper Geyser Basin, where Old Faithful's reliability has lured millions of visitors from the world over. For a geyser treat unfettered by crowds, try the 17-mile roundtrip hike into Shoshone Geyser Basin near Grant's Pass. If you're extremely lucky, you'll be in Yellowstone for a rare eruption of Steamboat Geyser near Norris. At up to 300 feet high, it reigns as the world's largest geyser. Don't hold your breath: Steamboat can go as long as 50 years without blowing its top, and as of the fall of 2007, it had waited more than two years.

* **Hot springs**: They're the same as geysers, without the drama. Most of Yellowstone's hot springs merely spill out of the ground at temperatures nearing 200 degrees, though Crested Pool has been known to explode even though it has no constrictions. The Rockies and Cascade Range of Oregon and Washington are dotted with thousands of hot springs, many offering a welcome respite for the sore muscles of hikers, skiers, boaters, etc. But anyone looking for such relief in Yellowstone will be—pardon the pun—sorely disappointed. For safety reasons, the park does not allow soaking in thermal pools, even in the backcountry. Tourists have scalded themselves and even died. Some springs carry potentially deadly microorganisms. Besides, finding the right temperature mix is a challenge: Most springs are too hot, and the stream water too cold. A pleasurable exception is Boiling River, which spills into the Gardner River just inside the North Entrance at Gardiner, and a few renowned swimming holes on the Firehole River.

* **Fumaroles**: These are geysers without the water, much of which has been vaporized by the time it reaches the surface. Fumaroles are known for their hissing sounds and rotten-egg smell of hydrogen sulfide, most notably at Soda Butte in the Lamar Valley. The appropriately named Roaring Mountain, just north of Norris on the east side of the road, is the most prominent example of fumaroles.

* **Mud pots**: Take a hot spring, add mud and subtract a consistent water source. Presto, you've got a mud pot. Mud pots rely on snow and rain for subsistence. The bubbling, which has the look of a witch's brew, is from escaping gasses. Add minerals to the recipe, and you've got a colorful paint pot. Check out the Artist's Paint Pots southwest of Norris, the Fountain Paint Pot Nature Trail in Lower Geyser Basin and the West Thumb Paint Pots.

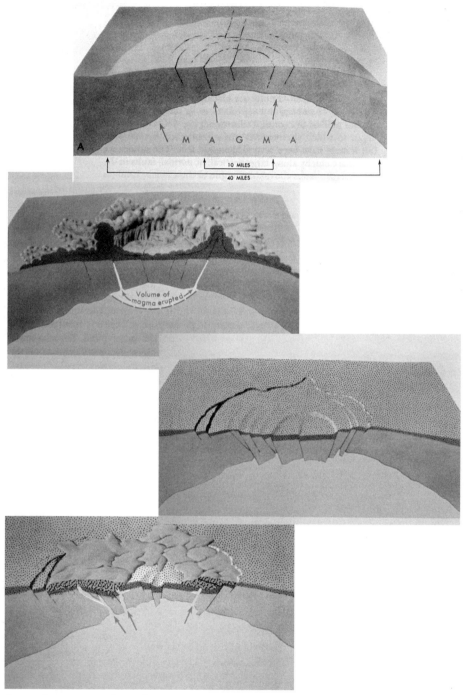

Super-volcano eruptions begin when magma rises to create a boiling reservoir at the Earth's crust. The reservoir expands dramatically until the violent pressure causes an eruption. The Yellowstone super-volcano has erupted three times in the past 2.1 million years. Each formed a large caldera. Yellowstone caldera illustrations 1–4 show how the super-volcano erupted 2.1 million, 1.4 million and 640,000 years ago. National Park Service

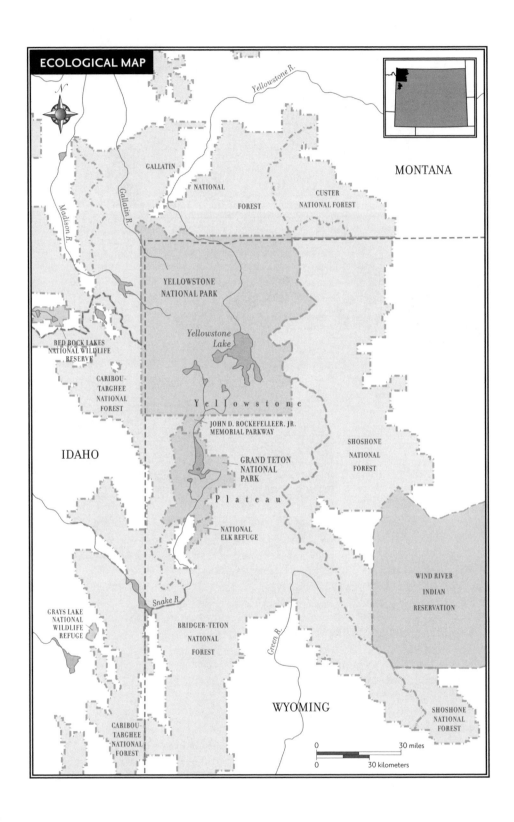

ECOLOGICAL MAP

N

MONTANA

GALLATIN

NATIONAL

FOREST

CUSTER
NATIONAL FOREST

Yellowstone R.

Gallatin R.

Madison R.

YELLOWSTONE
NATIONAL PARK

*Yellowstone
Lake*

RED ROCK LAKES
NATIONAL WILDLIFE
RESERVE

CARIBOU-
TARGHEE
NATIONAL
FOREST

Y e l l o w s t o n e

JOHN D. ROCKEFELLEER, JR.
MEMORIAL PARKWAY

GRAND TETON
NATIONAL
PARK

SHOSHONE

NATIONAL

FOREST

IDAHO

P l a t e a u

NATIONAL
ELK REFUGE

WIND RIVER

INDIAN

RESERVATION

Snake R.

GRAYS LAKE
NATIONAL
WILDLIFE
REFUGE

BRIDGER-TETON

NATIONAL

FOREST

Green R.

WYOMING

SHOSHONE

NATIONAL
FOREST

CARIBOU-
TARGHEE
NATIONAL
FOREST

0   30 miles

0   30 kilometers

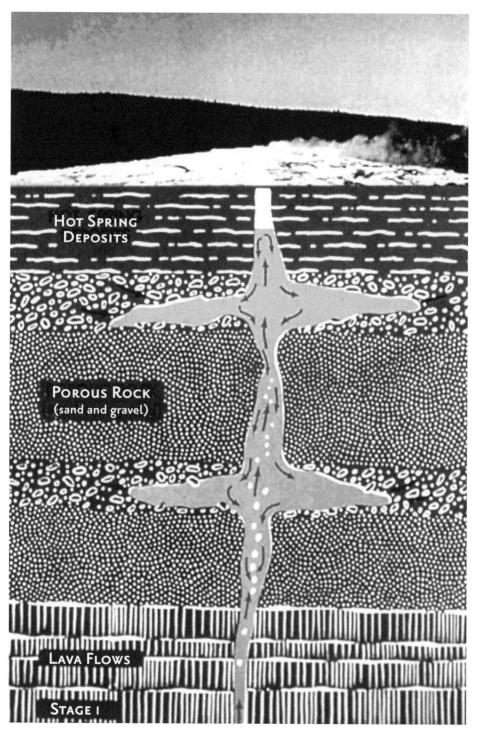

How geysers work. National Park Service

Yellowstone's geothermal activity is also at least initially responsible for the park's most breathtaking feature: the Grand Canyon of the Yellowstone. Twenty miles long, up to 1,200 feet deep and ranging from 1,000 to 4,000 feet across, the Grand Canyon's story begins with the arrival of glaciers whose impact would be felt as far south as the Tetons. The glaciers dammed the Yellowstone River, forming lakes. When they retreated, water poured forth and eroded lava rocks made vulnerable by the hot gasses just beneath the surface. The rocks, called rhyolite, weren't always so submissive to the onrushing water in two notable spots—one at the edge of the caldera, the other at the meeting point of two different types of rhyolite. These spots are now recognized as the Lower Falls (308 feet) and Upper Falls (109 feet) of the Yellowstone. Both are favorites of the tourist's camera because of the dramatic drops, colorful hues of the canyon walls and mists that can create surreal light at the right moments. Small wonder that the most popular vantage points are called Inspiration Point, Artist Point and Grandview. Both falls are near Canyon Village in the heart of the park, and accessible from the road.

Also inspiring is the northern range, generally the one part of the park where visitors will find the type of towering mountains they might expect from a western vacation. This region is no less extraordinary for the dramatic gap in age between the Gallatin and Absaroka Mountains on the west, north and east, and the Washburn Range and Red Mountains to the south. Both tower above the Yellowstone, Gardner and Lamar River Valleys. Yet the Gallatins and Absarokas are about 50 million years old; meanwhile, the area between the Washburns and Reds, best seen from 8,859-foot Dunraven Pass, is a product of Yellowstone's most recent major eruption 640,000 years ago. The hike to the top of 10,243-foot Mount Washburn just north of the caldera provides a dramatic look at this explosive past. Rivulets of water cascade down these high peaks into the Lamar River, which cuts a sagebrush plain renowned for its wildlife, including the most prolific wolf sightings anywhere on the planet over the past 10 years.

Grand Teton National Park/Jackson Hole

Surrounding Yellowstone's caldera are some of America's most dramatic, rugged and wild mountain ranges, some almost 80 million years old. Though each is unique in its splendor, none has captured imaginations and photographers' lenses like the Tetons, which tower abruptly from the floor of Jackson Hole in a jaw-dropping display of glacier-carved rock and ice. It's fitting that Grand Teton National Park is 57 years younger than the world's first national park just to the north because it's also a relative baby geologically.

The youngest of the Rocky Mountains were born in a geological nanosecond some 9 to 13 million years ago, when the east and west sides of a 40-mile north-south fault decided, mostly via earthquakes and other released tensions, to go their separate ways: Up on the west, down even more dramatically on the east. Imagine an aboriginal photographer's nirvana then. By the time the fault-blocking and glacial carving had concluded, Grand Teton had risen from 6 miles underground to more than 5 miles above what would eventually be named Jackson Hole.

In the millions of years since, erosion of the limestone peaks of Grand Teton, Middle Teton, Owen and Moran have combined with sedimentation in Jackson Hole to begin an inevitable reunion of the two land masses; Grand Teton has slipped to 13,770 feet above sea level, less than 1½ miles above the rising town of Jackson. Along the way, glaciers carved the jagged ridges and outcroppings that left the Tetons with unique contours once the last ice floe disappeared about 13,000 years ago. Today, the Tetons are one of the world's most

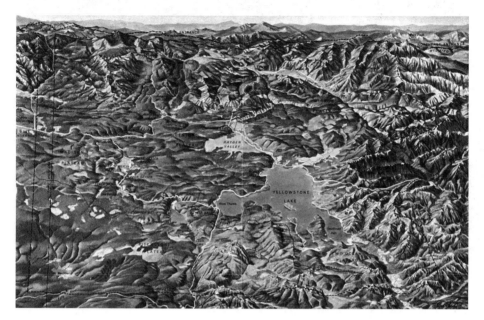

Relief map of Yellowstone National Park. National Park Service

spectacular visual wonders, especially from the east, where that dramatic fault-blocked rise and fall left no foothills to mar the views across sage plains and lodgepole forests.

Eventually, Jackson Hole will rise and meet the tips of the Tetons, until the next great earthquake separates them again. Of course, when Yellowstone finally blows its top, any movement to the south may be the geological equivalent of rearranging the Titanic's deck chairs.

Those of us living in the vicinity can at least hold out hope that Yellowstone's caldera will keep its relative cool just a little longer. After all, the "hot spot" underfoot is moving southwest at the expeditious rate of about an inch per year. In no time at all, it'll be Nevada's problem.

CULTURAL HISTORY

Yellowstone National Park

Imagine that you've migrated across the frozen Bering Strait, crossed the wilds of what is now Alaska and British Columbia and ventured south into what would be called Montana in about 11,000 years. Along the way, you've traversed retreating glaciers from an ice age, evaded saber-toothed cats and feasted on woolly mammoths. Suddenly you come across a trembling landscape unlike any you've ever known. Hissing, steaming, snorting—all just reemerging after thousands of years of being trapped restlessly in icy seclusion under the glaciers.

Thus was the genesis of the physical and spiritual reverence humans have had toward Yellowstone. The awe continued with latter-day Native Americans and the first Anglos who arrived in the 18th century. Food riches beckoned those first humans, known as the

The Bannock Indians who inhabited the Yellowstone region were descendents of the Sheepeaters. They frequently mingled and traded with white settlers. National Park Service

Folsom and Clovis cultures. If archaeologists are correct, the earliest residents used obsidian to hunt mammoth, camels, mastodons, beaver and bighorn bison that, compared to today's descendents, would have looked as if they were on steroids. Those first humans might also have used the same tools to fend off attacks from lions, bears and wolves that also scarcely resembled the liked-named carnivores roaming what is now Yellowstone National Park.

After the ice departed, it probably ushered in a 2,000-year period during which the land was delicate tundra. Only after gradual warming did Yellowstone begin to take on its current profile, about 9,000 years ago. Lodgepole pine appeared, along with Engelmann spruce and whitebark pine, whose nuts became a favorite of the grizzly bear. Blood found on arrowheads, knives, rocks and other tools scattered throughout the region suggests that deer, elk, rabbit, sheep and bear were plentiful. In an ominous precursor of our current overconsumption habits, evidence also suggests that these cultures pillaged their bounty. The decline of game populations caused dramatic social restructuring and forced a focus on smaller game and plants for food.

Today's visitors would be surprised to learn they might not be the first to complain about summer crowds, though climates were so harsh that only the Sheepeater Indians—bighorn-eating ancestors of Idaho's Shoshone and Bannock tribes—made permanent homes in Yellowstone and the Grand Teton region. Hundreds of fire rings, wickiups, campsites, petroglyphs, tipi rings, obsidian points, burial sites and buffalo kill sites have been discovered, and archaeological mapping has barely begun. Researchers also believe most evidence of those long-ago residents has been lost to harsh climes and time. The whereabouts of other existing remote religious sites remain a mystery because today's native inhabitants, mostly the Crow and Shoshone Indians, still use them. All evidence suggests that these were bustling summer grounds.

To the south, lack of hot springs, geysers and other warming features apparently limited human winter habitation of the Grand Teton/Jackson Hole area even more than Yellowstone, largely because big game migrated to lower elevations and less-harsh climes. The ancestors of what would become the Crow, Bannock, Shoshone and Blackfeet would feast on summer roots on the plateaus, then cross the Continental Divide to wait out the deep snows of the Little Ice Age that ended in the decades just before Yellowstone was established in 1872. Other Indians would winter in the broad valley north of what is now Gardiner, where buffeting winds scoured the Yellowstone River Valley of its snow and left a paradise of native grasses and small animals. As the climate continued to warm in the past 2,000 years, large game returned and Indian populations followed.

The first Anglos to arrive were French-Canadian fur trappers in search of beaver pelts in the late 1770s. They came up the Missouri River and dispersed up its tributaries, including the Yellowstone, Madison and Gallatin Rivers, which are birthed on the Yellowstone plateau. Their legacy remains in some of the names still gracing towns, rivers and mountains. The Yellowstone, known by the Indians as Elk River, was named *Rive des Roches Jaunes* (literally "river of yellow rock") by the French, probably because of the amber rimrock downstream near present-day Billings but possibly because of similarly hued outcroppings near the confluence of the Missouri in North Dakota. The French influence is most notable in the Tetons themselves, christened *Les Trois Tétons* (the three breasts) by trappers no doubt yearning for female companionship.

The trappers and Indians had the woods and rivers to themselves in a tenuous détente until the Lewis and Clark Corps of Discovery passed through the region in 1803, after President Thomas Jefferson ordered exploration of the Louisiana Purchase country. Lewis and Clark never saw the Yellowstone or Teton country, but they heard frightful Shoshone and Nez Perce tales of rolling thunder emanating from the mystical land to the south; indeed, by this time many Indians were reluctant to sleep near the geyser basins because they believed spirits inhabited them. Lewis and Clark's reports of bountiful resources in the area began to pique a nation's interest, and one of the trip's members, John Colter, returned to Yellowstone five years after the expedition to trap beaver. But it wasn't until 1827 that Americans on the East Coast received their first detailed description of the Yellowstone-Teton region, thanks to trapper Daniel Potts's vivid accounts in a Philadelphia newspaper.

Colter and Potts were just two of many fur-trapping mountain men whose tales of the northern Rockies grew to mythical proportions back East. Though their era lasted only until about 1840, such names as Jim Bridger, Jedediah Smith and the Sublette boys live on, their legacies perpetuated in western art, folklore and such movies as *Jeremiah Johnson*. For about 15 years, Anglo and Indian trappers would gather for annual rendezvous that were whiskey-drinking, arm-wrestling, skirt-chasing, gun-dueling, poker-playing precursors to some of the tamer frontier-day festivals many small western towns stage today.

The next wave of explorers came after the Civil War. Easily the most significant was a group formed at the behest of the Northern Pacific Railroad, which sought a route across Montana and needed publicity to entice investors. In 1870, the railroad bankrolled the 19-member Washburn-Langford-Doane Expedition. The group planned to follow a route detailed a year earlier by the Folsom-Cook-Peterson expedition, whose account of the region in a popular magazine had rekindled flagging interest. East and West Coast media accounts of the Washburn Expedition ensured that Yellowstone would forever be in the national consciousness. Annual tourist visits began to skyrocket from the average of 500 who soaked at Mammoth Hot Springs during the Civil War era.

Many famous people have visited Yellowstone, including President Calvin Coolidge in 1927. National Park Service

In 1872, thanks to attention drawn to the area by the compelling images of landscape painter Thomas Moran and photographer William Henry Jackson, the U.S. Congress was moved to designate Yellowstone as the world's first national park. President Ulysses S. Grant signed the Yellowstone Act that year. The region was ultimately and ironically saved from development by its own ruggedness. Amid the nation's headlong rush to exploit the West's resource wealth, Yellowstone was deemed so remote and harsh that protecting it couldn't possibly hinder progress. This utilitarian philosophy toward the earth would last another century, when adjacent lands protected under the 1964 Wilderness Act were mostly rock and ice, and deemed either unfit or uneconomical for resource extraction.

"Protection" was a misnomer, however. For nearly a decade after its formation, the park was under such siege from poaching, squatters and vandalism that the U.S. Cavalry was called in to quell the lawlessness and land grabbing. For three more decades, the cavalry patrolled the park on horseback, first from Camp Sheridan and then from Fort Yellowstone, now the park's current headquarters at Mammoth. Their role was a far cry from Yellowstone's current mission. The cavalry built roads and fought fires. It also protected elk and bison from poaching and eliminated such natural predators as coyotes, wolves and mountain lions by using poisons. The cavalry's presence ended in 1916 with the formation of the National Park Service.

The next major players in the Yellowstone region were the railroads. By the early 1880s, Jay Cooke's Northern Pacific had reached Livingston, Montana, and Averill Harriman's Union Pacific had driven its golden spike in northern Utah. Despite opposition from hunters, railroad spurs were built from Livingston to Gardiner and from Pocatello, Idaho, to present-day West Yellowstone, Montana. At the turn of the century, more than 80 percent of the tourists arrived by train and entered the park in carriages or on horseback. Railroad barons had grand visions of development within Yellowstone's borders, including building a dam at the falls in the Grand Canyon of the Yellowstone River. But others vehement about keeping the park in its natural state stonewalled their attempts.

The railroads' era lasted about as long as that of the mountain man. Construction of the Grand Loop Road was finished in 1905, and the first automobile entered Yellowstone legally in 1915. Within a quarter-century, more visitors had entered the park via car than by train, and rail service ended in 1960. Today, all that remains of the railroad's influence is visible remnants of the old grades, renovated historic stations at West Yellowstone and Gallatin Gateway, and the Railroad Ranch along the Henry's Fork of the Snake River, a world-renowned dry-fly fishing shrine. Meanwhile, Yellowstone now has 370 miles of roads and five entrances, with the north station at Gardiner open year-round.

The park's mission continues to evolve. The age-old debate over recreational values versus intrinsic values took a surprising turn in 2006 when new Interior Secretary Dirk Kempthorne, a Republican former governor of Idaho and a George W. Bush appointee, announced that natural values would take precedence. This was a dramatic reversal of philosophy. No longer was the prevailing sentiment "how can the park serve the people"; now it was, "how can people serve the park." While welcome in many quarters, the sentiment hasn't been universally applauded. It was especially disappointing for snowmobile enthusiasts, whose access to Yellowstone already had been dramatically reduced because of pollution concerns and stress on wildlife. This has in turn affected the economy of West Yellowstone, which is redefining itself after relying heavily on the spending habits of snowmobilers since the early 1960s.

Along similar lines, the concerted effort to eliminate predators, culminating with the extinction of wolves in the 1920s, came full circle after their controversial reintroduction in 1995. Wolf researchers had no idea what to expect when they released 31 grays near the

Yellowstone's first superintendent, Horace Albright, and President Herbert Hoover, after a day of trout fishing in 1928. National Park Service

Lamar Valley that January. To their surprise, the wolves have been highly visible, seen by thousands of visitors through scopes, binoculars and sometimes out the windows of their cars. The result is a bustling winter tourist trade for such winter hamlets as Cooke City, Silver Gate and Gardiner.

Other wildlife are benefiting as well.

Where once bears gathered at park entrances for handouts, now feeding and/or approaching them is strictly prohibited, for the protection not only of visitors but the bears themselves. "A fed bear is a dead bear" is the parks' motto, and the last bear-feeding show took place in 1941. Bear-proof garbage bins and regulations about food storage are just two ways park officials are attempting to preserve the wildness of the grizzly and black bear.

Where once bison were reduced to a handful at what is now the Yellowstone Institute in the Lamar Valley, now they number in the thousands and range far and wide—sometimes too far and wide. Bison that leave the park near West Yellowstone and Gardiner are considered a brucellosis threat to cattle. Today, park officials first try "hazing" them back into the park with helicopters and on horseback. Montana tried a "hunt" in the mid-1990s, but national media pictures of stationary bison being gunned down struck a chord with Americans bearing lingering guilt over the wholesale buffalo slaughter of the 1800s. Some bison are still rounded up and sent to slaughterhouses, and a hunt has returned to Montana under much stricter, and quieter, conditions. But the public let its feelings be known in the spring of 2007 when 300 wandering bison, including more than 100 calves, were given a death sentence. The fear was that cattle migrating to summer grazing ranges would contract brucellosis, which causes cows to abort calves. The resulting outcry led to

Wildlife officials deliver wolves into the heart of Yellowstone for release in January of 1995. In a controversial move, 31 gray wolves from Canada were introduced into the park. Now more than 500 roam the ecosystem.
National Park Service

two hazings that returned the bison to the park. Current conservation efforts on the behalf of bison include buying rangelands where cattle feed. An example is the work of media mogul Ted Turner, who raises bison on his huge spread between the Gallatin and Madison Rivers.

Where once park officials attempted to extinguish fires, now there is the so-called "let-burn" philosophy, a misnomer given that all fires are monitored and some extinguished. The policy made national headlines in the summer of 1988, when the media descended on the lightning-induced inferno that Yellowstone had become. Images of towering smoke, vast wastelands with the ghostly spire remnants of lodgepole pine, and flames nipping at the fringes of Grant Village and Cooke City dominated TV screens. Once the hysteria died with the last smoldering ember, and after an astonishing 800,000 acres was scorched, cooler heads began trying to understand what happened and why. Turns out the devastation was partly a function of the failed old Smokey the Bear doctrine that the only good fire is an extinguished fire. Ever since the first humans arrived, Mother Nature had cleansed the ecosystem of bugs, disease and deadfall with fire; suppression had created the perfect recipe for devastation. Well before 1988, scientists recognized that prescribed burns were necessary for the health of the forest, and that what happened that summer was inevitable.

The hue and cry over the fires lasted for years, ranging from visitors lamenting the perceived loss of a national icon to right-wing politicians clamoring for logging the park's charred timber. But the drama has largely subsided with the park's remarkable "recovery." Two decades later, the spires of 200-year-old lodgepoles stand over verdant understories that provide browse for wildlife. Teen-aged pines are rising in the shadows. Wildflowers are abundant. Animals are thriving and the park is closer to a natural balance than at any time since the post–Civil War era. An ominous note was struck in April 2007 when a lightning-caused fire was recorded, the earliest in the year within memory. Clearly, Yellowstone isn't out of the woods, so to speak, when it comes to fire. Climate change and lingering drought have created yet another tinder box just waiting for a careless smoker or series of lightning strikes. Scientists say conflagrations akin to 1988 had happened before, and they surely will happen again, regardless of man's intentions. The good news is that nature heals quickly and provides an education along the way.

Other challenges remain as well. Limited funding has created infrastructure concerns that some believe was a covert attempt by a Republican-dominated government to privatize the park. A ray of hope did emerge in 2007 from President Bush, who in acknowledging the importance of national parks, called for increased financial backing in his annual budget. Whitebark pines dying from beetle and fungus cast an ominous shadow over the threatened grizzly bear, which ironically was removed from the federally protected list in 2007. The endangered Yellowstone cutthroat trout's future is further at risk because of the illegal introduction of lake trout in the frigid waters of Yellowstone Lake. Anti-wolf groups are ever vigilant, looking for any morsel of news they might use to sway public sentiment toward a second eradication. Their recent focus has been on the reduced numbers of the once-overpopulated northern range elk herd, which wolf opponents are quick to blame on *Canis lupus*. Some in Wyoming have even called for the construction of a fence around the entire park to keep wildlife in, à la Theodore Roosevelt National Park in North Dakota, ostensibly creating the world's largest drive-thru zoo.

Though only 1 percent is intensely developed and 90 percent of visitors limit themselves to these areas, the park remains in danger of being loved to death by its overwhelming number of summer visitors. Perhaps even greater threats are coming from outside the

Yellowstone's North Entrance near the town of Gardiner. National Park Service

park's borders. Logging and mining have subsided, but oil and gas wells might soon cover northern and western Wyoming in unprecedented numbers, threatening wildlife corridors and pristine waters. Housing developments are sprouting on the fringes of both parks, compromising the wildness and isolation that lured people here in the first place.

Even at 2.2 million acres, Yellowstone is an island, cut off from the endless wild country to the north, its ecosystem fragile. Its challenges remain as great today, perhaps even greater, than when it was founded more than a century ago.

Grand Teton National Park/Jackson Hole
One look at the jagged peaks of Grand Teton, Middle Teton and Mount Moran would seem sufficient evidence to instantly declare the awe-inspiring area south of Yellowstone a national park. And in fact, early Yellowstone superintendents and Wyoming politicians periodically proposed expanding the park's boundaries southward; the U.S. House of Representatives even approved setting aside the rock and ice of the Teton Range plus eight glacial lakes as a national park in 1929.

If only it were that easy.

More than 75 years of controversy, political wrangling and compromise would pass after the rubber-stamp creation of Yellowstone before an increasing tide of tourists empowered Washington in 1950 to create the Grand Teton National Park we know today. As much as wilderness purists blanch at the expanding town of Jackson and its trendy faux western boutiques, they would have cringed at what Jackson Hole had become at the beginning of the 20th century.

The utilitarian vision for the region south of Yellowstone first took hold in 1910 with the construction of 70-foot-high Jackson Lake Dam on the Snake River. The dam flooded 7,200 acres of lodgepole pines and backed up enough water to supply potato and beet farmers on the other side of the mountains in Idaho. In an ironic twist, the dam may well have planted the seed for the park's creation a half-century later: As an ugly town housing construction workers sprang up overnight, and dead and dying trees poked through the surface of Jackson Lake, the scene quickly sparked an emotional preservation versus development debate.

Like those who appreciated Yellowstone's wonders, some entrepreneurs gazed at the grandeur of the Tetons and envisioned multitudes coming west to escape life's workaday pressures. The vacation dude ranches so prevalent in the region today actually had their genesis at the time the dam was built. Their owners saw the need to preserve the scenic qualities of the area and began the long, winding and bumpy road to protection from overdevelopment.

The first step toward protection was a visit in 1926 by millionaire John D. Rockefeller, at the behest of Yellowstone superintendent Horace Albright and a coalition of dude ranchers, cattlemen and others who feared commercial exploitation of the valley. One glance at the growing commercialization was enough to persuade Rockefeller to purchase 35,000 acres of delinquent ranches with the intent of donating the land to the newly created Park Service to add to the existing park. Knowing a giveaway to the federal government wouldn't sit well with cattlemen who used the rocky valley as a cattle thoroughfare between summer and winter grazing lands, he bought the land covertly, under the name of a company that implied his group might operate as a ranch.

The deal was complete in 1930 before locals knew what hit them, and many of the state's politicians and ranchers were furious. After Rockefeller's end run, opposition to protection of surrounding lands intensified. The ire was so fierce that the feds wouldn't even accept his donated land. Park opponents opined that expanding the boundaries would lock up the land from development and put ranches out of business. For 13 years, they had their way.

In 1943, with the country distracted by World War II, President Franklin D. Roosevelt used his popularity to rebuke Congress and accept Rockefeller's 35,000-acre gift. Roosevelt took another 130,000 acres of U.S. Forest Service land and created the Jackson Hole National Monument, again with a predictable reaction. Wyoming politicians repeatedly introduced legislation to overturn the monument, only to be rebuffed in Washington, D.C.

Ultimately, tourists saved a valley now threatened by their very passion for it. The money they brought during a celebratory post–World War II travel boom eased local economic fears. In a move that would aid in the creation of future national parks and wilderness areas, the federal government compromised by "grandfathering" in the right of ranching families to run cattle within the park's borders. On September 14, 1950, Rockefeller's donated land and the national monument were incorporated into the national park, bringing Grand Teton National Park to its present size.

Today, nobody is more grateful that the land was saved from commercialization and that proposed dams were thwarted than the residents of Jackson Hole. Until the gas-and-oil boom that enveloped other parts of Wyoming in 2005, no region of the state had a more bustling economy. Tourism flourishes at unprecedented levels. Jackson consistently ranks among the top communities in America for wealth. Though sprawl is evident, the park boundary, mountains to the west and the National Elk Refuge to the north have limited Jackson's growth and kept it more intimate than other destination resorts. And even that old eyesore, Jackson Lake Dam, was rebuilt in the late 1980s so that it better meshes into the landscape. Visitors to sprawling Jackson Lake Lodge, once a controversial building itself, now gaze over Willow Flats and shimmering lake waters to towering mountains that form one of the most breathtaking backdrops in America.

THE FIRES OF 1988

The Perfect Firestorm

The morning of June 21, 1988, arrived with characteristic sun-kissed bliss in Yellowstone National Park. That all changed in one afternoon with the flick of a cigarette on the Targhee National Forest, just west of the park boundary.

Before the day was out, howling winds, high temperatures and the worst drought in Yellowstone's history had conspired to set 460 acres ablaze. Before the week had ended, lightning would start two more fires in different corners of the park, creating an eerie glow that would last for months. And before the summer breathed its last, more than 800,000 acres—about one-third of the park—would be consumed by 51 conflagrations, the devastation sensationally transmitted into America's living rooms each night by network television.

For nearly three months, from the moment that firewood-cutter's tiny cigarette butt ignited that first fire until September's snows blanketed the park, the "tragedy" in Yellowstone was the buzz of an upset and angry nation. Government officials argued over policies that had ranged from the old Smokey the Bear suppress-every-fire philosophy to the inaccurately nicknamed "Let Burn" doctrine of 1972, which guided the decisions made 16 years later. Residents of such gateway communities as Cooke City and West Yellowstone expressed anger as they watched the flames draw nearer, their livelihoods and lives threatened. Tourists in the park and folks back home watched in shock and sadness as America's first and most cherished national park went up in smoke, never to be the same again.

They saw the tens of millions of scorched trees. They saw the charred remains of fleeing elk. They saw the smoldering remnants of cabins. And they bristled as more than 25,000 firefighters lived in grimy tent cities and battled the flames in utter futility, at an astronomical $125 million cost to the taxpayer. How could this happen, Americans wondered, and more to the point, how could the Park Service let this happen?

When the winter snows mercifully halted the carnage, reporters packed their notebooks, TV trucks lowered their satellite dishes and government officials turned to other matters, leaving the rest of the Yellowstone story untold. What Americans wouldn't see on TV or in the headlines for the next 20 years—except on nature programs and in special reports buried in newspaper travel sections—was the miracle of regeneration, a turnaround so rapid and remarkable that even many biologists were awestruck. Missed all along, though, was the irony: The fires were exacerbated, not only by record winds, stifling heat and 20 percent of normal rainfall, but by years of fire suppression that allowed for dense undergrowth, acres of timber dying in aging forests, and beetle infestations that killed lodgepole and whitebark pine.

Fire, we discovered too late, was not a detriment to forest health, it was a necessity.

By the spring of 1988, a mild winter and lingering drought had set the stage for the perfect firestorm; many of the park's dead and dying lodgepoles had as little as 6 percent moisture content, or about the same as a kiln-dried two-by-four. At midsummer, when afternoon thunderstorms with their accompanying high winds and lightning are almost a daily occurrence, the park was a tinderbox.

A crown fire rages out of control near Dunraven Pass. About 41 percent of the 1988 fires were crown fires, which leave little in their wake. Remarkably, less than 1 percent of the park's soils were sterilized by the heat, and the park has undergone a self-restoration. National Park Service

Since 1972, when the so-called "Let Burn" policy was instituted, less than 2 percent of the park had burned, about 35,000 acres total. Before then, the largest fire ever recorded in the park was 20,000 acres, at Heart Lake in 1931. A week into the Fires of 1988, the combined figure was already 50,000. The North Fork/Wolf Lake fire started by the careless woodcutter eventually grew to 500,000 acres (much of it outside the park; indeed, of the seven fires responsible for 95 percent of the burn, five started outside the park).

Nobody paid much attention until mid-July when the Shoshone Fire, which started near Lewis Lake, jumped the road south of Old Faithful and aimed its fury at Grant Village. There, firefighters removed debris, hosed down buildings and dropped pink fire retardant through the smoky haze, ultimately saving the historic site. All three major TV networks descended on the park, focusing their cameras on Grant Village, Old Faithful and Cooke City, which in a fit of gallows humor renamed itself "Cooked City" as flames moved within a mile. Donald Hodel, the interior secretary under the first President Bush—who, coincidentally, had a planned a Yellowstone vacation in 1988—declared that all fires would be suppressed until further notice.

It didn't matter. Mother Nature was playing by her own rules. By August, some 25 fires were burning a mosaic across the park. Ash fell 100 miles to the east and smoke plumes 27,000 feet high could be seen 500 miles away. On August 20, called Black Saturday, hurricane-force winds forced officials to close the park completely for the first and only time in its history. On September 7 alone, almost 100,000 acres burned, taking 20 cabins near Old Faithful with it.

Regardless of human efforts, the siege wasn't about to end until nature counterpunched with cooler temperatures and precipitation. Finally, three months and 1.4 million charred Greater Yellowstone acres later, the last embers flickered and died after a snowfall

A bull elk lounges on a grassy knoll spared by the 1988 fires. Of the remarkably low 400 large mammals that perished in the fires, about two-thirds were elk—most victims died of smoke inhalation. National Park Service

Tourists snap photos of the charred remnants of a forest shortly after the 1988 fires scorched about 800,000 acres in the park and 1.4 million acres in the Greater Yellowstone ecosystem. National Park Service

on September 11, leaving park officials and park lovers fearful for the park's future.

They didn't have to wait long for their first hopeful sign, in a count of blackened animal carcasses. In all, fewer than 400 large mammals perished, about two-thirds of them elk. Less than one out of every 1,000 elk in the park was lost. Only a handful of bison, bear, moose and deer were killed, most from smoke inhalation.

Then came more news that brought the fires into context: Less than half of the acreage was lost in "crown" or "canopy" fires, which race from treetop to treetop in a deadly firestorm that leaves nothing in its wake. Another one-third was a tolerable combination of crown and ground fire. The remainder was the kind of healthy, regenerating burn that had been suppressed for so many years. Most important, only a tiny fraction of soil was sterilized by the intense heat, meaning virtually the entire park was poised for a rebirth.

Two decades later, that rebirth is astonishing. Wildflowers like fireweed and Indian paintbrush, along with grasses and forbs, were the first flora to come back, providing forage for deer, elk and bison in places where they once wouldn't roam because of the tangled understory. Millions of lodgepole cones opened and rooted, with many of those stands now reaching 20 feet tall. Weaker wildlife ultimately perished at the paws of predators in the harsh winter of 1988–89, leaving the fit to survive, leading to today's flourishing populations.

The fires did result in a slight change to the government policy. Natural fires are still allowed to burn, especially in the backcountry, but they are watched carefully. As had always been the case under the so-called "Let Burn" policy, man-caused fires are immediately doused.

Though at first area residents feared that Yellowstone would cease to be one of America's favorite destinations, visitors still come in greater droves than ever, the still-

The people of Cooke City tried to maintain a sense of humor in 1988, even as fires licked at their doorstep. In the end, the town and its residents were spared. National Park Service

visible burned areas more a source of fascination than disappointment. Wildlife gravitates to the burns, making it more visible to happy tourists. Gateway communities thrive as never before.

The upshot: The ecosystem works. And even periodic cataclysmic fires are part of the ecosystem—always have been, always will be. A typical plot of Yellowstone land has burned at least 30 times since the last Ice Age some 10,000 years ago. A typical year will see 22 lightning-caused fires.

A year later, at least one prominent media outlet offered a mea culpa for the industry's blatantly sensationalist coverage.

"Reports of the park's death," the *Washington Post* wrote, "were greatly exaggerated."

Thus, today, words like "destruction," "devastation" and "catastrophic" so common in 1988 are no longer part of the Fires of '88 lexicon. They have been replaced by words like "dramatic," "awe-inspiring" and "the way it was meant to be."

Transportation

No national park embodies the idyllic family vacation more than Yellowstone. Countless millions have planned and saved, then hopped into the family vehicle—once a station wagon, today a minivan—and crossed the fruited plain to the strains of "This Land Is Your Land." For many, a journey to Yellowstone marks their first glimpse of snowcapped mountains, rising dramatically in the distance. Along the way are the obligatory stops that serve as a peek into this new world: Mount Rushmore, Wall Drug, prairie-dog towns, the Badlands, Devil's Tower and the sprawling Little America motel complex in western Wyoming.

Small airports with regional airlines serve several communities in the surrounding area, all with rental cars available. A century ago, trains were the most popular and efficient transportation to Yellowstone's gateway communities, but today only remnants of those rail beds are visible, used as hiking and mountain biking trails. Tour buses are another popular way to see the parks.

But as much as times and technology have changed, the automobile is still the most memorable way to get to Yellowstone, Grand Teton and Jackson Hole, as well as the most convenient and economical.

What follows is a closer look at transportation to and around America's first national park and her sister park 8 miles to the south.

Getting to Yellowstone, Grand Teton and Jackson Hole

By Car

From the Midwest and East Coast

If your vacation is more about the destination than the journey, the interstate highway system is the quickest way to Yellowstone's doorstep. Interstates 70, 80 and 90 stretch from the eastern seaboard to the Rockies, and beyond, some to the Pacific Coast. Speed limits reach 75 in North Dakota, South Dakota, Wyoming, Montana and even Colorado, which once strictly enforced the old 55-mph federal limits. A word of advice for anyone coming from the Midwest or Northeast: Avoid the inevitable bottleneck around the south side of Chicago, if at all possible. Idling for hours in bumper-to-bumper traffic on a stifling July day, still two days away from the parks, is no way to start a vacation. It's worth the extra mileage to dip south to I-70 west to Indianapolis, and then angle northwest on I-74 to the junction of I-80 at the Quad-Cities of Iowa and Illinois.

INTERSTATE 80

I-80 might be the starkest of the east-west interstates, but it's also the quickest to Yellowstone and Grand Teton. About midway through Wyoming, at the dusty high desert

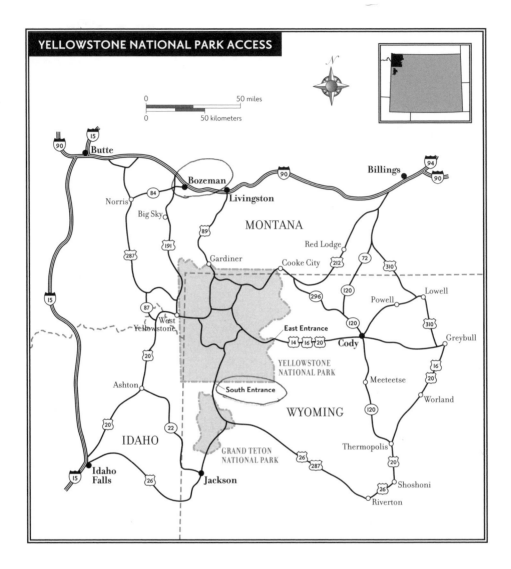

town of Rawlins, head north on US 287, the first Grand Teton-Yellowstone exit. After crossing the desolate Great Divide Basin, where waters go to die, you'll appreciate the views of the lengthy and mystical Wind River Range out the driver's side window upon reaching the charming outdoor-recreation haven of Lander. This route traverses the red-rock country along the Wind River through the gateway community of Dubois to scenic Togwotee Pass, then down to Moran Junction and the first awe-inspiring views of the Tetons.

INTERSTATE 90

This is our recommended route—so long as you meet up with I-90 west of Chicago. No highway provides a better gradual evolution to western landscapes. The farmlands of southern Minnesota and eastern South Dakota give way to rolling prairie, the pine-carpeted Black Hills, the rugged cowboy country of northeast Wyoming and finally a first teasing view of the burly Bighorn Mountains. Be sure to stop at the Badlands, Leadville and Mt. Rushmore in South Dakota. From there, it doesn't take much imagination to envision a band of Sioux Indians appearing over a nearby rise. At Buffalo, Wyoming, there are two ways to reach Yellowstone: Stay on I-90 as it veers north to Sheridan and Dayton, then head west on US 14 through Lovell and Powell to the gateway community of Cody, named for Buffalo Bill. Or, leave I-90 at Buffalo and cross the Bighorns on US 16, where you'll zig and zag through Ten Sleep and Greybull en route to Cody. At Cody, US 16 and US 14 join to follow the picturesque Shoshone River to Yellowstone's East Entrance. A less-traveled route well worth the extra time and effort is to go north out of Cody on WY 296 through spectacular Sunlight Basin to Cooke City and Yellowstone's Northeast Entrance.

Another option is to continue northward on I-90 to Billings, Montana. Once there, decide between driving another 100 miles west to Livingston or head south on US 212 through Red Lodge for the unforgettable journey over the spectacular Beartooth Pass to the Northeast Entrance—though be aware that the 10,974-foot pass typically is open only from late May until early October. If you continue west from Billings to Livingston on I-90, turn

Snowmobiles line up at the West Entrance at West Yellowstone in the days before limits were placed on entry. More than 1,500 snowmobilers would enter the park on its busiest days, most from West Yellowstone. National Park Service Photo by Jane Doe

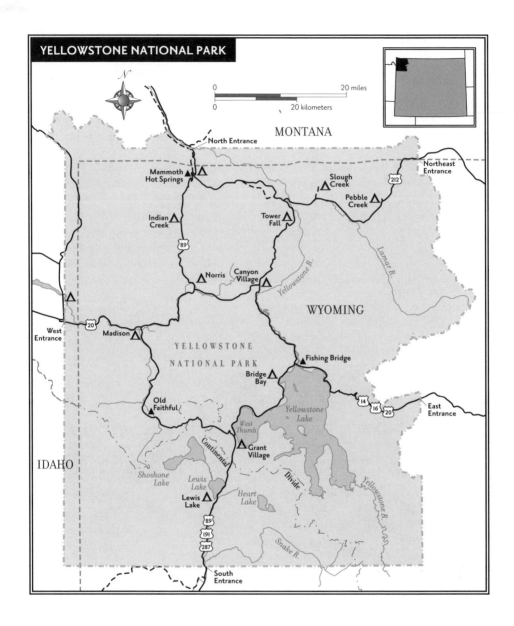

0   20 miles

0   20 kilometers

MONTANA

North Entrance

Mammoth
Hot Springs

Slough
Creek

Northeast
Entrance

212

Pebble
Creek

Indian
Creek

Tower
Fall

89

Norris

Canyon
Village

Yellowstone R.

Lamar R.

WYOMING

West
Entrance

20

Madison

YELLOWSTONE

NATIONAL PARK

Fishing Bridge

Bridge
Bay

Old
Faithful

Yellowstone
Lake

14

East
Entrance

16 20

West
Thumb

Continental

Grant
Village

IDAHO

Shoshone
Lake

Lewis
Lake

Divide

Yellowstone R.

Lewis
Lake

Heart
Lake

89

191

287

Snake R.

South
Entrance

south on US 89 and follow the Yellowstone River along the base of the Absaroka Range
through the aptly named Paradise Valley to the North Entrance at Gardiner. Or stay on I-90
to Bozeman and go south on US 191 through the narrow Gallatin River canyon to the West
Entrance at West Yellowstone.

INTERSTATE 94

If it's isolation you crave, this is your route. Miles of endless North Dakota prairie eventually give way to rolling rangeland and the badlands of Teddy Roosevelt National Park, a
rarely visited gem just east of the Montana border. Here, behind the fences of Teddy

Roosevelt along the interstate, is where you'll likely see the first wild bison. Underappreciated eastern Montana is C. M. Russell cowboy country at its finest, with coulees, pine-dotted rimrock and lush cottonwood draws along the meandering Yellowstone River. At Billings, I-94 ends when it meets with I-90. Here, you can continue west on I-90 to Livingston or Bozeman, or turn south to Red Lodge for the stunning drive over the Beartooths.

From the Southeast

A variety of interstates ultimately lead to Denver, most notably I-70, though the most appealing route is I-40 west to Amarillo. Veer north at Amarillo on US 287, which goes through the high plains of north Texas, west Oklahoma and southeast Colorado before meeting up with I-25 at Denver. If you have the time, the most scenic route is to take US 40 into the Rockies through Steamboat Springs, Colorado, and the Dinosaur National Monument to Vernal, Utah. Turn north on US 191, which passes through Rock Springs, Wyoming, en route to the Teton gateway community of Jackson, Wyoming. Or, continue north on I-25 from Denver and then make a decision at Cheyenne, Wyoming: I-80 west if your first destination is the Tetons and Jackson Hole, or I-25 north to Buffalo or Sheridan if it's Yellowstone.

From the Southwest and California

All roads lead to Salt Lake City, the one major metropolitan area within striking distance of the parks. From the Southwest and Southern California, take Interstate 15 through southern Utah to Salt Lake City (make a note to visit the state's stunning canyonlands on another trip). To reach Yellowstone, continue north on I-15 to Idaho Falls, then follow US 20 north

Cars enter through the Roosevelt Arch at the North Entrance in 1903. This was as far as cars were allowed until 1915. National Park Service

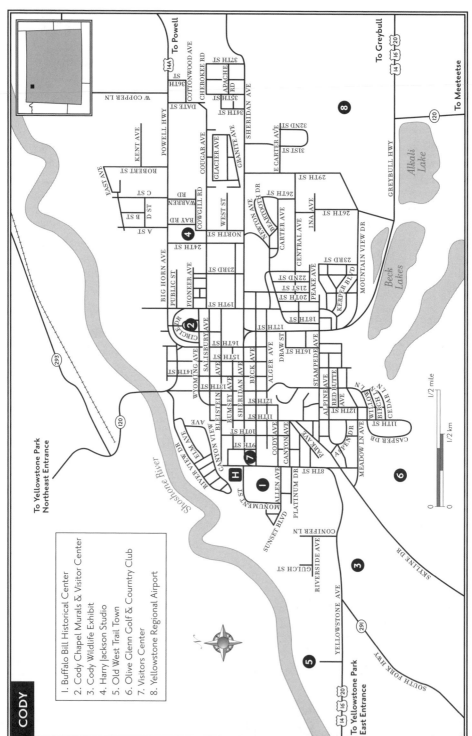

CODY

1. Buffalo Bill Historical Center
2. Cody Chapel Murals & Visitor Center
3. Cody Wildlife Exhibit
4. Harry Jackson Studio
5. Old West Trail Town
6. Olive Glenn Golf & Country Club
7. Visitors Center
8. Yellowstone Regional Airport

To Yellowstone Park
Northeast Entrance

To Yellowstone Park
East Entrance

To Powell

To Greybull

To Meeteetse

Shoshone River

Alkali Lake

Beck Lakes

1/2 mile
1/2 km

CPI12.05 Cody

to Ashton and beyond to West Yellowstone. You can also reach Jackson by taking US 26 east over the mountains from Idaho Falls. A more scenic route to Jackson is to leave I-15 just before Tremonton, Utah, and take US 89 through Logan, Utah, and northward through what has become rapidly expanding oil and gas country. If you're coming from Northern California, take I-80 east through arid Nevada to Salt Lake City.

From the Pacific Northwest

From Portland and Seattle, the fastest way to Yellowstone and Grand Teton is I-90 east through Spokane, Washington, and Butte, Montana. From Portland, take I-84 to the junction of I-82 and go north to Tri-Cities, Washington, where you'll veer off onto US 395 and continue another 70 miles north to its junction with I-90. From Seattle, take I-90 the entire route.

After crossing Homestake Pass just east of Butte, you'll have several options: Take US 287 through the broad Madison River Valley to West Yellowstone, continue to Bozeman and take the narrow US 191 through the Gallatin Canyon to West Yellowstone, or keep going to Livingston and take US 89 south to Gardiner. If you're coming from Boise, Idaho, it's worth leaving the interstate for US 20/26 at Mountain Home for a quick tour of Sun Valley and Craters of the Moon National Monument.

By Bus

If you go **Greyhound** (800-231-2222; www.greyhound.com), you can at least get in the neighborhood of Yellowstone and Grand Teton. To the north of Yellowstone, Greyhound has stations in Billings, Livingston, Bozeman and Three Forks, Montana. To the west, the closest stop is in Idaho Falls. On the east, it's Cody, Powell, Lovell, Riverton and Thermopolis, Wyoming. Greyhound does not serve Jackson. From any one of these destinations, you'll need a tour bus, taxi or rental car.

By Train

Back in a more romantic era, either the Northern Pacific, Union Pacific or Burlington railroads brought a majority of visitors to Yellowstone. Rail spurs took passengers to the edge of the park at Gardiner and West Yellowstone, as well as close to the park at Gallatin Gateway west of Bozeman. Today? Don't bother. **Amtrak's** Empire Builder from Chicago to Seattle cuts across northern Montana through Glacier National Park, but it's a five-hour drive from the train station nearest to Yellowstone. The California Zephyr from Chicago to the Bay Area stops in Salt Lake City. If you're coming from the Midwest, neither offers the scenery or efficiency to make this an adventure worth undertaking. This could change, however. In the summer of 2007, Montana lawmakers were making rumblings about renewing service on the Montana Rail Link route paralleling Interstate 90 through Billings, Livingston and Bozeman.

By Plane

Thanks to the popularity of Yellowstone, Grand Teton and Jackson Hole and the growth of destination ski resorts, surrounding communities have a surprising array of airline service given their size. Commercial air services are available in Bozeman, Cody, Jackson, Idaho Falls/Pocatello and West Yellowstone. Billings and Salt Lake City also put the traveler within short driving distances of the parks.

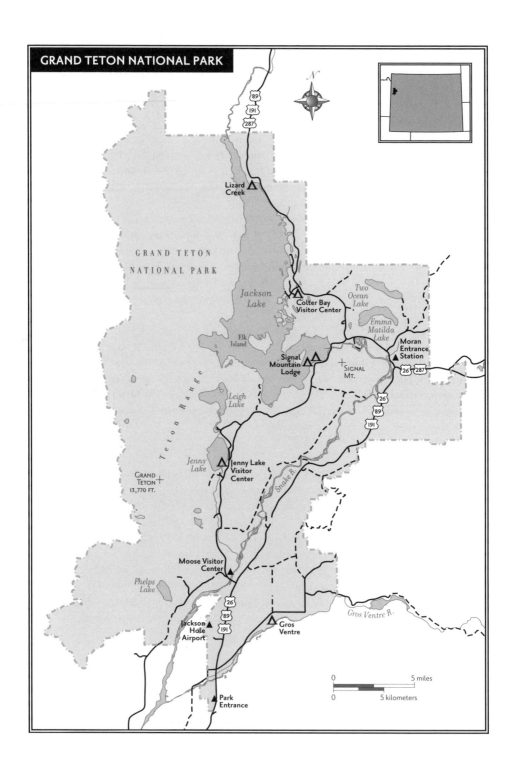

GRAND TETON NATIONAL PARK

89
191
287

N

GRAND TETON
NATIONAL PARK

Lizard
Creek

Jackson
Lake

Two
Ocean
Lake

Colter Bay
Visitor Center

Emma
Matilda
Lake

Elk
Island

Moran
Entrance
Station

26 287

Signal
Mountain
Lodge

SIGNAL
MT.

Teton Range

Leigh
Lake

26

89

191

Jenny
Lake

Jenny Lake
Visitor
Center

GRAND
TETON
13,770 FT.

Snake R.

Moose Visitor
Center

Phelps
Lake

Gros Ventre R.

26
89
191

Jackson
Hole
Airport

Gros
Ventre

0   5 miles

0   5 kilometers

Park
Entrance

Former CBS newsman Charles Kuralt dubbed the Beartooth Highway "The most beautiful roadway in America." The highway rises above 10,000 feet between Red Lodge and Cooke City, Montana. National Park Service

BOZEMAN

Picturesque Gallatin Field (406-388-8321; www.gallatinfield.com), located 8 miles to the northwest of Bozeman in Belgrade and about 90 miles from Yellowstone's West Entrance, is served by five airlines. **Horizon Airlines** (800-547-9308), a subsidiary of **Alaska Airlines**, has four flights daily originating in Seattle, two stopping in Butte. **Northwest Airlines** (800-225-2525) has three flights daily from Minneapolis, a direct Saturday flight from Detroit and also partners with **SkyWest/Delta Connection** (800-221-1212), which has six daily flights from Salt Lake City. **United Express** (800-241-6522 or 800-864-8331) has four flights daily from Denver and one direct flight from Chicago, increasing to two in the summers. **Delta Airlines** has direct flights to and from Atlanta on Saturdays, Sundays and Tuesdays in the summer. **Big Sky Airlines** (800-273-7788) has one direct flight daily from Boise.

CODY

Yellowstone Regional Airport (307-587-5096; www.yra.com) is 52 miles from the East Entrance to the park. **SkyWest/Delta Connection** (800-221-1212) has two daily flights from Salt Lake City and **SkyWest/United Express/Mesa Airlines** (800-864-8331) has one from Denver.

IDAHO FALLS/POCATELLO

Idaho Falls Regional Airport (208-612-8221) is served by five regional airlines, all subsidiaries of major carriers. **Northwest Airlines** (800-225-2525) has a daily flight from Minneapolis. **SkyWest/Delta Connection** (800-221-1212) has six daily flights from Salt Lake City. **Horizon Airlines** (800-547-9308) has three flights daily from Boise. **United**

Express (800-864-8331) has two daily and a Saturday flight from Denver. **Allegiant Air** (702-505-8888) has Monday and Friday flights from Las Vegas.

Jᴀᴄᴋsᴏɴ

Jackson Hole Airport boasts perhaps the most scenic setting in America, thanks to the majestic Tetons just off the wing. It is the only commercial airport in America located inside a national park. Eight airlines provide service to Jackson, much of it seasonal. **SkyWest/Delta Connection** (800-221-1212) has four daily flights from Salt Lake City, a Saturday flight in the winter from Cincinnati and twice-weekly service from Atlanta. **United Express** (800-864-8331) has three daily flights from Denver. **American Airlines** (800-433-7300) has a flight from Chicago O'Hare and one from Dallas/Fort Worth. **Big Sky Airlines** (800-273-7788) has one direct flight daily from Boise. A direct flight from New York City reportedly is in the works. Book a seat on the right side of the airplane for incoming and left side for departure.

Wᴇsᴛ Yᴇʟʟᴏᴡsᴛᴏɴᴇ

SkyWest/Delta Connection (800-221-1212) flies from Salt Lake City into West Yellowstone Airport (406-646-9321) three times daily from June to September. The airport is closed from October until May.

By Taxi

Unless you're flying into Jackson, a taxi is an expensive way to get around Yellowstone and Grand Teton. Following are the taxi services in Jackson.

Airport Shuttle Service: 307-730-3900
Cowboy Cab Co.: 307-734-8188
Allstar Taxi & Transportation: 307-733-2888
Buckboard Cab: 307-733-1112
Bullseye Taxi: 307-730-5000
Custom Cab: 307-413-4302
Snake River Taxi: 307-732-2221
Teton Taxi & Backcountry: 307-733-1506
Tumbleweed Taxi: 307-739-7167
Westbank Cab: 307-690-0112

Gᴇᴛᴛɪɴɢ ᴀʀᴏᴜɴᴅ Yᴇʟʟᴏᴡsᴛᴏɴᴇ, Gʀᴀɴᴅ Tᴇᴛᴏɴ ᴀɴᴅ Jᴀᴄᴋsᴏɴ Hᴏʟᴇ

By Rented Car

This is easily the way to go if you plan to see as much of Yellowstone, Grand Teton and Jackson Hole as possible. Note that rates for SUVs and four-wheel-drives can spike in winter. If you're looking to rent an RV, try **Cruise America** (480-464-7300; www.cruise america.com), a national company based in Mesa, Arizona.

Bᴏᴢᴇᴍᴀɴ Aɪʀᴘᴏʀᴛ

Avis: 406-388-6814; www.avis.com
Budget: 406-388-4091; www.budget.com
Dollar: 406-388-2313; www.dollar.com

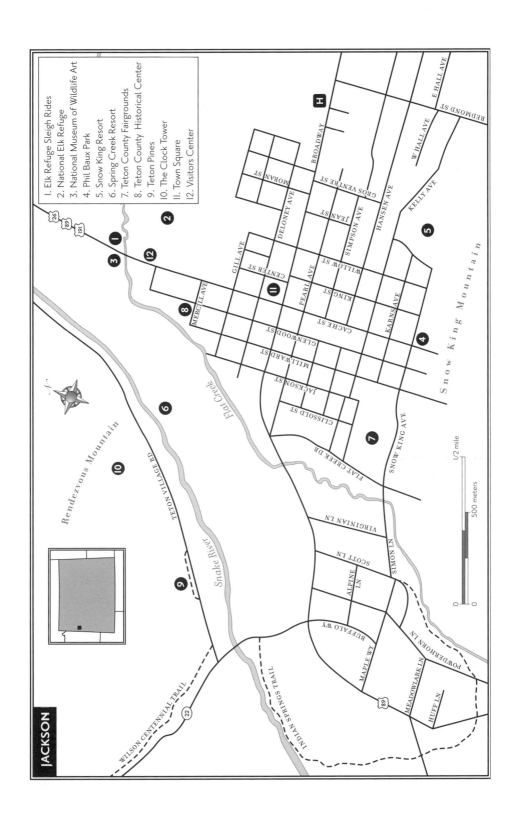

JACKSON

1. Elk Refuge Sleigh Rides
2. National Elk Refuge
3. National Museum of Wildlife Art
4. Phil Baux Park
5. Snow King Resort
6. Spring Creek Resort
7. Teton County Fairgrounds
8. Teton County Historical Center
9. Teton Pines
10. The Clock Tower
11. Town Square
12. Visitors Center

Enterprise: 800-261-7331; www.enterprise.com
Hertz: 406-388-6939; www.hertz.com
National; Alamo: 406-388-6694; www.nationalcar.com (off-site/shuttle required)
Payless: 406-388-9669; www.paylesscarrental.com
Thrifty: 406-388-3484; www.thrifty.com

Cody Airport
Budget: 307-587-6066
Hertz: 307-587-2914
Rent-A-Wreck: 307-527-5549
Thrifty: 307-587-8855

Idaho Falls/Pocatello Airport
Alamo: 208-522-0340
Avis: 208-522-4225
Budget: 208-522-8800
Enterprise: 208-523-8111
National: 208-522-5276
Thrifty: 208-522-1298

Jackson Airport
Alamo: 800-327-9633
Aspen: 307-733-9224
Avis: 800-831-2847
Budget: 800-527-0700
Eagle: 307-739-9999
National: 800-227-7368
Thrifty: 800-367-2277

West Yellowstone
Big Sky: 406-646-9564; 429 Yellowstone Ave.
Budget: 800-231-5991; 131 Dunraven St.

Tour Buses
Alta
Grand Targhee Resort: 307-353-2300; P.O. Box SKI, Alta, WY 83422.

Ashton
Back Country Sports: 208-652-3385; P.O. Box 773, Ashton, ID 83420.

Big Sky
Wild Trout Outfitters/Mountain Taxi: 406-995-4895; P.O. Box 160003, Big Sky, MT 59716.
Yellowstone Tour Guides: 888-493-2260; P.O. Box 160654, Big Sky, MT 59716.

Billings
Northwest Passage/Silver Eagle Shuttle: 406-254-2900; P.O. Box 23333, Billings, MT 59103.

BOZEMAN
Karst Stage: 800-287-4759 or 406-388-2293; Belgrade, MT 59714.
Off the Beaten Path: 406-586-1311; 7 East Beall St., Bozeman, MT 59715.
Yellowstone Guidelines: 800-314-4506; 16634 Bridger Canyon Rd., Bozeman, MT 59715.
Yellowstone Safari: 406-586-1155; P.O. Box 42, Bozeman, MT 59771.

CODY
Grub Steak Expeditions: 307-527-6316; P.O. Box 1013, Cody, WY 82414.

GILLETTE
Powder River Transportation Services: 307-682-0960; P.O. Box 218, Gillette, WY 82717.

JACKSON
Alltrans: 307-733-4325; P.O. Box 411, Jackson, WY 83001
Callowishus Park Touring Company: 307-733-9521; P.O. Box 2281, Jackson, WY 83001.
Outdoor Adventures/Upstream Anglers: 307-733-8057; P.O. Box 30106, Jackson, WY 83001.
Personal Guide Service: 307-733-6312; P.O. Box 1440, Jackson, WY 83001.

WEST YELLOWSTONE
Buffalo Bus Touring Company: 406-646-9353; P.O. Box 580, West Yellowstone, MT 59758.
Yellowstone Tour & Travel: 406-646-9310; P.O. Box 410, West Yellowstone, MT 59758.

By Bicycle

The Jackson Hole area offers some of the finest mountain-biking terrain in the world. Yellowstone and Grand Teton National Parks provide picturesque cycling, but caution is urged because of traffic and narrow shoulders. The town of Jackson has embarked on an ambitious Pathways System designed to make it easier for cyclists and walkers to get around without having to fight motorized traffic. More details on cycling appear in Chapter 6, "Recreation."

On Foot

Hiking is, of course, a primary reason to visit these parks. More on hiking in the Recreation chapter. Maps of the Jackson Hole Community Pathways System are available via mail at P.O. Box 1687, Jackson, WY 83001 or by phone at 307-732-8573.

The interior of the Old Faithful Inn towers seven stories and is fondly called "the old house." National Park Service

3

LODGING

You didn't come to Yellowstone or Grand Teton to sit inside a hotel room, and the accommodations generally reflect this philosophy. Much of the lodging in Yellowstone does its best to coax visitors outside to experience the natural wonders. Technological amenities are limited or nonexistent. No televisions, few telephones. Internet connections—where available—are slower than the average Conestoga wagon. Nevertheless, whatever level of rustic luxury you desire is at hand. In Yellowstone, you can get back to nature within four walls at rustic and remote Tower/Roosevelt or bask in luxury in suites at Mammoth and Old Faithful. Lodging is more limited in Grand Teton, but much of it is upscale, especially the cabins and lodge at Jenny Lake.

Not surprisingly, given the limited seasons in Yellowstone and Grand Teton, most summer lodging is booked well in advance. Park officials recommend securing reservations at least six months before your Yellowstone visit and at least nine for Grand Teton. Rooms are more readily available in gateway communities, but thinking you can drive into town and find a room in the summer can lead to frustration. All park lodging is closed for portions of the spring and fall as they gear up for busy summer and, in some cases, winter seasons. In Yellowstone, only Old Faithful and Mammoth are open in winter, and only Mammoth is accessible by car.

Gateway-community lodging can tend to be basic as well, though upscale accommodations are available, especially in Jackson and Teton Village. For a unique western experience, try one of the dozens of dude ranches scattered throughout the region. These typically are all-inclusive, with meals and many activities as part of the rates, which typically start in the low four figures for a minimum week stay.

Most of Yellowstone's concessions, including its nine lodges (spaced about 20 miles apart because that's how far stagecoaches could go in a day) and five of its campgrounds are handled by Xanterra Parks and Resorts. Reservations are made through Xanterra at 866-GEYSERLAND, www.travelyellowstone.com or at reserve@travelyellowstone.com. Call 307-344-7901 for same-day reservations on the off chance there's a cancellation. Reservations for three of the five lodges inside Grand Teton—Colter Bay, Jackson Lake and Jenny Lake—are made through Grand Teton Lodge Company (800-628-9988).

Credit Cards

AE—American Express
CB—Carte Blanche
D—Discover
DC—Diner's Club
MC—Master Card
V—Visa

LODGING IN YELLOWSTONE NATIONAL PARK

Canyon Lodge & Cabins
Managers: Xanterra Parks & Resorts
307-344-7901
www.travelyellowstone.com
In the heart of Yellowstone, 16 miles north of Yellowstone Lake, 19 south of Tower-Roosevelt
Rates: $65–155
Credit Cards: AE, CB, D, DC, MC, V, JBS International
Handicapped Access: Yes (first floor of Dunraven and Cascade lodges)
Seasons: Early June to mid-Sept.

Sprawling Canyon has two newer lodges with 80 western rooms and 540 cabins, all built about a half-century ago. It is ideally situated for short drives or hikes to the Grand Canyon of the Yellowstone, Mount Washburn and wildlife viewing, cycling or fishing in Hayden Valley. All rooms and cabins have private baths. The Cascade and Dunraven lodge rooms are appealing for their modern log décor. The Pioneer cabins are the most primitive and least expensive. The Frontier and Western cabins are more plush. A gift shop, cafeteria, restaurant and deli also are on site.

Grant Village
Managers: Xanterra Parks & Resorts
307-344-7901
www.travelyellowstone.com
Southwest shore of Yellowstone Lake, just south of West Thumb
Rates: $123 and $131
Credit Cards: AE, CB, D, DC, MC, V, JBS International
Handicapped Access: Yes
Seasons: Late May to late Sept.

This could've been the original Motel 6: Six stark, motel-style buildings with 50 rooms each, none designed to fit Yellowstone's persona. Grant Village is for lake lovers who couldn't get a room at Lake Village. It is the closest Yellowstone lodging to Grand Teton and Lewis Falls, but otherwise Grant is nondescript and a last resort, so to speak.

Lake Lodge Cabins
Managers: Xanterra Parks & Resorts
307-344-7901
www.travelyellowstone.com
West shore of Yellowstone Lake
Rates: $65 and $130
Credit Cards: AE, CB, D, DC, MC, V, JBS International
Handicapped Access: Yes
Seasons: Mid-June to late Sept.

The quintessential Yellowstone cabins, with a choice between rustic and more modern, on the west shore of Yellowstone Lake. The inviting main lodge has two stone fireplaces, log

The Lake Lodge cabins aren't the most attractive in the park, but they serve the budget-conscious traveler.
National Park Service

beams and the type of furnishings that make you want to curl up with a good book in front of the fire. The cafeteria overlooks the lake. The 1920s cabins offer two choices: the primitive and less-expensive Pioneer and the more-spacious Western. Lake Lodge Cabins offer a sense of solitude yet are a short walk from the more vibrant happenings at the stylish Lake Yellowstone Hotel.

Lake Yellowstone Hotel & Cabins
Managers: Xanterra Parks & Resorts
307-344-7901
www.travelyellowstone.com
West shore of Yellowstone Lake
Rates: $109–$516
Credit Cards: AE, CB, D, DC, MC, V, JBS International.
Handicapped Access: Yes
Seasons: Mid-May to early Oct.

Antebellum meets the northern Rockies. The face of the Lake Yellowstone Hotel has changed dramatically with time, and this grand building now looks as if it was plucked from an estate in the Deep South. The 158 rooms are comfortable and charming, but what makes the hotel most appealing is the ambience. Lake views are superb from the Sun Room, where music from a grand piano serves as a soothing backdrop for a game of chess, a good book and a glass of wine. For the more economically inclined, the refurbished Lake Yellowstone Hotel Annex doesn't have views but it does have comfortable environs that

The Lake Yellowstone Hotel is the oldest in the park. The hotel is an oddity with its Southern colonial archi-tecture, but offers terrific views of the lake and an appealing lobby area with a grand piano. National Park Service

include phones. Even gentler on the budget are the Lake Yellowstone Hotel Frontier Cabins, duplex units that were built in the 1920s but remodeled in 2004.

Mammoth Hot Springs Hotel

Managers: Xanterra Parks & Resorts

307-344-7901

www.travelyellowstone.com

5 miles south of North Entrance to Yellowstone National Park

Rates: Inexpensive to expensive; rates substantially reduced in winter

Credit Cards: AE, CB, D, DC, MC, V, JBS International

Handicapped Access: Yes

Seasons: Late May to mid-Sept. and mid-Dec. to mid-Mar.

Welcome to the 1930s, when the North Entrance was Yellowstone's primary traffic corridor and Mammoth was the park's hub of activity. The rooms provide simple elegance, and with a little imagination you can picture Calvin Coolidge resting in the next room after arriving on a train for a few days of fly fishing. The hotel rooms come with a bed, washbasin and phone. Showers and bathrooms are down the hall. Cabins on the grounds run the gamut. There are two "luxury" suites with phone, cable TV and a private bedroom. The Frontier Cabins have showers. A bare-necessities option offers a sink, with a community bath-room. This is a place to escape the outside world; only two luxury suites have TV, radio and Internet. There's no air-conditioning, either, though at 6,400 feet you rarely need it. Excellent food is across the parking lot in the restored dining hall. There's a small bar on the main floor with TV and appetizers. A quiet lounge next to the lobby features a grand piano and giant carved wood inlay map of the United States. Tours can be arranged here as well. Mammoth quiets down early, but don't expect to sleep in: The paper-thin walls reverberate in the morning with the echoes of people eager to take in Yellowstone's treasures. Mammoth featured a geothermal pool in the 1930s, but the closest you'll get today is a hot tub on a few cabin porches. Locals like Mammoth for a quick getaway in winter, when room rates are substantially reduced. There's a gift shop in the lobby, but one of the best gifts is right out the front door, where a large elk herd frequently grazes.

Old Faithful Inn
Managers: Xanterra Parks & Resorts
307-344-7901
www.travelyellowstone.com
Southwest side of the park, 30 miles from West Entrance and 39 from South Entrance
Rates: $90–449
Credit Cards: AE, CB, D, DC, MC, V, JBS International
Handicapped Access: Yes
Seasons: Mid-May to early Sept.

The Grand Dame of Yellowstone, now a National Historic Landmark, turned 100 in 2003 and remains the most visited man-made attraction in Yellowstone, thanks partly to a somewhat-popular geyser with the same name just out the back door. As such, it's also the most difficult lodging to secure in the park. Inside the lobby, it's the Swiss Family Robinson meets Jeremiah Johnson. The inn's original log structure, fondly called "The Old House," towers seven stories with a mosaic of lodgepole staircases and walkways designed by architect Robert C. Reamer to reflect nature's perfect imperfections. The centerpiece is

Elk are frequent visitors to the grassy areas between the cabins at Mammoth Hot Springs in Yellowstone. Mammoth features a number of cabins and a no-frills 1930s-style hotel. National Park Service

a massive stone fireplace. At the top, some 92 feet from the floor, is a "crow's nest" where musicians once played. Despite the heavy foot traffic between Memorial Day and Labor Day, it's still possible to find a cozy corner to sit in a log rocker and read a book by the fire. Wings were added in the two decades after the original construction. The lodge now has 327 rooms, many with original plumbing, including claw-footed tubs. The old building has survived the area's frequent earthquakes, including the famed 1959 temblor that collapsed the dining-room chimney. Old Faithful Inn also came perilously close to being reduced to cinders in the 1988 fires—remnants can still be seen from the inn—but she has endured. Periodic remodeling continued through the summer of 2007, limiting the summer seasons. The inn features a restaurant, a deli, and souvenir stores. Interpretive tours can be arranged at the inn. It is closed in winter, but is accessible by snow coach or via cross-country skis. The nearby Old Faithful Snow Lodge and Cabins are open from mid-December until mid-March.

Old Faithful Lodge Cabins

Managers: Xanterra Parks & Resorts

307-344-7901

www.travelyellowstone.com

Southwest side of the park, 30 miles from West Entrance and 39 from South Entrance

Rates: $66 and $102

Credit Cards: AE, CB, D, DC, MC, V, JBS International

Handicapped Access: Yes, but limited

Seasons: Mid-May–late Sept.

The Old Faithful Lodge. National Park Service

The recently constructed Old Faithful Snow Lodge caters to winter visitors who arrive in snowcoaches and on cross-country skis. National Park Service

For the budget-conscious who want the amenities of the Old Faithful Inn and access to the geysers and fishing on the Firehole River, there are the Old Faithful Lodge Cabins next door. The Old Faithful Lodge might be the stepchild of Old Faithful Inn, but it certainly isn't ugly. It has the best views of the geyser from its cafeteria. There are no rooms in the lodge, but this is the hub for 130 cozy cabins. The primitive Budget cabins are standard motel-style units with a sink and toilet; communal showers are in the main lodge. The Pioneer cabins are also rustic, but have showers. A store, gift shop and recreation hall are in the main lodge.

Old Faithful Snow Lodge & Cabins
Managers: Xanterra Parks & Resorts
307-344-7901
www.travelyellowstone.com
Southwest side of the park, 30 miles from West Entrance and 39 from South Entrance
Rates: $90–185 summer, $85–171 winter
Credit Cards: AE, CB, D, DC, MC, V, JBS International
Handicapped Access: Yes
Seasons: Early May–late Oct., late Dec.–mid-Mar.

Yellowstone's newest lodge was constructed in 1999 to blend seamlessly with its lodgepole and geyser surroundings. Though modern, one can imagine nearby Old Faithful Inn looking and feeling much the same when its fresh timbers, stone fireplace and frontier furnishings were installed a century earlier. What sets the Snow Lodge & Cabins apart is its winter season. From the warm and cozy confines, winter adventurers are destined for a treat: Solitude amid steamy geysers and congregating wildlife, especially bison. Getting here in winter is the challenge. Snowcoaches bring in most tourists from West Yellowstone some 20 miles away, though some intrepid visitors will arrive via snowmobile or even cross-country skis. The lodge features 100 attractive rooms with full baths. The Western cabins are akin to staying in a comfortable motel room. The Frontier cabins are duplexes; they're more vanilla, but still comfortable. A store and dining room also are on site. Special packages are available in winter.

Roosevelt Lodge Cabins

Managers: Xanterra Parks & Resorts
307-344-7901
www.travelyellowstone.com
North side of the park, 23 miles from North Entrance and 29 from Northeast Entrance
Rates: $63 and $102
Credit Cards: AE, CB, D, DC, MC, V, JBS International
Handicapped Access: Yes, but limited
Seasons: Early June to early Sept.

Ask any Yellowstone regular or seasonal employee about the best place to get away from it all, and the answer, hands down, will be Roosevelt. It's isolated from prime park attractions, close to such wildlife havens as the Lamar Valley and Hayden Valley, and the lack of any upscale lodging usually ensures that your neighbors are like-minded. A perfect day at Roosevelt would consist of early-morning wolf watching in the Lamar followed by exceptional fly fishing on the nearby Yellowstone River, an afternoon horseback ride, an evening wagon ride and cookout, followed by watching the sun set from a log rocker on the front

Rustic Roosevelt Lodge offers the most serene accommodations in Yellowstone and is a favorite of park employees for its isolation and Old West feel. Book this one at least a year in advance. National Park Service

porch. The two styles of cabins are rustic, especially the Roughrider, which has no bathroom and is heated by a wood-burning stove. Then again, that's precisely the point. Be sure to book these a year in advance.

LODGING IN GRAND TETON NATIONAL PARK

Colter Bay Village
Managers: Grand Teton Lodge Company
800-628-9988 or 307-543-3100
www.gtlc.com/lodgeCBV.aspx
On the east shore of Jackson Lake, a few miles northwest of Jackson Lake Lodge
Rates: $41–165
Credit Cards: AE, D, DC, MC, V
Handicapped Access: Yes
Seasons: Late May to late Sept.

Quaint, comfortable and more geared toward families than Jackson Lake and Jenny Lake lodges (see next two entries), this actual village features 166 comfortable log cabins suitable for two to six people as well as tent cabins, 112 RV spaces and a campground. Colter Bay is an ideal spot for families, and its location at the north end of the park makes it a great base for scouting Yellowstone National Park as well. All amenities are on site.

Jackson Lake Lodge
Managers: Grand Teton Lodge Company
800-628-9988 or 307-543-3100
www.gtlc.com/lodgeJac.aspx
On a bluff overlooking Jackson Lake, 26 miles north of the Jackson Hole Airport
Rates: $189–625
Credit Cards: AE, D, DC, MC, V
Handicapped Access: Yes
Seasons: Mid-May–late Sept.

The signature, if somewhat controversial, lodge in the park. Who hasn't seen a photo taken from the 60-foot picture window in the main lodge overlooking Jackson Lake and featuring a jaw-dropping view of the Tetons? The main lodge has 37 guest rooms and is flanked by 348 guest cottages that look more like mountain motel rooms. The architecture is decidedly the antithesis of national park themes, but in many respects this is the hub of Grand Teton National Park. The lodge has a Mural Room and Pioneer Grill for food and a cocktail lounge that features regular entertainment, not to mention astounding views from inside or the outdoor patio. Most rooms are under $200, with view rooms costing slightly more. This is the place for visitors who like to be at the center of the action, and it's easy to spend hours in the lodge gazing at the lake and mountains or watching moose browse in Willow Flats.

Jenny Lake Lodge
Managers: Grand Teton Lodge Company
800-628-9988 or 307-543-3100

www.gtlc.com/lodgeJen.aspx
About halfway between the Jackson Airport and Jackson Lake Lodge, on the east shore of Jenny Lake
Rates: $525–750
Credit Cards: AE, D, DC, MC, V   *Too expensive*
Handicapped Access: Yes
Seasons: Early June to early Oct.

Rustic western luxury at its finest. If you're not bothered by the steep prices, Jenny Lake Lodge's 37 cabins provide the consummate Teton vacation and might be the finest lodging anywhere in the national park system. The rooms are beyond comfortable and the cost includes an exceptional breakfast and five-course dinner. Free bicycling and horseback riding are included in the amenities. The views are spectacular and Jenny Lake is the prettiest lake in the park. Hiking is nearby and the service is a cut above.

Dornan's Spur Ranch Cabins

307-733-2522
www.dornans.com/cabins
200 Moose St., Moose, WY 83012
Rates: $175–205 summer and $125–150 winter and shoulder season for one-bedroom cabins, $175 and $250 for two-bedroom cabins
Credit Cards: AE, D, MC, V
Handicapped Access: No
Pets: Yes, with restrictions
Seasons: Year-round

This appealing family-owned spread near the park headquarters at Moose features eight newer one-bedroom and four two-bedroom cabins with lodgepole pine furniture and modern amenities, all on the banks of the Snake River. Kitchens are fully equipped and patios face the Tetons. There are barbecues but no TVs in the cabins. It's all part of a 10-acre complex that includes a restaurant, the largest wine shop in the region and a wide variety of recreation rentals. The minimum stay in summer is three nights.

Flagg Ranch Resort

800-443-2311 or 307-543-2356
www.flaggranch.com
P.O. Box 187, Moran, WY 83013
Located between Yellowstone and Grand Teton National Parks on the John D. Rockefeller Memorial Hwy.
Rates: $165–175.
Credit Cards: AE, D, MC, V
Handicapped Access: Yes
Pets: Yes, with restrictions
Seasons: Mid-May–mid-Oct.

The oldest continually running lodge in upper Jackson Hole. It features newer fourplex log cabins that are comfortably furnished and include patios. All other amenities are available in the main lodge, including a lounge, restaurant, deli and gift shop.

Signal Mountain Lodge
Manager: Forever Resorts
307-543-2831
www.signalmountainlodge.com
South shore of Jackson Lake
Rates: $117–150 for one-bedroom cabins, $161–171 two-bedroom cabins, $151 Country
Rooms, $201 Deluxe Country Rooms, $161–247 bungalows, $222–237 Lakefront Retreats
(rates are to increase 5–10% for the summer of 2008)
Credit Cards: AE, D, MC, V
Handicapped Access: No
Pets: Yes, except for the upper Lakefront Retreats
Seasons: Early May–mid-Oct.

This collection of 1930s rooms, cabins and houses runs the gamut, though none are luxurious. Rooms are motel-style with microwaves and fridges. Some have fireplaces. The
Lakefront Retreats are cozy and offer great views of the lake which is less than 100 feet
away. A marina, store and other amenities are on site. In keeping with the park's policies,
there are no televisions in the rooms.

LODGING IN YELLOWSTONE NATIONAL PARK GATEWAY COMMUNITIES

Cody, Wyoming   *to Old Faithful – 117 miles (2 hrs 49 min)*

To many Yellowstone visitors, Cody personifies the Old West, starting with the name.
Colonel William "Buffalo Bill" Cody first came to this arid region of northwest Wyoming
in the 1870s with a professor from Yale University. He quickly became enamored of the
area and its development possibilities, vowing to return. A decade later he did, with devel-
opers who began the town on the east end of the Shoshone River canyon (the town was
later moved to the present-day west end). Cody built the town's first hotel, the Irma,
named after his daughter; he coaxed the Burlington Railroad to build a spur to his new
town; he persuaded a good friend named Teddy Roosevelt to build a federal dam on the
river west of the city; he orchestrated the construction of the scenic road to what is now
Yellowstone's East Entrance; and he founded the town's newspaper, the Enterprise, which
still serves the city. Small wonder that in 1895 the town's fathers voted to name the new
settlement Cody. His influence didn't stop at the town's edge: Through Roosevelt, he
helped establish the country's first national forest, the Shoshone, and its first ranger station, at Wapiti. Though known as a proud frontiersman on horseback, Buffalo Bill also was
an early champion of Indian rights, women's suffrage and environmental causes. His name
lives on throughout the region, including the famed Cody Nite Rodeo, which began in 1922
and is surely the first rodeo the majority of Americans witness. Some of the town's charm
has been lost with the arrival of big-box stores, chain restaurants and motels, but seeing
the nightly gunfight outside the Irma is an entertaining reminder of the town's origins.
A wide variety of lodging options are available in town, most of it standard fare, with plenty
of national chains. For a closer look at what's available, go to www.codychamber.org/
visitcody/lodging.htm.

Motels

Big Bear Motel
Managers: Bill and Jodi Holly
800-325-7163 or 307-587-3117
www.bigbearmotel.com
139 W. Yellowstone Ave., Cody, WY 82414
Rates: $36–125
Credit Cards: AE, D, MC, V
Handicapped Access: Yes
Pets: Yes
Season: Year-round

This truly unique mom-and-pop motel has 47 rooms with six suites and one three-bedroom townhome. Bill and Jodi live on the 4-acre property so they like to keep it interesting. Pony rides, and sing-alongs with Helen Carter (who sang in the Grand Ole Opry) are regular events along with the Wyoming Pony Ride for the young at heart and small of size. Other amenities include outdoor heated swimming pool, continental breakfast (sometimes featuring Helen's famous sticky buns), wireless Internet, air-conditioning, smoking and nonsmoking rooms.

Bison Willy's Base Camp
Owner: Kenny Gasch
877-587-0629 or 307-250-0763
www.bisonwillys.com
1625 Alger Ave., Cody, WY 82414
Rates: $20–89 (per person)
Credit Cards: MC, V
Handicapped Access: No
Pets: Yes
Season: Year-round

Two distinct facilities based on the European hostel model. Base camp is a 1,100-square-foot upscale house with two rental units inside: a two-bedroom section with private bath, and a one-bedroom section that sleeps four in bunk beds and has a private bath. Both sections share the living room, full kitchen, dining room, sun porch and back deck with barbecue. The spike camp is a spartan 400-square-foot cottage with six bunk beds, full kitchen and a bathroom. Bring your own bedding. Willy's caters to international travelers as well as ice climbers and kayakers.

Buffalo Bill's Antler's Inn
Manager: Carlene Roemmich
800-388-2084 or 307-587-2084
1213 17th St., Cody, WY 82414
Rates: $45–90
Credit Cards: AE, D, MC, V
Handicapped Access: Yes
Pets: No
Season: Summer

Forty western-themed, affordable rooms with handmade burl wood furniture patterned after the historic works of Thomas Molesworth. Each room offers the typical amenities and wireless Internet. Formerly known as the Burl Inn.

Buffalo Bill Village Resort

Cody's only downtown full-service resort is a large complex that includes two major chain motels and a village of cabins that operate independently but in coordination. Ticket sales for anything that goes on in town may be purchased at the resort. Special Group or tour rates are available by calling the main office. The QT Restaurant, Bottoms Up Lounge and an outdoor heated pool are on the premises for all three motels. Wireless Internet is available in each room. There is meeting and banquet space for 350. Motels included in the resort are:

Comfort Inn at Buffalo Bill Village Resort

Manager: Pernille Swienink
800-527-5544 or 307-587-5556
www.blairhotels.com
Address: 1701 Sheridan Ave., Cody, WY 83414
Rates: $79–179
Credit Cards: AE, D, MC, V
Handicapped Access: Yes
Pets: No
Season: Year-round

The Comfort Inn has 75 rooms available from May through October, then 49 rooms during the off-season. A free continental breakfast is offered.

Holiday Inn at Buffalo Bill Village Resort

Manager: James Blair
800-527-5544 or 307-587-5555
www.blairhotels.com
1701 Sheridan Ave., Cody, WY 82414
Rates: $79–189 (suite is $50 more)
Credit Cards: AE, D, MC, V
Handicapped Access: Yes
Pets: No
Season: Year-round

The Holiday Inn features 189 deluxe rooms in the summer, then scales down to 132 in the winter. The inn is surrounded by the Buffalo Bill Village cabins and is the center of the complex.

Buffalo Bill Village Cabins at Buffalo Bill Resort

Manager: Judy Blair
800-527-5544 or 307-587-5544
www.blairhotels.com
1701 Sheridan Ave., Cody, WY 82414
Rates: $99–159

Credit Cards: AE, D, MC, V
Handicapped Access: Yes
Pets: No
Season: May through Sept.

The 83 refurbished cabins were originally built for workers in Buffalo Bill's circus. They offer some semblance of privacy in a busy area, with cowboy-style décor. Cabins vary in size and sleep from two to eight. Each features air-conditioning, cable TV, a full bath and a coffeepot.

Cody Legacy Inn & Suites
Managers: Kellie and Bryan Edwards
307-587-6067
www.codylegacyinn.com
1801 Mountain View Dr., Cody, WY 82414
Rates: $139–169 June 12–Aug. 13, $99–129 May 29–June 11 and Aug. 14–Sept. 30, $79–105 May 1–28, $68–79 Oct. 1–Dec. 20 and Jan. 3–Apr. 30.
Credit Cards: AE, D, MC, V
Handicapped Access: Yes
Pets: No
Season: Year-round (Closed Dec. 22–Jan. 2)

One of the newest lodging options in Cody, the Legacy Inn and Suites offers modern western-themed rooms with an antler chandelier and stone fireplace dominate the lobby where black-and-white photos of some of the town's famous names grace the walls. The inn added a fitness center and two family suites in the spring of 2007. A swimming pool and hot tub are on site. Complimentary breakfast. A conference room is also available.

Irma Hotel
Owner: John Darby
800-745-4762 or 307-587-4221
www.irmahotel.com
1192 Sheridan Ave., Cody, WY 82414
Rates: $95–145
Credit Cards: AE, D, MC, V
Handicapped Access: Yes
Pets: Yes ($25 fee)
Season: Year-round

Built in 1902, Cody's signature hotel was the first building in town. Built by Buffalo Bill Cody himself and named after his daughter, it remains rustic with a hunting-lodge décor and some of the original furniture and photos. Rooms have private baths and TV. The historic rooms are furnished in much the same manner as Buffalo Bill had them. A newer addition to the hotel features more contemporary furniture. A restaurant, saloon and gift shop are downstairs. Wireless Internet is available. If you hear gunshots out front on summer evenings, don't be alarmed: From June through Oct. 1, a western gunfight is reenacted at 6 PM on the wood-planked veranda. For more on the Irma, see "Historic Sites" in Chapter 4, "Attractions."

Bed and Breakfasts

Angel's Keep

Owners: Barbara and Robert Kelley
877-320-2800 or 307-587-6205
www.angelskeep.com
1241 Wyoming Ave., Cody, WY 82414
Rates: $85–145
Credit Cards: MC, V
Handicapped Access: No
Pets: Considered
Season: Year-round

Set within a former church, each of three rooms has a TV, VCR, air-conditioning and private bath. A complete country gourmet breakfast is served each morning, and cookies are always available. Antiques and primitives are sold in the gift shop.

Chamberlin Inn

Owners: Ev and Susan Diehl
888-587-0202 or 307-587-0202
www.chamberlininn.com
1032 12th St., Cody, WY 82414
Rates: $145–165 for standard queens, $235 for Hemingway Suite, $265 for Queen Suites, $285 for King Suites, $235–285 for apartments, $650 for Courthouse
Handicapped Access: Limited
Pets: No
Season: Year-round

The Chamberlin Inn in Cody is a historic hotel that has been renovated and refurbished to blend modern amenities with a sense of history.
Courtesy Chamberlin Inn

Eighteen rooms on two floors are decorated in a Victorian western theme reminiscent of an Old West hotel. In fact, the brick building is an old boarding house started by Agnes Chamberlin, who worked for Buffalo Bill Cody at the Cody Enterprise in 1900; she opened the boarding house three years later. Eventually, it became a hotel and was expanded to include the Cody Circuit Judge Courthouse. The hotel's old guest registry includes such names as Ernest Hemingway and Marshall Fields. Hemingway stayed at the hotel in 1932 and finished his manuscript for *Death in the Afternoon* there. He went to fish the Clark's Fork of the Yellowstone River, returned to mail the manuscript and then downed a few cold ones at the Irma Bar a block away before heading back to the Clarks Fork. His room has been refurbished to reflect his lifestyle. The hotel eventually fell into disrepair, was jump-started under another name in the mid-1970s and then changed back to the Chamberlin Inn when Ev and Susan Diehl purchased it in 2005. They completely restored it to expertly mesh history with modern conveniences. Lodging is also available in Cody's original courthouse, a garden cottage, garden apartment and garden loft apartment.

K3 Guest Ranch

Owners: Jerry and Bette Kinkade
888-587-2080 or 307-587-2080 or 307-587-4550
www.k3guestranch.com
30 Nielsen Trail, Cody, WY 82414
Rates: $150–200, $25 each additional person
Credit Cards: D, MC, V
Handicapped Access: No
Pets: Yes, but kept outside or in vehicle at night. Horses are kept in corrals
Season: Year-round

This former small cattle operation turned guest ranch was featured in *Bed and Breakfast America* magazine in the fall of 2006. Peter Greenburg (the Travel Detective for NBC) also featured the K3 Guest Ranch as one of the four unique Bed and Breakfasts in the world, and the most unique in the United States. In the spacious Chuckwagon and Rocky Mountain rooms, guests sleep in real ranch wagons fitted with comfy pillow-top mattresses. Each room sleeps up to 6. The smaller Teton Room features a Teton Mountain mural with a pole fence frame and life-sized Rocky Mountain trout carved into the bathroom tiles. The Big Chief Teepee (under construction) will offer a queen bed, full bath and another great way to experience the real West. Breakfast is cooked over an open fire and served outdoors. Two streams for fishing are within 100 feet of the 3,500-square-foot lodge. Buddy and two trick horses will entertain kids of all ages. The ranch is six minutes from Cody, but seems like 600 miles.

Lambright Place

Owners: Jim and Mary Crow
800-241-5310 or 307-527-5310
www.lambrightplace.com
1501 Beck Ave., Cody, WY 82414
Rates: $65–160
Credit Cards: MC, V
Handicapped Access: No
Pets: No
Season: Year-round

The K3 Guest Ranch has been honored as one of the most unusual places to stay in the world Courtesy of K3 Guest Ranch

This 1924 Victorian home on a street corner in downtown Cody offers three rooms with private baths and queen beds, one with a daybed for an accompanying child. A separate bunkhouse sleeps five and has a bath. It is furnished with Victorian antiques and has warm, sunny rooms. A full gourmet breakfast is served. Specialties include artichoke soufflé and crème brûlée french toast. The inn is within walking distance of the Buffalo Bill Historical Center.

Southfork
Owners: Donna and Brian Lloyd
307-587-8311
www.southforkbb.com
797 South Fork Rd., Cody, WY 82414
Rates: $125
Credit Cards: D, MC, V
Handicapped Access: No
Pets: No
Season: Year-round

Formerly a private estate, the Southfork is a large home with a guest and residential wing flanking a common area. Three rooms are available for rent. Located 8 miles from town, with 360-degree views of the mountains, the guest lodge sits among ranchettes and homes in a part of Cody most tourists don't see. Co-owner Brian Lloyd is a retired chef who enjoys preparing a full, tantalizing breakfast. Amenities include high-speed Internet, a home theater, satellite TV, a lodge atmosphere with a huge stone fireplace, mission furniture, stain-glass lighting, and collectible Indian artifacts and western art.

Robin's Nest
Managers: Robin and Bob Berry
866-723-7797 or 307-527-7208
www.robinsnestcody.com
1508 Alger Ave., Cody, WY 82414

Rates: $135–145
Credit Cards: AE, D, MC, V
Handicapped Access: No
Pets: Yes
Season: Year-round

This two-story brick home built in 1926 has three rooms available, all decorated in distinct styles. One features the 1920s furniture that belonged to co-owner Robin Berry's grandmother. Another room has a Paul Bunyan–sized log bed. The breakfast menu includes bison sausage and a French praline upside-down toast. The Berry motto: "Come as tourist . . . leave as family."

The Mayor's Inn
Owners: Bill and Dale Lee
888-217-3001 or 307-587-0887
www.mayorsinn.com
1413 Rumsey Ave., Cody, WY 82414
Rates: $120–210 summer, $80–160 winter
Credit Cards: AE, D, MC, V
Handicapped Access: No
Pets: No
Season: Year-round

The Mayor's Inn is a restored historic home with four rooms in the main house and a carriage house that sleeps four and has a full kitchen. Jacuzzi and hot tub suite are available and one room has a claw-foot tub in the bathroom. It has central air-conditioning, wireless Internet and heated bathroom floors for cold winter nights. Their signature breakfast is a stack of sourdough flapjacks with a side of buffalo sausage. The inn is located one block off Main Street and within walking distance of all downtown activities.

Cooke City, Montana   *101 miles to Old Faithful (2 hrs 40 min)*

When they say, "meet me at the end of the road," they really mean it in Cooke City. At least that's true in the winter, when the road really does dead end in a pile of snow. The plowing from Gardiner through Yellowstone National Park ends here at this narrow strip town with mostly motels, restaurants, a couple of gas stations and a few homes for the 100-plus hearty year-round residents. In the late 1800s, Cooke City—named for a Northern Pacific president who never visited the place and refused to build a railroad to the site, much to the citizenry's dismay—was a bustling gold-mining town with two smelters, two sawmills and two hotels. In winter, the main drag in this old mining town is abuzz with snowmobiles, most of them headed east on the Beartooth Highway. In the past decade, they've shared the road with Subaru wagons toting wolf-spotting scopes and cameras. In summer, it's more of a standard tourist community, the first and only significant town between the park and Beartooth Pass. Like Silver Gate, the town typically gets tons of snow, with remnants often lingering until June. Evidence of the 1988 fires is starkly evident in what was then morbidly referred to as "Cooked City," when the old mining town was sure it was destined to meet its maker. Miraculously, the fires skirted the town's northern edge.

Just east of Yellowstone's Northeast Entrance, Cooke City is the end of the road after the snow falls. The small town's motels cater to snowmobilers and wolf watchers in winter. National Park Service

Alpine Motel
Owner: Gerlie Weinstein
888-838-1190 or 406-838-2262
www.cookecityalpine.com
105 Main St., Cooke City, MT 59020
Rates: $50–155
Credit Cards: AE, D, MC, V
Handicapped Access: Yes
Pets: Yes (fee)
Seasons: Year-round

The Alpine features single rooms plus apartment units with two bedrooms and kitchen in typical western decor. Wireless Internet and guest laundry are on site. More amenities are offered with extended stays. ATV and hiking trails on the Gallatin and Custer National Forests are right out the front door.

Antlers Lodge
Owners: Bill and Kay Whittle
866-738-2432 or 406-838-2432
www.cookecityantlerslodge.com.
311 Main St. E., P.O. Box 1152, Cooke City, MT 59020
Rates: $55–125
Credit Cards: MC, V
Handicapped Access: No

Pets: Yes
Seasons: Year-round

The Antlers is comprised of 18 log cabins and a historic (1913) lodge with a hearty mountain feel, right down to the stone fireplace and elk racks on the log walls. Some cabins have full kitchens, a few with satellite television. The lodge has wireless Internet. The Antlers bar and restaurant is on site. This place fills fast during the summer (June–September) and winter (December–March) seasons.

Big Moose Resort

Owner: Bev Chatelain
406-838-2393
www.bigmooseresort.com
Colter Pass, Cooke City, MT 59020
3 miles east of Cooke City on the Beartooth Hwy.
Rates: $75–100
Credit Cards: D, MC, V
Handicapped Access: No
Pets: Yes
Seasons: Year-round

With a wide array of newer and older cabins, the Big Moose is a solid bang for the buck, and far enough away from Cooke City to avoid the constant buzz of snowmobiles. Each cabin has satellite TV, wireless Internet and gas/log fireplaces, and a few have kitchenettes. Hot tub and Swedish massage by appointment are among the amenities.

Blue Sky Wonder

Manager: Florence Zundel
406-838-2153 or 360-331-7607
www.blueskywonder.com
P.O. Box 1146, Cooke City, MT 59020
Rates: $180 (three-night minimum), $1,000/week, $800/month for a three-month minimum stay
Credit Cards: AE, D, MC, V
Handicapped Access: No
Pets: No
Seasons: Year-round

A cozy, two-bedroom upstairs apartment nests above a log home. Decked out with modern and attractive furnishings, the special feature of this wonder in the sky is a completely outfitted kitchen, including stainless-steel appliances and gas range. Extended stays by the week or month can be accommodated.

Buns 'N' Beds

Managers: Leo and Jan Gaertner
406-838-2030
201 Main St., P.O. Box 1018, Cooke City, MT 59020
Rates: $60 (two people), $100 (four)

Credit Cards: MC, V
Handicapped Access: No
Pets: Yes
Seasons: Year-round

The three functional and rustic cabins behind the restaurant were built in 1938. Two have a microwave and fridge, the third a kitchenette. The popular restaurant is open year-round and is known for its barbecue cheddar bomb sandwich.

Elk Horn Lodge
Owners: Suzy and John Hahn
406-838-2332
www.elkhornlodgemt.com
103 Main St. E., P.O. Box 1178, Cooke City, MT 59020
Rates: $63–94 (rooms), $78–104 (cabins)
Credit Cards: MC, V
Handicapped Access: No
Pets: Yes (with permission)
Season: Year-round

These two quaint log cabins come with two beds, a full bath, Direct TV and kitchenette. Six deluxe rooms also come with two beds, full bath, Direct TV, small fridge and coffeemaker. All lodging is nonsmoking and comes with wireless Internet. Owner Suzy Hahn is director of the Chamber of Commerce and offers handy tips and information, including snow reports. Discounts are offered for off-season and extended stays.

Grizzly Pad & Cabins
Owner: Janet Burbach
406-838-2161 or 406-838-2065
P.O. Box 1124, Cooke City, MT 59020
Rates: $85
Credit Cards: MC, V
Handicapped Access: Restaurant only
Pets: No
Season: Dec. 27–Apr. 1 and Memorial Day Weekend–Oct. 1

Convenience is the buzzword at the Grizzly Pad, which offers two log cabins with satellite TV and full kitchens plus a restaurant in front that serves breakfast, lunch and dinner and features a kids' menu. Favorite items include pizza, hamburger, fries and shake special, and local Wilcoxson ice cream. Sack lunches are available. The restaurant closes for the season when the cabins shut down.

Skyline Guest Ranch
Owners: Liz and Victor Jackson
877-238-8885
www.flyfishyellowstone.com
31 Kersey Lake Rd., P.O. Box 1074, Cooke City, MT 59020
Rates: $83–105

Credit Cards: MC, V
Handicapped Access: Limited
Pets: No
Seasons: Summer and winter

The Skyline is a six-year-old, three-story lodge with five spacious guest rooms, each with private bath. A full, hot breakfast is included; dinner is served by reservation. Shared areas include living room, game room, deck and hot tub. Family outfitters for 50 years, the Jacksons offer trail rides, backcountry camping and hiking, lake and stream fly fishing, and hunting expeditions. Skyline Guest Ranch & Guide Service Inc. operates under permit of the Gallatin National Forest, the Custer National Forest and Yellowstone National Park.

Soda Butte Lodge, Tavern & Casino
Manager: Lorraine Kokkler
406-838-2251 or 800-527-6462
www.cookecity.com
209 US Hwy. 212, P.O. Box 1119, Cooke City, MT 59020
Rates: $65–120
Credit Cards: AE, D, MC, V
Handicapped Access: Yes
Pets: Yes
Seasons: Year-round

An old-style western motel, the Soda Butte on the upper east end is the most conspicuous in Cooke City. The Prospector Restaurant and Ore House Bar are on site. An inside hot tub is open part of the year. A large suite with Jacuzzi is also available. Don't expect a quiet sleep, especially if you're close to the tavern and casino. This Cooke City mainstay can get rowdy into the wee hours.

Stillwater Outfitters
Owners: Matt and Mary Robison
888-341-2267 or 406-838-2267
www.stillwateroutfitters.com
714 US Hwy. 212, P.O. Box 1029, Cooke City, MT 59020
3 miles east of Cooke City on the Beartooth Hwy.
Rates: Cabins start at $65; varies by season
Credit Cards: MC, V
Handicapped Access: No
Pets: Considered
Seasons: Summer May–Sept., winter Dec.–Mar.

Six rustic, clean log cabins come with private baths; two have full kitchens, making them ideal for families or large groups. Breakfast is offered in the summer and full meals in the winter. Full outfitting for horseback pack trips and river, stream or lake fly-fishing are offered. The outdoor hot tub is always open. Formerly known as Big Bear Lodge.

Super 8 Motel

General manager: Bob Smith
877-338-2070 or 406-838-2070
www.cookecitysuper8.com
303 E. Main St., Cooke City, MT 59020
Rates: $75–95
Credit Cards: AE, D, MC, V
Handicapped Access: Yes
Pets: No
Seasons: Year-round

The most modern motel in Cooke City has 33 rooms, in décor that fits the surroundings. The familiar chain motel—the only one in Cooke City—features smoke-free rooms, wireless Internet, complimentary continental breakfast and conference room. Kids stay free. Super 8 Motels aren't fancy, but they're the one place where you know what you're getting up front.

Yellowstone Yurt Hostel

406-838-2349
www.hostels.com
West Broadway, Cooke City, MT 59020
Rates: $14
Credit Cards: No
Handicapped Access: No
Seasons: Year-round (except May, June and Oct.)

For the absolutely budget-minded, this true Mongolian yurt sleeps six. There's a kitchen with Coleman stove, shower and toilet behind the yurt. The views alone are worth the $14, which is paid on the honor system inside the yurt.

Gardiner, Montana   *57 miles to Old Faithful (1hr 45 min)*

Of all the gateway communities to Yellowstone, Gardiner in many ways feels like the most authentic frontier town, with a rugged and raw persona befitting its semiarid region. It feels as if the town would be here even if there weren't a park—which can't necessarily be said of West Yellowstone, Cooke City or Island Park. Nonetheless, Gardiner was created in 1880 entirely for the purposes of serving visitors coming to the park's original entrance, though mining, ranching and fur trapping certainly have had significant influences. The town was laid out hard against the park's northern border, reputedly by an irate local man angry with park officials for tossing him out of Mammoth, 5 miles to the south. Today, Gardiner is perched above steep banks on both sides of the frothy Yellowstone River, the old part of town facing the park and connected to the newer section along US 89 by one bridge. It is best known as the site of the stone Roosevelt Arch and was the hub of park activity for a half-century after the Northern Pacific Railroad arrived from Livingston. By 1883, Gardiner had 21 saloons serving about 200 full-time residents. Rail service ended in the 1950s. Today, it has its share of motels and touristy knickknack shops, but it's also where the majority of the park's employees live. Stop in the fall and watch an eight-man football game at the high school, where an occasional pronghorn or rutting bull elk has been known to wander across the field.

Motels

Absaroka Lodge

Managers: Richard and Irene Herriford
800-848-7414 or 800-755-7414
www.yellowstonemotel.com
310 Scott St. W., P.O. Box 10, Gardiner, MT 59030
Rates: $95–105
Credit Cards: AE, D, DC, MC, V
Handicapped Access: Yes
Pets: Yes
Seasons: Year-round

Email reservations balconies

The Absaroka is popular because all rooms have an attached balcony with exceptional views high above the Yellowstone River. It's also known for making the cover of *National Geographic* magazine once, though the stars of the photo were two bison.

Chico Hot Springs Resort

Owners: Mike and Eve Art
Manager: Colin Davis
800-468-9232 or 406-333-4933
www.chicohotsprings.com
1 Old Chico Rd., P.O. Box 29, Pray, MT 59065
About 30 miles north of Gardiner off East River Rd.
Rates: $49–345
Credit Cards: AE, D, MC, V
Handicapped Access: Yes
Pets: Yes
Seasons: Year-round

looks beautiful

Hot springs pools included in stay

Houses/Cottages/Chalets –
Chalet I – 3 queens – lof $199 (8)
Chalet I – sleeps 10 $229   3 queens/1o 2 singles
Fisherman's Lodge – 2 queen beds – room $115   1 queen downsta
Lower Lodge – 2 queens – $125
Warren's Wing – one king – 2 queens $125
Main Lodge – small rooms – $89 – no bath

It's worth a stop in the heart of Paradise Valley just to soak in the thermal waters of the out-door swimming pool. The main lodge oozes history, from its uneven floors and huge elk mount in the cozy lobby to the black and white photos of the late actor Warren Oates, once a Chico regular. The bar is close to the soaking pool and offers pool, darts and live music. The restaurant is renowned for some of the finest gourmet dining in the Northern Rockies. There is also a poolside grill that offers lunch and snacks. Rooms in the main lodge are quaint and cozy, many without bathrooms, but a bargain starting at $49 during the off-season. Rates increase but are still reasonable in the more modern Warren's Wing, Lower Lodge and Fisherman's Lodge. For those who want privacy and views of the Absarokas and Gallatins, six houses, cottages and chalets can accommodate up to 16. A gift shop, day spa, horseback riding and other activities are on site. Pool guests can be served at the bar through a service window. Added to National Register of Historic Places in 1999, it's as popular with locals as out-of-towners.

Comfort Inn

Managers: Rod and Jill McAllister
800-4-CHOICE or 406-848-7536
www.yellowstonecomfortinn.com

107 Hellroaring St., P.O. Box 268, Gardiner, MT 59030
Rates: $69.99–154.99
Credit Cards: AE, D, MC, V
Handicapped Access: Yes
Pets: No
Seasons: Year-round

Grayling MT
Island Park, ID

This log-style motel on the north end of town has 77 rooms appointed with rustic log furniture. The Antler Pub & Grill, a full-service restaurant, is on site. Three indoor hot tubs are part of the amenities, and Jacuzzi suites are available. Wireless Internet can be accessed in the lobby.

Hillcrest Cottages

Owners: Art and Annie Bent
800-970-7353 or 406-848-7353
www.hillcrestcottages.com
200 Scott St. W., P.O. Box 430, Gardiner, MT 59030
Rates: $60–150
Credit Cards: D, MC, V
Handicapped Access: Limited
Pets: Yes, with restrictions
Seasons: June–Nov.

Small "urban" cottages

These 12 modern cottages with a total of 17 units (some are duplexes) are urban by Gardiner standards. It's a family-owned operation across from a gas station, just over the Yellowstone River bridge. Rooms are clean, comfortable and most have kitchenettes with microwave and fridge, but no views.

Riverside Cottages

Managers: Edie and Laura Cox
877-774-2836 or 406-848-7719
www.riversidecottages.com
521 Scott St. W., P.O. Box 677, Gardiner, MT 59030
Rate: $69–159
Credit Cards: MC, V
Handicapped Access: Limited
Pets: Yes ($5 fee)
Seasons: Year-round

Looks very sparse $129-149 also

These cute cabins consist of a fourplex and a family suite perched high above the Yellowstone River. The Gardiner Chamber of Commerce gushes that the Riverside has "the best views in Gardiner," including Electric Peak in the Gallatin Range. It's hard to argue the claim.

Yellowstone Basin Inn

Owners: Greg and Sabrina Strauss
800-624-3364 or 406-848-7080
www.yellowstonebasininn.com
4 Maiden Basin Dr., Gardiner, MT 59030

B & B amenities w/ private rooms

5 miles north of North Entrance, just off US 89 at Mile Marker 5
Rates: $67–325
Credit Cards: AE, D, MC, V
Handicapped Access: Yes
Pets: No
Seasons: Year-round, with limited availability in winter

Eleven rooms are ideally situated for anyone wanting contemporary western environs away from the hum of Gardiner. The inn's porch, decked with bistro tables and hot tub, is on a ridge overlooking the Yellowstone River and Electric Peak. Vistas of the surrounding ranch lands enhance that sense of being away even as you remain close to the park. Each room is nonsmoking, exceptionally clean and features wireless Internet. Dinner can be arranged with advance notice. Forest Service trailheads are nearby and the Strausses are eager to provide helpful information.

Yellowstone River Motel
Manager: Betty Deweese
888-797-4837 or 406-848-7303
www.yellowstonerivermotel.com
14 E. Park, P.O. Box 223, Gardiner, MT 59030
Rates: $50–88
Credit Cards: AE, D, DC, MC, V
Handicapped Access: Yes
Pets: Yes
Season: May–Oct.

basic hotel style rooms

A string of 38 clean and comfortable units sit on a bank of the Yellowstone River; you can't sleep much closer to the river in Gardiner. One family suite is available, and there is a picnic patio overlooking the river. In-room wireless Internet is available.

Bed and Breakfasts

Diamond Bar-D Guest Ranch & Hunting Lodge
Owner: Cheryl Standish
406-223-0148
www.diamondbardguestranch.com
384 Crevice Rd, P.O. Box 461, Gardiner, MT 59030
9 miles east of Gardiner, 5 miles past Jardine
Rates: $200 per 2-person stay, includes breakfast and dinner. Children $25
Credit Cards: AE, D, MC, V
Handicapped Access: No
Pets: Yes (if they don't chase deer, chickens, ducks or cats)
Season: June 1–Sept. 15, Dec. 1–Apr. 1

This remote outpost puts visitors as close to the Yellowstone backcountry experience as possible. Located on Crevice Mountain (8,300 feet elevation) and an elk migratory route, the property is on the site of an old mining town. Hunters use it as a base for pursuing elk in the fall, but wildlife watchers and photographers will think they have found nirvana. Traditional western log cabins sleep up to six, and trails out the back door lead directly into the park. The Diamond Bar-D is prized for its unstructured environment, seclusion, home-cooked healthy meals and nightly campfires with the occasional educational talk. Three more cabins and a wedding chapel were under construction in the summer of 2007.

Gardiner Guest House
Owner: Nancy and Richard Parks
406-848-7314
www.gardinerguesthouse.com
112 Main St., P.O. Box 173, Gardiner, MT 59030
Rates: $65–125 summer, $65–105 off-season
Credit Cards: MC, V
Handicapped Access: No
Pets: Yes
Season: Year-round

Four rooms in a quaint historic home provide a calm haven in downtown Gardiner. A detached 100-year-old, two-story cabin in the back sleeps four. The entire house can be rented for a special event. Hearty breakfasts are served and special dietary needs are considered. Nancy runs the B&B while Richard operates a fly shop on the property. Either one will happily suggest a hike or fishing hole. Cross-country ski rentals are available in winter for adventures within or around the park.

Headwaters of the Yellowstone
Managers: Merv and Joyce Olson
406-848-7073 or 888-848-7220; fax 406-848-7420
www.headwatersbandb.com
9 Olson Lane, P.O. Box 25, Gardiner, MT 59030
3 miles north of Gardiner on US 89
Rates: $120–175
Credit Cards: AE, D, MC, V
Handicapped Access: Yes
Pets: No
Season: Year-round

The Headwaters features four first-floor rooms in a home overlooking the Yellowstone River, plus a Riverview Cabin that sleeps six and a Mountainview Cabin sleeping four. Each room includes a private bath, breakfast and exceptional views. Breakfast is available for cabin guests at an additional charge. Cabins are available year-round, but the Olsons sometimes close the main house during the off-season for routine maintenance. Their piece of riverfront includes a sandy beach with chairs and fire pit.

Yellowstone Suites B&B
Owner: Julie Sharkich
406-848-7937 or 800-948-7937
www.yellowstonesuites.com
506 Fourth St. S., P.O. Box 277, Gardiner, MT 59030
Rates: $105–150 summer, $75–98 off-season
Credit Cards: MC, V

Handicapped Access: No
Pets: No
Season: Year-round

Four rooms of this century-old three-story home near Roosevelt Arch are appointed with antique touches. Two rooms are on the second floor and two on the third; one room on each floor has a private bath and all have views of Electric Peak. Country breakfasts served each morning. Entire floors or the house can be rented. The Yellowstone Suite includes a full kitchen. Stones used for the top two floors of the house are leftovers from the arch's construction. Stones for the bottom half of the house are from the Yellowstone River.

Guest Ranches

Mountain Sky Guest Ranch
Manager: Yancey Arterburn
800-548-3392 or 406-333-4911
www.mtnsky.com
P.O. Box 1219, Emigrant, MT 59027
About 20 miles north of the park
Rates: $3,045–3,745 per person per week (summer), $335 per night off-season. Includes all meals, gratuity and all on-ranch activities
Credit Cards: MC, V
Handicapped Access: Yes
Pets: No
Season: May 1–Oct. 15

This classic western guest ranch, once a working ranch, is tucked along a creek in a picturesque Gallatin Range canyon off a gravel road, 4.5 miles from Paradise Valley. Thirty guest cabins with one, two and three bedrooms are sprinkled among pine and fir trees. For a true mountain getaway experience, two cabins are located on remote portions of the ranch, including one on a creek; they are available June 10–Aug. 26. Rates include all meals and use of tennis courts, heated pool, sauna, horseback riding (seven-year-olds and up; six-year-olds arena-individualized instruction; five-and-under access to horses by lead line) and trout pond (with instruction), yoga, fitness room and extensive hiking program. The main lodge has classic log beams, stone fireplace and authentic dining room with a bunkhouse atmosphere. Minimum stay is one week during summer season. *28 miles to West Yellowstone*

Island Park, Idaho *59 miles to Old Faithful (1hr 25 min)*

Island Park boasts of having "The Longest Main Street in America," a 33-mile north-south ribbon of US 20 that cuts a narrow incorporated swath through lodgepole pine roughly paralleling the Henry's Fork of the Snake River, a fly-fishing shrine. The town, no more than 500 feet wide in places, was incorporated in the 1940s for ease of licensing businesses scattered throughout the area. From the name, you'd expect to see a series of islands in the Henry's Fork, but the moniker is actually for the meadows, or "islands" of open land, amid the thick forests of the Yellowstone caldera. Travelers through this country would "park" in these meadows for overnighters before moving on to the next "island." Much of the area's focus was resource extraction—mining, timber, ranching—until a realignment of values beginning in the 1970s. *Lakeside Lodge*

Sawtelle Mtn Resort $
89 - 2 queen beds

Island Park has an interesting mix of tourists. Harriman State Park and the Box Canyon section of the Henry's Fork lure fly fishermen and their Orvis togs from the world over. Toward the north at Macks Inn, the woods, some heavily logged, are a labyrinth of snowmobile and ATV trails, their use increasing in recent years with restrictions placed on snowmobiles in the park. The "town" is still a place with periodic "islands" in which to "park," only now those parks feature motels, gas stations and sporting goods stores. The post office is in the "island" of Island Park, but the community also has services at Macks Inn and Last Chance. The area is chock full of private cabins available for rent. Call 208-558-9675 or go to www.islandparkidaho.com/Yellowstone_cabin_rentals.html for more information.

Anglers Lodge at Henry's Fork

too expensive

208-558-9555
www.anglerslodge.net
3363 Old Hwy. 191, Island Park, ID 83429
Rates: $139.95 (regular suites), $149.95 (kitchenettes), $169.95 (Jacuzzi suites)
Credit Cards: AE, D, MC, V
Handicapped Access: Yes
Pets: Yes
Season: Year-round

Located just off US 20, this attractive 15-room motel with log accents sits hard on the east bank of the Henry's Fork, with all rooms and the restaurant looking over the meandering stream. Three cabin rentals and a vacation home also are available through Angler's Lodge. Snowmobile rentals are offered on site.

Last Chance Lodge

fly fishing packages

Owner: Lamoyne Hyde
800-428-8338 or 208-558-7068
www.hydeoutdoors.com/lodge
3350 US Hwy. 20, Island Park, ID 83429
Rates: $75–120 for rooms and $140 for cabin in summer, $49–69 in winter
Credit Cards: AE, D, MC, V
Handicapped Access: No
Pets: Yes ($20 fee)
Season: Year-round

This two-story log motel with 10 lodge rooms and 12 stand-alone cabins is across the street from the Henry's Fork. There's a fly shop on-site, and you can arrange for guided fishing trips on the Henry's Fork, Madison and Teton Rivers. The restaurant serves breakfast and dinner for guests only.

The Pines at Island Park

$359 - 2 bdrm
$149 1 bdrm - 4 max

Owners: Rick and Sheila Egan
888-455-9384 or 208-558-0192
www.pinesislandpark.com
3907 Phillips Loop Rd., P.O. Box 421, Island Park, ID 83429
Rates: $169–359 summer, $169–359 winter, $109–229 spring, $129–299 fall
Credit Cards: AE, D, MC, V

Handicapped Access: Not yet
Pets: No
Season: Year-round

Handcrafted log cabins—one-bedroom, two-bedroom and three-bedroom—are tucked into the lodgepoles near Island Park Reservoir and Henry's Lake, each come with satellite TV and private hot tubs. Historic Phillips Lodge houses the check-in. The Lodgepole Grill features a credible wine menu.

Trout Hunter Lodge
208-558-9900
www.trouthunt.com
3327 N. US Hwy. 20, Island Park, ID 83429
Rates: $89.95–150, more for guided trips
Credit Cards: AE, D, MC, V
Handicapped Access: No
Pets: No
Season: Year-round

$150 2 night min

Another clean, attractive motel with 11 rooms on the banks of the Henry's Fork, with rates for the budget-minded fisherman. Each room has a fly-tying desk. Guided fishing trips are offered for up to six nights, and a vast array of fly-fishing equipment is available in the full-service store on site. The lodge features a bar and grill and large outdoor spa.

Silver Gate, Montana *99 miles (2 hrs 30 min)*

Peace and proximity are the draws of Silver Gate, a tiny hamlet less than a mile from the Northeast Entrance and 3 miles from the hum of Cooke City, a snowmobiler's paradise. Motors aren't endorsed in Silver Gate, except on the cars and trucks passing through. The Absaroka Mountains surrounding the town are some of the most dramatic around Yellowstone and create a distinct alpine feel. Bring your camera: It isn't unusual to see a moose, mountain goat or even an occasional grizzly bear wandering through town. The town was barely spared from the 1988 fires, which are evident in the ghostly spires of lodgepole to the north and east of town.

Silver Gate received its name for the silver haze that seems to hang over the 10,000-foot peaks to the immediate southwest. One man determined to maintain the wildness surrounding Silver Gate and the rustic quality of the buildings owns much of the town .

Silver Gate and Pine Edge Cabins
Managers: Bob and Holly Thompson
406-838-2371
www.pineedgecabins.com
www.silver-gate-cabins.com
HC 84 Box 48, Silver Gate, MT 59081
Rates: $75–150 for cabins, $72 for motel rooms adjacent to store.
Credit Cards: MC, V
Handicapped Access: No
Pets: Yes
Seasons: Year-round

These 25 clean, quaint, attractive and functional log cabins across US 212 from Soda Butte Creek are tucked against a hillside in this high (7,400 feet) forested valley just outside Yellowstone's lightly used Northeast Entrance. You'll have to crane your neck to see the jagged tops of the Absaroka Mountains towering over the village. Nature and tranquility are the buzzwords here, especially in winter. Silver Gate, with a year-round population of 7, is an eco-oriented community that waves snowmobiles and 4-wheelers on up the road to Cooke City. The log cabins, built in the 1930s but currently undergoing renovations, maintain their rustic wilderness appeal, as mandated by the town's architectural covenants. The seven motel rooms are basic. All lodging has kitchenettes with cooking utensils. Say "howdy" to Bob and Holly, who are always available even in the darkest and snowiest days of winter, and they'll eagerly provide the story of Silver Gate's rich mining legacy while fixing you up with a spotting scope for wolf watching. The recently renovated old log dance hall on the property, once a bordello, has served up an eerie assortment of ghostly tales. The store provides general needs, including bear spray. Don't be surprised to find moose wandering through the front yard.

Grizzly Lodge
Owner: Hays Kirby
Manager: Stacy Harrison
406-838-2319 (summer) and 520-290-3647 (winter).
www.yellowstonelodges.com
Grizzly Lodge Rd.
HC 84 Box 9, Silver Gate, MT 59081
Rates: $66–80
Credit Cards: D, MC, V
Handicapped Access: Yes
Pets: Yes
Seasons: June 1–Oct. 1

These attractive motel-like rooms are nestled on horseshoe-shaped land along Soda Butte Creek, with a stunning Absaroka Mountain summer backdrop. Updated rooms, with cedar and stone exterior, blend with conifer surroundings to maintain a look similar to the original mid-1850s construction, when Silver Gate was a mining town. Two-room suites and rooms with kitchenettes are available. A large, grassy picnic area stretches along the creek, which has several outstanding trout "honey" holes just off the property. On the property you'll find grills and a fire pit stocked with wood. The attraction is solitude, proximity to the park's Northeast Entrance and Lamar Valley. Silver Gate has few amenities; groceries and gas are 3 miles up US 212 in Cooke City.

Log Cabin Cafe Bed & Breakfast
Manager: Kay King
406-838-2367 and 402-464-7762 (winter)
HC 84 Box 22, Silver Gate, MT 59081
Rates: $85
Credit Cards: MC, V
Handicapped Access: Yes (in the cafe)
Seasons: June 1–Oct. 1

These decidedly cozy, small cabins were initially bought in 1990 for family and friends of the owners of the cafe, built in 1937. They are log-hewn and rustic, but they fit the peaceful ambience of Silver Gate. The rate includes full breakfast.

Sunlight Basin, Wyoming   *117 miles (Cody) 2 hrs 50 min*

Lightly used, underdeveloped and spectacularly beautiful—that's Sunlight Basin, the stark and rugged country squeezed on two sides by federal wilderness areas, between Cody and Yellowstone's Northeast Entrance. It's far from the crowds of Old Faithful and as close to seeing the Yellowstone country the way John Colter saw it as you can get without actually being in the park. The Clark's Fork of the Yellowstone Wild & Scenic River cuts a spectacular 1,200-foot canyon as it leaves Montana's highest mountains and ventures east. The area is characterized by vast tracts of sage, pine and rugged multihued 3.2-billion-year-old rock. Stop at Sunlight Creek and gaze over the tallest bridge in Wyoming. Chief Joseph and his band of Nez Perce came this way on their ill-fated 1877 journey to Canada, knowing they could hide and slip away from the cavalry in the dramatic canyons.

Guest Ranches

Hunter Peak Ranch
Owners: Louis and Shelley Carey
307-587-3711
www.hunterpeakranch.com
4027 Crandall Rd., Cody, WY 82414
Rates: $130 for one-bedroom cabins, $190 for two bedrooms, $130–170 for two-bedroom suites, $410 for five-bedroom suite
Credit Cards: MC, V
Handicapped Access: Yes
Pets: Yes
Season: Year-round

The ranch, 60 miles northwest of Cody, offers seven cabins—five in one unit and two standing alone on Clark Fork of the Yellowstone. All cabins on the neatly manicured grounds have undergone recent renovations. Meals are by reservation only; the nearest restaurant is one mile away.

K Bar Z Ranch
Manager: Dawna Barnett
307-587-4410
www.agonline.com/kbarz
3477 Crandall Rd., Cody, WY 82414
Rates: $90 per cabin nightly, $1,200 per person all-inclusive per week
Credit Cards: AE, D, MC, V
Handicapped Access: Limited
Pets: Yes
Season: May–Sept., and hunting season Sept.–Dec. 7

The seven authentic, rustic log cabins, most built in the 1940s, are located 24 miles from the park. Family sit-down meals are the norm, with horseback riding, fishing, hiking on the activities menu. Pack trips can be arranged.

Seven D Ranch

Managers: Chuck and Kerry Gunther
888-587-9885 or 307-587-9885
www.7dranch.com
774 Rd 7GQ, Cody, WY 82414
Rates: $1,770 per person all-inclusive (decreases with number in party).
Credit Cards: MC, V
Handicapped Access: Limited
Pets: No
Season: Mid-June–mid-Sept.

Eleven guest cabins, sleeping from two to eight, are located on a 270-acre ranch in the midst of an unburned section of the Shoshone National Forest, with no other property in sight. Activities include horseback riding, fly fishing, hiking, cowboy sing-alongs, line dancing and a sweat lodge. The year 2008 marks the ranch's 50th anniversary.

Wapiti Valley, Wyoming

For most Americans, this winding, rugged 50-mile stretch from Cody to the East Entrance along the tumbling Shoshone River is the route taken on their first trip to the Yellowstone/Teton/Jackson Hole area, in part because a stop in Cody provides an obligatory western tune-up. This is stark and dry country, with pines dotting volcanic hills, cliffs and hoodoos. The "Warning: Grizzly Bear Country" signs let you know you're at the edge of Yellowstone's remotest wilderness. As the name implies—"wapiti" is Indian for "elk"—the magnificent and proud ungulate is frequently visible here, especially in winter. Look for bighorn sheep and moose as well. Stop and toss a fly in the Shoshone; it's a blue-ribbon trout stream. There are few motels here, mostly guest ranches and lodges.

Motels

Green Creek Inn and RV Park

Managers: Laurie and Chip Ash
877-587-5004 or 307-587-5004
www.greencreekinn.com
2908 North Fork Hwy., P.O. Box 421, Cody, WY 82450
Rates: $50–127 cabins, $33 RV sites
Credit Cards: AE, D, MC, V
Handicapped Access: Limited
Pets: Yes
Season: May 1 to Nov.

This facility, located in a quiet mountain valley, offers 17 rooms adorned with log furniture, tile bath and shower. For families, there are two suites with bunk beds. Rooms are air-conditioned and some have wireless Internet, as does the office. The nine RV sites feature full hookups, horseshoe pits, picnic tables and a playground on the property. A restaurant is one mile down the road.

Wapiti Lodge & Steakhouse

Owner: Gina O'Connell
307-587-6659
3189 Yellowstone Hwy., Cody, WY 82414.
Rates: To be determined.
Credit Cards: MC, V.
Handicapped Access: No.
Pets: To be determined.
Season: Restaurant is open year-round, so cabins most likely will be, too.

Owner Gina O'Connell recently purchased the original lodging cabins that were moved off the property more than two decades ago. She found postcards of the cabins on eBay and is determined to restore them authentically. Restoration began in the fall of 2007 and the cabins are scheduled to open in 2008. The steakhouse, a local landmark, is open Wednesday through Sunday for western-style dining; it's known for hand-cut Angus steaks, but they also serve chicken, seafood and pasta. A bar services the restaurant and often features live music on the weekends.

Yellowstone Valley Inn & RV

Managers: Ron and Kyla Jordan
877-587-3961 or 307-587-3961
www.yellowstonevalleyinn.com
3324 Yellowstone Hwy., Cody, WY 82414
Rates: $99–169 summer, $49–69 off-season
Credit Cards: MC, V
Handicapped Access: Limited
Pets: Cabins only
Season: Apr. 15–Oct. 15

Mountain views in all directions, along with trout fishing on the premises, are the hallmarks of these rustic digs. Ten log cabins feature modern amenities, and most of the 15 motel rooms offer views of the Shoshone River. Amenities include a new heated pool, indoor hot tub, dance hall and a banquet room where sing-alongs are staged each night. The RV park has 57 sites—19 with full hookups, 38 with electric and water. A dump station is on site.

Lodges

Absaroka Mountain Lodge

Managers: Kerry and Theresa Boyd
307-587-3963
www.absarokamtlodge.com
1231 North Fork Hwy., Cody, WY 82414
Rates: $106–185
Credit Cards: D, MC, V
Handicapped Access: No
Pets: No
Season: Mid-May through Sept.

Operated by permit on Shoshone National Forest land, the lodge has 17 log cabins along a mountain stream. The owners stress a family atmosphere while offering a wide variety of horseback riding opportunities and nightly campfires. A full-service restaurant serving breakfast and dinner is on site. Packages are available.

DNR Ranch at Rand Creek
Managers: Rick and Dollie Horst
888-412-7335 or 307-587-7176
www.dnrranch.com
3064 North Fork Hwy., Cody, WY 82414
Rates: $109–259
Credit Cards: MC, V
Handicapped Access: Limited
Pets: Ask
Season: May–Nov.

The DNR Ranch is literally halfway between Cody and Yellowstone. Most of the cabins have full kitchens; four are more like a home. Wednesday and Sunday nights are reserved for a guest barbecue. H&F Outfitters offers horseback pack trips through the ranch. Family-oriented fun is the theme here. Rates include breakfast.

Goff Creek Lodge
Manager: Seven Mazzone
800-859-3985 or 307-587-3753
www.goffcreek.com
Address: 995 North Fork Hwy., Cody, WY 82414
Rates: $89 ($339 for large cabin that sleeps 10)
Credit Cards: AE, MC, V.
Handicapped Access: Yes
Pets: Yes, with restrictions
Season: May 1–mid-Oct.

Family-run, -owned and -oriented, this lodge features 12 cabins in a mountain setting along Goff Creek. Cabins are rustic in appearance but have all the modern amenities. The lodge is located on Shoshone National Forest land, with 2½ million acres to roam out the back door. The full-service restaurant in the lodge serves breakfast, lunch and dinner. Guided fishing and horseback trips can be arranged to some of the best-kept secret trails on the Shoshone.

Pahaska Tepee
Owner: Bob Coe
800-628-7791 or 307-527-7701
www.pahaska.com
Address: 183 Yellowstone Hwy., Cody, WY 82414
Rates: $62.95–$149.95
Credit Cards: D, MC, V
Handicapped Access: Yes
Pets: In cabins, with restrictions

[handwritten notes:] 66 miles · (1hr 48 min)

2 queen beds + 2 twin beds – available

Deluxe condo $575

standard Room $169.95

1 queen standard – available $109.95
2 queen standard – available $134.95

Season: May 1–mid-Oct.

Listed in the National Registry for Historic Places, Pahaska Tepee was built in 1904 by Buffalo Bill Cody himself and offers the closest accommodations to the park's East Entrance. A wide array of accommodations will suit different budgets and the makeup of your group. Among them are the original 1903 homesteaders' cabins. Modern amenities have been added—water, heating, even phones—but there's no need for air-conditioning in the high mountain setting. A modern-style Reunion Lodge is designed for large groups, family gatherings or corporate retreats. The property features a gift shop, restaurant and bar, and convenience store. Trail rides and tours of the original lodge can be arranged.

Shoshone Lodge
Manager: Mike Christiansen
307-587-4044
www.shoshonelodge.com
349 Yellowstone Hwy., Cody, WY 82414.
Rates: $90–275 peak season, $80–245 off-season
Credit Cards: AE, MC, V
Handicapped Access: No.
Pets: Yes
Season: May 1–Oct. 15

The Shoshone consists of 18 log cabins, most of them stand-alone, with queen pillow-top beds, bathrooms, phone, microwaves and fridges. Some have kitchenettes. No TVs. Horseback riding and fishing the Shoshone River and Grinnell Creek are highlights.

Guest Ranches

Bill Cody Ranch
Owner: Waiyee Bonneau
800-615-2934 or 307-587-6271
www.billcodyranch.com
2604 Yellowstone Hwy., Cody, WY 82414
Rates: $130–250
Credit Cards: D, MC, V
Handicapped Access: Yes
Pets: No
Season: Mid-May through Sept.

The Bill Cody is a classic rustic western guest ranch set amid pines and fir halfway between the town of Cody and the park's East Entrance. There are 17 one- and two-bedroom log cabins and duplexes, and some stand-alones. What makes the Bill Cody unique is that no minimum stay is required. A dining room serves breakfast and dinner daily. Traditional, family-style campfire cookouts and chuckwagon barbecues are staged Wednesday and Saturday nights.

Elephant Head Lodge
Managers: Kevin and Debbie Millard
307-587-3980
www.elephantheadlodge.com
1170 Yellowstone Hwy., Cody, WY 82414
Rates: $110–300
Credit Cards: MC, V
Handicapped Access: Limited
Pets: No
Season: May through Nov.

The Elephant Head consists of 15 cozy cabins that sleep anywhere from two to eight. A restaurant, lounge and family room are on the premises, along with a horse concessionaire. Located on national forest land, the lodge and many cabins are on the National Historic Registry because the restaurant, lodge and Trapper Cabin were built by Buffalo Bill Cody's niece. The name comes from a decidedly elephant-shaped rock overlooking the property.

Red Pole Ranch
Owners: Don and Patty Jo Schmalz
800-587-5929 or 307-587-5929
www.redpoleranch.com
574 Stagecoach Trail, Cody, WY 82450
Rates: $89–129
Credit Cards: AE, D, MC, V
Handicapped Access: No
Pets: No
Season: Year-round, though dates vary in winter

The Red Pole is a working guest ranch with eight log cabins dressed in western motif, all in a broad valley at the base of sage and pine hills. Some cabins have kitchens; all have fridges, microwaves, bath and shower. Located near Sheep Mountain, the ranch is surrounded by 2,500 acres of national forest and BLM land. The owners are retired outfitters and happily offer advice on outdoor activities; they might even disclose some favorite hidey holes on the Shoshone or other nearby streams.

Rimrock Dude Ranch
Managers: Dede and Gary Fales
800-208-7468 or 307-587-3970
www.rimrockranch.com
2728 North Fork Hwy., Cody, WY 82414
Rates: $1,475 per week for adults, children (6–18) $1,275 all-inclusive
Credit Cards: MC, V (for deposits only)
Handicapped Access: Limited
Pets: No
Season: May–Sept.

These rock and log cabins straddle Canyon Creek in the heart of the Absaroka Mountains. The cabins have private baths and fridges. Each guest gets a horse and trail rides, all coming in a variety of sizes and shapes geared toward a rider's skill level. A nightly rodeo is for watching—and even guest participation. Day trips to Yellowstone and fishing and float trips on the Shoshone are some of the featured activities. There is a heated pool, hot tub and game room, and airport transportation from Cody is available.

UXU Ranch
Manager: Tuff Flaharty
800-373-9027 or 307-587-2143
www.uxuranch.com
1710 Yellowstone Hwy., Cody, WY 82414
Rates: $1,695 per week for adults, $995 for children all-inclusive
Credit Cards: MC, V
Handicapped Access: Yes
Pets: No
Season: Year-round

The UXU's 10 log-sided guest cabins have recently been upgraded to include tongue-and-groove wood-paneled walls. Two gourmet chefs on staff prepare three meals a day, and guests can complete their meal by choosing their favorite red or white from a 1,500-bottle wine cellar. Activities include morning jogs and runs, horseback riding, hiking, mountain biking, softball, Yellowstone Park excursions, wildlife talks and fly fishing with a professional guide. The ranch's motto: "It's your vacation, so you call the shots."

West Yellowstone, Montana   *31 miles to Old Faithful (54min)*

No gateway community has more of a theme-park atmosphere than West Yellowstone, which seems to have sprung from a lodgepole pine forest simply to serve park tourists. Indeed, that's precisely what happened. In the late 1800s, visitors to the West Entrance came to this broad, forested bowl via wagon from Virginia City, Montana, about 70 miles to the northwest. After the turn of the century, Union Pacific Railroad president E. H. Harriman saw a business opportunity and punched a rail line from Pocatello, Idaho, to the town's current site hard against the park's western boundary. The line was finished in 1907, and West Yellowstone was carved out of Forest Service land in 1908. The town originally was named Riverside after a soldier's station inside the park, even though the Madison River is 2 miles away. However, having two Riversides was confusing, so in 1910 the town was renamed Yellowstone. Alas, it only created more confusion, this time between the town and park. Finally, in 1920, "West" was added to the name.

In the early years, heavy snows and winter temperatures that frequently were the lowest in the nation sent residents scurrying for warmer climes. Once the state began plowing US 191 north to Bozeman, the town grew into a year-round playground. Rail passenger service ended in 1960, but the introduction of snowmobiles a few years later created a new prosperity. That lasted for four decades, until tourist complaints about noise, pollution and stress to animals moved the Park Service to ban the machines in the park. Today, a limited number of quieter, clean machines are allowed in Yellowstone, albeit only with guides. Thus, West has been forced to diversify and reinvent itself, a reality that only exacerbates the region's ubiquitous government mistrust and gives the town a decided edginess. In the summer, West is a fly-fishing hub, renowned for such angling legends as Bud Lilly and Bob Jacklin. Lodging is functional, with an endless array of homespun operations that contribute to the town's western theme-park persona. West Yellowstone does have a central reservations system (888-646-7077, 406-646-7077; www.yellowstonereservation.com; 211 Yellowstone Ave., West Yellowstone, MT 59758) with access to more than 500 rooms.

Motels

Golden West Motel

[handwritten: website doesn't work]

Managers: Kurt and Michele Marsden
406-646-7778
www.goldenwestmotel.com
429 Madison Ave., P.O. Box 637, West Yellowstone, MT 59758
Rates: $45–95
Credit Cards: MC, V
Handicapped Access: No
Pets: No
Seasons: Closed in Nov.

Twelve clean rooms with the basics for the budget-minded. Located on Madison Avenue, a few blocks off the main strip, Golden West is recognized for its manicured front lawn and clean and tidy appearance. Some rooms have kitchenettes, and all have cable TV access. A comfortable patio and barbecue area are available for guest use. Also available are two townhouse condos (one that sleeps up to 10 people) ideal for a retreat or family gathering. This motel caters to hikers, bikers, skiers and snowmobilers.

Gray Wolf Inn & Suites

Manager: Lori Depweiler
800-852-8602 or 406-646-0000
www.graywolf-inn.com
250 S. Canyon St., West Yellowstone, MT 59758
Rates: $169–299
Credit Cards: AE, D, MC, V
Handicapped Access: Yes
Pets: Yes
Seasons: Year-round

[handwritten: 24th - NO ROOMS; 25th - Rooms available; standard 2 queen rooms or 2 bedroom suite (Double beds) or 1 king bed + sofa bed]

Located slightly off the well-worn path but directly across from the Grizzly Wolf & Discovery Center, this hotel offers 102 spacious rooms and one- and two-bedroom suites, some with kitchens. Winter visitors will appreciate the heated underground parking garage. For summertime, there is an unheated indoor pool. A hot tub, sauna and a deluxe continental breakfast buffet round out the list of amenities.

Hadley's Motel

[handwritten: no availability]

Owner: Norma Salmon
Manager: Alyn Salmon
866-291-5235 or 406-646-9534
www.hadleysmotel.com
29 Gibbon Ave., West Yellowstone, MT 59758
Rates: $70–115

Credit Cards: AE, D, MC, V
Handicapped Access: Yes
Pets: Yes
Seasons: May–Oct.

Family owned and operated for three generations, this small retro-style, budget motel offers 18 clean and quaint rooms. They're equipped with fridge, microwave and cable TV, but no phones. Gracie's Gifts offers a wide selection of jewelry, trinkets and souvenirs.

Hebgen Lake Mountain Inn

[handwritten: left message one bedroom suite – 2 queen beds + hide a bed]

Owners: Klungervik Family
Managers: Tahni and Rin
866-400-4564 or 406-646-5100
www.happyhourbar.com
15475 Hebgen Lake Rd. (US Hwy. 287 north), West Yellowstone, MT 59758
Rates: $165 summer, $95 Oct. 1–May 15

[handwritten: looks very plain but clean]

Credit Cards: AE, D, MC, V
Handicapped Access: Yes
Pets: Limited, with fee
Seasons: Year-round

[handwritten: need to call — can't check availability online]

This recently built two-story motel with a non-western motif is across US 287 from Hebgen Lake. Sixteen rooms have fully equipped kitchens and semiprivate decks. An indoor pool and spa complete the scene. The infamous Happy Hour Bar and Restaurant directly across the highway offers lunch and dinner overlooking the lake. Known for hand-cut steaks, shrimp, and pasta dishes as well as a sometimes-rowdy atmosphere and some R-rated photos on the walls, courtesy of the occasionally uninhibited patron. The restaurant and bar close for six weeks each fall and spring.

Hibernation Station

[handwritten: 3 night minimum $300 night for 3 queen beds]

Manager: Katrina Mann
800-580-3557 or 406-646-4200
www.hibernationstation.com
212 Gray Wolf Ave., West Yellowstone, MT 59758
Rates: $119–300 summer, $119–299 winter, $89–200 shoulder seasons
Credit Cards: AE, D, MC, V
Handicapped Access: Yes
Pets: Yes
Seasons: Year-round

[handwritten: Queen bed, Queen bunk bed (6) $269⁰⁰]

Hibernate for a night or a week in one of the 50 newer cabins, each with homey log interiors. Some come with kitchenettes and fireplaces. A family condo unit sleeps eight and features a fireplace, kitchen and jetted tub. Soak under the stars in the outdoor spa. One of the largest bronze elk sculptures in the world—weighing in at 5,000 pounds—stands guard over the premises.

Kelly Inn West Yellowstone

Managers: Tom and Linda Thompson

[handwritten: Moose Creek Inn]

800-259-4672 or 406-646-4544
www.yellowstonekellyinn.com
104 S. Canyon St., West Yellowstone, MT 59758
Rates: $179–259 summer, $79–229 winter
Credit Cards: AE, CB, D, MC, V
Handicapped Access: Yes
Pets: Yes
Seasons: Year-round

[handwritten: Double smoke free standard rooms indoor pool not available]

Seventy-eight spacious rooms are even more comfortable after a recent remodeling that included all new carpeting in the rooms. Jacuzzi suites are available. The Kelly, perhaps the most distinguishable lodging in West Yellowstone, features a large indoor pool, sauna and hot tub. The inn offers wireless Internet in rooms and a guest computer in the lobby. The continental breakfast has recently been expanded.

Kirkwood Resort & Marina

Owner and Manager: Pam Sveinson
877-302-7200 or 406-646-7200
www.kirkwoodresort.com
11505 Hebgen Lake Rd., West Yellowstone, MT 59758
Rates: $71–100
Credit Cards: AE, D, MC, V
Handicapped Access: Yes
Pets: Yes
Seasons: Cabins are year-round; RV park closes at the end of September

[handwritten: Basic looking w/ 2 beds room w/ 1 bed NO availability]

The Kirkwood is comprised of 11 cabins, some with kitchens and some with multiple rooms. The property also has 15 RV hookups and a marina. Dock rent and launching are offered, along with boat rental and a convenience store that sells fuel. Pete Owens runs Paddle On Adventures out of the marina and can be reached at 406-209-7452 or www.paddleonadventures.com. The resort offers recreational kayak rentals with hardtop carriers and also organizes guided trips on the lake in summer.

Madison Hotel & Gift Shop

Manager: Linda Christensen
800-838-7745 or 406-646-7745
www.madisonhotel.com *[handwritten: www.madisonhotelmotel.com]*
139 Yellowstone Ave., P.O. Box 1370, West Yellowstone, MT 59758
Rates: $25–46 (hostel), $65–126 (motel)
Credit Cards: AE, D, MC, V
Handicapped Access: No
Pets: No
Season: May 25–Oct. 10

[handwritten: hotel & motel = public bath beds only available on dates]

This historic hotel, built in 1912, offers a variety of options for the budget-minded traveler. The fourteen hostel and economy rooms require using a shared bathroom down the hall. The 17 standard and deluxe motel rooms all have private baths and Internet access. Former president Warren G. Harding as well as actors Wallace Beery and Gloria Swanson have stayed at the Madison. The gift shop is reputed to offer Montana's largest selection of regional knickknacks.

Sleepy Hollow Lodge
Owner: Larry Miller
406-646-7077
www.sleepyhollowlodge.com
124 Electric St., P.O. Box 1080, West Yellowstone, MT 59758
Rates: $84–102
Credit Cards: MC, V
Handicapped Access: No
Pets: No
Season: May–Oct.

[handwritten notes: Sent email request — one queen = $107; one queen + one double - 2 rooms $127; 2 doubles - 2 rooms $127; one queen - 2 twins - 2 rooms $127; add $10 for each person over #2 ($40); Senior discount 15%; Booked up]

Traditional, hand-hewn, log cabins are furnished with handmade furnishings, some of them antiques. A lodging retreat, touted as "a real gem" by another well-known travel guide, features a total of 14 cabins. Seven cabins range from one queen bed with no kitchen to two queen beds with kitchen. There are no phones in the cabins. An informal continental breakfast is served in the summer and fall season. Miller, a guide and outfitter in the area for more than 40 years, offers fly-fishing services.

Stagecoach Inn
Manager: Lynne Kelly
800-842-2882 or 406-646-7381
www.yellowstoneinn.com
209 Madison Ave., P.O. Box 169, West Yellowstone, MT 59758
Rates: $69–139 summer-winter, $49–79 spring-fall
Credit Cards: AE, D, MC, V
Handicapped Access: Yes
Pets: Yes (smoking rooms)
Seasons: Year-round

[handwritten notes: Standard hotel rooms, nice lobby, Grand staircase, no availability]

The Stagecoach is a large motel with 88 western-style rooms and heated underground parking. It features a comfortable lobby with old stone fireplace, sweeping staircase and mounted wildlife heads. Two hot tubs and a dry sauna complete amenities, with a restaurant soon to be built.

Super 8 West Yellowstone Lionshead
Manager: Mike Jaskson
406-646-9584 or 800-800-8000
www.super8.com
1545 Targhee Pass Hwy., West Yellowstone, MT 59758
Rates: $58.95–$92.95 double occupancy, $5 each additional person
Credit Cards: AE, D, MC, V
Handicapped Access: Yes
Pets: Yes ($30 deposit)
Seasons: May to mid-Oct.

[handwritten note: none available]

What makes this 44-room chain motel unique is its isolated location, far from the buzz of West Yellowstone, about 8 miles west of town. Indeed, the familiar Super 8 sign on the highway even seems out of place here. The motel offers a continental breakfast, spacious suites, nonsmoking rooms, sauna, guest laundry and wireless Internet.

Three Bear Lodge
Manager: Jan Stoderd
800-646-7353 or 406-646-7353 or 800-221-1151
www.threebearlodge.com
217 Yellowstone, P.O. Box 519, West Yellowstone, MT 59758
Rates: $49–168
Credit Cards: AE, D, MC, V
Handicapped Access: Yes
Pets: Yes
Seasons: Year-round

[handwritten: No availability]
[handwritten: 6 person small suite 2 queens 1 Double 2nd Room $138]
[handwritten: 1 king suite $158 2 queens in 2nd Room]

The Three Bear's 73 rooms come with natural pine furnishings and all the modern amenities. Some units have jetted tubs. Two-room suites sleep six and have microwaves and fridges. There are four indoor hot tubs and an outdoor pool in summer. The Three Bear Restaurant on site is known for steak and prime rib. The Lodge is a proud sponsor of the Where the Painted Buffalo Roam Project. Check the website for "bearly believable deals."

Wagon Wheel Campground & Cabins
Manager: Ken Herman
406-646-7872
www.wagonwheelrv.com
408 Gibbon, West Yellowstone, MT 59758
Rates: $89–150 cabins, $26.95–37.95 campground
Credit Cards: None
Handicapped Access: No
Pets: Yes (in campground, not in cabins)
Seasons: Memorial Day weekend through Sept.

[handwritten: Rustic wagon 1 queen $95]
[handwritten: Booked called - none available for more than one night - won't rent only one night]
[handwritten: Minimum 3 & 5 night stay]

The Wagon Wheel's 10 attractive cabins are surrounded by shade trees, with picnic tables and gas barbecues nearby. Cabins have kitchenettes. Bring your own bedding and save money on smaller camp cabins. A three-bedroom cabin features a full kitchen and sleeps six. A four-night minimum stay is required in summer. Call for possible winter availability; seasons are weather-dependent.

Whispering Pines
406-646-1172
321 Canyon St., West Yellowstone, MT 59758
Rates: $50
Credit Cards: MC, V
Handicapped Access: No
Pets: Yes
Seasons: Year-round

[handwritten: no website]

Rustic one-, two- and three-bedroom cabins with TVs. The property borders the national forest on the north end of town, giving it a feel of seclusion. They have no Web site, so this could be West Yellowstone's best kept secret for lodging.

Yellowstone Cabins & RV Park

Manager: B. J. Eller
866-646-9350 or 406-646-9350
www.yellowstonecabinsandrv.com
504 US Hwy. 20, P.O. Box 627, West Yellowstone, MT 59758
Rates: $60–80 cabins, $25–30 RV sites
Credit Cards: MC, V
Handicapped Access: No
Pets: No
Season: Year-round

[handwritten: Have to call]
[handwritten: 2 queens - $88, 1 queen - $77, 1 full - $65, Basic $5.00 each person over 2+]
[handwritten: $100 - 6, $65 - 1, left message]

Eight RV sites (limited to 40 feet and shorter) and seven efficient duplex camp cabins all come with private bathrooms and cable TV. Gas grills and picnic tables are for guest use.

Yellowstone Holiday RV Campground & Marina

Managers: Jim and Eileen Albin
877-646-4242 or 406-646-4242
www.yellowstoneholiday.com
16990 Hebgen Lake Rd., West Yellowstone, MT 59758
Rates: $62–110 cabins, $35–45 RVs
Credit Cards: D, MC, V
Handicapped Access: No
Pets: Yes
Seasons: Mid-May to mid-Sept.

[handwritten: no bedding or towels]

Located on the north shore of Hebgen Lake, this facility caters to families and reunions, and includes a central cooking facility for large groups. Lodging accommodations include 24 camp cabins, some with private baths, and an apartment that sleeps up to 10 and has a full kitchen and bathroom. There are 36 large RV sites with full hookups accommodating rigs up to 75 feet. Some are on the lake, with beachfront access. Internet access is available.

Yellowstone Village Inn

Manager: Shea Unger
800-276-7335 or 406-646-7335
www.wyellowstone.com/yellowstonevil
85 Buffalo Dr., P.O. Box 973, West Yellowstone, MT 59758
Rates: $120–175 summer, $95–150 spring, $95–150 fall and winter
Credit Cards: AE, D, MC, V
Handicapped Access: Yes
Pets: Yes ($25 fee)
Season: Year-round

[handwritten: website doesn't work]

Welcome back to the 1980s with retro-chic furnished condos featuring from one to 12 units, all with kitchens and fireplaces. They are located about 10 miles from the park. The inn has no phones or Internet, but there is excellent wildlife viewing from the lobby, while enjoying the warmth of the stone fireplace. In summers, an outdoor pool is open, along with a year-round hot tub. The inn also sports two tennis courts.

Guest Ranches

Bar N Ranch

Not available

Managers: Mike and Gayle Gavagan
406-646-0300; fax 406-646-0301
www.bar-n-ranch.com
890 Buttermilk Rd., P.O. Box 250, West Yellowstone, MT 59758
6 miles from West Yellowstone
Rates: $234–363 summer, $216–339 winter, $139–262 spring/fall
Credit Cards: AE, D, MC, V
Handicapped Access: Yes
Pets: Yes
Season: Year-round

The Bar N features seven lodge rooms, four one-bedroom cabins and three two-bedroom cabins, all with private outdoor hot tubs. Wireless Internet is available in main lodge. A Montana country-style breakfast is served each morning. The first-rate gourmet restaurant with wine list is open daily from June 1 to Sept. 30, then Wednesday–Sunday from Oct. 1 to May 31. The South Fork of the Madison River, a blue-ribbon trout stream, flows through the 200 acres.

Parade Rest Guest Ranch

too expensive

Manager: Marge Wanner
406-646-7217
www.paraderestranch.com
7979 Grayling Creek Rd., West Yellowstone, MT 59758
10 miles from West Yellowstone, 1 mile from the junction of US 287 and US 191
Rates: $178 per person, $112 off-season
Credit Cards: AE, D, MC, V
Handicapped Access: No
Pets: Limited
Season: Mid-May–late Sept.

Located on a historic Bannock Indian migration route, the Parade Rest has 14 cabins, a dining hall, recreation room, outdoor hot tub and equestrian facilities. The cabins range from the original 1912 Homestead Cabin to more modern buildings. Some are in the main ranch area, others on a ridge overlooking a horse pasture and a creek. Accommodations are available for parties ranging from two to eight.

Vacation Rentals

If you're looking for a vacation home, condo or cabin, check out **Yellowstone Vacation Rentals** (406-646-7865; www.yellowstonerental.net), **Yellowstone Townhouses** (406-646-9331; www.yellowstonetownhouses.com) or **Yellowstone Village Condominiums** (800-276-7335; www.westyellowstonerenals.com).

LODGING IN GRAND TETON NATIONAL PARK GATEWAY COMMUNITIES

Alta/Grand Targhee, Wyoming   128 miles (3 hrs 8 min)

When you say Alta, you really mean Grand Targhee. The ski area is why this little mountain community exists. It has no stores, one restaurant/bar/grill and a handful of lodging possibilities. You can't beat the location in the undulating pine- and aspen-bathed foothills of the Tetons, about 6 miles east of Driggs, Idaho, just inside the Wyoming border.

Alta Lodge B&B

Owner: Dee Cotton
877-437-2582 or 307-353-2582
www.pdt.net/altalodge.com
590 Targhee Town Rd., Alta, WY 83414
Rates: $75–150
Credit Cards: No
Handicapped Access: No
Pets: No
Season: Year-round

The Alta is an adults-only B&B with four bedrooms and a large, comfortable house with direct views of the west slope of the Tetons through large picture windows. A full country breakfast is served, with emphasis on Idaho spuds. Some rooms look out on the Tetons, some the Luscious Valley, all are meant to pamper your senses. The Alta is an 8-mile drive from Grand Targhee.

Targhee Lodge Resort

Owner: George Gillette
800-827-4433 or 307-353-2300
www.grandtarghee.com
3300 E. Ski Hill Rd., Alta, WY 83414
Rates: $79 and up
Credit Cards: AE, D, MC, V
Handicapped Access: No
Pets: No
Seasons: June–mid-Sept., Nov.–mid-Apr.

The Targhee Lodge Resort is actually three lodges in one: The Targhee, Sioux Lodge and Teewinot Lodge. Check-in is at the same desk for all three. The Targhee is lodging for the budget-conscious, with 15 standard motel rooms. The outdoor pool and hot tub are shared by all three properties. There are four restaurants on site, and at least two are always open. Each property has cable TV and free wireless Internet. All three are ski-in and ski-out to Grand Targhee's nearby lifts. Rental home properties in Driggs are also available through the lodge.

Sioux Lodge

Rates: $129 and up, depending on season
The Sioux has 32 suites with microwaves and fridges in spacious higher-end rooms with more modern accommodations.

Teewinot Lodge
Rates: $109 per night to $416 per person
The showiest of the three was remodeled in 2006 and has 48 deluxe rooms with more spacious and rustic luxury furnishings. The slope-side lodge has a lobby with stone fireplace and comfortable seating, and an indoor hot tub for Teewinot guests only. Amenities include flat-screen TVs, full bath with tub and a ski-in/ski-out option.

Teton Teepee Lodge
Manager: Amanda Conner
800-353-8176 or 307-353-8176
www.tetonteepee.com
470 W. Alta Rd., Alta, WY 83414
Rates: $178 double, $128 single private room, $70 adults/$55 kids for dormitory style
Credit Cards: AE, D, MC, V
Handicapped Access: No
Pets: No
Season: Thanksgiving–mid-Apr., or depending on ski season

Breakfast, dinner and beverages are included in the deal for lodging in this 35-year-old building whose core is shaped like a teepee. The lodging is in a circular format, with a center fireplace. The basement has the dormitory-style bunk beds with a game room featuring table tennis and shuffleboard. Upstairs, there are two lofts, one with a pool table. There is an outdoor hot tub, wireless Internet, Dish Network for TV and hearty family-style hot breakfasts. Dinner is an Italian-cuisine buffet. The Teton Teepee Lodge is geared to skiers and snowboarders.

Wilson Creekside Inn B&B
Owner/manager: Janice Wilson
307-353-2409
www.wilsoncreeksideinn.com
130 N. Alta Rd., Alta, WY 83414
Rates: $75–90
Credit Cards: No
Handicapped Access: No
Pets: No
Season: Year-round

A 180-acre working sheep ranch and country farm home have been turned into a bed and breakfast, with the same magnificent views of Grand Teton. The house has four rooms for rent, one with a king bed and private bath. Three rooms are upstairs, one sleeping four and the others fitting two. The upstairs rooms share a bath. A full country breakfast is served. The home is on Teton Creek, surrounded by mature cottonwoods and pines. At 6 miles away, it is the closest lodging to Grand Targhee. Skiers are welcome.

Driggs, Idaho   126 miles (3hrs)
Once a picturesque farming and ranching community in Idaho's potato country, Driggs is now experiencing the benefits and costs of being discovered by the outside world. For that, the town of 1,100 can thank—or blame—the spillover from Jackson. At first, it was an

affordable outlying area where service workers could live and commute over Teton Pass without busting their bank accounts. Now, with only 3 percent of Jackson's county in private hands and land prices skyrocketing, Driggs is evolving into what Jackson was in the 1970s: a recreation haven for the wealthy.

Driggs, Victor and Tetonia are pastoral little communities on ID 33, in the heart of a largely flat agricultural valley between the Tetons and Big Hole Mountains. Lodging is still limited, but you can expect that to change as more tourists appreciate the Teton Valley's serenity and access to the Teton and Yellowstone parks. For the truly budget-conscious ski bum, the Movin' Sol Hostel once offered a place to grab a shower and bunk, but the hostel is out of business. Affordable lodging can still be had, however.

Teton Valley Cabins
Owner: Vertical Investments
General manager: Lisa Ridenour
866-687-1522 or 208-354-8153
www.tetonvalleycabin.com
34 E. Ski Hill Rd., Driggs, ID 83422
Rates: $70–99
Credit Cards: AE, D, MC, V
Handicapped Access: No
Pets: Yes
Season: Year-round

These 20 units include 14 deluxe rooms with kitchenettes. A bunk cabin sleeps six. The six standard motel rooms have microwaves and fridges. Seven log duplexes share a porch. There is an outdoor hot tub, laundry, high-speed Internet and HBO. Located 1 mile from downtown Driggs. Formerly the Intermountain Lodge.

The Pines Motel Guest Haus
Owners: John and Nancy Nielson
800-354-2778 or 208-354-2774
105 S. Main St., Driggs, ID 83422
Rates: $40–90
Credit Cards: AE, D, MC, V
Handicapped Access: Limited
Pets: Yes ($10)
Season: Year-round

This European-style guesthouse offers seven small rooms attached to a log cabin, each with fridge, microwave, cable TV and phone. A large hot tub is outside. A country breakfast is served in the log portion of the building for $15 for adults and $7.50 for children under 16.

Dubois, Wyoming
123 miles to Old Faithful (2 hrs 42 min)

Like Cody, Dubois (pronounced DOO-boys) is just far enough from the park to retain a frontier persona, perhaps even more than most communities that try harder for the look. Few of the gateway communities have the wide-open spaces and big-sky feel of Dubois. This decidedly western community has a long main drag in US 26/287, along the Wind River. By this point, tourists coming from the southeast notice the Absaroka Range on the right and Wind Rivers on the left beginning to pinch the river, providing a stunning back-drop to the multihued badlands of the valley, a generous portion of which is checkerboard state and Bureau of Land Management country. The loggers who cut the high country for railroad ties christened the town "Never Sweat" in 1886. It was so named because the con-stant winds and dry air kept them from sweating, even on the hottest days. When the Postal Service refused to put an office in a town with such a zany name, it was changed to Dubois, inexplicably named for an Idaho senator (there's an eastern Idaho town called Dubois as well). Famous folks who once put their boots up here include Butch Cassidy, Jim Bridger and Kit Carson. Once a logging and ranching town, Dubois transformed itself after its sawmill closed in 1987, using its 300 days of sunshine, balmy banana-belt temperatures and breathtaking surroundings to turn itself into an outdoor-recreation hub. Retirees are even finding peace in the "Valley of the Warm Winds," where frequent winter Chinooks howl in from the Wind Rivers and keep the ground free of snow.

Motels

Branding Iron Inn
Owner: Anna Colson
Manager: Sue Harris
888-651-9378 or 307-455-2893
www.brandingironinn.com
401 W. Ramshorn St., Dubois, WY 82513
Rates: $49–90
Credit Cards: MC, V
Handicapped Access: Limited
Pets: Yes ($5 fee)
Season: Year-round

You won't find any lodgings like these 23 well-maintained, 1940s Swedish Cope, hand-hewn cabins. All units are available in the summer and 17 are open in the winter. All come with such basic modern conveniences as TVs, phones, fridges, microwaves and coffee pots. Some have kitchenettes. Guests may stable their horses for free in the corrals. Barbecues, picnic tables and horseshoe pits are on the premises. The large parking area makes suit-able for horse-trailer parking.

Chinook Winds Mountain Lodge
Owner: Debi Young
866-455-2987 or 307-455-2987
www.rainbow-village.net
640 N. First St., Dubois, WY 82513
Rates: $60, $125 for cabin
Credit Cards: AE, D, MC, V
Handicapped Access: Limited
Pets: Yes ($5 fee)
Season: Year-round

The Chinook Winds has recently built pine motel rooms with two beds each, all with a fridge, microwave, cable TV, coffee pot and iron. There's a king suite with a kitchenette and seven rooms with one bed (full or queen). A covered outdoor Jacuzzi is on the banks of the Wind River and the lodge is 50 yards from the river. A one-bedroom cabin with a fireplace and full kitchen on several acres also is available for rent. The lodge is located on the edge of town and is integrated with the Meadowlark Retreat Center, a healing center.

Stagecoach Motor Inn

Owners: Rene and Debbie Suda
800-455-5090 or 307-455-2303
www.stagecoachmotel-dubois.com
103 Ramshorn St., Dubois, WY 82513
Rates: $59–125, seasonal rates available
Credit Cards: AE, D, MC, V
Handicapped Access: Yes
Pets: Yes (fee)
Season: Year-round

This multistory 47-unit motel has been family owned and operated for 31 years. It has a swimming pool and hot tub for summers, and a coin-operated laundry. The suites have fully loaded kitchenettes, and the King Suites overlook Horse Creek. Located in the heart of Dubois, the Motor Inn offers old-fashioned comfort.

Trail's End Motel

Owner: Tammy and Scott Bushnell
888-455-6660 or 307-455-2540
www.trailsendmotel.com
511 W. Ramshorn St., Dubois, WY 82513
Rates: $69–149 peak season, $59–119 all other times
Credit Cards: AE, D, DC, MC, V
Handicapped Access: Yes
Pets: No
Season: Year-round

Nineteen log-built units are in three separate buildings, including two that are stand-alone. The Trail's End touts itself as the only lodge actually on the Wind River. Eight units have fridges, microwaves, coffee makers, an iron, bathrobes, slippers and 27-inch flat-screen TVs. All rooms have a large TV and fridge. Paved parking is at your door. Wireless Internet is free and laundry services are on the premises. The motel is close to the town's new river walk. Airport transportation is provided and in-room massage therapy is available by appointment. Outdoor weight and exercise equipment are on site. Note: The Trail's End was planning to change its name and Web site in early 2008.

Twin Pines Lodge and Cabins

Owner: Mike Slider
800-550-6332 or 307-455-2600
www.twinpineslodge.com
218 W. Ramshorn St., Dubois, WY 82513
Rates: $60–90 single, $70–100 double, $80–120 suites
Credit Cards: AE, D, MC, V

Handicapped Access: Yes
Pets: No
Season: Year-round

History and modern conveniences mesh comfortably in this 1934 lodge with cabins and a rich rustic flavor. A full continental breakfast is served. Wireless Internet is available and some rooms have Jacuzzi tubs. There are 16 units—five in the lodge and 11 cabins. The property features a large playground for the kids.

Resorts

Brooks Lake Lodge
Manager: Adam Long
307-455-2121
www.brookslake.com
458 Brooks Lake Rd., Dubois, WY 82513
Rates: $300/person per night for lodge rooms, $375 for suites, $325 small cabin, $350 for one-bedroom cabin, $1,600 for two-bedroom cabin. $225/$275 in winter for lodge rooms and suites.
Credit Cards: AE, D, MC, V
Pets: No
Handicapped Access: No
Season: Mid-June—mid-Sept., mid-Dec.—mid-Mar.

The historic Brooks Lake Lodge, refurbished in the 1980s with all modern log amenities, sits in a forest and sage valley halfway between Dubois and Grand Teton National Park. There are seven rooms and eight cabins with a maximum group capacity of 36. Lodging includes three meals with extensive menu and such activities as horseback riding, fly fishing, guided hiking and canoeing. It also offers use of the spa, workout room, Jacuzzi and steam room. Alcoholic beverages, massage therapy and summer pack trips into the Pinnacle and Brooks Ranges are not included in the rate. Snowmobiles are available for rent in winter. Snowshoeing, cross-country skiing, ice fishing and the Jacuzzi are part of the winter package. A two-night minimum stay is required in winter, three in summer. A children's activity coordinator is on site in the summer. The ranch is located on 25 remote acres, about one-quarter mile from Brooks Lake.

Bed and Breakfasts

The Stone House
Owner: Grace Whalen
307-455-2555
www.duboisbnb.com
207 S. First St., Dubois, WY 82513
Rates: $65—85
Credit Cards: MC, V
Handicapped Access: Limited
Pets: No
Season: May 1—Oct. 31

A historic stone and quarry-block home with three rooms sits on a quiet acre and offers mountain views, yet is within easy walking distance of downtown Dubois. A three-room, stand-alone cottage on the property features a microwave, fridge and coffeepot. The house offers a two-room suite with bath and two other rooms that share a bath. A full breakfast includes fruit, cereal, an egg dish, breakfast meat and pastry. There is ample parking, and the stone construction ensures peaceful sleeping even though the home is near the main highway through town.

Guest Ranches

Bitterroot Ranch

Owners: Mel Bayard and Richard Fox
800-545-0019 or 307-455-2778
www.bitterrootranch.com
1480 East Fork Rd., Dubois, WY 82513
Rates: $1,950/person per week all-inclusive
Credit Cards: D, MC, V
Handicapped Access: Limited
Pets: No.
Season: Year-round

The Bitterroot is one of the more extraordinary dude ranches anywhere, which explains why one noted author included it among his "1,000 places to see before you die." The 1,400-acre Bitterroot a working cattle ranch for 36 years, is now turned dude ranch with emphasis on equine activities. The ranch has 170 horses to split among 30 guests. The goal is to introduce guests to the pleasures of riding, regardless of skill level, and they're serious about it. The Bitterroot refuses to join the Dude Ranch Association because the group doesn't require horseback riders to wear helmets. The ranch itself is in pristine forest and sage country, 17 miles from the closest paved road. Cabins are spaced for privacy. After a day of riding, special emphasis is placed on meals, with extra attention paid to wines. There are 17 unique and rustic cabins on a trout stream, all coming in a variety of sizes. Guests can participate in an actual cattle drive the last week in September and help move them between grazing areas from July to September. The Bitterroot Ranch is 16 miles up the East Fork Road, almost due east of Dubois.

CM Dude Ranch

Managers: Kass and Mike Harrell
800-455-0721 or 307-455-2331
www.cmranch.com
P.O. Box 217, Dubois, WY 82513
Rates: $1,500/person per week, $1,210 children 12 and under
Credit Cards: MC, V
Handicapped Access: No
Pets: No.
Season: June–mid-Sept.

The CM is a guest ranch that has been offering dude-ranch vacations at the mouth of the Jakeys Fork tributary of the Wind River since 1927. It sits in a remote location at the edge of national forest and wilderness. Three full meals a day are served with emphasis on healthy and hearty. Horseback riding, fishing and other family-oriented activities are regularly scheduled. Overnight pack trips are offered. A heated swimming pool and hot tub are on site. Three 1920s cabin-style homes are above the main lodge and come in two and three bedrooms, with all the necessary amenities. There are a number of various sized cabins dotting the property. The ranch can house up to 50 people and a one-week minimum stay is required. Weddings and pack trips can also be accommodated.

Lazy L&B Ranch

Owner: Lee and Bob Naylon
800-453-9488 or 307-455-2839
www.lazylb.com
1072 East Fork Rd., Dubois, WY 82513
Rates: $1,350/person adults, $1,250 children all-inclusive
Credit Cards: MC, V
Handicapped Access: No
Pets:Considered
Season: Summers

These 12 log cabins are rustic but feature all modern necessities. Three family-style meals are served daily, with accommodations made for vegetarian diets. Activities include horseback riding, a swimming pool with hot tub, fishing the East Fork of the Wind River and a stocked trout pond. The 150-acre ranch is completely surrounded by public lands, with riding trails in every direction. The Lazy L&B also runs the Bear Basin Wilderness Camp (www.bearbasincamp.com), which offers wilderness pack trips through the summer and fall for $225 per day per person. The four- to six-day trips accommodate up to eight people who stay at a base camp with wall tents, wood-burning stoves, a cook and a wrangler.

Mackenzie Highland Ranch

Managers: Tom and Ruthie Verheul
307-455-3415
www.mackenziehighlandranch.com
3945 US Hwy. 26, Dubois, WY 82513
Rates: $175–245
Credit Cards: MC, V
Handicapped Access: No
Pets: Yes
Season: Year-round

Eight cabins ranging from one to four bedrooms are available in the summer and five are operating in winter on this small family guest ranch. The emphasis is on self-sufficiency. Each cabin has a full kitchen and laundry facility. Guests do their own housekeeping. The ranch is 16 miles west of Dubois on 120 acres and surrounded by the Shoshone National Forest, with serene views, lots of wildlife and Wind River frontage. A three-night minimum stay is required. Activities include fly fishing, hunting and guided horseback rides. Paddocks or corrals are available for those who bring their own horses. ATV rentals are offered in summer.

T Cross Ranch

Managers: Mark and Gretchen Cardall
877-827-6770 or 307-455-2206
www.tcross.com
P.O. Box 638, Dubois, WY 82513
Rates: $700/person for three nights, $1,400 for six
Credit Cards: MC, V
Handicapped Access: No
Pets: No
Season: June through Sept.

Eight 1920s and '30s log cabins with a maximum capacity of 24 guests dot this 160-acre pine-covered spread. Prime activities are horseback riding and fly fishing, with evening entertainment around the campfire. A hot tub is on the premises and the cook prepares traditional ranch cuisine. This is a historic family-oriented dude ranch, rich in tradition and local folklore.

Triangle C Dude Ranch

Owner: Cameron Garnick
800-661-4928 or 307-455-2225
www.trianglec.com
3737 US Hwy. 26, Dubois, WY 82513
Rates: $2,100/person, $1,700 children six nights; $1,750/$950 three nights
Credit Cards: AE, D, MC, V
Handicapped Access: No
Pets: No
Season: Memorial Day–mid-Oct.

The Triangle C focuses on families in the summer and hunters after Labor Day. The 8,000-square-foot main lodge includes a saloon, dining hall and recreation area. The 17 relatively new cabin units with private baths have a maximum group capacity of 45–50 guests. The Wind River runs through the property. A hot tub and guest laundry are on site. Pack trips are available in the summer; after Labor Day, three- and six-night hunting packages are offered.

Jackson, Wyoming 97 miles to Old Faithful (2hus 21min)

The first admonition you'll hear from anybody who lives in the region is this: Jackson and Jackson Hole are *not* the same. Jackson is the town; Jackson Hole is the entire valley. You'll hear it from longtime or outlying residents who aren't enamored with the deep-pocketed eastern influences brought on Lear jets to this ruggedly beautiful region. You'll also hear it from nouveau Jacksonites who find the outlying areas, and even some of the in-town locales, a tad too primitive for their liking. What they have in common is an appreciation for one of the most spectacular settings in the world, even if they cherish it for different reasons. And they weren't the first. Indians came to Jackson Hole in summers to hunt the bountiful wildlife. It wasn't until 1807, when John Colter veered south from the Lewis and Clark Expedition on its return trip to St. Louis, that the first Anglos saw the region. Fur trappers soon followed to pursue beaver, and many a mountain man converged for regular rendezvous in the "hole" between the Teton and Gros Ventre Ranges. Serious settlement didn't begin until the 1880s, when the creation of Yellowstone National Park sparked interest in the area to the south. Jackson was created in 1894 as a hub for the cattle-ranching industry and a destination for wealthy eastern hunters. Remnants of a few of the original buildings remain in the town's renowned Town Square, known best for the elk-antler arches at each of the four corners. That this would be no ordinary town first became apparent in 1920—a year after women were given the right to vote nationally— when Jackson democratically picked an all-woman city council, a first for the country. A tow was constructed at Teton Pass in 1937 and Snow King opened a few years later as the first ski area in Wyoming.

The movie industry certainly contributed to making Jackson what it is today. *Nanette of the North* was filmed in Jackson Hole in 1921, John Wayne's first speaking part was in Jackson in 1932, and *Shane* was produced near Kelly two decades later. Henry Fonda's *Spencer's Mountain* in 1963 is another flick that brought the region to the big screen. Today it's a renowned haven for artists, writers and other creative types as well as high-powered, deep-pocketed fast-trackers from elsewhere. Celebrities flock to Jackson each summer and winter, grateful that it's one of the few places where their arrival at a restaurant is greeted by little more than a nod. It's part of what has helped Jackson retain some of its charm, even as real estate has exploded off the charts, periodically ranking the town as the most expensive in the nation. This phenomenon is due partly to the area's beauty and partly to limited elbow room; only 3 percent of the county is privately owned. Galleries blend seamlessly with curios shops, cosmopolitan restaurants flourish next to busy barbe-cue joints and the rich mingle comfortably but sometimes tenuously with carefree outdoor lovers with holes in their jeans.

This unique blend is reflected in the town's lodging. Though there's no shortage of swanky resorts, such as the Four Seasons (the largest building in Wyoming), Jackson also has a surprising number of affordable accommodations. We can offer just a sampling of the more unique here. For renting vacation homes or condos, contact Jackson Hole Resort Lodging at 800-443-8613 or 307-733-3990, or go to www.jhresortlodging.com.

Motels

Anglers Inn
Manager: Debra Currier
800-867-4667 or 307-733-3682
www.anglersinn.net
265 N. Millward St., Jackson, WY 83001
Rates: $65–160
Credit Cards: AE, D, MC, V
Handicapped Access: Yes
Pets: No
Season: Year-round

Each of the 28 nonsmoking rooms at this otherwise standard motor inn has lodgepole pine furniture and fly-fishing decor. Each room has a mini-fridge, coffeemaker, microwave, hairdryers, iron, TV with HBO and wireless Internet. Flat Creek meanders by the property, creating a sense of rural retreat in the midst of the city.

Buckrail Lodge

Owner: Janet Colonel

307-733-2079

www.buckraillodge.com

110 E. Karns Ave., Jackson, WY 83001

Rates: $80–120

Credit Cards: AE, D, MC, V

Handicapped Access: Accessible, but not equipped

Pets: No

Season: May–mid-Oct.

Located five blocks south of town at the base of Snow King mountain, this family-owned and -operated lodge consists of a row of 12 cedar log cabins with rooms. Coffee and tea is available in the rooms and lobby. There's a spacious yard with mature spruce and aspen trees, providing a private setting in a not-so-private town. So authentic is this lodge, it was used for one of the settings in the Clint Eastwood movie *Any Which Way You Can.*

Bunkhouse

Manager: Alton Parker

800-234-4507 or 307-733-3668

www.anvilmotel.com

215 N. Cache, Jackson, WY 83001

Rates: $25

Credit Cards: D, MC, V

Handicapped Access: No

Pets: No

Season: Year-round

Jackson's least expensive place to stay offers dormitory-style rooms, with semiprivate bunks. Lockers and linens are provided. A locker room has a place for ski waxing. The large lounge has a TV with HBO. Walk-ins only; reservations are not accepted.

Cottages at Snow King

Manager: Angie Watson

307-733-3480

470 So. King St., Jackson, WY 83001

Rates: $78–105 nightly in summer, $600–900 per month in winter

Credit Cards: AE, D, MC, V

Handicapped Access: No

Pets: Yes

Season: Year-round

The Cottages at Snow King are actually 22 small economy hotel rooms, each with microwaves and fridges. Some have kitchen units; none have phones. Situated four blocks from downtown, the Cottages at Snow King have some of the lowest rates in Jackson—and you get what you pay for. Though older and more rustic than most area lodging, the rooms are well kept and great for the bargain hunter or guests who don't plan to spend much time in their rooms.

Cowboy Village Resort

Managers: Dave Palmer or Cherisse Haws
800-483-8667 or 307-733-3121
www.townsquareinns.com
120 South Flat Creek Dr., Jackson, WY 83001
Rates: $80–180
Credit Cards: AE, D, MC, V
Handicapped Access: Yes
Pets: Yes
Season: Year-round

These 82 individual log cabins all feature kitchenettes and sofa sleepers. Each cabin deck has a charcoal barbecue grill and picnic table. A hot tub, swimming pool and guest laundry are on site. A free continental breakfast is served in winter. There also is a meeting room, business center and wireless Internet available throughout the facility.

Elk Country Inn

Owner: Wendy Meadows
Manager: Dan Winder
800-483-8667 or 307-733-2364
www.townsquareinns.com
480 W. Pearl. St., Jackson, WY 83001
Rates: $42–100 summer, $80–208 winter
Credit Cards: AE, D, MC, V
Handicapped Access: Yes
Pets: Yes, except in cabins
Season: Year-round

The Elk Country has an eclectic array of lodging, including 16 stand-alone cabins with two queen beds or a kitchen. There's a picnic park with barbecue grills and a playground, and a hot tub on the grounds. A ski wax room, winter car plug-ins and complimentary ski shuttles complete the list of winter amenities. Located next to Cowboy Village cabins.

Elk Refuge Inn

Owner: Ron Miller
Manager: David Gamaleri
800-544-3582 or 307-733-3582
www.elkrefugeinn.com
1755 N. US Hwy. 89, Jackson, WY 83002
Rates: $69.95–$225.95
Credit Cards: AE, D, MC, V
Handicapped Access: Yes
Pets: No
Season: Year-round

Views of the National Elk Refuge from each room are the hallmark of this inn, a 24-room lodge that features three suites and 10 balcony rooms with kitchenettes. Eleven rooms have patios and come with a king-sized bed or two double beds. Barbecue grills and a small fire pit are available in the picnic area. For elk hunters, the inn offers horse corrals and a hanging post. The refuge is just across the highway, providing excellent viewing opportunities to view elk and bison.

Golden Eagle Inn
Owners: Jim and Dood Loose
888-748-6937 or 307-733-2042
www.goldeneagleinn.com
325 E. Broadway Ave., Jackson, WY 83001
Rates: $60–140 (call for quote on house and family units)
Credit Cards: AE, MC, V
Handicapped Access: No
Pets: No.
Season: Apr. through Oct.

This standard two-story has 23 rooms, all with a fridge, microwave and coffeepot. An outdoor heated pool provides lounging space for a respite in a busy tourist town. A large family unit sleeps up to eight, and a two-bedroom house is also available upon request. Family owned and operated, this friendly motel offers unusually affordable lodging for Jackson.

Grand Victorian Lodge
Owners: Tom and Nancy Stodola
800-584-0532 or 307-739-2294
www.grandvictorianlodge.com
85 Perry Ave., Jackson, WY 83001
Rates: $99–334
Credit Cards: AE, D, MC, V
Handicapped Access: Yes
Pets: No
Season: Year-round

As the name suggests, this is a Victorian-style small luxury hotel with a bed and breakfast ambience. Eleven rooms are individually decorated and appointed in a homey style. A chef-prepared breakfast is served in the fireside dining room. Godiva chocolates, gourmet coffee and tea, and homemade cookies await your arrival in the lobby. An outdoor spa is on site as well as concierge service. The lodge is a replica of an 1880 Queen Anne home and is within walking distance to the Town Square.

Hoback River Resort
307-733-5129
www.hobackriverresort.com
11055 S. US Hwy. 89, Jackson, WY 83001
Rates: $75–95 motel rooms, $130–180 cabins
Credit Cards: AE, D, MC, V
Handicapped Access: No
Pets: No
Season: Year-round (motel), June 1–Oct. 1 (cabins and cottages)

Sixteen comfortable motel rooms and 10 cabins and cottages are perched on a bluff over-looking the Snake and Hoback Rivers near the Snake River canyon. The cottages have full-size stove and fridge, and include all linens and cookware. The grass lawn in front offers picnic tables and barbecue grills for freshly caught trout. Cottages are one- and two-bedroom. Cabins are closer to the river and are fully furnished. The river has a sandy beach for swimming and boat launching.

Homewood Suites by Hilton
Manager: Joe Medera
800-225-5466 or 307-739-0808
www.homewoodsuites.com
260 N. Millward St., Jackson, WY 83001
Rates: $289–319 summer, $239–279 winter, $169–189 off-season
Credit Cards: AE, D, MC, V
Handicapped Access: Yes
Pets: Yes
Season: Year-round

This chain motel features 41 suites with full kitchen, living room and fireplace. Perks include an indoor swimming pool, hot tub and wireless Internet. A hot breakfast is served each morning, and light dinners are served 5:30–7:30 PM Mondays through Thursdays in the reception area. Free athletic club passes also are available.

Inn on the Creek
800-669-9534 or 307-733-1565
www.innonthecreek.com
295 N. Millward Dr., Jackson, WY 83001
Rates: $179–469
Credit Cards: AE, D, MC, V
Handicapped Access: No
Pets: No
Season: Year-round

Though just three blocks from Town Square, this rustically elegant inn feels secluded. A variety of tastefully appointed rooms have a touch of luxury, ranging from the down comforters and fireplaces to the box of chocolates, terry robes and views of Flat Creek. Complimentary breakfasts can be delivered to your room. An outdoor Jacuzzi is on the banks of the creek. Some rooms have creek-side balconies or patios, and one has a full kitchen. Wireless Internet is available.

Jackson Hole Lodge
Owner: Jicarilla Apache Nation
Managers: Outrigger Lodging Services
800-604-9404 or 307-733-2992
www.jacksonholelodge.com
420 W. Broadway Ave., Jackson, WY 83001
Rates: $59–319
Credit Cards: AE, D, MC, V

Handicapped Access: Yes
Pets: In standard lodge rooms
Season: Year-round

This gray two-story building with log façade contains 60 units, the standard lodge rooms coming with various bed sizes. Condo suites have deluxe queen beds, full kitchen, fireplace, eating area and writing desk. One-bedroom suites also have a washer and dryer, a small deck or patio and two full baths. The largest unit is two stories with two bedrooms; it has a fully equipped kitchen and two bathrooms and sleeps up to eight. On site are a 40-foot heated indoor pool, two heated Jacuzzis, a dry sauna and game room with table tennis and foosball. Wireless Internet and a computer are available in the lobby.

Kudar Motel
Owners: Joe and Ron Kudar
Manager: Scott Alexander
307-733-2823
260 N. Cache St., Jackson, WY 83001
Rates: $85–120
Credit Cards: MC, V, D
Handicapped Access: No
Pets: No
Season: Mid-May–mid-Oct.

One of Jackson's oldest motels, the Kudar was built in the 1940s but was recently refurbished. Fourteen motel rooms and 17 cabins retain an authentic frontier feel. An old motor court features a grassy area with picnic tables in the center of a circular driveway. An original owner, the legendary Mrs. Kudar, turned 97 in November 2007. This nonsmoking motel is suited for the budget-conscious. Many families have been coming to the cabins since the 1950s and '60s.

The Lodge Best Western
Manager: Dayne Benoit
800-458-3866 or 307-739-9703
www.lodgeatjh.com
80 S. Scott Lane, Jackson, WY 83002
Rates: $119–249
Credit Cards: AE, D, MC, V
Handicapped Access: Yes
Pets: No
Season: Year-round

A complimentary hot buffet breakfast is part of the bargain at this 153-room motel known for its carved wooden bears. The swimming pool is half indoors and half outdoors and includes a hot tub and sauna. All king-sized rooms have jetted tubs. Each room features a fridge, microwave and coffeepot. There is a two-room suite for $329 a night that sleeps up to six people comfortably.

Parkway Inn & Spa

Owner and General Manager: Jacquie Riley
800-247-8390 or 307-733-3143
www.parkwayinn.com
125 N. Jackson St., Jackson, WY 83001
Rates: $109–339
Credit Cards: AE, D, MC, V
Handicapped Access: No
Pets: No
Season: Year-round

The Parkway is an early-20th-century Victorian-style hotel with handmade quilts and American antiques throughout the 47 rooms and suites. Renovated rooms are designed in a newer western motif. An indoor lap pool is complemented by two jetted spa tubs. Cable TV, coffeemakers and hairdryers are in the comfy and spacious rooms. An expanded continental breakfast is included in the rate.

Ranch Inn

Manager: Cindy Carson
800-348-5599 or 307-733-6363
www.ranchinn.com
45 E. Pearl St., Jackson, WY 83001
Rates: $105–175
Credit Cards: AE, D, MC, V
Handicapped Access: Yes
Pets: No
Season: Year-round

This nonsmoking facility features six suites, six luxury rooms, 17 standard rooms and 28 spacious tower rooms on the second and third floors, with balconies that face the Snow King ski area. A honeymoon suite features a full kitchen with a fireplace and huge balcony. A former mayor owns the property and is determined to keep it appealing and affordable. A continental breakfast with fresh fruit is served.

Rusty Parrot Lodge & Spa

Manager: Kevin Kavanaugh
800-458-2004 or 307-733-2000
www.rustyparrot.com
175 N. Jackson St., Jackson, WY 83001
Rates: $205–700
Credit Cards: AE, D, MC, V
Handicapped Access: No
Pets: No
Season: Year-round

This downtown log lodge is the only four-star hotel in Jackson. A full chef-prepared breakfast at the Wild Sage Restaurant on site is included. The Rusty Parrot also features full concierge service. An outdoor hot tub overlooks the town. Rooms offer down comforters and gas fireplaces. Body Sage, the first full-service spa in Jackson, is a part of the lodge. Therapeutic treatments can be custom-made and arranged by appointment.

Sundance Inn
Owner: Casey and Amy Morton
888-478-6326 or 307-733-3444
www.sundanceinnjackson.com
135 W. Broadway Ave., Jackson, WY 83001
Rates: $59–109 winter, $69–169 summer
Credit Cards: AE, D, MC, V
Handicapped Access: No
Pets: No
Season: May through Oct., Dec. through Mar.

This 27-room downtown inn offers cozy accommodations and homemade continental breakfast. All rooms are individually decorated and feature private baths and air-conditioning. An outdoor hot tub is on site. The owners have operated the motel for 21 years and have developed a loyal clientele. The motel, a Jackson stalwart, was built in the 1950s and maintains its art-deco theme from the time period.

Teton Gables Motel
Manager: Scott Anderson
307-733-3723
www.tetongables.com
1140 W. Hwy. 22, Jackson, WY 83001
Rates: $79–120, depending on season (all rooms one price)
Credit Cards: AE, D, MC, V
Handicapped Access: Limited
Pets: Yes ($10 fee)
Season: Year-round

Don't expect many frills in this 28-room motel, which prides itself on clean rooms, friendly staff and some of Jackson's most competitive rates. It is located at the junction of WY 22 and US 89, 2 miles from Town Square. The rooms have one or two queen beds, and each room has a TV, phone and alarm clock. The newer Fine Spotted Cutthroat restaurant and bar are on site, offering reasonably priced breakfast and a cold beer with dinner.

Trapper Inn & Suites
Managers: Dianna and Tim Waycott
888-771-2648 or 307-733-2648
www.trapperinn.com
285 N. Cache Dr., Jackson, WY 83001
Rates: $189–249 peak seasons, $119–249 off-seasons
Credit Cards: AE, MC, V
Handicapped Access: Yes (four rooms ADA-approved)
Pets: No
Season: Year-round

One of Jackson's newer lodgings is an all-suite hotel, with 90 rooms total. They include courtyard rooms, luxury kings, standard suites and a few specialty rooms. Each room comes with the usual amenities including a fridge, coffeemaker, microwave, cable TV and HBO; some have kitchenettes. A conference room with full kitchen is also on site.

Virginian Lodge

Manager: Jim Triplet
800-262-4999 or 307-733-2792
www.virginianlodge.com
750 W. Broadway Ave., Jackson, WY 83001
Rates: $108–210 summer, $59–164 winter
Credit Cards: AE, D, MC, V
Handicapped Access: No
Pets: No
Season: Year-round

The Virginian Lodge looks like something straight out of Route 66, a throwback to the days when Jackson was largely a collection of motor lodges serving Grand Teton visitors, hunters and fishermen. The sprawling complex features 170 guest rooms, 105 RV spots, a saloon, liquor store, hair salon and outdoor heated pool open in summers, and a hot tub. The lodging features eight types of room, ranging from standard doubles to a kitchenette and two-bedroom suites. You'll mingle with locals in the Virginian Saloon, under bighorn ram mounts and surrounded by other regional artifacts. The Virginian is situated seven blocks from Town Square on the main drag toward Wilson.

Wagon Wheel Village

800-323-9279 or 307-733-2357
www.wagonwheelvillage.com
435 N. Cache Dr., Jackson, WY 83001
Rates: $90–165 (Dec. 16–Apr. 1), $50–95 (Apr. 1–May 15 and Oct. 1–Dec. 15), $90–157.50 (May 16–June 14 and Sept. 16–30), $100–175 (June 15–Sept. 15)
Credit Cards: AE, MC, V
Handicapped Access: Yes
Pets: No
Season: Year-round

A popular complex, this establishment offers varying lodging arrangements ranging from deluxe three-bedroom units to camping on the creek. Also on the premises are the Route 89 Smokehouse Restaurant, a saloon, a liquor store, a western gift shop and a Laundromat. Note: The Wagon Wheel was scheduled to be sold in October 2007.

Wort Hotel

Director of guest relations: Christy Reinhardt
800-322-2727 or 307-733-2190
www.worthotel.com
50 N. Glenwood St., Jackson, WY 83001
Rates: $169–699
Credit Cards: AE, D, MC, V

Handicapped Access: Yes
Pets: No
Season: Year-round

This English-Tudor revival style brick and stucco hotel, which takes up an entire city block, is a National Historic Landmark. Remnants of its years as an illegal gambling hall remain throughout, including an old roulette wheel, blackjack table and historic photos. The bar is adorned with 2,032 inlaid silver dollars, and there are 300 original silver dollars displayed throughout the dining area. The lobby is filled with locally made log furniture. A large rawhide chandelier with iron cutouts greets visitors. The original staircase and fireplace survived a devastating second-floor fire in 1980. The full-service hotel's 59 classy rooms come with valet parking and a fresh rose. Six different types of rooms, ranging from deluxe ($169–289) to the fit-for-a-king Silver Dollar Suite ($699), feature either two queens or a king bed, granite and marble in the bathrooms, plush carpet and luxurious bedding topped with a stuffed bear for company. Larger suites are up to a rustically elegant 500 square feet and include a wet bar. The property features a fitness center, two Jacuzzis, a bar and a restaurant that prepares regional meats such as elk and bison.

Resorts

Alpenhof Lodge
General Managers: Mark and Ann Johnson
800-732-3244 or 307-733-3242
www.alpenhoflodge.com
3255 W. Village Dr., Teton Village, WY 83025
Rates: $209–589 winter, $229–529 summer, $159–409 off-seasons
Credit Cards: AE, D, DC, MC
Handicapped Access: No (Dining room only)
Pets: Dogs
Season: May 1–mid-Oct., Dec. 1–early Apr. (typically follows opening and closing of Jackson Hole Mountain Resort)

The Alpenhof is one of the older lodges serving the ski area. It has 43 rooms, including a two-bedroom suite. Rates typically include hot and cold European breakfast, delivered to rooms in the shoulder months between busy seasons. There is an outdoor heated pool that remains open during the winter, plus an outdoor hot tub, indoor sauna and massage. Wireless Internet is available throughout. Breakfast is served at the Alpenrose Restaurant, with a distinct German and Austrian flair. A bistro on the second floor serves lunch and a casual dinner. Live entertainment often enhances the ambiance during ski season.

Amangani Hotel
Manager: Stuart Lang
877-734-7333 or 307-734-7333
www.amanresorts.com
1535 Northeast Butte Rd., Jackson, WY 83002
Rates: $565–1,660
Credit Cards: AE, D, MC, V
Handicapped Access: Yes

Pets: No
Season: Year-round

This elegant 40-suite hotel was opened in 1998 and is the only North American property in the Singapore-based Amanresorts chain. It is located on a 1,000-acre wildlife sanctuary that's a migratory route for mule deer and elk between Jackson and Teton Village. Built mostly from redwood and Oklahoma sandstone, the resort includes a full-service spa, a pool and a health center. A 65-seat bar, restaurant and a grill are on site. The views of the Tetons are as spectacular as the accommodations.

Four Seasons Resort Jackson Hole
Reservations manager: Helen Blissitt
800-295-5281 or 307-732-5000
www.fourseasons.com/jacksonhole
7680 Granite Loop Rd., Teton Village, WY 83025
Rates: $575 up to $6,000 for a 5-bedroom penthouse in high season
Credit Cards: AE, D, MC, V
Handicapped Access: Yes
Pets: Yes (beagle-sized dogs or smaller)
Season: Year-round (closed for two weeks in spring and fall)

The name says it all, and the luxury comes in a wide array of room options in the largest building in Wyoming: Deluxe Executive Suite, Executive Suite, Premium, Deluxe, Superior and Standard. Suites are Presidential, Specialty, Premium or Deluxe. Two- to five-bedroom penthouses are available as well. Weddings, business retreats and other celebrations are commonly held here. There's a spa, restaurant and two lounges on premise. Ski-in and ski-out access to the mountain is one of the many perks. A variety of packages are available, including bed and breakfast.

Lost Creek Ranch & Spa
Manager: Mike Stevenson
307-733-3435
www.lostcreek.com
1 Old Ranch Rd., Moose, WY 83012
Rates: $6,200 per week (Sun. to Sun.), $14,545 for family of four
Credit Cards: AE, MC, V
Handicapped Access: No
Pets: No
Season: Late May through Sept.

Lost Creek is a deluxe ranch and spa with a maximum of 64 guests that can be accommodated in 10 luxury cabins. Lodging consists of two types: Duplex Cabins and Living Room Cabins. The Duplex Cabins are attached but independent of each other, so they may be rented separately. Each side has a queen and twin bed, a bathroom and a small fridge. One half-duplex, called the King Suite, features a king bed. Living Room Cabins feature two bedrooms and two baths, with a queen in each master bedroom and twins in the other room. They also have kitchenettes. Activities included in the rates are horseback riding, trips to both parks, scenic floats on the Snake River, guided hiking in the Tetons, cookouts, skeet shooting and a trip to the rodeo. Other activities can be arranged for extra charges. Gourmet food is a staple, and the spa is full-service, with facials, manicures, pedicures and massage by appointment. On site are an outdoor underground pool, hot-tub sauna, steam room, tennis court, basketball court, weight room, workout room and cardio deck with bicycles facing the Tetons. Yoga and Pilates classes convene three times a week.

Moose Head Ranch
Owner: Louise and Kip Davenport
307-733-3141 or 850-877-1431 (mid-Oct.–mid-May)
US Hwy. 89 N., Moose, WY 83012
Rates: $350 per person per night, $250 for kids 6 and under all-inclusive
Credit Cards: No
Handicapped Access: No
Pets: No
Season: Early June–mid-Aug.

The Moose Head is the last privately owned guest ranch completely surrounded by Grand Teton National Park. It features 14 log cabins, including a two-bedroom cabin that sleeps up to five with a living room, wood-burning stove, deck and porch. The smaller cabins sleep two. Trout ponds offer catch-and-release fly fishing (barbless dry flies only). Three chefs prepare gourmet meals three times daily. No structured programs are scheduled, but there are plenty of activities for the kids.

Snake River Lodge & Spa
General manager: Bruce Grosbety
800-445-4655 or 307-732-6090
www.snakeriverlodge.rockresorts.com
7710 Granite Loop Rd., Teton Village, WY 83025
Rates: $129–2,200.
Credit Cards: AE, D, MC, V
Handicapped Access: Yes
Pets: No
Season: Year-round (closed Nov. and a few weeks in Apr.)

The Snake River is yet another luxurious spa resort on the mountainside in Teton Village. This one features 140 rooms and several off-site condominiums, including two free-standing units. Lodging options range from the standard Lodge Room with obstructed views but plush king beds and granite countertops in the bathroom to two-bedroom penthouse suites with kitchen, gas fireplace and generous living space. The Residence Suites also house washers and dryers. On site are an indoor-outdoor heated pool, concierge services and full-service spa. The game-fish restaurant serves dinner with an emphasis on American western gourmet cuisine and such regional dishes as Wyoming beef, smoked game and native fish. In the Fireside Bar, a breakfast buffet will start your day right.

Snow King Resort
Manager: Dana Ahrensberg
800-522-5464 or 307-733-5200
www.snowking.com or loveridgelodge.com (condos)

400 E. Snow King Ave., Jackson, WY 83001
Rates: $200 single/$210 double for hotel rooms, $240–490 for condos depending on
number of bedrooms and location
Credit Cards: AE, D, MC, V
Handicapped Access: Yes
Pets: Yes (hotel only)
Season: Year-round

The Snow King offers one- to four-bedroom Loveridge condos, fully furnished in a western Wyoming motif and all privately owned. An outdoor swimming pool, two hot tubs and
tennis courts are located near the hotel lobby. The Atrium Restaurant and full-service
Olga's Day Spa and Gift Shop are on site, as well as a hair salon. In addition, the property
features a small game room and exercise facility. All guests renting condos are granted
access to amenities at the hotel, which features 204 appealing rooms with either king or
two queen beds. Cable TV and wireless Internet are in each room as well. A guest laundry
is on site. The hotel is located in a corner of town in a residential neighborhood, with ski-
in and ski-out to Snow King Mountain. Full concierge service is available.

Spring Creek Ranch

General manager: Stephen Price
800-443-6139 or 307-733-8833
www.springcreekranch.com
1800 Spirit Dance Rd., Jackson, WY 83001
Rates: $160–$2,250
Credit Cards: AE, D, MC, V
Handicapped Access: Limited
Pets: No
Season: Year-round

The Spring Creek Ranch has a spectacular setting above Jackson amid a wildlife preserve,
with 150 rooms. Also available are one-, two- and three-bedroom condominiums and
executive homes with up to five bedrooms. The hotel rooms are actually rustic cabins surrounding a trout pond, all on the edge of a cliff with views of the Tetons. Condos have full
kitchen, fireplace and living room, some larger than others and all with views of the sun
setting over the mountains. Six Executive Homes range from 4,300 to 6,500 square feet
and have four bedrooms and four baths. The ranch house has conference and meeting
facilities, and the ranch features on-site catering, tennis and a swimming pool. Activities
include horseback riding and sleigh rides in winter. The ranch has a hired naturalist who
gives talks, leads trips into Grand Teton National Park and assists with other activities.
Concierge service is available for any activity in the area. The Granary Restaurant serves
breakfast, lunch and dinner.

Teton Mountain Lodge & Spa

General manager: Steve Santomo
800-801-6615 or 307-734-7111
www.tetonlodge.com
3385 W. Village Dr., Teton Village, WY 83025
Rates: $259–$2,500 peak season, $199–2,000 off-season

Credit Cards: AE, D, MC, V
Handicapped Access: Yes
Pets: No
Season: Year-round

Luxury is the hallmark with these 129 rooms and suites, with seven different types of accommodations. Lodge rooms are traditional hotel rooms with mini-fridge and coffeemaker. Moran Suites are studio-style rooms with full kitchens, gas appliances and double-headed showers. The Sundance Junior Suites have king beds, gas appliances in the kitchenette and a whirlpool; they are located on the first or second floor facing the valley. One- and two-bedroom suites come with a full kitchen. The ultimate in luxury are the three-bedroom suites that sleep up to 12 and a two-level penthouse that sleeps 14. The facility features a fitness center, indoor and outdoor heated pool, massage and spa center, concierge services, steam room, and yoga and Pilates classes. The spa is located in a new larger building, and the fitness center has been upgraded. The Cascade Restaurant offers new western cuisine, with each entrée prepared on an outside heated patio, with views of Gros Ventre Mountains.

Triangle X Dude Ranch
Manager: Harold Turner
888-860-0005 or 307-733-2183
www.trianglex.com
2 Triangle X Rd., Moose, WY 83012
Rates: $2,220/person per week summers, $1,430 off-season; rates are all-inclusive
Credit Cards: MC, V
Handicapped Access: Yes
Pets: No
Season: Memorial Day weekend–mid-Oct., Dec. 26–mid-Mar.

One of few resorts entirely on national park land, the Triangle X accommodates up to 70 people in a series of log cabins. Amenities include three meals and two horseback rides per day. The ranch is casual and family-oriented, with wranglers specifically geared for kids' activities so parents can have some quality private time. Wildlife on the grounds is common, including elk, fox, pronghorn, moose and the occasional black bear. Horseback rides are tailored to meet skill level and interests. Guided fishing and float trips are available. Ten-mile float trips on the Snake River in the park are extra. A one-week minimum stay is required June 8 through Aug. 24; the minimum is four nights during the off-season and two nights during the winter.

Togwotee Mountain Lodge
Manager: Ben Wallace
800-543-2847 or 307-543-2847
www.togwoteelodge.com
27655 US Hwy. 26/287, Moran, WY 83013
Rates: $159–209 (cabins), $99–159 (lodge) in summer; cabins $99 in winter. Rates reduced in Apr., May, Oct. and Nov.
Credit Cards: AE, D, MC, V

Handicapped Access: Yes
Pets: No
Season: Year-round

This full-service resort offers such activities as dog-sledding, cat skiing, snowmobiling and tours into Yellowstone and other parts of the national forest. A travel agency books horse trips and other activities in Jackson Hole. Surrounded by the Bridger-Teton National Forest about 16 miles from the park, the lodge has 54 cabins and 28 lodge rooms, with six suites featuring loft rooms. Lodge rooms are on the second floor of the main lodge and feature two queen beds. The suites are on the third floor with a queen bed, sofa sleeper and bunk beds. Each cabin has a fully furnished kitchenette, two televisions, a dining area, living room, barbecue and seclusion amid the pines. The Grizzly Steakhouse and Red Fox Saloon are on site.

Bed and Breakfasts

Alpine House Country Inn
Manager: Brittany Senter
800-753-1421 or 307-739-1570
www.alpinehouse.com
285 N. Glenwood St., Jackson, WY 83001
Rates: $175–275
Credit Cards: AE, MC, V
Handicapped Access: Yes
Pets: No
Season: Year-round (closed a few weeks in Nov. and end of Apr. to late May).

With 22 rooms, this B&B feels more like an inn. Amenities include a hot tub, sauna and spa for facials and massages. Breakfasts are chef-prepared and are a full continental with two entrées: one savory and one sweet. Located three blocks from the Town Square.

Bentwood Inn
Manager: Susan Baratti
307-739-1411
www.bentwoodinn.com
4250 Raven Haven Rd., Jackson, WY 83001
Rates: $175–325
Credit Cards: AE, D, MC, V
Handicapped Access: Yes
Pets: No
Season: Year-round

The Bentwood has five rooms and offers hearty breakfasts. Most of the elegantly decorated rooms have jetted tubs and feature balconies or decks. Some have fireplaces. The inn is halfway between downtown Jackson and Teton Village on a wooded 3.5 acres with tall cottonwoods and views of the Tetons. The inn was built in 1995 using 200-year-old logs left over from the 1988 Yellowstone fires. *Country Inns* magazine recently rated it among the top 10 inns in the nation.

Sassy Moose Inn
Manager: Craig Kelley
800-356-1277 or 307-733-1277
www.sassymoose.com
3895 Miles Rd., Wilson, WY 83014
Rates: $79–199
Credit Cards: AE, D, MC, V
Handicapped Access: No
Pets: Yes
Season: Year-round

This log inn features stunning views of the Tetons. A stay includes an ample breakfast, an outdoor hot tub screened for privacy but still offering Teton views, and proximity to ski slopes. It's located in a rural setting west of Jackson.

Teton Treehouse
Owners: Denny and Sally Becker
307-733-3233
www.cruising-america.com/tetontreehouse
6175 Heck of a Hill Rd., Wilson, WY 83014
Rates: $195–230 and $425 summer, $175–210 late spring and early fall (mid-range prices offered for shoulder seasons)
Credit Cards: MC, V
Handicapped Access: No
Pets: No
Season: Year-round (was closed from October 2007 until May 2008)

Is this heaven? No, it just seems that way after you've climbed 95 steps through pine and fir forest to this hideaway in the trees. Owner Denny Becker started adding on to his hillside home three decades ago, and the former wilderness and river guide hasn't stopped. The result is six plush guest rooms with views of the valley and Sleeping Indian. You might need a map to navigate the twists and turns, and ups and downs, to find your room. Windows extend into the forest to offer a place to read or watch the wildlife, which includes dozens of birds and the occasional moose or deer. A heart-smart breakfast typically consists of fresh fruit, homemade porridge, homemade granola, yogurt, fresh hot bread and juices to jump-start a day of hiking, fishing or floating. Breakfast is served at 8 AM sharp so that guests may commune and exchange travel stories. As a longtime resident and former guide, Denny is eager to share the wonders of Jackson Hole with guests and might even invite you along for one of daily vigorous hikes.

Teton View Bed & Breakfast
Owners: Carol and Franz Kessler
866-504-7954 or 307-733-7954
www.tetonview.com
2136 Coyote Loop, Wilson, WY 83014
Rates: $159–269
Credit Cards: D, MC, V
Handicapped Access: No

Pets: Yes
Season: Summer and fall

This family-friendly B&B blends mountain hospitality with European flair. There is one guest room in the house, a two-room suite, and one cabin with a kitchen. A full breakfast is served. Special features include a large deck with views of the Tetons. The B&B is in a rural residential area halfway between the South Entrance to the park and Jackson and is near the mountains.

Trail Creek Ranch

Managers: Margaret Schultz and Alexandra Menolacino
307-733-2610
www.jacksonholetrailcreekranch.com
70100 Trail Creek Rd., Wilson, WY 83014
Rates: $225–425 summer, $175–350 late spring and early fall
Credit Cards: D, MC, V
Handicapped Access: No
Pets: No
Season: June 1–mid-Sept.

The remote Trail Creek Ranch fancies itself a bed and breakfast because that's the one meal they serve. The ranch features two private family cabins that sleep four to six apiece and a smaller recently built cabin for more romantic sorts. There are rooms available just off the main lodge, too, and the entire working ranch can be rented to accommodate as many as 20 guests. The ranch is hidden away on 280 acres in the mountains, yet only 10 miles from Jackson and just outside Wilson. All of the rustic cabins offer sweeping views of Sleeping Indian and the Gros Ventres from their porches. The ranch's dining specialty is a big breakfast with lots of choices. A heated swimming pool also is on the premises.

Wildflower Inn

Owners: Ken and Sherrie Jern
307-733-4710
www.jacksonholewildflower.com
3725 Teton Village Rd., Jackson, WY 83001
Rates: $300–400, depending on season
Credit Cards: MC, V
Handicapped Access: No
Pets: No
Season: Year-round

This gorgeous log inn on three acres has earned rave reviews in national magazines for reasons that quickly become apparent. The landscaping is colorful and immaculately manicured. The grounds are lush, wooded and include a pond. The rooms, so luxurious they've earned plaudits from *Bon Appétit, Sunset* and *Glamour,* have private decks and bathrooms. There are four single rooms and a two-room suite. Beds are handcrafted and feature down comforters. Wireless Internet is accessible throughout.

Cabins

Buffalo Valley Ranch

Managers: Karen and Jesse Rodenbough
888-543-2477 or 307-543-2062
www.buffalovalleyranch.com
16985 Buffalo Valley Rd., Moran, WY 83013
Rates: $129–219
Credit Cards: AE, D, MC, V
Handicapped Access: No
Pets: No
Season: Year-round

Three well-kept, recently remodeled, apartment-like cabins overlooking the Buffalo Fork River are halfway between Jackson and Yellowstone National Park. Designed to get guests outdoors, there are no phones or televisions, just a washer and dryer for cleaning up after a day in the mountains or on the river. The larger cabin is two-bedroom and sleeps eight, with a living area and country kitchen with a cookstove and fridge. The two smaller cabins have a fridge and cookstove and sleep four. Views of the Buffalo Valley and Tetons are terrific from the deck. The Buffalo Valley Cafe and fly shop are nearby, and float trips, horseback rides and fishing trips are offered. The site was originally homesteaded in 1908.

Camp Creek Inn

Owner: Johnny Upsher
307-732-2222
www.campcreekinn.com
12330 S. US Hwy.191, Jackson, WY 83001
Rates: $95–105
Credit Cards: AE, D, MC, V
Handicapped Access: No
Pets: Yes (with deposit)
Season: Year-round

Seven rustic wooden cabins are located next to a bar and restaurant 4 miles south of Hoback Junction. The cabins have no phones or cable TV, but there is a VCR for movies. A continental breakfast is included.

Luton's Teton Cabins

Owners: Brad and Joanne Luton
307-543-2489
www.tetoncabins.com
P.O. Box 48, Moran, WY 83013
Rates: $225–386
Credit Cards: No
Handicapped Access: Yes
Pets: No
Season: May 15–Oct. 30

Thirteen attractive, authentically western log cabins are situated 4 miles east of Moran, near Grand Teton's North Entrance. The smaller cabins are one-bedroom and sleep two or three. Larger cabins sleep six. A laundry is on site, and the lodge features a small library. There are no TVs or phones in the cabins, and no food service. The location, surrounded by national forest, is renowned for its seclusion, quiet, central location and views of the Teton Range.

Moulton Ranch Cabins
Owners: Hal and Iola Blake
307-733-3749
www.moultonranchcabins.com
Mormon Row Grand Teton National Park, Kelly, WY 83011
Rates: $75–195
Credit Cards: MC, V
Handicapped Access: No
Pets: No
Season: Memorial Day weekend–Oct. 1

These five nonsmoking log cabin units feature fantastic views of the Tetons and are completely surrounded by the park, about 13 miles north of Jackson. The cabins sit at the base of Blacktail Butte on one acre and often receive bison visitors. Each cabin has a kitchen and sleeps from two to six. All have grassy yards. They are about 100 yards south of the famous Moulton Barn, which can be used for a dance hall or other special events.

Guest Ranches

Flat Creek Ranch
Owner: Joe Albright
Manager: Shelby Scharp
866-522-3344 or 307-733-0603
www.flatcreekranch.com
P.O. Box 9760, Jackson, WY 83002
Rates: $560
Credit Cards: MC, V
Handicapped Access: Yes
Pets: No
Season: Memorial Day weekend through Sept.

Five historic guest cabins, with a total maximum capacity of 15 people, are on 160 acres at the end of a bumpy four-wheel-drive road, surrounded entirely by public lands. Rates include fly fishing, horseback riding, and shuttles to and from town and the airport. Swimming and canoeing on a nearby lake are other perks. Cabins are rustic, with antique tubs and handheld nozzles for showers, though a separate Wash House for traditional showers is also on the premises. A minimum three-night stay is required. Also available are four- and seven-day stays starting on Monday or Friday. A Wilderness Camp with even more primitive environs is 6 miles west of the ranch and set up with tents and thick mattresses. The family has owned the ranch since the 1920s. The entire ranch can be rented for special events.

Goosewing Ranch
Owner: Francois Corrand
888-733-5251 or 307-733-5251
www.goosewingranch.com
P.O. Box 4084, Jackson, WY 83001
Rates: $699–999 per person (three nights), $1,399–1,999 per person (seven nights) all-inclusive
Credit Cards: AE, MC, V
Handicapped Access: No
Pets: Upon approval, but not allowed in buildings
Season: Closed in Oct., Nov., Apr., May

This remote 50-acre ranch in the Gros Ventre River Valley, surrounded by wilderness and national forest, offers scenery, wildlife and horseback riding. There are eight guest cabins and a larger home, with a total capacity of 30 guests. Other activities include archery, hiking, mountain biking, fishing, wagon rides, cookouts, soaking in the hot tub and swimming in an outdoor heated pool. The main lodge, with its fireplace and pool table, is the primary gathering spot. The menu is eclectic, and there's plenty of beer and wine. A three-night minimum stay is required.

Gros Ventre River Ranch
Owners: Karl and Tina Weber
Resident manager: Sean McGough
307-733-4138
www.grosventreriverranch.com
P.O. Box 151, Moose, WY 83012
Rates: $1,575–2,675 per week high season, $1,420–2,365 early and late season; $240–395 per night early and late season (weekly only June 17–Sept. 2)
Credit Cards: No
Handicapped Access: No
Pets: No
Season: Mid-May–early Oct.

Four log cabins and five log lodges are aligned along the Gros Ventre River, surrounded by the Gros Ventre Wilderness and Bridger-Teton National Forest. The cabins were brought to the site from the second-oldest dude ranch in the valley and remodeled for a contemporary western look and feel. The log lodges were built in 1987 and feature all the modern amenities of the cabins, plus kitchenette, fireplace and wood-burning stove. Rates include meals, wine, horseback riding, canoeing, floating, fishing on the river and cookouts. Meals range from casual gourmet to western barbecue. The ranch just missed getting buried by the 1925 landslide that created Slide Lake. The slide area is visible from the lodge.

Heart Six Ranch
Managers: Karen and Jesse Rodenbough
888-543-2477 or 307-543-2477
www.heartsix.com

P.O. Box 70, 16985 Buffalo Valley Rd., Moran, WY 83013
Rates: $1,850 per week adults, $1,550 children 6–13, $925 children 3–5 all-inclusive during the summer season
Credit Cards: AE, D, MC, V
Handicapped Access: Yes
Pets: No
Season: Year-round

The Heart Six Ranch in the Buffalo Valley features 14 modern western cabins. The ranch is family-oriented and prohibits smoking on the grounds. There are no TVs or phones, but wireless Internet is in the lodge. Activities include horseback riding, archery, target shooting, float trips, fishing the Buffalo Fork River, backcountry adventures and campfires with nightly entertainment. In winter, the focus shifts to snowmobiling. Hunters come in the fall to traverse the nearby Bridger-Teton National Forest and wilderness area. The ranch has hundreds of horses and mules for packing on thousands of acres of public lands. Options are more flexible and meals are offered à la carte after August. A six-night stay is required from June 1 through August.

Red Rock Ranch

Owners: David and Debbie McKenzie
Manager: Douglas Hare
307-733-6288
www.theredrockranch.com
P.O. Box 38, Kelly, WY 83011
Rates: $1,200–2,200 per person five nights, $1,200 children all-inclusive
Credit Cards: AE, D, MC, V
Handicapped Access: Limited
Pets: No
Season: Late June–mid-Sept.

This dude ranch along Crystal Creek in the Gros Ventre Mountains offers 10 cabins and can accommodate groups of up to 25. The typical stay is five nights, though a Saturday and Sunday night stay can be worked out. Activities include horseback riding, hiking, trout fishing on Crystal Creek, mountain biking, swimming in the ranch's pool, soaking in the hot tub, cookouts, campfires and nature activities. Gourmet meals are served family style twice a week, and there are regular cookouts. Separate kids' wranglers are on staff so adults can enjoy alone time. The one- and two-bedroom log cabins are each named after an Indian tribe and feature a sitting room, wood-burning stove, fridge and porch. The ranch is above Lower Slide Lake, surrounded by national forest and wilderness.

Spotted Horse Ranch

Manager: Kevin Watkins
800-528-2084 or 307-733-2097
www.spottedhorseranch.com
12355 S. US Hwy. 191, Jackson, WY 83001
Rates: $1,725/person per week for four or more, $2,650/person single all-inclusive; $275/$450 daily

Credit Cards: MC, V
Handicapped Access: No
Pets: No
Season: Mid-May through Oct.

This sprawling ranch about 16 miles south of Jackson is geared more toward adults (indeed, only adults are allowed in September and October). The Spotted Horse has 10 cabins and can accommodate up to 35. The entire ranch and its 55 horses can be rented for $51,750 per week. Activities primarily are horseback riding, Orvis-endorsed guided fishing trips and big-game hunts in the backcountry. On the premises are volleyball, billiards and a saloon, sauna, whirlpool, laundry and video library. The ranch also has a pond stocked with trout. Cookouts are regular fare, and three hearty meals are served every day. Cabins are spacious and modern with a western flair. The Hoback River runs through the ranch, which is surrounded by national forest and is just downstream from Granite Hot Springs. From mid-May to June there's a three-night minimum, and from June through August the minimum stay is a week. In September and October it's back to three nights.

Turpin Meadow Ranch
General Manager: Dennis Jordan
800-743-2496 or 307-543-2000
www.turpinmeadowranch.com
24505 Buffalo Valley Rd., Moran, WY 83013
Rates: $300/person per night Memorial Day–Labor Day all-inclusive (six-night minimum), $109–129 winter modified all-inclusive
Credit Cards: AE, D, MC, V
Handicapped Access: Limited
Pets: No
Season: Year-round

Turpin Meadows is on 32 acres and features 13 log cabins with a rustic lodge and restaurant that serves three meals a day. Activities are horseback riding, fly fishing, snowmobiling and cross-country skiing on the property. One- and two-bedroom wood cabins are cozy and charming, with full baths. The ranch, near the confluence of the Buffalo Fork and Snake Rivers, has great views of the Tetons and is surrounded by the Bridger-Teton National Forest in a remote area. Hunting, fishing and snowmobiling packages are available through the ranch.

Victor, Idaho 122 miles to Old Faithful (2hrs 53min)
Victor is the first town you'll see after arriving over Teton Pass from Jackson, and there isn't much in this little roadside community of less than 1,000 except for a couple of interesting sporting-goods stores, a theater, cafe, soda fountain and two microbreweries. Once upon a time, when it was a major railroad stop between Teton Pass and Swan Valley, the town had more hustle and bustle than it does today. It had hotels, cafes, a theater and the only bank for miles. The town was a railroad hub for cattle and sheep ranchers, and the folks who mined the stone that can still be seen in some of the area architecture.

Kasper's Kountryside Inn
Owner: Shona Kasper
208-787-2726
www.tetonvalleychamber.com/kountrysideinn.htm
915 S. 100 W, Victor, ID 83455
Rates: $89–109 summer, $69–89 all other times
Credit Cards: D, MC, V
Handicapped Access: No
Pets: No
Season: Year-round

The Kountryside features two units separate from the main home. Three-room suites have tasteful furnishings and large viewing windows. Each suite has a living room and a fully-stocked kitchen with hickory cabinets and sofa sleeper queen bed in the bedroom. There is a stove, fridge, microwave and dishwasher, laundry facility in the bathroom, coffeepot, satellite TV and free movie rentals. Coffee, hot chocolate and popcorn are provided for movie watching. The chef's choice of a hot breakfast is $5 per person and is delivered whenever guests want it. Extended stays are possible. The inn is about a half-mile from the state highway, providing peace and privacy.

Teton Springs Golf and Casting Club
Director of operations: John Pinardi
888-761-7429 or 208-787-8008 ext. 17
www.tetonspringresort.com
10 Headwaters Dr., Victor, ID 83455
Rates: $225–890, depending on room and season
Credit Cards: AE, MC, V
Handicapped Access: Limited
Pets: No
Season: Year-round

Teton Springs is a gated community featuring luxury 3,000-square-foot designer-appointed homes with one to five bedrooms. All are privately owned. There's a swimming pool, tennis courts, basketball and fitness center, all surrounded by a Byron Nelson golf course. Also on the premises is a heliport for heli-skiing. Fully groomed cross-country skiing trails are on the property, as well as several fly fishing ponds; instruction is available. Privately owned hotel rooms and condos are scheduled for completion in the winter of 2007. The Headwaters Grill serves breakfast, lunch and dinner, depending upon the season. A shuttle service is provided from the Teton Valley airport and to Grand Targhee. The property is bordered by national forest.

Trails End Motel
Owner/manager: Roy Bell
208-787-2973
10 N. Main St., Victor, ID 83455
Rates: $79.95
Credit Cards: AE, D, MC, V

Handicapped Access: No
Pets: No
Season: May through Oct.

Three little log cabins are located in back of the Evergreen 66 gas station on Main Street. Two sleep four and one sleeps two. Each has a shower/tub, microwave, fridge, TV with cable, air-conditioning and heat. No phones. The name says it all.

4

ATTRACTIONS

You likely have heard about the reliable outbursts of Old Faithful. You probably have seen pictures of the Tetons. You no doubt have some vague sense of the northern Rockies being cowboy and rodeo country. And you might be well aware of the extraordinary wildlife viewing in Yellowstone and Grand Teton National Parks. Yet there is so much more to a region with surprising diversity, thanks to the influx of upscale populations to the gateway communities such as Jackson, which is frequently rated the richest community in the nation. In how many places can you watch a rodeo in the afternoon and dine at a five-star restaurant the same evening? Old Faithful is the signature geyser in Yellowstone, but you might be surprised to learn that it's not the biggest or most active. The Tetons are the Rockies' showcase mountains, but you might be surprised to know the Absarokas are bigger and older. Rodeos are widely associated with the northern Rockies, but just as numerous are film and art festivals.

For all the natural attractions in the region, there are as many cultural attractions.

FAMILY FUN

JACKSON

Alpine Golf (800-522-5464; www.snowking.com; 400 E. Snow King Ave.) An 18-hole miniature golf course next to the Alpine Slide. Price: $8 adults, $6 juniors (6–13).

Alpine Slide (800-522-5464; www.snowking.com; 400 E. Snow King Ave.) Snow King Mountain's 2,500-foot alpine slide starts with a ride up the mountain on a chairlift. Next comes a half-mile of twists and turns through forest and sage. Speed is controlled by riders, so it's suitable for all ages. Price: $12 single ride, $50 for five rides, early and late season; $15/$65 mid-June–August.

Amaze'n Jackson Hole (307-734-0455; 85 Snow King Ave.) Race against the clock and your friends in a large maze. Squirt guns are allowed by day and flashlights by night. Includes candy store and shaved ice. Also in West Yellowstone. No credit cards accepted.

Ripley's Believe It Or Not (307-734-0000; www.conceptattractions.com/html/Jackson .htm; 140 N. Cache St.) Here you'll find everything zany and wacky, much of it connected to the region, like the Flip-Flop Lodge and Bizarre Forest. Price: $9.95 adults, $7.95 juniors (5–12).

Snow King Chairlift (800-522-5464; www.snowking.com; 400 E. Snow King Ave.) Ride to the top of Snow King Mountain for scenic views of Jackson Hole and the Tetons.

Black bears look for a handout on a Ford in the 1920s. "A fed bear is a dead bear" is the park's current motto, and feeding bears from cars stopped in the early 1970s. National Park Service

Trails branch off from the summit. Open 9 AM–6 PM daily from late May to early September. Price: $25 adults, $22 seniors, $20 children (6–13) early season; $29/$27/$25 mid-June–August.

WEST YELLOWSTONE

Amaze'n Yellowstone (406-646-4321; 140 Madison Ave.) Race against the clock and your friends in a large maze. Squirt guns allowed by day and flashlights by night. Includes candy store and shaved ice. Also in Jackson.

FESTIVALS

ALTA

Grand Targhee Bluegrass Festival (800-827-4433) Three days of bluegrass music, arts and crafts, food booths, and children's entertainment. Mid-August.

CODY

Buffalo Bill Art Show and Sale (888-598-8119 or 307-587-5002; www.buffalobillart show.com) This show benefiting the Buffalo Bill Historic Center features fine art with western themes. Buffalo Bill Historic Center, late September.

Cowboy Songs and Ballads (307-587-4771; www.bbhc.org/events) Listen to authentic cowboy music, poetry and stories from local ranchers, cowboys, musicians and storytellers. Buffalo Bill Historical Center, second weekend in April.

Old West Show and Auction (307-587-9014; www.codyoldwest.com) This popular event features collectors from around the country gathering to buy old cowboy gear.

Robbie Powwow Garden, Buffalo Bill Historical Center, late June.

Plains Indian Museum Powwow (307-587-4771; www.bbhc.org/events) Singing, dancing, arts and crafts, Indian food from all over the region. Robbie Powwow Garden, Buffalo Bill Historical Center, mid-June.

Rendezvous Royale (888-598-8119 or 307-587-5002; www.rendezvousroyale.org) A celebration of the arts that combines the Buffalo Bill Art Show and Sale, Buffalo Bill Historical Center's Patrons Ball fundraiser and the Western Design Conference, which features western fashions. Riley Arena, late September.

Yellowstone Jazz Festival (307-587-4771; www.yellowstonejazz.com) Jazz aficionados have converged here from around the nation for 20 years. Funded by Wyoming Arts Council. Cody City Park, Buffalo Bill Historical Center, Powell High School, mid-July.

COOKE CITY/SILVER GATE

Fireman's Picnic Cooke City, Fourth of July.
Shakespeare in the Park Silver Gate, late July.
Fish Fry and Big Fish Contest Cooke City, mid-August.

DUBOIS

Dubois Antler Rendezvous (307-455-2556) Five days of selling antlers gathered after winter. Dubois town park, mid-May.

Swedish Smorgasboard (307-455-3429; www.duboiswyoming.org/smorgasbord.htm) This five-day event honors the Swedish loggers who worked in the area a century earlier. Headwaters Art Center, mid-June.

Winterfest (307-455-2556; www.dteworld.com/wedo/dubois.html) This three-day event features sled-dog racing, skijoring, cowboy lore and a hootenanny to brighten up the winter. Headwaters Arts Center and Sheridan Creek Oval, first weekend in February.

GARDINER

Brew Fest (406-848-7971; www.gardinerchamber.com) Microbrewers from the area show off their wares, with the help of live bands and food, starting at 2 PM and running until dark each day. Arch Park, Labor Day weekend.

Yellowstone Music Festival (www.yellowstonemusicfest.com) Live bluegrass, rock and folk music in the shadows of the famed Roosevelt Arch. Arch Park, Labor Day.

JACKSON

Elkfest (307-733-3316; www.elkfest.org) An elk-antler auction and mountain-man rendezvous are the highlights of the annual Elkfest. The antlers shed by the elk each year are collected by Boy Scouts from the nearby Jackson Hole National Elk Refuge and sold to help with the feeding of the elk. Teton County Fairgrounds, third weekend in May.

Grand Teton Music Festival (307-733-1128; www.gtmf.org) Nightly classical-music concerts feature internationally renowned symphony musicians in a newly renovated hall. Walk Festival Hall, Teton Village, mid-July–late August; free concert each July 4.

Jackson Hole Film Festival (800-733-8144 or 307-733-8144; www.jhff.org) Each year, some 80 independent films are screened for competition in seven categories. Roundtable discussions and other events are included. Center for the Arts, downtown; early June. Admission: $200 for festival pass; individual tickets available 15 minutes prior to start of films.

Jackson Hole Fall Arts Festival (307-733-3316; www.jacksonholechamber.com) This 11-day event features "visual, contemporary, culinary, western and Native American arts." There's a wide array of music, cowboy poetry and cuisine, along with gallery walks, workshops, artist receptions. The highlight is the "Taste of the Tetons" food expo. Early September.

Jackson Hole Scottish Festival (www.wyohighlanders.net) People of Scottish ancestry celebrate their roots with a variety of events and attractions over two days, including vendors, drumming, dancing, music, sports and clan-related events. The Wyoming Highlanders are a nonprofit group that celebrate the Scottish and Celtic mountain men who came to northwest Wyoming more than 200 years ago. Teton County Fairgrounds, 305 W. Snow King Ave., mid-August. Admission: $5 per day.

Jackson Hole Wildlife Film Festival (307-733-7016; www.jhfestival.org) Some 700 filmmakers from more than 30 countries gather every other year with scientists, naturalists and other wildlife enthusiasts. The event concludes with an awards ceremony. Jackson Lake Lodge, early October in odd-numbered years.

Mountain Artist's Rendezvous Art Show (307-733-8792; www.artassociation.org) Competitive arts and crafts fair. Miller Park, late July.

Micro-Brew Festival Brew specialists from a number of regional breweries show off their skills. Includes food and music. Teton Village, early August.

Old West Days (307-733-3316; www.jacksonholechamber.com/old_west_days/old-west days.php) Lots of Old West activities, including a mountain-man rendezvous, chuckwagon dinners, horses, shootouts, etc. Teton County Fairgrounds, Memorial Day weekend.

Spring Earth Festival (307-739-2246; www.muriecenter.org/programs.html) The conservation-oriented Murie Foundation offers the Teton Sustainability Project and other adventures. Culminates every spring in an ECO-fair. The Murie Center, Moose, mid-April.

Teton County Fair (307-733-5289; www.tetoncountyfair.com) This weeklong event includes the usual fair fare: rodeo, 4-H competitions, beauty queens, demolition derby, wildlife, food, music and exhibits, with a western flair. Teton County Fairgrounds, 305 W. Snow King Ave., late July. Admission: Varies by event.

TETON VALLEY

Spudfest (www.spudfest.org) A film festival focusing on documentaries, short films and independent movies, some shown at the Spud Drive-In—a fitting name in a region dominated by potato growers. The festival was founded by Dawn Wells, the actress who played country-girl Mary Ann on *Gilligan's Island*. Spud Drive-In, mid-August.

Teton Valley Summer Festival (208-354-2500; www.tetonvalleychamber.com) Famed for the launch of hot-air balloons, this festival also features a crafts fair, parade, fireworks and other events. Airport, early July.

WEST YELLOWSTONE

Knothead Jamboree (406-646-1093; www.westyellowstonechamber.com) Up to 1,000 square dancers have been gathering annually for a half-century. So-named because once upon a time anybody who journeyed more than 100 miles to go square dancing was considered a "knothead." Union Pacific Dining Lodge, Labor Day weekend.

World Snowmobile Expo (406-646-7701; www.snowmobileexpo.com) Six days of racing take place in the self-proclaimed snowmobile capital of the world. Expo Central, Snocross track and airport, mid-March.

Yellowstone Ski Festival (406-646-7097; www.yellowstoneskifestival.com) More than 3,000 Nordic skiers gather to celebrate the beginning of the season. The festival includes races, shows, sales and other attractions. Rendezvous Ski Trails, late November.

GONDOLAS/CHAIRLIFTS/PARAGLIDING

JACKSON HOLE

Jackson Hole Bridger Gondola (307-739-2654) After considerable review, Jackson Hole Mountain Resort made the difficult decision in October 2006 to close the 40-year-old aerial tramway from Teton Village up to the 9,095-foot gondola summit on Rendezvous Mountain. Construction of a newer, faster tram that carries 100 passengers at once and 600 per hour was to begin in 2007 and be completed for the 2008–09 winter season.

JH Paragliding (307-690-4948) Tandem paragliding rides from Snow King Mountain over Jackson Hole. Make your reservations at Cafe 6311 in the Bridger Center in Teton Village. Instruction is available.

Snow King Scenic Chairlift (307-733-5200) The chairlift provides panoramic views of Jackson Hole and access to hiking trails and picnic areas.

Teewinot Chairlift (307-739-2587) This chairlift is in Teton Village and takes mountain bikers to trails along the Teton front. Tickets and bike rentals are at Jackson Hole Sports in the Bridger Center.

Historic Sites

Yellowstone National Park

Old Faithful Inn

The National Historic Landmark turned 100 in 2003 and remains the most visited man-made attraction in Yellowstone, thanks partly to a certain geyser with the same name just out the back door. As such, it's also the most difficult lodging to secure in the park. Inside the lobby, it's the Swiss Family Robinson meets Jeremiah Johnson. The inn's original log structure, fondly called "The Old House," towers seven stories with a mosaic of lodgepole staircases and walkways designed by architect Robert C. Reamer to reflect nature's perfect imperfections. The centerpiece is a massive stone fireplace. At the top, some 92 feet from the floor, is a "crow's nest" where musicians once played. Despite the heavy foot traffic between Memorial Day and Labor Day, it's still possible to find a cozy corner to sit in a log rocker and read a book by the fire. More rockers are lined up on a long porch facing the geyser. Wings were added in the two decades after the original construction. The lodge now has 327 rooms, many with original plumbing (see Chapter 3, "Lodging"), including claw-footed tubs. The old building has survived the area's frequent earthquakes, including the famed 1959 temblor that collapsed the dining-room chimney. Old Faithful Inn also came perilously close to being reduced to cinders in the 1988 fires—remnants can still be seen from the inn—but she has endured. A three-year renovation project designed to improve the safety of the building in the event of an earthquake is expected to be complete in the summer of 2008. The inn features a restaurant, deli and souvenir stores. Interpretive tours can be arranged at the inn. It is closed in winter, but it is accessible by snowcoach or via cross-country skis.

Lake Hotel

Yellowstone's oldest surviving hotel—guests were first accepted in 1891—and now the second largest wood-frame building in North America was built by the Northern Pacific Railroad at the popular site of rendezvous between mountain men, trappers and Indians. Its southern colonial look was created 12 years later by Robert Reamer, who built the Old Faithful Lodge. Renovations have continued through the years, especially after the hotel began to fall apart in the 1960s. By the 1980s, the hotel had been restored to the elegant, if seemingly out of place, yellow structure visitors see today. It's certainly the most modern hotel in the park, and the views of Yellowstone Lake through picture windows are unmatched. Historical tours are offered at 5:30 PM each day.

Lake Ranger Station

This classic log cabin, with its large stone fireplace, was completed in 1923 and recently added to the National Register of Historic Places.

Albright Visitor Center

This old stone building, which serves as park headquarters at Mammoth, features a quaint collection of exhibits with mounted animals, books, theater and information desk, as well as restrooms downstairs. Albright provides a quick snapshot of the park and is a great place to get information before heading deep into the park. Watercolor paintings by the renowned Thomas Moran and photos by William H. Jackson are the featured highlight here.

Fort Yellowstone

Many of the buildings constructed for the army's reign at the turn of the previous century remain, providing a lingering aura of that era. Many of the two-story square buildings served as homes for officers. Today's park administration building was the barracks where soldiers stayed.

Mammoth Hot Springs Hotel

History still oozes from the creaking floors of a hotel built in 1911 and reconstructed in 1937. One wing of the original hotel remains. Inside, check out the huge inlay map of the United States, made from 15 varieties of wood.

Grand Teton National Park

Jackson Lake Lodge

Depending on one's perspective, this is either an icon of modern construction brilliantly designed to highlight the views across Jackson Lake to the Tetons . . . or an architectural abomination that no more belongs in a western national park than a fire lookout in Times Square. When it was completed in 1955, many national park enthusiasts accustomed to the rustic and stately elegance of Yellowstone's Old Faithful Inn and Oregon's Crater Lake Lodge were aghast at renowned architect Gilbert Stanley Underwood's monstrosity. Underwood used massive amounts of concrete, and the buildings are mostly odd-shaped rectangles, leading some to compare it to a bomb shelter. Nevertheless, first-time and annual visitors alike can't help but stop in their tracks after ascending a flight of stairs into a lobby that features 60-foot-high picture windows that frame the lake and snowcapped Grand Teton. The full-service resort has 348 guest cottages and 37 rooms in the main lodge, which blends more comfortably into its surroundings now that the lodgepole pines have matured. The Mural Room features above-average dining—no extra charge for the Teton view and moose browsing in Willow Flats. The facility also has a grill, a popular bar

The U.S. Cavalry established Fort Yellowstone in 1886 to help prevent lawlessness in the park, including poaching and squatting. The army stayed until 1916, when the National Park Service was formed. National Park Service

with outdoor patio (famed for huckleberry daiquiris/margaritas), conference rooms, a gift shop, stores and other amenities. At least the accommodations are in the national park spirit: no TVs or radios, though there are phones and data ports (see Chapter 3, "Lodging"). There have been occasional calls to tear down the sprawling structure, but it's too late: The Jackson Lake Lodge became a National Historic Landmark in 2003.

Chapel of the Transfiguration
This log Episcopal church is still active and is even the site of an occasional summer wedding. It was built in 1925, through donations from a California family that summered at nearby dude ranches. The chapel is known for its views of the Tetons through large windows in the back. Eucharist services are at 8 and 10 AM Sundays during the summer.

Bill Menor Cabin and Ferry
In the early 1890s, a homesteader named William D. Menor put down roots in the sage soil and built a cable ferry to get back and forth across the Snake. For some 25 years, it was the only way to cross the river for miles. Menor charged 50 cents for wagons, 25 cents for horses. The store Menor built still stands and is a museum of sorts, housing a collection of artifacts from early area settlers. A replica of the old ferry is still used to carry tourists across the river, conditions permitting.

Cunningham Cabin
Pierce Cunningham and his wife, Margaret, built his sod-roofed log cabin amid the sage in 1890. It's accessible today by a short trail at the end of a gravel road 6 miles south of Moran Junction. The Cunninghams are known for having built the type of split-rail fence that has become a modern fixture in Jackson Hole. The cabin's interior is empty, but a peek inside offers a sense of what it was like to be here a century ago. Note: The Cunninghams were early proponents of preserving the area as a national park, though they weren't around to see it come to fruition.

Historic Sites in the Parks' Gateway Communities

CODY
The Irma Hotel (800-754-IRMA or 307-587-4221; www.irmahotel.com) was built in 1902 by Buffalo Bill Cody, architect of the city. Cody, who named the hotel after his youngest daughter, called the Irma "just the sweetest hotel that ever was." He maintained two suites and an office in the hotel. Today, the Irma still oozes history, and guests will find plenty of Old West charm in the upstairs rooms. There's a bar and a lounge on the first floor. The hotel stages gunfights out front daily at 6 PM, Monday through Saturday.

ISLAND PARK
Harriman Railroad Ranch (208-558-7368) is 3 miles south of Island Park. The serene sage and lodgepole ranch was founded in 1902 by the Guggenheim family and Averill Harriman, owner of the Union Pacific Railroad. Harriman, who also founded Idaho's Sun Valley resort, built a spur line from Pocatello to West Yellowstone. The area is renowned for its world-class dry-fly fishing on the Henry's Fork of the Snake River, which serpentines through the property. Today the land is owned by the state of Idaho. A bunkhouse is available for weekend retreats.

WEST YELLOWSTONE

Quake Lake (406-682-7620), about 25 miles northwest of West Yellowstone, is worth the
drive for an eerie perspective on recent history. On Aug. 17, 1959, two faults just outside
of Yellowstone moved simultaneously and caused an earthquake that registered 7.5 on
the Richter scale. A massive landslide into the Madison River just west of Hebgen Lake
roared down Sheep Mountain at 174 mph, killing 23 unsuspecting campers at a campground in eight seconds. Five more campers were washed away in a flood as waters
raged over the dam at Hebgen. Some 370 aftershocks were counted, and 298 geysers in
the area erupted, some for the first time in recorded history. The landslide became a
natural dam on the Madison and created a 38,000-acre lake that's 190 feet deep and 6
miles long; the spires of drowned trees still stand like sentinels above the water, and
the site of the landslide is still obvious. Just how powerful was the quake? Water-
softener magnate Emmitt Culligan had a home on Hebgen Lake built to withstand a
nuclear attack. Unbeknownst to Culligan and his architect, the home was constructed
on a fault line. When the earth quit trembling, one side of the house was 15 feet higher
than the other. A Forest Service visitor center has been built at the site of the slide, with
a boardwalk, exhibits and video room helping visitors relive Mother Nature's awesome
power. The center is open 8:30 AM–6 PM daily from Memorial Day through mid-
September. The fee is $3 per car, $1 per hiker/biker.

*Remnants of the 1959 earthquake at Golden Gate Bridge in Yellowstone. The quake killed 28 people and
dammed the Madison River, creating Quake Lake.* National Park Service

MUSEUMS AND DISCOVERY CENTERS

Yellowstone National Park

MAMMOTH

Albright Visitor Center and Museum

307-344-2263
www.yellowstone.net/visitorcenters/albrightmammoth.htm
Open: 8 AM–7 PM (late May–late Aug.), 9 AM–5 PM (late Aug.–late Oct.)
Admission: Free

The center offers a quick overview of Yellowstone history, covering Native Americans, the military, mountain men, early explorers and the Park Service. It includes a theater and gift shop. The visitor center was the quarters of bachelor officers when the army oversaw the park.

NORRIS

Museum of the National Park Ranger

307-344-7353
www.yellowstonenationalpark.com/visitorcenters.htm
Open: 9 AM–5 PM (June–Sept.)
Admission: Free

The museum is housed in a rebuilt 1908 cabin that was one of the first soldier stations in the park. Exhibits show the evolution of the park ranger and include a 25-minute movie, *An American Legacy*. Retired Park Service employees comprise most of the staff.

Norris Geyser Basin Museum

307-344-7353
www.yellowstonenationalpark.com/visitorcenters.htm
Open: 10 AM–5 PM (June–Sept.)
Admission: Free

Geothermal geology is the focus in this stone and log structure. Built in 1930, this National Historic Landmark is noted for the popular "parkitecture" construction of that era. Exhibits were renovated in the mid-1990s. There's an information desk and bookstore.

MADISON JUNCTION

Madison Museum

307-344-2821
www.yellowstonenationalpark.com/visitorcenters.htm
Open: 9 AM–5 PM (June–Sept.)
Admission: Free

This National Historic Register building contains just a few touchable items. The Park Service had plans to add information panels in the summer of 2007. The Madison Museum also serves as an information station and bookstore.

GRANT VILLAGE

Fishing Bridge Museum & Visitor Center

307-242-2450

www.yellowstonenationalpark.com/visitorcenters.htm

Open: 8 AM–7 PM (late May–Sept.)

Admission: Free

This is another stone and log structure from the early Great Depression era. Exhibits center on Yellowstone wildlife, mostly birds. A stuffed grizzly sow and two cubs provide an intimidating greeting. Nightly slide shows are offered by rangers.

Museums in the Parks' Gateway Communities

CODY

Buffalo Bill Historical Center

800-227-8483 or 307-587-4771

www.bbhc.org.

720 Sheridan Ave.

Open: 8 AM–8 PM (May 1–Sept. 15), 8 AM–5 PM (Sept. 15–Oct. 31), 10 AM–5 PM (Nov. 1–Mar. 31), 10 AM–5 PM (Apr. 1–May 1). Note: Closed Mon. in winter.

Admission: $15 adults, $13 seniors, $10 students (13–17), $6 children (5–12), $40 families. Members free. Admission is good for two days

This impressive collection of western historical artifacts is actually five museums under one 300,000-square-foot roof: The Buffalo Bill Museum, Plains Indians Museum, Cody Firearms Museum, Whitney Gallery of Western Art and Draper Museum of Natural History. It began as the Buffalo Bill Museum across the street, in a log cabin that has since become the Chamber of Commerce offices. The Buffalo Bill Museum features artifacts once owned by Cody as well as essays written about him and other famous Westerners. The Plains Indians Museum, opened in 2000, highlights the years after the Indians were subdued by the military, mostly from 1880–1930; focus is on the Crow, Lakota Sioux, Arapaho, Cheyenne and Shoshone. The Draper Museum emphasizes the region's natural history, conservation and ecology. Visitors will be treated to the works of the West's most famous artists and photographers—Thomas Moran, C. M. Russell and Fredric Remington, among many others—at the Whitney Gallery of Western Art. And not to be outdone, the Cody Firearms Museum has the largest collection of American firearms in the world, most notably the renowned Winchester Collection. Volunteers and docents are especially helpful and friendly. Expect crowds, especially in the summer. Nearly a quarter of a million visitors annually pass through what is sometimes called "The Smithsonian of the West."

Foundation for North American Wild Sheep

307-587-5508

www.fnaws.org

720 Allen Ave.

Open: 7 AM–5 PM Mon.–Fri.

Admission: Free

This nonprofit organization supports research and education on the bighorn sheep with the goal of increasing populations for conservation and hunting. The site offers a free visitor center with a gift shop, a wild-sheep movie and mounted exhibits of the four types of wild North American sheep.

Harry Jackson Art Museum
307-587-5508
www.harryjackson.com
602 Blackburn St.
Open: 8 AM–5 PM Mon.–Fri.
Admission: $8

Harry Jackson was 14 years old when he left his Al Capone–ruled mafia family in Chicago for a new life in the West. His work ranges from World War II paintings to sculptures of Sacajawea. Jackson is still alive and lives part-time in Cody, part-time in Italy.

Heart Mountain Center
307-754-2689
www.heartmountain.net
15 miles northeast of Cody

Heart Mountain was an internment camp where 10,700 Japanese-American citizens were relocated during World War II. The site currently features a few empty buildings and a brick hospital chimney, but plans for an interpretive center are under way. The site is on public land, and visitors can view the memorial adjacent to the camp, read the interpretive signs and explore the area.

Old Trail Town/Museum of the Old West
307-868-2111 or 866-868-2111
www.museumoftheoldwest.org
2 miles west of Cody
Open: 8 AM–8 PM mid-May–Sept.
Admission: $7 adults, $6 seniors, $3 children under 13

This is a collection of 26 Old West buildings from as far back as 1879 and as recent as 1901. Also featured are horse-drawn carriages, Native American artifacts and other frontier memorabilia, including a cabin once inhabited by Butch Cassidy and the Sundance Kid. The site is where Buffalo Bill Cody originally laid out the town named after him. The small cemetery out back is the resting place of many western luminaries, including Jeremiah "Liver Eating" Johnson, made famous by the movie of the same name. As of spring 2007, the Museum of the Old West, a newer log cabin located in the center of Old Trail Town, was attempting to raise the funds to purchase the surrounding town.

Dubois

Dubois Museum
307-455-2284
www.duboismuseum.org
909 W. Ramshorn St.

Open: 9 AM–6 PM (summer), 10 AM–4 PM Tues.–Sat. (winter)
Admission: $1 adults, 50 cents children

Immerse yourself in the history of the colorful Wind River Valley and Wind River
Mountains. Displays range from Sheepeater Indian pictographs to the construction of the
railroad into the valley.

National Bighorn Sheep Interpretive Center
307-455-3429 or 888-209-2795
www.bighorn.org
907 W. Ramshorn St.
Open: 8 AM–7 PM (summer), 9 AM–5 PM (winter)
Admission: $2 adults, 75 cents children, $5 families, members free

The bighorn sheep was once close to extinction. See how it was saved, through exhibits,
videos and displays. The center offers tours and features a gift shop and memberships.

GARDINER

Heritage and Research Center
307-344-2664
www.nps.gov/yell/historyculture/collections.htm
200 Old Yellowstone Trail
Open: 8 AM–5 PM Mon.–Fri. (library 9 AM–4 PM)
Admission: Free

A new, state-of-the-art, 32,000-square-foot facility houses a wide variety of artifacts,
photographs, journals and other items of historical value involving the park. Though
mostly for research and storage, visitors are welcome to view displays. Appointments can
be made to do research in the archives and museum collections. Public tours are Tuesdays
and Thursdays at 10 AM from Memorial Day through Labor Day.

JACKSON

Jackson Hole Museum
307-733-9605
www.jacksonholehistory.org
105 Glenwood St.
Open: 9:30 AM–6 PM Mon.–Sat., 10 AM–5 PM Sun. (late May to early Oct.)
Admission: $3 adults, $2 seniors, $1 children, $6 families

This nonprofit museum founded in 1958 features artifacts once owned by local legend W.
C. "Slim" Lawrence, many dating back to the first humans to walk the area. Collections
range from Native American pottery, tools and weapons to items from the fur-trapping era
and early pioneer settlement. Many exhibits are permanent; some change with the seasons. Walking tours of the town of Jackson are offered four days a week.

Jackson Hole Historical Society
307-733-9605
www.jacksonholehistory.org
105 Mercill Ave.

Open: 8 AM–5 PM Mon.–Fri. (June–Sept.)
Admission: Free

Exhibits range from the history of Plains Indians to the creation of Grand Teton National Park. It also features a research library.

National Museum of Wildlife Art

307-733-5771 or 800-313-9553
www.wildlifeart.org/Frame_HomePage.cfm
2820 Rungius Rd.
Open: 8 AM–5 PM daily (summer), 9 AM–5 PM (winter), 9 AM–5 PM Mon.–Sat. & 1–5 PM Sun. (spring/fall)
Admission: $6 adults, $5 children, $14 families

This beautiful museum overlooking the National Elk Refuge features 12 galleries with more than 4,000 works of wildlife art, including paintings and sculptures. The stone and wood building was carefully constructed to fit into the sage hillside above the refuge and embody the countryside. With its rounded corners, it has the feel of a Native American kiva. In a concerted effort to avoid being known only as a tourist stop, the museum allows residents of Jackson free admission on Sundays. The building also houses a popular restaurant.

Moose

Murie Center

307-739-2246
www.muriecenter.org
South of visitor center
Free tours at 3 PM Mon. and Wed., May–Oct.

A ranch once owned by environmental pioneers Olaus and Mardy Murie is preserved as a place for lodging, meals, historical exploration and seminars. Olaus Murie founded the Wilderness Society; Mardy was the first female graduate of the University of Alaska. Their fingerprints are on a wide range of land-preservation efforts in Alaska and the Northern Rockies. The facility is open to the public, but appointments are recommended.

Teton Science School

307-733-4765
www.tetonscience.org
Past town of Kelly off Gros Ventre Rd., about 8 miles east of Moose, with another new facility just west of Jackson on WY 22

Learn about nearly every aspect of the natural processes taking place in the Greater Yellowstone ecosystem. The classes are geared to kids and young adults in their college years. Seminars ranging from one to five days are offered during the summer tourist season, and simple lectures for a nominal fee are available, too. The Murie Natural History Museum is on site.

West Yellowstone

Museum of the Yellowstone

406-646-1100
www.yellowstonehistoriccenter.org

104 Yellowstone Ave.
Open: 9 AM–9 PM (May–Sept.)

Admission: $6 adults, $5 seniors, $4 children and students, $15 families
Take a closer look at the cultural history of the park and the events that have shaped it. The museum is located in the old Union Pacific building.

Grizzly & Wolf Discovery Center
406-646-7001 or 800-257-2570
www.grizzlydiscoveryctr.org
201 Canyon St.
Open: 8 AM–dark (summer); winter hours vary
Admission: $9.75 adults, $9 seniors, $5 children (5–12)

Here is the easy and safe way to get up close and personal with two of Yellowstone's more famous denizens. The center features eight grizzlies, including "101," who lived in the wild for 20 years before human carelessness allowed her and her cubs access to pet food. Six wolves form the domestic Gallatin Pack, all born in captivity and thus unable to survive in the wild. The center contributes somewhat to the theme-park atmosphere, but it does provide educational information on two key predators that have had their struggles in the park.

Others Worth Seeing along the Way
Museum of the Mountain Man (877-686-6266; Pinedale, WY) An overview of the western fur trade's place in the northern Rockies. $5 adults, $4 seniors, $3 children (6–12).
Museum of the Rockies (406-994-2251; Bozeman, MT) Step back through four billion years with fossils, pioneer buildings, regular exhibits. $9.50 adults, $6.50 children (summer); $8 adults, $4 children (winter).
Idaho Museum of Natural History (208-282-3317; Pocatello, ID) Here you can take a closer look at native species no longer with us. $5 adults, $4 seniors, $3 students, $2 children.
Jefferson County Historical Museum (208-745-8243; Rigby, ID) It's worth a stop just to see the birthplace of television.
Teton Flood Museum (208-359-3063; Rexburg, ID) The story of the 1976 Teton Dam collapse is vividly told in this museum in the basement of the Rexburg Tabernacle.
T-Rex Natural History Museum (307-655-3359; Ranchester, WY) A complete T-Rex skull is the highlight of exhibits that include fossils, minerals and lecture programs.
World Museum of Mining (406-723-7211; Butte, MT) This museum focuses on the history and technology of mining and includes the 3,200-foot Orphan Girl Mine on site. $7 adults, $6 seniors, $5 youths, $2 children.

NATURAL WONDERS

Yellowstone National Park
Grand Canyon of the Yellowstone
For all its scenic beauty, Yellowstone is more savored as an ecosystem where the natural world still works, mostly unhindered by humanity. An exception is the gaping Grand Canyon of the Yellowstone River, between Canyon and Tower. For 10,000 years, the river

has been carving a riveting chasm in the geothermally weakened rhyolite walls, creating a 1,000-foot-deep canyon that's 20 miles long and as much as 4,000 feet wide. It's the one place where visitors stand and stare in awe at the rich hues of sheer orange, pink, tan and yellow canyon walls, from many different angles. How such a dramatic landscape occurred on a river that mostly meanders isn't entirely clear. Scientists speculate that when glaciers retreated some 11,000 years ago, they left ice dams at the mouth of Yellowstone Lake. Melting of the ice was like pulling a cork, sending mountains of water northward and scouring the canyon out at the weakest point in the rock. There has likely been more than one such catastrophic flood caused by the melting of glaciers. Today, the river continues to work its erosive magic, digging the canyon deeper for future civilizations.

The most famous place to view the canyon is Artist Point on the South Rim. Stop there, and along with the rest of the crowd you will instantly recognize the snapshot. Another worthwhile endeavor for fitter tourists is the 328-step descent on the metal stairs of Uncle Tom's Trail. Inspiration Point on the North Rim is equally mesmerizing. For a different perspective that could turn your legs to jelly, take the half-mile paved walk to Brink of the Lower Falls, where from the platform you'll look directly over the lip of 308-foot Lower Falls. It isn't for the faint of heart; these falls are twice the height of Niagara Falls. Look for osprey riding the thermals and searching for fish in the tumultuous waters below.

Hoodoo Basin

Hoodoos are bizarre, almost ghostlike volcanic rock formations carved by winds and rains for thousands of years. These monoliths are especially mesmerizing in Hoodoo Basin, a

Hoodoos in the Yellowstone backcountry were sculpted by wind and rain, creating an eerie landscape.
National Park Service

Peering over the Brink of the 309-foot Lower Falls in the Grand Canyon of the Yellowstone River is not for the faint of heart. National Park Service

remote part of Yellowstone near where the Lamar River begins its journey off the rugged western slopes of the Absaroka Range. For those willing to hike or pack some 18 miles into the backcountry, the hoodoos, meadows and mountain peaks will take your breath away.

Lewis Falls

For the many visitors who first arrive through the South Entrance, Lewis Falls is the first major scenic attraction, unless they've encountered a moose chomping on willows along the Lewis River. The 29-foot falls are a favorite of photographers. They're about 10 miles into the park from the South Entrance, just before Lewis Lake. They were named for Meriwether Lewis, father of the Lewis and Clark Expedition—though Lewis never came far enough south to see his namesake falls.

Mammoth Hot Springs

If there's a close runner-up to Old Faithful in terms of natural wonders that define Yellowstone, it's Mammoth Hot Springs, about 5 miles south of the North Entrance at Gardiner. Nowhere in the world is there a better example of travertine terraces at work. These ever-evolving springs above park headquarters at Mammoth are split into upper and lower terraces. All have excellent boardwalk access and viewing platforms with interpretive sites. The dominant white rock is the result of deposits left by the rain and snow runoff that has passed through the fissures in the earth's surface and reemerged as carbonic acid. The stunning variety of colors, ranging from brown and yellow to azure and teal, are attributed to the dramatic array of microorganisms living in the hot water, along with temperature variances and acidity. The dead lodgepoles protruding from pools on the upper terrace are stark evidence of just how rapidly these terraces change. Calcium car-

The Minerva Terrace at Mammoth Hot Springs produces a ton of travertine per day. National Park Service

bonate (travertine) accumulates rapidly, forming lips that dam the water and kill vegetation. Terraces can grow as much as 8 inches in one year and some two tons of travertine are dispersed throughout the springs each day. Pools that exist today may be gone in 5 or 10 years. If you're short on time, don't miss the New Blue Spring on the upper terrace. Other pools of note are Canary Spring, Angel Terrace and Palate Spring. Between the terraces and the commercial area, you'll notice an erect hunk of 2,500-year-old dormant travertine called Liberty Cap. It was named by the Hayden exploration party in 1871 for its resemblance to French military caps.

Old Faithful

Nothing says Yellowstone like Old Faithful, the park's best-known and first-named geyser. Though it isn't the largest geyser—that distinction belongs to Steamboat Geyser—it has faithfully erupted in front of crowds for better than 150 years, first coming to national attention in 1870 when the Washburn party named it. Crowds gather every hour outside the Old Faithful Inn, where a clock lets visitors know about when to expect the next eruption. But don't rely entirely on the clock—contrary to the myth that it erupts every hour, Old Faithful actually can spew anywhere from every 45 minutes to 95 minutes. Currently, the wait is about 92 minutes. Researchers believe frequent earthquakes in the area have added distance to the average time between eruptions. Still, the geyser never disappoints, typically sending some 4,000–8,000 gallons of scalding water to heights of up to nearly 200 feet for anywhere from 90 seconds to five minutes. Benches forming a half-moon around the geyser on the south and east sides offer prime viewing for tourists who come pouring out of the gift shops and restaurants. Upstairs in the lodge is another excellent place to watch.

Petrified Tree

Petrified trees aren't uncommon in the Greater Yellowstone Ecosystem, but most require some effort to see. This one is about a mile west of Tower, just off the road from Mammoth. These redwood trees—yes, the same redwoods that now grow along the California coast—were preserved when volcanic activity covered them in ash, their organic structure replaced by minerals. Eventually, the ash eroded, leaving the tree remnants. Once, there were three petrified trees in the vicinity. Unfortunately, visitors took them apart piece by piece for souvenirs. Thus, the remaining Petrified Tree is fenced to protect it from vandals. A more remarkable place to see petrified works of nature is deep in the park at Specimen Ridge above the Lamar Valley, where 27 forests are stacked on top of one another. Preserved trees there include redwoods, oaks, mangroves and breadfruit.

Roaring Mountain

It's quickly obvious how Roaring Mountain got its name. This barren, steamy 400 feet of mountainside just west of the road between Mammoth and Norris hisses as you drive by. Named in 1885 by park geologists, Roaring Mountain sends the remnants of 200-degree water into the air as steam, making it a classic example of a fumarole.

Steamboat Geyser

The granddaddy of all the world's geysers, Steamboat launches its spray up to 400 feet in the air—typically twice or three times as high as Old Faithful—with some eruptions lasting 40 minutes. Trouble is, Steamboat is not particularly . . . faithful. When it's in the mood,

A petrified redwood tree on Yellowstone's Specimen Ridge. The ridge features 27 forests stacked on top of one another, preserved by 50 million years of volcanic activity. Preserved trees include magnolia, breadfruit, mangrove, redwood and oak, none of which are native to the region today. National Park Service

loud eruptions take place every four days or so at its location just west of Norris. When it's not, visitors can wait as long as 50 years; Steamboat actually was dormant from 1911 to 1961. The geyser was silent from 1991 until 2000, then erupted five times from April 2002 to May 2003. If you happen to count yourself among the fortunate few to see Steamboat erupt, you're in for an unforgettable treat. Chances are better of seeing an occasional burp in which the geyser sends water 10–15 feet skyward for a few seconds.

Thorofare Region

This isn't really a specific natural wonder, yet the Thorofare area in the park's southeast corner warrants mention simply for its unfettered wildness. There are no roads in the area. The Thorofare Ranger Station is the farthest inhabited dwelling from a road in the Lower 48. Eagle Peak, at 11,358 feet the highest point in the park, is here. Grizzlies, wolves, moose, mountain lions and other wild creatures roam without intrusion from man, save for the occasional backcountry hiker or poacher. It's 18 miles from the closest road trailhead to Two Ocean Pass, where waters in a high-altitude marsh part ways, some headed for the Atlantic and some for the Pacific. The Thorofare region does have 15 backcountry campsites for hikers and packers, including a platform at the ranger station. Nowhere in Yellowstone is it more important to observe rules regarding storing food from bears. Nobody who takes the time and effort to traverse the Thorofare will ever forget it.

Grand Teton National Park

Teton Viewpoints

OK, so they're only natural in that the views are of the Tetons, which are prolific in and around the park. Still, there are at least three places that are a must-see, if only because others have made them famous. The first is the Snake River Overlook halfway between Moose and Moran, the place where Ansel Adams immortalized the park in 1942. His black-and-white photo of the Tetons under brooding skies is seen just about everywhere that has the name "Grand Teton" attached to it. Another fine spot with a familiar view is the Oxbow Bend Turnout, just west of Moran. Finally, if you've seen photos that look slightly different from Adams's but are nearly as renowned, they were probably taken near Schwabacher Landing, a boat launch just south of the Snake River Overlook.

RODEOS

Is there anything that says "Old West" like a rodeo? The dusty cowboy of frontier lore comes to life every day in the summer in Montana, Wyoming and Idaho. Family vacations to Yellowstone and Grand Teton aren't complete without a night at the Cody Nite Rodeo in Cody, Wyoming, which calls itself the "Rodeo Capital of the World." Many real cowboys and cowgirls still come from real ranches to compete, though a growing number hail from the ranchettes springing up all over the New West. If you can get past the occasional dreary Brokeback Mountain joke, you'll appreciate the skill required to stay aboard an irate bull for eight seconds or to rope a sprinting calf's hind legs in half the time.

Cody Nite Rodeo (800-207-0744; www.codyniterode.com; Rodeo Grounds, Cody) The 5,500-seat Rodeo Grounds on Cody's west strip are the venue for the nightly PRCA Rodeo June 1–Aug. 31. Tickets are $16. The Buffalo Bill Cody Stampede Rodeo takes place over the Fourth of July. Cody Country Classic Pro Bull Riding is Labor Day. This rodeo featuring mostly local talent is a staple of Yellowstone visitors as they arrive from the east.

Ennis Fourth of July Rodeo (406-682-4700; Ennis Rodeo Grounds, Ennis) This is an NRA-sanctioned event that draws most of the top cowhands in Montana. It takes place on Fourth of July afternoon following a morning parade through town. Tickets are $10 reserved seating, $8 general admission.

Gardiner Rodeo (406-848-7971; Jim Duffy Arena, Gardiner) This rodeo takes place in mid-June in the arena just off US 89 north of town. It features top Northern Rodeo Association cowboys and cowgirls. A parade crosses the bridge high over the Yellowstone River.

Livingston Roundup (406-222-3199; Park County Fairgrounds, Livingston) This century-old PRCA event on Fourth of July weekend is rated one of the country's 10 best and typically lures top cowboys. The talent is so strong that even the best Montana cowboys struggle to make finals. Payoffs push $175,000. Starts with a parade featuring floats, bands, antique cars, etc.

Wild West Yellowstone Rodeo (406-560-6913; www.yellowstonerodeo.com; Rodeo Arena, off Yellowstone Ave., West Yellowstone) A series of 10 weekend rodeos throughout the summer leads to the finals in mid-Aug. Tickets are $15 adults for grandstand, $10 general admission; children are $8 for grandstand, $5 general admission. Adult season passes are $180 for grandstand, $120 general admission; children's passes are $90 for grandstand, $60 general admission.

Wyoming Rodeo (307-733-2805; www.jhrodeo.com; Jackson Hole Rodeo Grounds, 2 blocks W. of Snow King Ski Resort, Jackson) This rodeo features younger cowboys and cowgirls and is open to all comers. Wed. and Sat., Memorial Day to Labor Day. Tickets $14 reserved, $11 general admission, $8 children (4–12).

SCENIC DRIVES

Let's start with the supposition that any drive in Yellowstone, Grand Teton and Jackson Hole is, by definition, scenic. That's why they are called national parks. Here is a closer look at the different driving segments in Yellowstone, and what you can expect to find there:

Yellowstone National Park

Mammoth to Tower-Roosevelt (18 miles) A mix of conifer, sage and high plains, with a dramatic crossing of Gardner River and views across Yellowstone River canyon. Highlights: Blacktail Plateau Drive, Undine Falls, Petrified Tree, Blacktail Pond, Wraith Falls.

Tower-Roosevelt to Northeast Entrance (29 miles) Best known for the Lamar Valley, though it becomes more forested and breathtaking as the Northeast Entrance nears. Barronette Peak is perhaps the park's most dramatic mountain. Highlights: Lamar Valley, Soda Butte, Yellowstone Association Institute (Buffalo Ranch), Slough Creek, Barronette Peak, Icebox Canyon, wildlife (wolves, bears). Open in winter.

Tower-Roosevelt to Canyon Village (19 miles) Pretty, mountainous route over Dunraven Pass with terrific views of pine-bathed hills. Highlights: Tower Fall, Mount Washburn, Dunraven Pass, Calcite Springs.

Canyon Village to Norris (12 miles) Largely forested middle section of the figure-8 highway shape in central Yellowstone, most just inside the north edge of the caldera. This is a good place to examine the remnants of the 1988 fire. Highlights: Virginia Cascades, wildlife (bison, elk).

Mammoth to Norris (21 miles) Scenic north-south road takes in much of what Yellowstone symbolizes, from mountains and thermal features to wildlife and Golden Gate, site of one of the more dramatic construction projects in park history. The ghostly shaped Hoodoos between Golden Gate and Mammoth are a sneak peek at similar configurations in the backcountry. Highlights: Bunsen Peak, Golden Gate, Sheepeater Cliff, Willow Park (look for moose), Roaring Mountain, Rustic Falls, Hoodoos, Obsidian Cliff.

Norris to Madison (14 miles) One of the more rugged sections of highway, this stretch offers a vivid picture of the caldera's edge at 84-foot Gibbon Falls, where the Gibbon River pours into the caldera and meanders toward a meeting with the Madison. Highlights: Gibbon Falls, Gibbon Meadows (look for elk), Artist Paint Pots, Chocolate Pots, Steamboat Geyser, Beryl Spring, Porcelain Basin.

Madison to Old Faithful (16 miles) This is the famed geyser section of the park. The road follows the aptly named Firehole River to Lower Geyser Basin and Fountain Flat Drive. Highlights: Grand Prismatic Spring, Great Fountain Geyser, Fountain Paint Pot, Midway Geyser Basin, Sapphire Pool, Upper Geyser Basin, Firehole Lake Drive (Firehole Falls), Firehole swimming hole.

Yellowstone's Geyser Basin on a rainy day. The park has more than 10,000 thermal features, more than any place in the world. National Park Service

The Yellowstone River serpentines through the Hayden Valley, a wildlife mecca. National Park Service

Old Faithful to West Thumb (17 miles) This forested mountain drive crosses the
Continential Divide twice north of Shoshone Lake. Highlights: Old Faithful, Kepler
Cascades, Lone Star Geyser, Craig Pass.

West Thumb to Fishing Bridge (21 miles) A scenic drive along Yellowstone Lake.
Highlights: Yellowstone Lake, Natural Bridge.

Fishing Bridge to Canyon Village (16 miles) This pretty drive follows the meandering
Yellowstone River through the wildlife-rich Hayden Valley, where the soil is too thick
for trees to grow. The route climaxes at the Grand Canyon of the Yellowstone.
Highlights: Grand Canyon of the Yellowstone vista points, Mud Volcano, Sulphur
Caldron, LeHardys Rapids (spawning trout), wildlife viewing.

Fishing Bridge to East Entrance (27 miles) Views of Yellowstone Lake and lots of forest
that offer a glimpse at the park's remote southeast corner. Highlights: Sylvan Pass,
Avalanche Peak, Sylvan Lake, Lake Butte Overlook.

West Thumb to South Entrance (22 miles) Lots of lodgepole pine and marshland heading
toward Grand Teton National Park. Highlights: Lewis Lake, Lewis Falls, Moose Falls,
Continental Divide, wildlife (look for moose browsing on willows).

Madison to West Entrance (14 miles) Forested drive along the Madison River, with eagles
and elk. Highlight: Eagle nesting site along Madison.

Mammoth to North Entrance (5 miles) Rapid descent from park headquarters to the arch
and confluence of the Yellowstone and Gardner Rivers at Gardiner. Highlights: Boiling
River, Gardner River, bighorn sheep, elk. The more adventurous might consider the

one-way gravel road that parallels the main road, out of sight, from Mammoth to Gardiner. Open in winter.

Grand Teton National Park

Moran to Moose (18 miles) A largely straight shot on a sagebrush bench above the Snake River and accompanying cottonwoods. Highlights: Cunningham Cabin, Triangle X Ranch, Snake River Overlook, Blacktail Ponds, Hedrick Pond (*Spencer's Mountain* with Henry Fonda was filmed here), Schwabacher viewpoint, views of the Tetons the entire route. Open in winter.

Moran to Jackson Lake Junction (5 miles) Lots of lodgepole and the meandering Snake River just below the dam. Highlights: Oxbow Bend, Jackson Lake Lodge, trailheads to Emma Matilda and Two Ocean Lakes. Open in winter.

Jackson Lake Junction to Moose (20 miles) This is the Teton Park Road through the heart of the park, mostly through sagebrush but also stands of lodgepole and aspen. Highlights: Jackson Lake, Chapel of the Sacred Heart, Signal Mountain Road, Jenny Lake, Menors Ferry, numerous viewpoint turnouts and trailheads. Closed in winter.

Moose to Gros Ventre Junction (8 miles) Sagebrush plains past the Jackson Hole Airport. Highlight: Views, wildlife (elk, bison).

Moose-Wilson Road (6 miles) A narrow, winding road through aspen and lodgepole forest that continues on to Teton Village and Wilson. The first 4 miles from Moose are paved;

A Yellowstone cutthroat trout navigates LeHardys Rapids just north of Fishing Bridge. National Park Service

then the road becomes gravel for several miles to the Granite Canyon Entrance Station. Highlight: Wildlife viewing. Closed in winter.

Jackson Lake Junction to North Entrance (16 miles) Forested road mostly follows east shore of Jackson Lake, past Colter Bay Village and Leeks Marina. Highlights: Colter Bay Village, marina, views of Mount Moran.

Others:

Antelope Flats Road just north of Moose leads to Mormon Row, where remnants of early settlements remain. Also in the vicinity is **Shadow Mountain Road**, which makes you work to get to the summit, but once you do the view of the Tetons to the west across Jackson Hole is spectacular (not recommended for RVs and trailers).

Gros Ventre Road follows the river along the edge of the Elk Refuge into the Bridger-Teton National Forest. Check out the funky little settlement of Kelly along the way; it's known for its unusual dwellings, including yurts. Keep going past Kelly on Gros Ventre Road to the park boundary, where you can still see the decaying cabin used to film the western classic *Shane* with Alan Ladd in 1951. Just outside the park boundary is the Gros Ventre Slide, where an entire mountainside slid about 1½ miles into the river in 1925, forming Slide Lake. Two years later, the natural earthen dam collapsed, sending a wall of water through Kelly and into the Snake River, killing six people. Learn more about this natural phenomenon on the Gros Ventre Geological Trail, just past what is now Lower Slide Lake.

Gnarly **River Road** follows the Snake from just north of Moose to a junction with Teton Park Road just south of Signal Mountain Lodge. Four-wheel-drive is required on a road more suited for mountain biking.

Outside the Parks

Beartooth Highway, US 212, Cooke City to Red Lodge (54 miles; 3 hours minimum) One journey to the sky quickly reveals why former CBS newsman Charles Kuralt dubbed the Beartooth the "most beautiful roadway in America." The Beartooth Mountains are Montana's highest, and instead of the craggy peaks associated with the Absarokas and Wind Rivers, this ancient range looks as if a giant decided to take a nap before stepping across the Rockies. The road, built in 1936, winds through forests, past pristine lakes and near glaciers to above timberline and climaxes at 10,974 feet before flattening out amid snowfields. You'll feel like you're on top of the world, with precipitous half-dome drops resembling Yosemite's El Capitan. Look for mountain goats and maybe even a wayward grizzly bear. The window of opportunity isn't large: The highway generally is open from June to October, though it was shut down for the entire summer in 2005 by a landslide on the Red Lodge side.

Buffalo Bill Cody Scenic Byway Road, US 14/16/20, Cody to Yellowstone East Entrance (52 miles; 1.5 hours) Teddy Roosevelt didn't have the Beartooth Highway to wax poetic about, but he did have the winding route through the Wapiti Valley along the North Fork Shoshone River. He called it "the most scenic 52 miles in the United States." This is the dry side of Yellowstone, so the stark cliffs and rock outcroppings are especially colorful as the road traverses the Shoshone National Forest from high desert to pine. Frequent signs warning about grizzly bears reveal the wildness of the country, and indeed, the park's Thorofare area southwest of the highway is Yellowstone's most remote. Bring a fly rod for the North Fork, one of the premier trout streams in the Greater Yellowstone ecosystem.

Chief Joseph Scenic Highway, WY 120 and WY 296, Cody to US 212 (47 miles; 1 hour)
File this one under best-kept secrets. Understandably, most tourists arriving at
Yellowstone's East Entrance travel straight west from Cody and visitors coming from
Red Lodge typically ride the Beartooth Highway straight to Cooke City. They're missing
out on the starkly beautiful, rugged, almost moonscapelike Sunlight Basin terrain that
Chief Joseph and his Nez Perce band used in 1877 in a valiant attempt to escape the U.S.
Cavalry. The views west to the park from Dead Indian Pass are striking. As the road
continues its elevation gain, it nears the rugged Clarks Fork of the Yellowstone River
canyon.

Gallatin Canyon Road, US 191, West Yellowstone to Bozeman (89 miles; 2 hours)
Dramatically different from the sweeping Yellowstone and Madison River Valleys on
either flank, the Gallatin is narrow, winding and beautiful, and it's the one road that
provides free access to Yellowstone. Gaze at the pristine emerald waters of the Gallatin
as it glides under spruce, fir and pine. If it seems familiar, you might recognize it from
the movie *A River Runs Through It,* much of which was filmed in the lower canyon near
Storm Castle. Look for wolves and moose along the upper stretches, where US 191 slices
off the northwest corner of the park. The Gallatin might be the premier road-accessible
whitewater-rafting stream in Montana when the water's high in the spring and early
summer. Pull off at House Rock, just north of Big Sky, and watch rafters and kayakers
navigate the Mad Mile. It's worth the 9-mile side trip from the stoplight at Big Sky up to
the ski areas in the shadow of Lone Peak.

Grassy Lake Road from Flagg Ranch to Ashton (52 miles; 2 hours minimum) This
seldom-used gravel back road offers a distinct feeling of remoteness, which explains its
appeal to mountain bikers. Four-wheel-drive vehicles are best, though the typical
sedan can make it, too. No trailers or RVs. Check out Huckleberry Hot Springs and
Squirrel Meadows Guard Station, which is available for rent from the Caribou-Targhee
National Forest.

Mesa Falls Scenic Byway, ID 47, Island Park to Ashton (29 miles; 1 hour) Most visitors
zoom past this area on US 20 without giving much thought to what they're missing in
the lush forests just to the east. Stop and smell the pines, and experience the grandeur
of Upper and Lower Mesa Falls on the Henry's Fork of the Snake River—one of the many
blue-ribbon trout streams in the region. The river drops dramatically out of Yellowstone's caldera onto the Snake River Plain at Upper Mesa Falls. It's believed to be the
last falls undisturbed by man in the Columbia River system.

Paradise Valley, US 89, North Entrance at Gardiner to Livingston (62 miles; 1 hour)
Even though this gorgeous valley has been carved up into ranchettes for log mansions,
it's still worth the drive to absorb the towering Absaroka and Gallatin mountains rising
above the meandering Yellowstone River. To get some sense of what this valley was like
before it was discovered in the mid-1990s, veer off on East River Road about 20 miles
north of the park and follow it along the base of the Absarokas until it rejoins US 89 just
south of Livingston. Keep your eyes open for eagles, bighorn sheep and elk. On US 89 at
Emigrant, look into the western foothills for the funky homes and bomb shelters of the
Church of Universalist Triumphant (CUT), which earned worldwide notoriety in the
mid-1980s when its leader predicted the world would end on a specific day. It didn't,
and the church has drifted into anonymity, but remnants remain.

Signal Mountain Summit Road, 1 mile south of Signal Mountain Lodge (5 miles one-
way; 20 minutes) This winding, narrow road curls to the top of Signal Mountain, some

800 feet above the valley floor, and offers views of the Tetons, Jackson Lake and good portions of Jackson Hole. No large motor homes or trailers are permitted.

Wyoming Centennial Scenic Byway, US 26/287, Moran Junction to Dubois (52 miles; 1 hour) This is best taken from Dubois to Moran to provide the most picturesque views of the Tetons from atop Togwotee Pass. The road narrows through the red-rock country along the Wind River, where it is pinched between the Wind River Mountains on the southwest and Washakie Wilderness on the northeast. Once over the pass, you've entered a different world of scenery.

Special Programs

Even if you've made regular sojourns to Yellowstone and Grand Teton National Parks, it's worth the time and expense to check out programs that both offer, to get a look at what makes these special places tick. Programs range from short ranger-led talks each evening to weeklong adventures into the backcountry guided by the Yellowstone Association Institute in the Lamar Valley.

Yellowstone National Park

Junior Ranger Programs (www.yellowstone-natl-park.com/ranger.htm) are for children ages 5–12 and their families. Activities include geyser monitoring, wildlife observation, hiking, skiing, snowshoeing and exploring. Programs are offered in summer and winter. The cost is $3.

Ranger-led activities (www.yellowstone-natl-park.com/ranger.htm) take place at Bridge Bay, Canyon, Fishing Bridge, Gardiner, Grant Village, Lake, Madison, Mammoth, Norris, Old Faithful, West Thumb and West Yellowstone. In addition, a Stars Over Yellowstone program is offered on weekends at the Madison Campground amphitheater. Also check out the Ranger Adventure Hikes at Canyon, Fishing Bridge, Mammoth, Old Faithful and Tower-Roosevelt. Reservations are required for many activities. Tickets are $15 for adults, $5 for children. Check the *Yellowstone Today* newspaper for updates on activities.

Yellowstone Association Institute (307-344-2294; www.yellowstoneassociation.org) in the heart of the Lamar Valley is a nonprofit outfit offering classes that have turned first-time Yellowstone visitors into lifelong supporters. Since 1933, the goal of the institute has been to partner with the Park Service to help visitors gain an understanding of the park's flora, fauna and geology. Spending a week's worth of nights in the institute's rustic cabins, amid the quiet of the Lamar Valley, assures a connectedness to the land. Opportunities range from in-depth field seminars and learning programs to private day tours and backpacking adventures. Membership levels range from $35 to $5,000. Some 22,000 people worldwide belong to the organization.

Grand Teton National Park

Ranger-led activities (www.grand.teton.national-park.com/cal.htm) start in late spring and continue into late fall. Activities take place at Colter Bay, Jackson Lake Lodge, Gros Ventre Campground, Signal Mountain Lodge, Lizard Creek Campground and Flagg Ranch. Guided hikes are available at Jenny Lake and Colter Bay. Junior Ranger Programs are offered for $1, which covers the cost of a ranger patch.

THEATERS

For those occasional rainy days, there are many places to sit back in a chair or on a bench and learn more about the parks—some with and some without popcorn and licorice.

CODY

Big Horn Cinemas (307-587-8009; www.bighorncinemas.net; 2525 Big Horn Ave.) Four screens showing mainstream movies.

Cody Gunfighters (800-745-4762 or 307-587-4221; www.irmahotel.com; 1192 Sheridan Ave.) Live reenactments of famous gunfights take place at 6 PM daily June through September on the steps of the Irma Hotel. An annual Gunfighter Festival in mid-September brings together competing teams from the United States and Canada. Admission is free.

Cody Stage (307-587-8274; 1110 Beck Ave.) Live performances. Check with the Chamber of Commerce (www.codychamber.org) for updated information and prices.

Cody Theater (307-587-2712; 1131 Sheridan Ave.) One screen showing mainstream movies.

GARDINER

Mountain Rose Theatre (406-223-5058; 210 Stone St.) The smallest theater in the West seats 77 and shows first-run movies.

JACKSON

Jackson Hole Playhouse (307-733-6994; www.jhplayhouse.com; 145 W. Deloney Ave.) Popular western-style family musicals such as *Seven Brides for Seven Brothers* play nightly. Dinner seating at 5 and 6:30 PM; showtime 8 PM. Reservations recommended. Prices: $50 adults for dinner/show, $35 children (12 and under). For show only, $25 adults and $18 children.

Jackson Hole Twin Cinema (307-733-4939; 295 W. Pearl Ave.) Two movie screens showing mainstream first-run movies. Prices: $7.50, $4 matinee (4:30 PM).

MovieWorks (307-733-4939; 860 S. US Hwy. 89) Four movie screens. Prices: $7.50, $4 matinee (4:30 PM).

Off Square Theatre Company (307-733-3670; www.offsquare.org; 265 S. Cache St.) Wyoming's lone year-round theater company stages comedies during the summer. Dramas are performed the remainder of the year. All productions take place at the Jackson Hole Center for the Arts. Reservations recommended. Prices: For dinner/show, $50 adults, $35 children (12 and under). For show only, $25 adults, $18 children.

Playmill Theatre (307-200-4407; www.playmilljackson.com; 50 W. Broadway Ave.) Open from early May to early September. Recent attractions have included Nunsense, Chaps and *The Music Man*. Prices: $25 adults, $20 children for center section; $20 adults, $15 children for sides.

Teton Theatre (307-733-6744; 120 N. Cache St.) One movie screen showing mainstream first-run movies. Prices: $7.50, $4 matinee (2:30 and 4:30 PM Saturday and Sunday).

VICTOR

Pierre's Playhouse (208-787-2249; www.pierresplayhouse.com; Main St., just north of the traffic light) Pierre's steps back into history with western melodramas Thursdays through Saturdays from mid-June to early September.

WEST YELLOWSTONE

Bear's Den Cinema (406-646-7777; 15 Electric St.) Year-round 125-seat theater shows mainstream films.

Playmill Theatre (406-646-7757; www.playmill.com; 29 Madison Ave.) The Playmill has been providing live stage shows since 1964, including musicals and comedies. Recent attractions have included *Footloose* and *Annie Get Your Gun*. Open Monday through Saturday from May to September. Reservations recommended. Prices: $9 adults, $8.50 seniors, $6.50 children (3–12).

Yellowstone IMAX (406-646-4100; www.yellowstoneimax.com; 101 Canyon St.) This six-story theater at the West Entrance gives visitors a bird's-eye view of the park on its giant theater. Among the features regularly playing is *Yellowstone.* Look for films on wolves and bears as well. Movies about places away from the park, such as Grand Canyon National Park and the Louisiana Bayou post-Katrina, also play. Features start every hour from 9 AM to 9 PM daily all year. Prices: $9 adults, $8.50 seniors, $6.50 children (3–12).

WILDLIFE VIEWING

For all the beauty, recreation and awe-inspiring natural features of Yellowstone and Grand Teton National Parks, wildlife surely ranks at or near the top of any list of favorite attractions.

For millions of people, Yellowstone is where they'll see their first wild bison, probably their first elk, almost surely their first bear and definitely their first wolf. Every day offers a new gee-whiz moment, whether it's seeing a grizzly sow with two cubs near Sylvan Pass, a giant bull elk with a massive antler rack at Madison Junction, or a pack of wolves in the Lamar River Valley.

As noted in Chapter 1, wildlife management has undergone dramatic changes in the history of both parks, but especially Yellowstone. Elk were hunted relentlessly and bison nearly went extinct from wholesale slaughter until the 1894 Lacey Act prohibited hunting of wildlife in the park. The law didn't prevent the concerted extirpation in the 1920s of the wolf, which was deemed a hunter of big game. Bear-feeding shows were conducted until 1941, and the bears were fed from cars at entrance stations until the early 1970s. Though Yellowstone can still feel at times like a drive-thru zoo, the evolution to a more natural management philosophy has enhanced the wildlife experience.

Because wildlife appears so docile, it's easy to be lulled into complacency. Don't be. As park literature constantly reminds visitors, these are wild animals. Don't leave your car and traverse a meadow to get closer to bear cubs; their mama won't like it. Don't put your young daughter on the back of a bison for a photo op; chances are you'll be gored. Don't try to get up-close-and-personal with a rutting bull elk; you'll lose body parts and the elk will lose its rack. Sound ridiculous? All of these scenarios have actually happened in Yellowstone. Give all animals at least 25 yards distance; make it 100 yards for bears. Don't feed any wildlife, even chipmunks or ravens. And don't try to call animals closer by bugling an elk or howling at a wolf.

What follows is a closer look at where and how best to view wildlife, with a few safety tips where appropriate. Purists cringe at the best advice for seeing wild animals, but it rings true: When you see cars pulled off the road, chances are there's something worth seeing. Early morning and toward dusk are the best times to see animals, when they often

Summer "bear jams" are common. Be sure to pull completely off the road so traffic can get past, and stay at least 100 yards from bears. National Park Service

feed in the open. If you do decide to stop, you're required to have all four tires off the road-way to keep traffic flowing smoothly.

Yellowstone National Park

Bears

Everybody wants to see bears, at least from a respectful distance or the safety of their car. Between 400 and 600 grizzlies and at least as many black bears roam the park, though sightings aren't as frequent at the height of summer when food sources are at higher eleva-tions. The best times are in the spring, when the bears are just coming out of hibernation and feasting on winterkill, and fall, when they're fattening up for hibernation in an annual gorge-fest called hyperphagia. Those also can be the most dangerous times because the bears become more aggressive in their singular search for food. In the fall of 2007, no fewer than six hunters were mauled by grizzlies just outside of Yellowstone's northern boundary; to grizzlies, the sound of a firearm is akin to the ring of a dinner bell. Bear attacks are exceedingly rare, but it's always advisable to use caution and bring bear pepper spray, especially when hiking the backcountry. Learn how to use it; some people have actu-ally sprayed it on themselves. Learn to identify the difference between black bears and grizzlies: It's not as easy as it seems because many black bears are cinnamon in color. Grizzlies have a hump behind their necks, a dish-shaped face and smaller, rounded ears. Stay on trails, hike in groups and make noise. Incidents are remarkably rare—about one per year—and only five fatalities from bear attacks have been recorded in the park's history, none since 1986. But attacks do occur, especially when a bear is surprised. If a black bear charges, make noise and look big. If a grizzly attacks, stretch out and play dead on your stomach, cover your neck and keep your backpack on. Don't run in either case; they'll be on you in a New York second. And always remember that a fed bear is a dead bear. Leaving food out will acclimate a bear to humans, ultimately leading to its demise because a confrontation is inevitable. If you plan to camp in the backcountry, hang your food at least 15 feet off the ground, at least 200 feet from your camp. Most backcountry sites provide food poles for this, but if a pole is not available, use a long rope and gunnysack to hang your food from a tree.

The grizzly's populations in Yellowstone apparently are solid enough that they are no longer threatened, but their future is by no means secure. A beetle and fungus are attacking whitebark pines, whose nuts are a prime source of grizzly food. Fortunately, the pine apparently produced a surprisingly bountiful crop in 2007, which park officials believe led directly to a record number of grizzly cubs (50) birthed. Climate change is another threat. And in the summer of 2007, the bears were delisted from the Endangered Species Act in a controversial move, meaning future hunts and lethal management is possible again. On the flip side, the reintroduction of the wolf has resuscitated riparian areas, including berries, providing a new food source. Prime viewing: Hayden Valley, Lamar Valley, Sylvan Pass.

Bighorn Sheep

These muscular creatures like the high country and other areas inaccessible to most humans, but it's possible to see some of the 250 or so that live in Yellowstone. They are

The grizzly bear inspires fear and awe in Yellowstone visitors lucky enough to see one. About 500 roam the Greater Yellowstone ecosystem. National Park Service

Bighorn sheep are a common sight in the Gardner River canyon and frequently cross the road for a drink.
National Park Service

recognizable by the curled horns used to do battle in mating season in November and December. Consider yourself extremely fortunate if you happen to come across two males ramming each other at high speeds as if auditioning for a documentary on *The Discovery Channel*. Prime viewing: Between the North Entrance and Mammoth along the Gardner River, Dunraven Pass, Lamar Valley, just outside the park north of Gardiner at Yankee Jim Canyon. Be especially careful when driving the Gardner Canyon because the sheep frequently cross the road to drink from the river.

Bison

The one exotic Yellowstone creature you're almost guaranteed to see, though most leave for higher ground in summer. At one time they were reduced by wanton slaughter in the United States to a total of 24—yes, 24—all at the Buffalo Ranch in Yellowstone's Lamar Valley. Now the herd of about 3,300 is so healthy that many wander out of the park, especially at West Yellowstone, where they're "hazed" back into the park to protect cattle from a disease called brucellosis, which causes cows to abort calves.

In the mid-1990s, Montana staged a "hunt" for animals that ventured across the park border near Gardiner. The national media caught wind of the event and descended on the area, causing a hue and cry that moved the state to cancel the hunt after the herd was thinned by about one-third. The hunt quietly returned in 2006, with more stringent regulations.

What to do with wandering bison remains a hot-button issue in Montana. In the spring of 2007, some 300 that migrated into West Yellowstone were slated for roundup and slaughter, including 100 calves. A public outcry moved government officials to continue hazing efforts. They appeared to work, though the bison seemed to get even by languishing on the road between Madison and Old Faithful, causing massive traffic jams in the summer.

Some bison are quarantined in pens north of the park. The hope is that they can be tested and certified brucellosis-free, then moved to bison conservation programs elsewhere. Montana Governor Brian Schweitzer and others are trying to push for a 50-mile bison buffer zone around the park so that the animals have more room to roam. Cattle ranchers leery of the state's losing its brucellosis-free status are balking at the idea. Today, there's a tenuous truce that allows bison outside park boundaries when cattle aren't present. Ironically, brucellosis is also present in elk. But because elk are such a favored target for hunters, there is no outcry about the ungulate roaming outside the park.

For tourists, the bison is the park's most dangerous animal. When provoked, it'll charge at speeds of up to 35 mph. As docile as they look, give them space. To learn more about issues involving the bison, contact the Buffalo Field Campaign (www.buffalofieldcampaign .com) in West Yellowstone. Prime viewing: Any valley, especially the Lamar, Hayden and Pelican near the north end of Yellowstone Lake. You'll see massive herds in winter; in summer, a few lone males will linger in lower country.

Coyotes

Not as commonly seen as the bison or elk, coyotes are still a regular sight even as wolf reintroduction has reduced their numbers. These resilient rascals have survived eradication programs to flourish throughout the park. It isn't uncommon to see then ambling along roadways looking for rodents or an unwitting pronghorn to herd. Some visitors confuse them with wolves, though once you've seen a wolf you won't make that mistake again. Though both look like large dogs, coyotes are smaller, less sturdy and have more pointed ears. Coyote numbers have been cut in half in Yellowstone's northern range by the presence of wolves but they are bouncing back as they adapt. Prime viewing: Lamar Valley, Hayden Valley and along the Madison, Firehole and Gibbon Rivers.

Eagles

America's symbol, and the best-known Endangered Species Act success story, is commonly seen in Yellowstone. Bald eagles are more numerous because golden eagles spend more time riding thermals in rugged mountains. The park now has more than two dozen nesting pairs, compared to 10 in 1986. Many of the younger birds tend to migrate out of the park in winter to Oregon and California, then return. Prime viewing: Along the Madison River between West Yellowstone and Madison Junction and along the Yellowstone River in Hayden Valley.

Elk

The stately ungulate is prevalent throughout the park, though more difficult to spot in summer when they head for the fresh grasses of the high country. Elk numbers are at about 30,000 in the park and 100,000 in the region despite the presence of wolves and its other primary predators, the grizzly and cougar. If you come to Yellowstone during the mating season (rut) in late autumn, you'll be treated to the primal sounds of males bugling and fighting each other with their massive racks during the rut. Such warfare often takes place on the grasses between the buildings in Mammoth. In winter, the big bulls hang together, often near the road between Mammoth and the Northeast Entrance. Hunters have decried a decline in the northern range herd since the wolf's return, but most wildlife biologists concede their numbers had been dramatically out of whack, to the detriment of the ecology. Such reasoning falls on deaf ears of those who simply want elk meat in their freezer and a rack over their fireplace. Prime viewing: Mammoth, Lamar Valley and Hayden Valley.

Moose

Another cantankerous animal to be watched from a safe distance. Bear won't attack unless startled, bison only when provoked and wolves never. A moose will come after you for no apparent reason, especially a cow with a calf or a bull courting a female. In 2005, a moose sent a morel mushroom hunter in the Gallatin Valley up a tree for hours, reappearing every time the man tried to come down. Look for moose around water, especially marshy areas where willows and aquatic plant life abound. These animals were perhaps hurt most by the prolific 1988 fires, which burned about one-third of the park's forests. Moose migrate to higher elevations in winter, where tree branches collect snow and make for easier movement. Without those trees, there is less prime moose habitat. Prime viewing: Just outside the Northeast Entrance, just inside the South Entrance, the Hayden Valley, south of Canyon and around Yellowstone Lake, and the willow thickets along the road between Norris and Mammoth.

Mountain Lion

Once hunted nearly to extinction in the park, these elusive and secretive cats, also called cougars, are rarely seen, even though one might be watching you if you venture into rocky areas. Like the wolf, the mountain lion was part of a predator-eradication program in the park at the turn of the previous century. Perhaps 25 of the animals live in Yellowstone. They can be found wherever mule deer roam, generally in the northern range. Consider

A bull moose browses on aquatic plants in the Hayden Valley. Look for moose in marshlands and anywhere willows grow. National Park Service

yourself lucky if you see one because cougars avoid humans if at all possible. No cougar attack on a human has ever been reported in Yellowstone. Prime viewing: Off the beaten path in the northern range.

Mule deer
Midwesterners and easterners are often surprised to discover that elk are more commonly seen than deer in Yellowstone. Mule deer, also called blacktail deer, are common. About 2,500 reside in the park. But because they tend to spend summers in the forest and high meadows, they're not as readily spotted. Prime viewing: Mammoth, along the Madison River and Blacktail Plateau.

Pronghorn
Often mistakenly called antelope, the graceful, speedy and colorful pronghorn is a denizen of sage prairies. Reaching speeds of up to 60 mph, they are the second-fastest animal on the planet, behind the cheetah. Predators such as the coyote have to catch them by surprise or use a tag-team approach. You'll see pronghorn by the hundreds or even thousands if you arrive from Wyoming, which has a herd of about 400,000. About 5,000 live in and around Yellowstone, though only a few hundred typically are within the park's borders. Prime viewing: The flat sage lands near the North Entrance at Gardiner and the Lamar Valley.

Trumpeter Swans
Yellowstone is critical habitat for the largest waterfowl in North America. Anywhere from 30 to 60 live there in summer; nearly twice that many convene in winter. These white birds were nearly hunted to extinction in the 1800s for plumage used to decorate women's hats. The park and wildlife refuges in surrounding areas have facilitated a tenuous rally. Prime viewing: Madison and Firehole Rivers, and the Yellowstone River near Canyon. In winter, look for them on the Henry's Fork of the Snake River in Island Park.

Wolves
Nowhere in the world is the wolf so readily visible in the wild than Yellowstone. The gray wolf was reintroduced to Yellowstone (and the wilds of central Idaho) in 1995 and 1996 after a seven-decade absence. Park naturalist James Halfpenny, a noted author on wolves, called it "the greatest ecological experiment of our time." Fourteen were brought from Alberta to Yellowstone in 1995, another 17 from British Columbia in 1996. A profound impact has been evident ever since. Start with tourism. Thousands of visitors come to Yellowstone each year, especially in the slower winter months, simply to see wolves. Such communities as Gardiner and Cooke City have especially savored a winter economic boon.

Scientists also believe the wolves are having a positive impact on the health of the Yellowstone ecosystem, thanks to what they call "trophic cascade." The wolf's place at the top of the food chain has rippled down to songbirds and trout. How so? Two Oregon State University plant researchers stumbled on this phenomenon quite by accident in the early 2000s. On separate projects in different parts of the park, they noticed that all aspen, cottonwood and willow they encountered were either more than 80 or less than 10 years old. After considering numerous explanations, they came back to a common theme: the wolf. Their theory: The presence of *Canis lupus* had instilled a long-lost fear in their favorite cuisine, the elk, which no longer could safely browse in the same places for hours. This "ecology of fear" has enabled the recruiting of aspen in the northern range and cottonwood and

Yellowstone chief ranger Sam Woodring plays with wolf pups in 1922. These pups, like all wolves in the park in those days, had a death sentence. Canis lupus was eradicated by the late 1920s and reintroduced in 1995. Hundreds roam the park today. National Park Service

willow in what had been an ailing valley. The return of such flora along the Lamar has in turn brought back the beaver, whose dams have created new habitat for trout. Also back are long-departed songbirds. And there's good news for the grizzlies: Berries growing along the banks are providing nutrition just when the whitebark pine appears to be in trouble.

Still, the wolf's place is not secure. Ranchers in the vicinity fear predation of their cattle and sheep because packs have spread beyond the park's borders. The environmental group Defenders of Wildlife pays ranchers for losses due to wolf predation, which isn't always easy to prove. Montana and Idaho proactively produced management plans that call for the shooting of wolves caught harassing livestock. As of press time, Wyoming, which wanted a shoot-on-sight policy for wolves outside the park, had yet to be approved by the feds to manage its populations.

The wolf is faring so well in central Idaho and Yellowstone that federal delisting from the Endangered Species Act is possible. For that to happen, a minimum of 10 breeding pairs—or about 100 wolves—had to be present in those two areas plus northwest Montana. The numbers are well past that, though Yellowstone had a brief scare in 2006 when parvo disease killed many pups. And contrary to fairy-tale lore, wolves are essentially harmless to humans. Prime viewing: Lamar Valley, early in the morning or at twilight. Helpful hint: Look for "The Wolf Man," Rick McIntyre, who drives a conspicuous yellow Nissan Xterra and pursues his research literally every day. Wherever the wolves go, the park's No. 1 wolf interpreter is sure to follow with a trail of "wolfers" behind him.

Other Animals

The fortunate visitor might see a wolverine, lynx, badger, fox, beaver, pika, sandhill crane, weasel, white-tailed deer or pine marten. More commonly seen are marmots, hawks,

Wolf watchers line up with spotting scopes in the Lamar Valley in the spring of 1996, just a few months after canis lupis *was introduced into Yellowstone and central Idaho.* National Park Service

ravens, red squirrels, osprey, river otters, white pelicans and chipmunks. The mountain goat, a snow-white favorite of visitors in Glacier National Park and even the mountains surrounding Yellowstone and Grand Teton, is not thought to inhabit these parks.

Grand Teton National Park

Bears

Black bears are a commonly seen resident of the aspen and pine forests of Grand Teton. As for the grizzly, it has spilled over from Yellowstone and is inching its way southward. Grizzlies are most common in the northern portions of the park, especially around Two Ocean and Emma Matilda Lakes. Prime viewing: None for grizzlies, Moose-Wilson Road for black bears. Keep a sharp eye out for either species on any trail into the high country or northeast corner of the park.

Bighorn Sheep

Chances are, you'll have to hike into the high country for a meeting with these muscular brutes. Most parts of the park above 9,900 feet are closed to winter travel to protect the bighorn. Prime viewing: Anywhere above 10,000 feet in the Tetons' alpine habitat.

Bison

Though not nearly as common as they are in Yellowstone, bison do roam the sage plains and benches along the Snake River. In winter, nearly 1,000 mingle with the wapiti for easy meals at the National Elk Refuge, creating the largest bison herd in any refuge. Prime viewing: Anywhere along the highway from Moran Junction to Moose Junction.

Coyotes

These animals can be found almost anywhere in the park, though they spend much of their time amid the sage, aspen and pine. Prime viewing: Anywhere sagebrush is found.

Eagles

The thermals created by the mountains plus an abundance of prey make the Tetons an excellent home for eagles. Prime viewing: For bald eagles, the cottonwoods lining the Snake River, especially at Moose, Oxbow Bend and Willow Flats at Jackson Lake; for golden eagles, elevations above 10,000 feet.

Elk

"Wapiti" are a common sight in Grand Teton, thanks in large part to the neighboring National Elk Refuge. In summers, they tend to disperse into the high country, though they are commonly seen amid the sage and aspen in the park. It's not uncommon to see a herd crossing Willow Flats. Prime viewing: Along Teton Park Road in summer, anywhere in Jackson Hole in winter, especially the refuge.

Moose

Whereas it can be an unexpected treat to see a moose in Yellowstone, they seem to be a part of the daily entertainment at Willow Flats, beneath Jackson Lake Lodge. With a taste for willow buds and aquatic plants, moose are found in marshlands. So they're more common in the northern part of the park, especially near the meandering Snake River and around Jackson Lake Lodge. Prime viewing: Behind Jackson Lake Lodge, in Willow Flats.

Mountain Lion

Though unlikely, the odds of encountering a cougar in Grand Teton are greater than in Yellowstone if you hike into the canyons above Jackson Hole. Still, though they'll keep an eye on you at a safe distance, don't bet on seeing one. Prime viewing: Rocky promontories in the upper elevations of the Tetons.

Mule Deer

Grand Teton provides a great deal of ideal terrain for the muley, which prefers rugged country. Look for them on benches or areas where the mountains meet the plains. Prime viewing: Teton Park Road, Moose-Wilson Road and Antelope Flats Road.

Pronghorn

This speedster is at home on the sage plains of Jackson Hole. They can be seen almost anywhere on the eastern side of the park. Prime viewing: Anywhere there's open sage country.

Wolves

It took three years for reintroduced wolf packs in Yellowstone to proliferate and migrate south into Grand Teton. In 1999, the Teton Pack took hold and gave birth to pups, the first in the park in more than 50 years. The pack appeared to be in peril when its alpha male was killed by a car on US 26/287 east of Moran in June of the same year. Conflicts with ranchers are a growing concern because they still graze cattle within the park's boundaries, a right "grandfathered" in to them as part of the park's establishment. Wolves are still infrequently seen in the park, though they continue to increase as packs expand. A wolf was shot and killed at Half Moon Lake in October 2005. In June 2006, a car on US 26/89/191 just south of Moran killed one. Unlike Yellowstone, where seeing a wolf is a realistic possibility, viewing one or more in Grand Teton would be a happy accident. Prime viewing: Anywhere along a road in the northern part of the park, or keep your eyes peeled at Pacific Creek Road.

Jackson Hole

National Elk Refuge (307-733-9212; www.fws.gov/nationalelkrefuge) provides a stunning sight when some 7,500 elk descend in late October from the mountains to their 25,000-acre winter-feeding grounds. It creates the largest concentration of wapiti anywhere in the world. The elk aren't alone for those six months; a winter drive or sleigh ride on the Refuge Road to Miller Butte is likely to turn up mule deer, moose and bison. They share the refuge, along with wolves that hang out on the fringes looking for an easy meal. Miller Butte typically features a readily visible concentration of bighorn sheep and recently had a mountain lion den. The animals concentrate here to escape the deep snows at higher elevations. When winters are especially harsh in the valley, U.S. Fish and Wildlife Service officials feed the elk. Before entering the refuge, stop at the Greater Yellowstone Visitor Center at 532 N. Cache Dr. in Jackson for updates and an overview. This is also the place to check in for horse-drawn sleigh rides (mid-December through early April), which bring tourists up close and personal with the elk. Limited elk hunts are allowed on portions of the refuge, as is trout fishing on Flat Creek. This is also a prime area for birders: Some 147 aviary species have been counted on the refuge. The National Elk Refuge was created in 1912 after a series of rugged winters threatened the area's herd of 25,000 elk. They are kept out of Jackson and off US 26/89/191 by 8-foot fences.

Jackson National Fish Hatchery (307-733-2510; www.fws.gov/jackson) about 3 miles north of Jackson is a unique place to understand the life cycles of the Snake River cutthroat trout that inhabit the Greater Yellowstone ecosystem. The hatchery features aquariums with vividly colored full-grown cutthroat and also has tanks packed with fingerlings. Eggs are taken from brood-stock trout and raised in the tanks, ultimately to be distributed to federal, state and tribal lakes and streams throughout Wyoming. About 400,000 young trout are released annually. Open daily from 8 AM–4 PM. Guided tours are available and the Sleeping Giant Pond was recently opened to fishing; a Wyoming license is required and there's a one-fish limit.

National Park Service

5

RESTAURANTS AND FOOD PURVEYORS

This is cowboy country, so you won't have any trouble finding a juicy steak or buffalo burger, baked potato on steroids and a cold beer to wash down a hearty meal. Restaurant food in the parks charts a similar course, with an emphasis on getting people in and out in a hurry. Burgers, fries, pie and a cola can be had just about anywhere, at modest prices.

That said, the dining landscape changes dramatically in Jackson, which squeezes more than 100 restaurants into a town of 8,000, many of them worthy of mention alongside the finest in Manhattan or San Francisco. Much of the cuisine prepared by nationally renowned chefs tends to be regional. Menus will include elk medallions, bison steak or some other wild game creatively presented. Yet even in Jackson, with all the money in the valley, the byword is casual and prices are surprisingly reasonable. Another unique feature of the region: Two of the finest restaurants are at small airports. Folks are known to fly in from all over the region for breakfast at Warbirds cafe in the Teton Valley airport in Driggs, Idaho. And T.J.'s Bettola at the West Yellowstone airport has fabulous Italian food, but drop in soon because the restaurant is moving into town.

If you're more comfortable with fast-food chains, you might be disappointed. Jackson and Cody have the usual suspects, and you can order from the Colonel or a McAnything in West Yellowstone. But most of the gateway communities are limited to small cafes, burger joints, saloons and country music. That's OK: The food is better and the ambience purely western.

Dining Price Codes
Inexpensive: Up to $15
Moderate: $15–30
Expensive: $30–65
Very Expensive: $65 or more

Credit Cards
AE—American Express
D—Discover
DC—Diners Club
CB—Carte Blanche
MC—Master Card
V—Visa
B = Breakfast, L = Lunch, D = Dinner

Restaurants in Yellowstone National Park

Dining Rooms

Grant Village Dining Room

307-242-3499 or 307-344-7311
1 Grant Loop Rd.
Price: Inexpensive to moderate
Season: June to Sept.
Hours: 6:30–10 AM, 11:30 AM–2:30 PM,
5:30–10 PM
Cuisine: Regional, Continental
Serving: B, L, D
Credit Cards: AE, D, MC, V
Handicapped Access: Partial
Reservations: Required

Typical park breakfast and lunch fare, with heaping helpings. Dinner can offer a surprisingly wide array, ranging from trout with crabmeat stuffing to platter-sized steaks. It's perhaps the most appealing family restaurant in the park for ambience and reasonable pricing.

Lake Yellowstone Hotel

307-242-3899 or 307-344-7901
Lake Yellowstone
Price: Inexpensive to expensive
Season: Mid-May to early Oct.
Hours: 6:30–10:30 AM, 11:30 AM–2:30 PM,
5–10 PM
Cuisine: Continental
Serving: B, L, D
Credit Cards: AE, D, DC, MC, V
Handicapped Access: Partial
Reservations: Required in summer

This is the crème de la crème of Yellowstone restaurants, and not just for the mesmerizing view from the north side of the lake. The spacious dining area provides a sense of privacy even when crowded. Entrees include bison, Idaho trout and a wide assortment of beef. For those seeking a break from typical regional meals, Lake Yellowstone features tofu

dishes, Asian vegetables, crab cakes, fettuccine and lobster ravioli.

Mammoth Hot Springs

307-344-7311
Mammoth
Price: Inexpensive to moderate.
Season: Early May to early Oct. and late December to early March.
Hours: 6:30–10:30 AM, 11 AM –2:30 PM, 5–10 PM (summer); 6:30–10 AM, 11:30 AM–2:30 PM and 5:30–8 PM (winter)
Cuisine: Continental
Serving: B, L, D
Credit Cards: AE, D, DC, MC, V
Handicapped Access: Partial
Reservations: Required for dinner in summer, suggested for dinner in winter

Mammoth offers a unique mix of casual and formal, with the area's 1930s history oozing from the walls. The breakfast buffet is ample, lunch is standard, and dinner features house-smoked entrées and a wide variety including vegetarian options.

Obsidian Dining Room

307-344-7901
Old Faithful Snow Lodge
Price: Inexpensive to moderate.
Season: Early May to mid-Oct. and Dec. to March
Hours: 6:30 AM–noon and 5–10 PM (summer); 6:30–10 AM, 11:30 AM–3 PM and 5–9:30 PM (winter)
Cuisine: Regional, Continental
Serving: B, D (Lunch in winter)
Credit Cards: AE, DC, D, MC, V
Handicapped Access: Partial
Reservations: Dinner reservations required in winter

New-and-improved from the cramped old snow lodge restaurant, with solid meals, western atmosphere and a wildlife motif. Try the seafood cioppino or braised lamb shanks. This is a great place to get away from the crowds at Old Faithful Inn.

Old Faithful Inn

307-545-4999 or 307-344-7311
Old Faithful
Price: Inexpensive to moderate
Season: Mid-May to mid-Oct.
Hours: 5–10 PM
Cuisine: Western American
Serving: B, L, D
Credit Cards: AE, D, MC, V
Handicapped Access: Partial
Reservations: Required in summer

The Old Faithful Inn is a classic western lodge setting featuring log furnishings, a stone fireplace and original oil paintings. Breakfast ranges from eggs anyway you want them to a buffet. Lunch also features a buffet with pan-fried trout or chicken sandwich, chili, salad, soup, coleslaw, etc. The more discerning palate might try the smoked Alaska salmon croustades for lunch or dinner. Familiar foods include burgers and fries; specialties include elk medallions, Montana Legend beef rib eye, pork osso buco as well as fish and chicken.

Roosevelt Lodge

307-344-7311
Tower-Roosevelt Junction
Price: Inexpensive to moderate
Season: June to Sept.
Hours: Subject to change; check on arrival.
Cuisine: Family-style Western
Serving: B, L, D
Credit Cards: AE, D, DC, MC, V
Handicapped Access: Partial
Reservations: No

Put on your 10-gallon hat, boots and spurs for this one. Start with a rustic log building, two stone fireplaces and a corral for aesthetics. Then toss in baby-back ribs, Roosevelt baked beans and fried chicken for grub. All you'd need to feel like a true-blue ranch hand is a few cattle to herd. For further authenticity, try Roosevelt Lodge's Old West Dinner Cookouts. You'll go by horseback or covered wagon through the sage and pine to a full meal deal of steak, potato salad, coleslaw, baked beans, apple crisp and coffee. Chances are a fiddle

Chuckwagon cookouts are part of the deal for guests at Roosevelt Lodge. National Park Service

player will come along for the ride. The cookouts are offered each afternoon from June to September.

Cafeterias

There are a number of cafeterias located throughout the park, for busy families wanting a quick but complete meal. Below are three examples. Be on the lookout for others as you drive through the park—they're all decent.

Lake Hotel Deli

307-344-7901
1 Grand Loop Rd.
Price: Inexpensive
Season: June to Sept.
Hours: 10:30 AM—9 PM
Cuisine: Deli
Serving: B, D
Credit Cards: AE, D, MC, V
Handicapped Access: Partial
Reservations: No

Healthy choices for folks on the go is what you'll find at this deli. Space is very limited so settle into comfy chairs in the immense lobby and piano room. Better yet, have your lunch on the patio overlooking the lake.

Lake Lodge Cafeteria

307-344-7311
1 Grant Loop Rd.
Price: Inexpensive to moderate
Season: Mid-June to late Sept.
Hours: 6:30 AM—9 PM
Cuisine: American, Continental
Serving: B, L, D
Credit Cards: AE, D, MC, V
Handicapped Access: Partial
Reservations: No

Inside the rustic log lodge you'll find family-style comfort with traditional American meals and an outstanding view of the lake.

Geyser Grill

307-344-7311
Old Faithful Inn
Price: Inexpensive

The Terrace Grill at Mammoth Hot Springs is a popular stop for regional food. National Park Service

Season: Mid-May to early Oct.
Hours: 10:30 AM—9 PM
Cuisine: Cafeteria
Serving: B, D
Credit Cards: AE, D, MC, V
Handicapped Access: Partial
Reservations: No

Cafeteria-style hot and cold entrees are offered, as well as sandwiches and snacks. Long tables and many chairs offer a place to view the famous geyser or take a break while awaiting the countdown.

Canyon Lodge Dining Room, Cafeteria and Deli

307-344-7901
Canyon Village
Price: Inexpensive to moderate
Season: Early June to mid-Sept.
Hours: 7—10:30 AM, 11:30 AM—2:30 PM,
5—10 PM
Cuisine: Casual American
Serving: B, L, D
Credit Cards: AE, D, MC, V
Handicapped Access: Partial
Reservations: No

You might feel like you're being herded onto an assembly line in a cafeteria where a small kitchen serves large, noisy crowds. But this is the place for the all-you-can-eat crowd: a breakfast buffet and a large salad bar. It's busy, but relaxed and spacious.

Grant Village Lake House

307-344-7901
1 Grant Loop Rd.
Price: Moderate
Season: May 25th to Sept.
Hours: 7—10:30 AM, 5:30—9 PM
Cuisine: Regional, Continental
Serving: B, L, D
Credit Cards: AE, D, MC, V
Handicapped Access: Partial
Reservations: Recommended

Located on the southwestern shores of

Yellowstone Lake, the dining experience is focused on the views. A breakfast buffet is offered for early risers. Lunch options include specialty sandwiches and soups. Palate-pleasing dinners range from wild Alaskan salmon to prime rib. Dinner reservations may be taken starting May 1 for the following year.

RESTAURANTS IN GRAND TETON NATIONAL PARK

Dining Rooms

Jenny Lake Lodge

307-433-4647
Jenny Lake
Price: Inexpensive to expensive
Season: Early June to early Oct.
Hours: 7:30—9 AM, noon—2:30 PM,
6—8:45 PM
Cuisine: Regional, Continental
Serving: B, D (Lunch is à la carte)
Credit Cards: AE, MC, V
Handicapped Access: Partial
Reservations: No

Five-course meals in a rugged national park? Yes. Breakfast is $19 and dinner $60, but if it's in your budget, you won't be disappointed. Try the elk carpaccio for an appetizer. Dinner specialties include venison, rabbit leg and pan-roasted squab (a pigeon that has yet to learn to fly). If you have reserved one night for dress up, this is it. Meals are included in the room charge for lodge guests. All in all, this is easily the finest meal in either park, and gives the top restaurants in Jackson a run for their money.

Mural Room

307-543-3100
Jackson Lake Lodge
Price: Inexpensive to expensive
Season: June to mid-Sept.
Hours: 7—9:30 AM, noon—1:30 PM, 5:30—9 PM

Cuisine: Regional
Serving: L, D
Credit Cards: MC, V
Handicapped Access: Partial
Reservations: Recommended for dinner

The famous view of the Tetons from Jackson Lake Lodge's giant picture window comes with dinner in the Mural Room. Continental breakfast features Belgian waffles and vegetarian eggs benedict. Tantalize your taste buds with the buffalo prime rib or rack of lamb for dinner. Keep an eye out for moose, elk and beaver in the willow flats between the lodge and Jackson Lake in the distance.

Peaks Restaurant

307-733-5470 or 307-543-2831
Signal Mountain Lodge
www.signalmountainlodge.com
Price: Inexpensive to moderate
Season: June to mid-Sept.
Hours: 7–10 AM, 11:30 AM–10 PM
Cuisine: Eclectic continental, regional
Serving: B, L, D
Credit Cards: AE, D, MC, V
Handicapped Access: Partial
Reservations: Required for breakfast and dinner

Signal Mountain Lodge's upscale dining experience emphasizes environmentally friendly foods such as free-range chicken. The Peaks is also well known for sunset viewing while dining in a casually rustic atmosphere. Other dinner specialties are filet mignon wrapped in applewood-smoked bacon and Mediterranean pasta.

Cafeteria/Deli

John Colter Cafe Court

307-543-2811
Colter Bay Village
Price: Inexpensive
Season: May to Sept.
Hours: 6 AM–10 PM

Cuisine: Deli
Serving: B, L, D
Credit Cards: MC, V
Handicapped Access: Partial
Reservations: No

This is a casual sit-down place for families who like inexpensive choices from a broad menu that includes pizza, sandwiches, soups, salads, chicken and vegetarian options.

Pioneer Grill

307-543-2811 ext. 3463 or 800-628-9988
Jackson Lake Lodge
Price: Inexpensive to moderate
Season: June to mid-Sept.
Hours: 6 AM–10:30 PM
Cuisine: American
Serving: B, L, D
Credit Cards: MC, V
Handicapped Access: Partial
Reservations: No

Grab a burger, fries and malt from a 1950s-style diner with round green stools and soda-fountain ambience. Try the bison burger for a real Wyoming experience. A rarely found kids menu is an added convenience for parents.

Deadman's Bar

307-733-5470 or 307-543-2831
Signal Mountain Resort
www.signalmountainlodge.com
Price: Inexpensive
Season: June to mid-Sept.
Hours: 11:30 AM–10 PM
Cuisine: Bar food
Serving: L, D
Credit Cards: AE, D, MC, V
Handicapped Access: Partial
Reservations: No

A bar famous for its blackberry margarita shouldn't be missed. Add a huge platter of nachos supreme and you have a satisfying lunch or light dinner. Regional beers are on draft or in bottle and one of the few televisions in the park can draw a crowd.

Leek's Pizzeria

307-733-5470
Colter Bay Village
Price: Inexpensive
Season: June to mid-Sept.
Hours: 11:30 AM–10 PM
Cuisine: Pizzeria
Serving: L, D
Credit Cards: MC, V
Handicapped Access: Partial
Reservations: No

Munch on a piping hot pizza and sip a draft beer while listening to the occasional live band on the patio at Leek's Marina. Inside and outside seating, sandwiches and large lake views are served up as well.

Restaurants in Yellowstone National Park Gateway Communities

Cody, Wyoming

Naturally, you won't have any trouble finding a sizzling steak or juicy buffalo burger in Cody. Though it isn't Jackson, options aren't merely limited to western fare, either. Cody has Cajun, Italian, Mexican and Chinese as well. Nothing too fancy, but just about anything a hungry tourist desires can be found here. And if you're in a hurry, Cody is one of two gateway communities—Jackson is the other—with the standard names in fast food.

Adriano's Italian Restaurant

307-527-7320
1244 Sheridan Ave.
Price: Inexpensive to moderate
Season: Year-round
Hours: 11 AM–9 PM Mon.–Thurs., 11 AM–10 PM Fri. and Sat.
Cuisine: Authentic Italian
Serving: L, D

Credit Cards: D, MC, V
Reservations: Suggested

You will find a definite Italian theme and cuisine at this restaurant; the owner and chef are both from Italy. Chicken Parmesan, veal Adriano and handmade pizzas are specialties. A limited bar menu with beer, wine and some cocktails round out the selections.

Beta Coffeehouse

307-587-7707.
1132 12th St.
Price: Inexpensive.
Season: Year-round
Hours: 7 AM–6 PM weekdays, 7 AM–4 PM weekends
Cuisine: Specialty beverages
Serving: B, L
Credit Cards: No
Reservations: No

This is the spot for hot and cold coffee drinks of all sizes and shapes. Fruit smoothies with fresh frozen fruit, plus herbal, white, green, black and Yerba Mate tea from South America, homemade Chai, hot chocolate and Italian sodas along with handmade pastries, scones, muffins, cinnamon rolls and bagels make menu decisions tough. Wireless Internet and seating for about 20 make this coffeehouse especially popular with the climbing set. A family of climbers owns the coffee shop and the name originates from a climbing term.

Black Sheep Restaurant/Gibs Sports Bar

307-527-5895
1901 Mountain View Dr.
Price: Inexpensive
Season: Year-round
Hours: Opens at 11 AM Mon.–Sat., noon Sun. Lunch 11 AM, dinner 5 PM
Cuisine: Steakhouse, bar food
Serving: L, D
Credit Cards: MC, V
Reservations: No

There's a dining room on one side, and a sports bar with two big-screen TVs and five more monitors on the other side. Hearty breakfasts, salad bar, fresh potatoes for home fries and smoked baked beans are among the specialties.

Bubba's Bar-B-Que

307-587-7427
512 Yellowstone Ave.
Price: Inexpensive to moderate
Season: Year-round
Hours: 7 AM–10 PM daily
Cuisine: BBQ
Serving: B, L, D
Credit Cards: AE, V, MC
Reservations: No.

In addition to pork, beef and chicken barbecue, sandwiches, burgers, steaks, salads and a huge salad bar, Bubba's offers a full breakfast menu. It's difficult, but try to save room for homemade desserts, especially the buttermilk pie. There are four other Bubba's locations, including one in Jackson.

Cassie's Supper Club

307-527-5500
214 Yellowstone Ave.
www.cassies.com
Price: Inexpensive to moderate
Season: Year-round
Hours: Opens at 11 AM daily
Cuisine: Steakhouse
Serving: L, D
Credit Cards: AE, D, MC, V
Reservations: Accepted

Opened in 1922 and renovated in 1995 to include three levels for dining, Cassie's was chosen as one of the top 20 steakhouses in the West by *Cowboys & Indians* magazine in 1999. A live band plays Thursdays through Saturdays.

Cody Coffee Company and Eatery

307-527-7879
1702 Sheridan Ave.
Price: Inexpensive
Season: Year-round
Hours: 7 AM–3 PM daily
Cuisine: Coffeehouse
Serving: B, L
Credit Cards: No
Reservations: Yes

Panini sandwiches of turkey, roast beef, ham and chicken pesto provide for a more continental menu. The Cody Coffee Company serves Ibis coffee from Utah, and homemade muffins, biscotti, and smoothies.

Granny's

307-587-4829
1550 Sheridan Ave.
Price: Inexpensive
Season: Year-round
Hours: 5 AM–10 PM Sun.–Thurs., 5 AM–11 PM Fri. and Sat.
Cuisine: American diner
Serving: B, L, D
Credit Cards: MC, V
Reservations: No

This full-service family diner caters to a blue-collar market and families with a limited budget. Their specialty is breakfast, but lunch and dinners can be ordered from 140 line items on the menu.

Irma Hotel Bar Restaurant and Grill

307-587-4221
1192 Sheridan Ave
Price: Inexpensive
Cuisine: Western American
Serving: B, L, D
Credit Cards: AE, D, MC, V
Reservations: Accepted for parties of 6 or more
Hours: 6 AM–10 PM daily
Season: Year-round

Authentic western-style dining and drinking is the order of the day at Bill Cody's Irma Bar and Restaurant. Begin your day with a plate of their famous steak and eggs or a Mexican green chili, hash brown and egg concoction served in a skillet. The flapjacks are made from a beer batter and offer that extra shot of the Wild West. Lunch entrees are fairly creative, including the local favorite, the Irma Philly. Prime rib is the dinner house specialty, but anything from salmon and Rocky Mountain trout to hand-cut chicken fried steak and buffalo rib eye are on the menu. There is also a breakfast buffet served daily and lunch buffet served Monday through Saturday. Kids will be pleased with a menu more suited to their tastes and tummy size, and they eat free if they are 6 or younger.

The Noon Break

307-587-9720
927 12th St.
Price: Inexpensive
Season: Year-round
Hours: 7 AM–2 PM
Cuisine: Southwestern
Serving: B, L
Credit Cards: No
Reservations: No

License plates on the walls provide a Route 66 style. Ask for the Code 10 Chili, if you can handle it lip-burning hot.

Our Place

307-527-4420
148 W. Yellowstone Ave.
Price: Inexpensive
Season: Year-round
Hours: 6 AM–2 PM daily
Cuisine: American diner
Serving: B, L
Credit Cards: No
Reservations: No

This locally popular family restaurant offers home-style cooking—burgers, steak and eggs, salads, sandwiches, a kids menu—and it's one of the last places in Wyoming, or maybe the nation, with 25-cent coffee.

Painter Outpost

307-527-5510
4 Van Dyke Rd.
www.painteroutpost.com
Price: Inexpensive
Season: Summer
Hours: 9–11:30 AM, noon–7 PM
Cuisine: Contemporary American
Serving: B, L
Credit Cards: MC, V
Reservations: No

The patio overlooks the Clark's Fork of the Yellowstone River in Sunlight Basin north of Cody. Part of an RV park and campground, you'll find exceptional atmosphere, outdoor dining, homemade soups and stews, beer, wine and other beverages. If you need to reconnect with the outside world, the Outpost has a big-screen television.

Proud Cut Saloon

307-527-6905
1227 Sheridan Ave.
Price: Inexpensive to expensive
Season: Year-round
Hours: 3–11 PM (closes at 10 PM Sun.)
Cuisine: Rodeo western
Serving: L, D
Credit Cards: D, MC, V
Reservations: Yes (if minors in group)

"Rodeo western" means hearty helpings: chicken, salads, sandwiches, half-pound burgers and huge prime-rib sandwiches for lunch. Steaks are mostly hand-cut and range from flat-irons to 22-ounce porterhouses. Tenderloins are served with a special house marinade. Other favorites offered include tempura-battered jumbo shrimp and homemade desserts such as peanut butter and hot fudge pie. There is a full bar, but children are not allowed in the saloon. Owner Peter Crump rode in the National Finals Rodeo, so tons of rodeo photos and memorabilia adorn the walls. Patio dining is available from the end of June through August.

QT's Restaurant

307-587-5555
1701 Sheridan Ave., in Holiday Inn
Price: Moderate
Season: Year-round
Hours: 6 AM–10 PM, shorter hours in winter.
Closed for lunch on Sat. in summer and
winter
Cuisine: American
Serving: B, L, D
Credit Cards: AE, D, V, MC
Reservations: No (except large groups)

Typically the last restaurant in town to
close, QT's serves up steaks, pasta, chicken,
salads, along with gourmets breads made
on site. Breakfast features omelets, French
toast, waffles and the ever-popular biscuits
and gravy. This is also the home of the
Buffalo Bill skillet, Angus beef burgers or
cheeseburgers that come with batter or
sweet potato fries. Children under 12 eat
free from a kids' menu.

Tommy Jack's Cajun Grill

307-587-4917
1134 13th St.
Price: Inexpensive
Season: Year-round
Cuisine: Cajun
Serving: L, D
Credit Cards: MC, V
Reservations: No

The only Cajun restaurant in the
Yellowstone region, Tommy Jack's was
opened by a husband-and-wife team from
Monroe, Louisiana, who brought their
Bayou tastes to the Rocky Mountain region.
Chances are this is the only place in the
Greater Yellowstone ecosystem serving
Bayou fried gator, which is basically a fried
strip of real alligator meat. The hearty
Louisiana gumbo, with spicy sausage and
chicken, is another favorite. And it would
be a shame to miss the crab-cake or Po-Boy
sandwich.

Wapiti Lodge and Steakhouse

307-587-6659
Price: Moderate to expensive
Season: Year-round
Hours: 4–10 PM Wed.–Sun.
Cuisine: Steakhouse, regional
Serving: D
Credit Cards: MC, V.
Reservations: Accepted.

True to its name, this eatery offers wapiti
(elk) medallions in marionberry demi-
glaze and wapiti-smoked pork ribs, along
with an extensive menu of additional
favorites. A lengthy list of enticing entrees
include: filet mignon, New York strip, rib
eye, buffalo rib eye, prime rib, shrimp, yel-
lowfin tuna (flown in from Hawaii), grilled
lamb chops, roasted pork tenderloin,
breast of duckling, chicken piccata, pasta.
You can even find a few vegetarian dishes.
Lighter fare includes sandwiches, salads,
burgers, and chicken tenders. There's a full
bar with local beers and a limited wine
selection.

Wyoming Rib and Chop House

307-527-7731
1367 Sheridan Ave.
Price: Moderate
Season: Year-round
Hours: 11 AM–10:30 PM Mon.–Fri., 4–10:30
PM Sat.–Sun.
Cuisine: Steakhouse, Cajun
Serving: L (Mon.–Fri.), D
Credit Cards: AE, MC, V, D
Reservations: Recommended

Award-winning baby-back ribs, hand-cut
certified Angus steaks, and fresh seafood
flown in several times a week are just a few
of the mouthwatering dinner selections.
Soups and sauces are made on the spot.
Choose from a customary wine, beer and
drink list, or a renowned 26-ounce margarita to wet your whistle. The Rib and
Chop House is a chain, but still worth a try
for the food and western aesthetics.

Zapata's

307-527-7181
1362 Sheridan Ave.
Price: Inexpensive to moderate
Season: Year-round
Hours: 11 AM–9 PM weekdays, noon–9 PM
Sat.
Cuisine: Mexican American
Serving: L, D
Credit Cards: AE, DC, MC, V
Reservations: Accepted

Zapata's is famous for a special chili relleno: two eggs cooked on the grill with chili and cheese added, somewhat like an omelet, and served with green chili sauce. You can also get enchiladas, chimichangas, flautas, sopaipillas, fried pie and fried ice cream. Wine, beer and house margaritas that come in array of fruity flavors (strawberry, peach, mango or raspberry) will complete your dinner. There are daily lunch and dinner specials, but Thursdays are always a huge hit with the chili relleno special.

Cooke City/Silver Gate, Montana

For a remote outpost known for catering to gearheads, (snowmobilers and ATV enthusiasts), Cooke City has some surprisingly sophisticated fare. Though the road east is closed by snow in winter, many restaurants are open and seat an eclectic mix that includes wolf watchers. Be advised that spring is a slow time here and not particularly appealing, especially during snowmelt. Open restaurants can be difficult to find during the shoulder seasons, especially in spring.

Bistro Café

406-838-2160
214 Main St., Cooke City
Price: Inexpensive to moderate
Season: Summers (a decision on winter is made each fall)
Hours: 7 AM–10 PM
Cuisine: Gourmet French, American
Serving: B, L, D
Credit Cards: D, MC, V
Reservations: Accepted

There is something about a bistro in the midst of all these motors that strikes a chord of civility. The menu is typical, with steaks, chicken, pasta, burgers, seafood and homemade soups, but the atmosphere and careful food preparation is truly unique for the area.

Buns 'N' Beds

406-838-2030
Main St., Cooke City
Price: Inexpensive
Season: Year-round
Hours: 10 AM–8 PM
Cuisine: Deli
Serving: B, L, D
Credit Cards: MC, V
Reservations: No

Barbecue, smoked meats, Cajun, Italian, soups, sandwiches and vegetarian items are happily made by hand and served with a side of warm smiles.

Miner's Saloon

406-838-2214
Main St., Cooke City
Price: Inexpensive to moderate
Season: Year-round
Hours: noon–2 AM, kitchen closes at 10 PM
Cuisine: Pizzeria
Serving: B, L, D
Credit Cards: No
Reservations: No

Surprisingly decent food can be had at this saloon, plus pool, keno, poker, foosball and live music on summer Saturday nights. Handmade pizzas, burgers, tacos and especially good fish tacos are a few of the favored menu items. Old West antiques, guns and mining equipment add to the authenticity.

Gardiner, Montana

If all you're looking for is a good burger and fries, or maybe a mom-and-pop breakfast, Gardiner is your place. Solid food, solid prices. No four-star restaurants, but that's not the reason you come to Yellowstone.

Antler Pub and Grill

406-848-7536
107 Hellroaring St., inside the Comfort Inn
Price: Inexpensive to moderate
Season: Apr.–Nov.
Cuisine: Western American
Serving: B, D (breakfast seasonally)
Credit Cards: MC, V
Reservations: No

Although the food is what you would expect (prime rib, BBQ, chicken, pasta, burgers) the views of the Yellowstone River from upstairs are the bonus here. For entertainment, video gambling and Texas Hold 'Em games are close at hand, or try identifying the numerous mounted species hanging on the walls.

Corral Drive Inn

406-848-7627
US Hwy. 89 S., across from Super 8
Price: Inexpensive
Season: Year-round
Hours: 11 AM–11 PM (summer), 11 AM–8 PM (winter)
Cuisine: Burgers
Serving: L, D
Credit Cards: MC, V
Reservations: Not unless you want a hateful laugh from Helen

The Corral is not much to look at, but that's not why folks stop. They come for "Helen's Hateful Hamburger" usually prepared by Helen herself. Helen's is the kind of place where your order is taken from a sliding window and you wait for half-pound burgers, milkshake or double dip cone on a well-used picnic table in the gravel parking area. Watch out for attitude and flying food at this one-of–a-kind burger stand.

K Bar Club

406-848-9995
US Hwy. 89 and Main St.
Price: Inexpensive to moderate
Season: Year-round
Hours: 11 AM–2 AM
Cuisine: Bar food
Serving: L, D
Credit Cards: MC, V
Reservations: No

The pizza at the K Bar is handmade and tastes exceptionally good after a long hike or day of car touring. They also offer burgers and Mexican food, along with billiards, a casino and a jukebox. Not much to look at inside (or out), but who cares after the nature viewing inside the park?

Gardiner Lighthouse Restaurant

406-848-2201
752 US Hwy. 89 S., 7.5 miles north of town at Corwin Springs
Price: Inexpensive to moderate
Season: Spring and summer
Hours: 5:30–9:30 PM daily
Cuisine: World
Serving: D
Credit Cards: AE, D, MC, V
Reservations: No

Lighthouse décor and atmosphere, serving a wide variety of cuisines and entrees ranging from sushi to lamb, prepared by five-star chef Victor Kaufman. Indian, Thai, Japanese cuisine and not to mention burgers and thick steaks make this possibly the most worldly menu in Montana. The Lighthouse, serving park visitors and local ranchers since 1928, was once operated by the Church Universal and Triumphant, an arm of the Summit Lighthouse religion. The restaurant lives on, however, and serves some of the best food in the Gardiner area. Don't expect to order a beer or glass of wine, however, as no alcohol is served on the premises.

Gardiner has plenty of casual places to eat, many of them open year-round. National Park Service

Park Street Grill and Cafe

406-848-7989
Price: Inexpensive to moderate
Season: Summers
Hours: Call for current hours
Cuisine: Italian
Serving: L, D
Credit Cards: MC, V
Reservations: No

Select from a menu of gourmet Italian entrées with wildly imaginative ingredients as well as names. Crazy Mountain Alfredo, one of the more popular pasta dishes, is named for the mountain range just north of the area and is a crazy concoction of sweet and hot peppers, spicy sausage and chicken. For the tamer appetites, there are a number of pork, chicken or beef meals prepared American-style. Save room for the huckleberry crème brûlée.

Pedalino's

406-848-9950
Price: Moderate to expensive
Season: Apr.–Summer
Hours: Call for current hours
Cuisine: Classic Italian
Serving: D
Credit Cards: MC, V
Reservations: Accepted

A complimentary bowl of authentic minestrone soup, served family style, is the first course to your meal. Served with warm crusty bread, it's almost a meal. But there's more, much more. Not just handmade pasta entrées, but tender steaks, succulent seafood and excellent salads provide a varied and full menu. Steve Pedalino also oversees the wine list, which is more than adequate and still reasonable.

Town Cafe

406-848-7322
120 E. Park St.
Price: Inexpensive
Season: Year-round
Hours: 6 AM–8:30 PM downstairs and 5:30 AM–9:30 PM upstairs
Cuisine: Western
Serving: B, L, D

Credit Cards: D, MC, V
Reservations: No

A western façade on the outside and gen-
uine western hospitality inside are the
markings of this family-style steakhouse
and cafe. Also on the complex are a lounge,
casino, gift shop and gas for sale. The Town
Loft is the steakhouse upstairs with a view
into the park. Downstairs is a family-style
café, which is more kid-friendly.

Tumbleweed Bookstore and Cafe

406-848-2225
501 Scott St.
Price: Inexpensive
Season: Year-round
Hours: 7 AM—9 PM summer, 7 AM—7 PM
Oct.–Dec., 11 AM—6 PM Jan.–Apr.
Cuisine: Deli, coffee shop
Serving: B, L
Credit Cards: MC, V
Reservations: No

A coffee shop offering fair-trade coffee
isn't what you'd expect to find in this gun-
toting, pick-up driving community. But
take it where you can get it. Along with a
fair cup of Joe, you'll find new and used
books, gift shop items and maybe some
peace and quiet.

Yellowstone Mine Restaurant

406-848-7336
US Hwy. 89 S.
Price: Inexpensive to moderate
Season: Year-round
Hours: 6–11 AM, 5–9:30 PM daily
Cuisine: Steakhouse
Serving: B, D
Credit Cards: AE, CB, DC, DI, MC, V
Reservations: No

Easily the most striking place in Gardiner,
Yellowstone Mine offers gold-mine decor,
breakfast buffet, full bar, gift store, beer,
wine and casino. You could even stretch it
to say that it offers some atmosphere

thanks to the large river rock fireplace.
Though this restaurant might be the best
known in Gardiner, it's also one of the most
expensive, with food that doesn't that
always live up to the price.

Island Park, Idaho

Island Park exists to serve tourists who are
just passing through, anglers eager to try
the world-famous waters of the Henry's
Fork of the Snake and snowmobilers who
have miles of relatively flat, remote terrain
just outside the park. The dining reflects
this life-on-the-go philosophy. The restaurants are largely the same, with appealing
western aesthetics and views of the meandering Henry's Fork. As one might expect,
you will find plenty of steaks, trout and
burgers.

A Bar Supper Club

208-558-7358
3433 Hwy. 20, in Last Chance
Price: Moderate
Season: Year-round
Hours: 10 AM—10 PM, longer hours in summer
Cuisine: American
Serving: B, L, D
Credit Cards: AE, MC, V
Reservations: No

The A Bar, on the banks of the Henry's Fork
of the Snake River, is known for its juicy
cheeseburgers, 14-ounce rib eye, and steak
and jumbo shrimp combo. Steak and halibut fingers are a local favorite. A simple
breakfast menu is offered for late-morning
starters.

Angler's Lodge Restaurant

208-558-9555
3363 Old Hwy. 191
www.anglerslodge.net/island_park_
restaurant.php
Price: Inexpensive to moderate
Season: Year-round (closed in Nov.)
Hours: 7 AM—11 PM

Cuisine: American
Serving: B, L, D
Credit Cards: MC, V
Reservations: No

Watch fly anglers on the Henry's Fork while dining in a great atmosphere that includes an authentic log interior and stone fireplace. In the summer, enjoy a steak, trout, a burger and beer or wine on the large deck overlooking the river.

Mack's Inn Dinner Theater/Henry's Fork Landing Cafe

208-558-7672
Macks Inn, on the north end of Island Park
Price: Inexpensive to moderate
Season: Year-round; dinner theater starts in May
Hours: Call for current hours
Cuisine: American
Serving: L, D
Credit Cards: AE, D, MC, V
Reservations: No, except for dinner theater

A dinner theater featuring western plays that show off the talents of regional actors sets the stage for a unique dining experience. Enjoy a hearty prime-rib supper while watching such productions as *The Robber Bridegroom* and *Dark Deeds at Swan's Place*. The actors, who earn roles through auditions, not only perform on stage, they serve food as well.

West Yellowstone, Montana

If you're looking for fine dining with elegant ambience, this isn't the place. The whole idea of being in Yellowstone is to experience the park and surrounding areas. Restaurants in West Yellowstone are in keeping with that theme: functional food, served quickly, in nondescript settings that won't encourage anybody to linger. One popular stop about 10 miles west of town was Alice's Restaurant, at the Lionshead RV Resort and Super 8 Motel, but it burned town in 2005.

Bar-N-Ranch

406-646-0300
890 Buttermilk Rd., 6 miles west of town off US Hwy. 20
www.bar-n-ranch.com
Price: Inexpensive
Season: Open nightly June 1–Sept. 30, Wed.–Sun. Oct. 1–May 31
Cuisine: Western
Serving: B, D
Credit Cards: MC, V
Reservations: Required

Chef Jack Cole has been with the restaurant since 2006 and is something of a West Yellowstone legend. His menu focuses on feeding the hard-working or -playing. On it you will find such interesting entrees as pecan-crusted French toast or omelets named for the nearby trout streams for breakfast and roasted Long Island duckling or Angel Hair Pomodoro for dinner. Not to worry, there are savory steaks for the beef lover. The restaurant is located in a lodge on the 200-acre ranch.

Bullwinkle's Saloon and Eatery

406-646-7974
19 Madison Ave.
www.yellowstonebullwinkles.com.
Price: Inexpensive
Season: Year-round
Hours: 11 AM–2 AM
Cuisine: Steakhouse, regional
Serving: L, D
Credit Cards: AE, D, MC, V
Reservations: Required for groups

A restaurant suitable for families, Bullwinkle's offers wild game, seafood and wine. The adjacent log annex is a curious mix of western decor and Green Bay Packers shrine. Sit on log chairs while dining amid Packers memorabilia, including an imposing blow-up doll wearing a green-and-yellow uniform and toting a football.

West Yellowstone's downtown offers standard dining options, ranging from fast food to casual atmosphere and featuring regional food. National Park Service

Eino's Bar
406-646-9344
8955 Gallatin Rd., off US Hwy. 191 9 miles north of West Yellowstone
Price: Inexpensive
Season: Closed between Thanksgiving and Christmas
Hours: Noon–9 PM peak season, noon–8 PM low season
Cuisine: Bar food
Serving: L, D
Credit Cards: No
Reservations: No

Off the beaten track and popular with locals, this bar conjures up images of cattle and sheep ranchers worn and weary from a hard day's work, ready for a simple but good meal. Eino's features a cook-your-own steak grill, a bar filled with menagerie and a couple of pool tables.

Gusher Pizza and Sandwich Shoppe
406-646-9050

40 Dunraven St.
Price: Inexpensive
Season: May–Oct., Dec.–March
Hours: 11:30 AM–10 PM
Cuisine: Pizzeria
Serving: L, D
Credit Cards: D, MC, V
Reservations: No

A place to share a pizza while on vacation, how American is that? The Gusher also serves sandwiches, burgers, steaks and seafood. The local favorite pie is the Gusher: a heaping eight toppings made mostly of meat, with some veggies thrown in. The burger of choice is the Poor Boy: an artery-clogging half-pounder topped with ham, egg and cheese. The pub and casino host video poker, keno and a pool table as well as electronic games for the kids. If you're staying nearby you can get your food to go or have it delivered to your motel for free.

Happy Hour Bar

406-646-5100
15475 Hebgen Lake Rd.
www.happyhourbar.com/bar
Price: Inexpensive to moderate
Season: Year-round, except for shoulder
seasons
Hours: Call for current hours
Cuisine: Steak, bar food
Serving: L, D
Credit Cards: MC, V
Reservations: No

Every hour is happy and the steaks are
thick, hand-cut and cooked to your specifi-
cations at the Happy Hour. Buffalo burgers,
onion rings, shrimp scampi and a salad bar
complete the limited but sufficient menu.
Not known for a kid-friendly atmosphere,
this well-known bar can get a little rowdy
and sometimes downright raunchy. It sits
on the bank of Hebgen Lake and is affili-
ated with the Hebgen Lake Mountain Inn,
newer lodging located across the highway.

Timberline Cafe

406-646-9349
135 Yellowstone Ave.
www.my.montana.net/timberlinecafe
Price: Inexpensive
Season: Early May–early Oct.
Hours: 6:30–11 AM, 11:30 AM–3 PM, 5–10 PM
Cuisine: American
Serving: B, L, D
Credit Cards: MC, V
Reservations: No

Steak, burgers, homemade soups, pies and
desserts all plated up in 1930s fashion.
Voted best pie in the state by *Montana
Magazine.*

T.J.'s Bettola

406-646-4700
Yellowstone Airport
Price: Moderate.
Season: Year-round
Hours 5–10 PM

Cuisine: Italian
Serving: D (possibly L)
Credit Cards: MC, V
Reservations: Yes

Italian and seafood specials are prepared
nightly. Bettola's recently earned one of the
few and coveted Montana liquor licenses.
Catering services offered can be useful for
large group gatherings. The restaurant
plans to change locations (move into town)
in the spring of 2008.

Wild West Pizza

406-646-4400.
20 Madison Ave.
www.wildwestpizza.com
Price: Inexpensive
Season: Year-round
Hours: Call for current hours
Cuisine: Pizzeria
Serving: L, D
Credit Cards: D, MC, V
Reservations: No

Pizzas made from scratch, starting with
Wheat Montana flour and using only the
best ingredients, make this one something
special. Routinely regarded and often voted
the best pizza in West Yellowstone, Aaron
Hecht claims the secret is in the sauce. It's
one that he grew up on. Great food takes
time to prepare, so settle back with a
refreshing beverage and take in the aromas
of the Wild West.

Wolf Pack Brew Pub

406-646-7225
139 N. Canyon St.
Price: Inexpensive to moderate
Season: Year-round
Hours: Noon–8 PM Mon.–Fri. (changes in
fall and winter)
Cuisine: American
Serving: L, D
Credit Cards: D, MC, V
Reservations: No

A brew pub can be a welcome sight after a long day of sightseeing. Wolf Pack brewing specializes in authentically brewed German beers made from imported German hops, malts and yeast. A bar menu allows you to match some appetizers with their hand-crafted brews. Their motto is "No whining, no drooling, no flat tires, no dead fish and no gimmicks."

RESTAURANTS IN GRAND TETON NATIONAL PARK GATEWAY COMMUNITIES

Jackson, Wyoming

Does anybody in Jackson have a kitchen? To be sure, each of the more than 100 restaurants have one. That's a staggering number of eateries for a town of 8,650, but then, few come to one of America's favorite year-round playgrounds to cook. And those who do have the cash to dine out regularly, do so. The result: more than a few dining establishments that could blend seamlessly into Manhattan or San Francisco. The competition is good news for diners. For such an affluent area, prices are surprisingly modest even at the finest restaurants.

Naturally, Jackson has its share of western-style eateries featuring bison, elk, trout and other wild game. Yet many restaurants also will make you forget you're in the land of rodeos, ranches and wild animals. Perhaps surprisingly, the area is lean on Mexican, Chinese, Japanese and other ethnic choices. And suffice it to say, Jackson has the run-of-the-mill fast-food chains for those who need the familiar. To help with choices, we've separated what we believe are the top 15 restaurants, followed by listings of others where you can't go wrong. The choices aren't entirely based on which have the best food; some are simply must-eat stops for their ambience, history and/or reputation. The list includes the communities of Wilson, Teton Village and Moose. Jackson is a year-round playground, so nearly all of its restaurants are always open as well.

The Fab 15

Backcountry Provisions

307-734-9420
50 W. Deloney Ave.
www.backcountryprovisions.com
Price: Inexpensive
Hours: Opens at 7 AM daily
Cuisine: Deli
Serving: B, L, D
Credit Cards: AE, D, MC, V
Reservations: No

Take-out sandwiches made with imported meats and cheeses, with an emphasis on helping outdoor enthusiasts prepare for backcountry adventures.

Bar | Chuckwagon

307-733-3370
Teton Village Rd., 6 miles west of Jackson and one mile north.
www.barjchuckwagon.com
Price: Moderate
Season: Memorial Day through Sept.
Hours: Doors open at 5:30 PM
Cuisine: Chuckwagon supper
Serving: D
Credit Cards: D, MC, V
Reservations: Strongly recommended

If you don't mind eating on speed dial, the Bar J is a unique frontier tourist-town experience not to be missed. Legend has it that the Bar J once served 500 patrons in nine minutes. Chuckwagon dining is complemented by a western show featuring story-telling, poetry, yodeling and music. Dinner is at 7 PM sharp, and though the Bar J seats 750 under cover, reservations are imperative through much of the summer. The meal features sliced beef in mild barbecue sauce, baked potatoes, Bar J beans, homemade biscuits, chunky apple sauce, spice cake, ranch coffee and lemonade. No alcohol is served.

Chicken, ribs and steak are available for an extra charge. The reasonable $18 ticket (summer 2007) includes dinner, Wyoming sales tax, gratuity and the show by the Bar J Wranglers. Tour groups are welcome.

Blue Lion

307-733-3912
160 N. Millward St.
Price: Moderate to expensive
Hours: Call for current hours
Cuisine: Eclectic American
Serving: D
Credit Cards: AE, D, DC, MC, V
Reservations: Recommended

Famed for its rack of lamb, steak, pasta, fresh fish, elk, salsas and vegetarian dishes, the Blue Lion is in a quaint, older, refurbished house. Specialties include mushrooms stuffed with crab cream cheese, specially prepared sauces, salads made with fresh greens and homemade desserts like tiramisu and mud pie. Outdoor patio dining is available in the summer and a private room upstairs can accommodate parties up to 28.

Bubba's Bar-B-Que

307-733-2288
515 W. Broadway Ave.
Price: Inexpensive to moderate
Hours: 6:30 AM–10 PM (summer), 6:30 AM–8:30 PM (winter)
Cuisine: BBQ
Serving: B, L, D
Credit Cards: AE, D, MC, V
Reservations: No

The motto here is "No whinin' while dinin'," and few people do, though many are moanin' because they're stuffed. This is definitely a family stop for the hungry and budget-conscious. The salad bar is all-you-can-eat and the portions are generous. You'll need plenty of napkins. For dessert, try their specialty, buttermilk pie. Bubba's is a regional chain and also has a restaurant in Cody.

Dornan's Moose Pizza and Pasta Company

307-734-2415, ext. 204
Grand Teton National Park entrance, Moose
Price: Inexpensive
Hours: 11:30 AM–9:30 PM (summer); 11:30 AM–3 PM Mon.–Fri., 11:30 AM–5 PM weekends (winter)
Cuisine: Pizzeria
Serving: L, D
Credit Cards: AE, CB, D, DC, MC, V
Reservations: No

Dornan's features carb-rich food and a bar with the largest wine selection in northwest Wyoming right next door. Buy a bottle of wine and bring it over for dinner . . . no corkage fee. Then add to your meal a dramatic view of the Grand Teton rising to a cobalt sky above the Snake River. It's so close it seems you can reach through the picture window and touch it. The food is above average and tastes especially good after a day hike or a scenic float on the Snake River.

Koshu Wine Bar

307-733-5283
200 W. Broadway Ave.
www.jhwine.com
Price: Moderate to expensive
Hours: Opens at 6 PM
Cuisine: Pan-Asian
Serving: D
Credit Cards: AE, D, MC, V
Reservations: Yes

The wine bar is in the back of the Jackson Hole Wine Company. This local favorite has metro-friendly décor in shades of slate and steel. The capacity doubles in summer with additional outdoor seating. The wine list is whatever is on the rack, plus a $10 corkage fee. By the glass, there are usually eight reds, eight whites and two to three roses, along with a few sparkling wines. Koshu is also known for inspired saki cocktails that use fresh ingredients, and an Asian fusion food menu.

Mountain High Pizza Pie

307-733-3646
120 W. Broadway Ave.
Price: Inexpensive to moderate
Hours: 11 AM—11 PM (summer), 11 AM—10 PM
(winter)
Cuisine: Pizzeria
Serving: L, D
Credit Cards: MC, V
Reservations: No

For many locals and tourists, there simply
is no other pizza parlor in Jackson.
Mountain High makes its own dough with
white or whole wheat flour for their crust
and breadsticks. Seating is limited inside
but expands to 12 picnic tables with checkered tablecloths outside. Beer and wine are
served. A delivery service to Teton Village
and Aspens is available after 5 PM. Owner
Bill Field likes to tell patrons that former
President Clinton once stopped in for a
pizza pie.

Nani's Genuine Pasta House

307-733-3888
242 N. Glenwood St.
www.nanis.com
Price: Moderate to expensive
Hours: Enoteca opens at 4 PM; dinner 5—10 PM
Cuisine: Classic Italian
Serving: D
Credit Cards: AE, MC, V
Reservations: Suggested

Each month Nani's features authentic food
and wines from one of Italy's 20 regions,
along with their regular Italian menu. Save
room for the Teton tiramisu, a heaping
helping of ice cream and whipped cream
oozing over three Lady Fingers in the shape
of the Grand, Middle and South Tetons. The
Enoteca Sicula is the wine bar at Nani's and
hosts happy-hour wine tastings from 4 to 6
PM for $10, along with 2-for-1 cocktails.

Nora's Fish Creek Inn

307-733-8288

5600 W. Hwy. 22, Wilson
Price: Moderate
Hours: Call for current hours
Cuisine: Steakhouse, regional
Serving: B, L, D
Credit Cards: AE, D, MC, V
Reservations: Recommended

On any list of don't-miss restaurants in
Jackson Hole, Nora's is always near the top.
House specialties include much more than
fish: elk tenderloin, free-range organic
half-chicken, rack of lamb and baby-back
ribs with Nora's special BBQ sauce. Trout is
served five ways and the sandwich menu
features that western favorite, the buffalo
burger. Breakfast is an event, with more
offerings than the prolific number of locals
dining here regularly. The log interior dotted with tiffany lamps features a slate and
metal fireplace created by a local artist.

Old Yellowstone Garage (OYG)

307-734-6161
175 Center St.
Price: Moderate to expensive
Hours: Call for current hours
Cuisine: Italian, regional
Serving: D
Credit Cards: AE, D, MC, V
Reservations: Suggested

Casually elegant might be the best way to
describe OYG, which started in Dubois and
moved to Jackson in 2000. The chef of OYG
is known for taking regional foods such as
elk shanks and preparing them in the style
of Italy's Piedmont region. Risotto, wood-
oven pizzas made with fresh herbs, fresh
seafood and slow-cooked lamb shank are
among patron favorites. More than 150
selections of wine are on the list, many
appealing to the budget-conscious.

Pica's Mexican Taqueria

307-734-4457 (Jackson), 307-734-7422
(Wilson)
1160 Alpine Lane (Jackson), 5755 W. Hwy.

22 (in Wilson's Stagecoach Bar)
Price: Inexpensive
Hours: Call for current hours
Cuisine: Traditional Mexican
Serving: L, D
Credit Cards: AE, D, MC, V
Reservations: No

For fresh fast food, Pica's is a hit for locals and tourists alike, especially before or after an exhilarating bicycle ride on Teton Pass. Pica's has a daily happy hour from 4–6 PM and is known for tacos al pastor, mahi and chipotle poblano. Tortas are served only at lunch and enchiladas only at dinner. The adjoining bar has two pool tables, and the outside patio is next to a volleyball court and sandbox. The restaurant in Jackson has a larger menu.

Pearl Street Bagels

307-739-1218 (Jackson), 307-739-1261 (Wilson)
145 W. Pearl St.
Price: Inexpensive
Cuisine: Bakery
Serving: B, L, D
Credit Cards: AE, D, MC, V
Reservations: No
Hours: 6:30 AM–6 PM

Pearl Street Bagels has limited seating, so expect to stand or lounge outside because this is the first place many go for their first shot of morning java, especially on weekends. It's a great place to read a newspaper, check the Internet or wind up for a day of outdoor activity. The handmade bagels are pretty fine, too.

Snake River Grill

307-733-0557
84 E. Broadway Ave.
www.snakerivergrill.com
Price: Moderate to expensive
Hours: Opens at 5:30 PM (summers), 6 PM (winters)
Cuisine: Fresh, regional, organic

Serving: D
Credit Cards: AE, DC, MC, V
Reservations: Required

No list of top restaurants in Jackson is complete without the Snake River Grill, one of the trendier and more intimate places to dine. Some would say it is the town's finest. This second-floor restaurant has an ever-changing, seasonal and organic menu with an emphasis on local, free-range ingredients and organic produce. The tables are linen-covered, the wine list award-winning and reservations a necessity because of the high volume of traffic at a restaurant well known beyond Wyoming's borders.

Sweetwater Restaurant

307-733-3553
Corner of King and Pearl
www.sweetwaterrest.com
Price: Moderate
Hours: 11:30 AM–3:30 PM, 5:30–10 PM (summer), 11:30 AM–2:30 PM, 5:30–9:30 PM (winter)
Cuisine: Regional, Mediterranean
Serving: L, D
Credit Cards: AE, D, MC, V
Reservations: Dinner only

This is a popular spot, with its intimate outdoor dining on a patio that's shaded by a large aspen tree in the center and enclosed by a tall hedge for privacy. The courtyard has about 15 tables covered by umbrellas. Sweetwater's menu is best known for the elk medallions and bison New York steak. For a Mediterranean flair, try a Greek salad, Greek lamb wrap or the Meze Platter appetizer with Greek olives, feta and baba ghanoush on toasted pita bread. Sweetwater features a solid wine and microbrew list as well.

The Bunnery

307-733-0075
130 N. Cache Dr.
www.bunnery.com

Price: Inexpensive
Serving: B, L, D (dinner in summers)
Credit Cards: D, MC, V
Reservations: No
Hours: 7 AM–3 PM year-round, plus 5–9 PM summers

The Bunnery is the best-known breakfast stop in a town known for its large breakfasts. Some of the breakfasts are geared to the health-conscious, and all the baked goods are top-shelf. Many bakery items are made from ingredients that the restaurant calls "O.S.M." (oats, sunflower and millet), including the bread for sandwiches. You can't go wrong, but if customers were to be polled, they'd eschew their normal calorie-counting regimen and splurge on the rich coffee cake. There's patio seating, a bakery and gift shop as well.

Honorable Mention

Bar-T-5 Cookout

800-772-5386 or 307-733-5386
812 Cache Creek Dr.
www.bart5.com
Price: Expensive
Hours: 5:15 PM and 6:30 PM Mon.–Sat. (mid-May to mid-Aug.); 4:45 PM and 6:15 PM (Aug. through late Sept.)
Cuisine: Chuckwagon
Serving: D
Credit Cards: DS, MC, V
Reservations: Yes

A live western show, covered-wagon ride into the Bridger-Teton National Forest, and western ballads from the Bar-T-Five Band come to make this a uniquely Wyoming dining experience. Horse-drawn wagons take guests into the Cache Creek Canyon for a hearty riverside cookout meal of Dutch oven chicken and roast beef, potatoes, corn on the cob, beans, rolls and brownies, all savored over gingham table covers. Along the way, you'll meet Indians, cowboys and a mountain man. Prices include sales tax but not gratuity. This Old West experience is more suited to younger children and families than some of the other chuckwagon dinner shows.

Cadillac Grille

307-733-3279
55 N. Cache Dr.
www.cadillac-grille.com
Price: Inexpensive to moderate
Hours: 11:30 AM lunch, 5:30 PM dinner
Cuisine: World
Serving: L, D
Credit Cards: AE, MC, V
Reservations: Recommended

The Cadillac Grille is actually four dining experiences in one complex, each dressed in western chic apparel. At the center is a distinguished and classy restaurant offering fine dining and an extensive menu. Billy's is a 1950s-style diner at the back of the storefront serving ginormous burgers made from lean ground chuck and accompanied by the usual sides. The Cadillac lounge serves beverages and food from Billy's menu. The Garden Terrace can stage group events under a heated cover. The restaurant likes to tout its "rustic Tuscan feel."

El Abuelito

307-733-1207
385 W. Broadway Ave.
Price: Inexpensive
Hours: 11 AM–11 PM Fri.–Sat., 11 AM–10 PM Sun.–Thurs.
Cuisine: Mexican American
Serving: L, D
Credit Cards: AE, D, MC, V
Reservations: Yes

Choices for Mexican food are limited in Jackson, and many locals consider El Abuelito, with its bright atmosphere, the best. The food is served Mex-American style on plates sprawling with the entrée, beans and lettuce. Try the Pulpo al Mojo de Ajo (octopus cooked in garlic butter) or a

RESTAURANTS AND FOOD PURVEYORS

seafood burrito stuffed with real crabmeat. Salad and French fries are available for patrons who don't want the cholesterol-free beans. Cerveza (beer), jumbo margaritas and daiquiris are available from the bar.

Kashman's Place

307-733-5600
325 W. Pearl Ave.
Price: Inexpensive to moderate
Hours: 6 AM–3 PM daily
Cuisine: Deli
Serving: B, L
Credit Cards: AE, D, MC, V
Reservations: No

Everything for breakfast from eggs cooked any style and buttermilk pancakes to French toast stuffed with cream cheese and homemade organic oatmeal makes Kashman's a hot morning ticket. Hot sandwiches include a turkey burger, buffalo burger and Pennsylvania baked ham and brie. Among cold sandwiches are Soho turkey with applewood bacon, Tribeca egg salad and Monsey's garden vegetables. The menu also features a wide range of salads topped with virtually every vegetable in the garden. The Espresso bar serves Seattle's Best coffee. Catering is also offered.

Merry Piglets Mexican Grill

307-733-2966
160 N. Cache
www.merrypiglets.com
Price: Inexpensive
Cuisine: Authentic Mexican
Serving: L, D
Credit Cards: MC, V
Reservations: No

Merry Piglets prides itself on serving authentic Mexican food in the valley for 36 years using no MSGs or lard. Homemade sauces include chipotle, green chile and ranchero. Check out Bug Hartnett's homemade chile con queso by the cup or the

bowl. The bar has a list of more than 30 tequillas.

Mizu Sushi

307-734-5205
3465 N. Pines Way
www.mizusushi.com
Price: Inexpensive
Hours: 5–10 PM Tues.–Sun.
Cuisine: Asian fusion
Serving: D.
Credit Cards: AE, MC, V
Reservations: Recommended

Jackson's newest full sushi bar features such unique Asian creations as Sake-steamed Chilean sea bass with shitake mushrooms and rib eye beef negi maki with enoki mushrooms, asparagus and scallions. Fresh fish and produce are delivered daily.

Rendezvous Bistro

307-739-1100
380 S. Broadway Ave.
Price: Moderate
Hours: 5:30–10 PM nightly, closed Sun. in winter
Cuisine: American bistro
Serving: D
Credit Cards: AE, D, MC, V
Reservations: Recommended

A sophisticated yet casual American bistro atmosphere where locals go to be seen, this spot features Jackson's only raw bar. Oysters on the half-shell, oyster shooters and tuna tartare are popular fare, as is such comfort food as meatloaf. Daily specials offered by chef Roger Freedman (originally from Snake River Grill) range from Wednesday's free-range fried chicken to Sunday's crispy striped bass. Private parties can be arranged.

Rising Sage Cafe

307-733-8649
2820 Rungius Rd., in the National Museum of Wildlife Art
Price: Inexpensive

Hours: 11 AM–3 PM daily
Cuisine: Deli
Serving: L
Credit Cards: AE, D, DC, MC, V
Reservations: No

The Rising Sage's meals are so highly regarded that locals will make the drive 2 miles north of Jackson to have lunch overlooking the National Elk Refuge. Try the Portobello mushroom burger, barbecue sandwich with hand-pulled beef brisket or homemade chili. Residents like to make a day of it on Sunday, when museum admission is free for locals. Tapas Tuesday is from 5:30–9 PM. Catering is also available.

Route 89 Smokehouse Diner

307-733-2492
445 N. Cache Dr.
Price: Inexpensive
Hours: 6 AM–10 PM (summer), 7 AM–9 PM (winter) daily
Cuisine: Traditional American
Serving: B, L, D
Credit Cards: AE, D, MC, V
Reservations: No

This is classic family-vacation dining in a diner atmosphere with barbecue, buffalo burgers, soup and salad bar and home-baked desserts. Slow-smoked prime rib is the Saturday night special. Breakfast is served until 4 PM on Saturdays. Beer, wine and cocktails are also on the menu.

Trio

307-734-8038
45 S. Glenwood St.
www.triobistro.com
Price: Inexpensive to moderate
Hours: Lunch 11:30 AM–2:30 PM Mon.–Fri., dinner 5:30 PM daily
Cuisine: American bistro
Serving: L, D
Credit Cards: AE, D, MC, V
Reservations: Recommended

Owned by three local chefs, the restaurant offers main courses ranging from buffalo burger and wood-fired half-chicken to sautéed trout almandine and linguini with mussels. Trio's extensive drink menu includes wine, elixirs, beer, malt scotch, cognac and liquors. Try the poached white peach or banana crepe for dessert.

The Best of the Rest

Alpenrose Restaurant/Alpenhof Bistro

307-733-3462 (restaurant), 307-733-3242 (bistro)
Teton Village, next to the clock tower
Price: Inexpensive to moderate
Hours: 7 AM–10 PM daily
Cuisine: German, Swiss
Serving: B, D (restaurant), L, D (bistro)
Credit Cards: AE, CB, D, DC, MC, V
Reservations: Yes

Dinners are prepared using Swiss recipes, and chef Steve Farlin prepares Alpine specialties such as Weiner schnitzel and Sauerbraten. Enjoy live music Thursdays, Fridays and Sundays in the bar during the winters. The house specialty is cheese and chocolate fondue for après ski.

Amangani Grill

307-734-7333
1535 N. E. Butte Rd.
www.amanresorts.com
Price: Moderate to expensive
Hours: Call for current hours; guests may order food at any time
Cuisine: Regional gourmet
Serving: B, L, D
Credit Cards: AE, D, MC, V
Reservations: Recommended

The cuisine is in complete harmony with its surroundings at Amangani. Menu selections change seasonally, utilizing fresh produce and regionally produced organic foods. An award-winning wine list will complement your selections. Receptions and private parties can be arranged. There are mountain views from the terrace.

Blu' Kitchen

307-734-1633
155 N. Glenwood St.
www.blukitchen.com
Price: Moderate
Hours: Call for current hours
Cuisine: Global
Serving: D
Credit Cards: AE, MC, V
Reservations: Recommended

This restaurant was opened in 2007 by chef Jarrett Schwartz, formerly of Mizu Sushi. Fresh ingredients, fireside dining, outdoor deck, wines, sake and a full bar make this a pleasurable evening out.

Bon Appe Thai

307-734-0245
245 W. Pearl Ave.
Price: Inexpensive
Hours: 7–11 AM breakfast, 11:30 AM–2:30 PM lunch, 5 PM dinner
Cuisine: Innovative authentic Thai, American
Serving: B, L, D
Credit Cards: D, MC, V
Reservations: Recommended

Bon Appe Thai is an intimate coffee-shop setting serving standard American for breakfast and lunch. Thai dinners include curries, stir fry and noodle entrées. Formerly called Two 45, it's one of the more appreciated ethnic restaurants in town.

Burke's Chop House

307-733-8575
72 S. Glenwood St.
Price: Moderate
Hours: 6 PM nightly
Cuisine: Steakhouse
Serving: D
Credit Cards: AE, D, MC, V
Reservations: Strongly recommended

Steaks, game, chops, pasta, seafood, wood-fired pizzas and such chef specialties as venison tenderloin, beef Wellington and halibut highlight a varied menu.

Camp Creek Inn

307-732-2222
12330 S. Hwy. 191, 15 miles south of Jackson
www.campcreekinn.com
Price: Inexpensive to moderate
Hours: 4 PM (bar), 5 PM (dining room)
Cuisine: Traditional Wyoming cowboy
Serving: D
Credit Cards: AE, D, MC, V
Reservations: Accepted

Camp Creek is home of the "No Mercy One Pound Burger." A restaurant that lists "grubs and suds" says casual fun and a great place to hang. Fish tacos, Idaho trout, prime rib, sleigh-ride dinners, homemade desserts and full bar service ensure everyone in your group will be satisfied.

Cascade Grill House & Spirits

307-732-6932
3385 W. Village Dr.
www.tetonlodge.com
Price: Inexpensive to moderate
Hours: 7 AM–10 PM daily
Cuisine: New Western, regional
Serving: B, L, D
Credit Cards: AE, D, DC, MC, V
Reservations: Recommended

Cascade features game, steaks and seafood entrées prepared over a fire grill. Mountainside dining with views of the Gros Ventres and heated outdoor patio add to the summer setting.

Choice Meats of Jackson Hole

307-739-1599 or 307-733-0450
974 W. Broadway Ave., inside Jackson Whole Grocer.
www.jacksonwholegrocer.com
Price: Inexpensive
Hours: Call for current hours

Cuisine: Take-out healthy deli
Serving: B, L, D
Credit Cards: AE, D, MC, V
Reservations: No

Choice Meats emphasizes healthy choices and caters especially to people looking to get out on the trail quickly. Deli choices are extensive, including free-range roasted chicken, slow-cooked Montana Legend beef, custom-built sandwiches, salads, smoothies and ready-to-go lunch-box specials.

Dornan's Chuckwagon

307-733-2415, ext. 203
In Moose, at south entrance to Grand Teton National Park
Price: Inexpensive to moderate
Season: Early June to mid-Sept.
Hours: 7–11 AM breakfast, noon–3 PM lunch, 5–9 PM dinner
Cuisine: Chuckwagon
Serving: B, L, D
Credit Cards: AE, D, DC, MC, V
Reservations: No

Serving western-style meals since 1948, this outdoor restaurant offers full breakfasts, lunch and Dutch oven dinners with fabulous views of the Tetons and Snake River.

43 Degrees North

307-733-0043
635 S. Cache Dr.
Price: Inexpensive to moderate
Hours: 11:30 AM–3 PM (lunch), 4:30–9:30 PM (dinner)
Cuisine: American
Serving: L, D
Credit Cards: AE, D, MC, V
Reservations: Recommended

43 Degrees North offers a pub atmosphere with its live music and full bar at the base of Snow King Mountain. Specialties include steaks, chops, burgers, pasta, salads and homemade chili.

gamefish

307-732-6040
7710 Granite Loop Rd., Teton Village, at Snake River Lodge & Spa
www.snakeriverlodge.com
Price: Moderate to expensive
Hours: 7–10 AM (breakfast), noon–2 PM (lunch), 5:30–9:30 PM (dinner)
Cuisine: Western American, regional
Serving: B, L, D
Credit Cards: AE, D, DC, MC, V
Reservations: Recommended

Sample entrées at this elegant restaurant at the Snake River Lodge include seared scallops in lobster glace, butternut squash lasagna, wapiti in spiked-cider reduction and Oregon beef short ribs braised in Zonker Stout. There is also a breakfast buffet, fireside bar and featured nightly dinner specials.

The Gun Barrel Steak & Game House

307-733-3287
862 W. Broadway Ave.
www.gunbarrel.com
Price: Moderate
Hours: Call for current hours
Cuisine: Western steakhouse
Serving: D
Credit Cards: AE, D, MC, V
Reservations: Suggested

Mesquite-grilled steaks, wild game, fried green tomatoes, venison bratwurst, velvet elk, buffalo prime rib and Rocky Mountain rainbow trout will make your dinner selection a challenge. Look for the famous bugling elk atop the building.

Jackson Hole Mountain Resort/Bridger Restaurant

307-739-2603
Jackson Hole Mountain Resort
www.couloirrestaurant.com
Price: Inexpensive to expensive (dinner

entrees are $75)
Hours: Call for current hours
Cuisine: World
Serving: L, D
Credit Cards: AE, D, MC, V
Reservations: Accepted

Dining at 9,000 feet after a ride on the Bridger Gondola, with views of the Tetons and Jackson Hole, is a rare experience. Three restaurants offer a variety of dining options. The Couloir offers fine dining, gourmet sandwiches are available at the Headwall Deli and the Mountain Servery is a cafe. The Couloir, which opened in June 2007, features the artistry of chef executive Wes Hamilton, who formerly worked at the Jenny Lake Lodge and Four Seasons. The regional menu offers three- and five-course meals emphasizing organic and locally grown foods. Specialties include prosciutto-wrapped Alaskan halibut, pan-roasted natural chicken and Moroccan spiced breast of duck. Hamilton also offers suggested wine pairings.

Jackson Hole Playhouse & Saddle Rock Saloon

307-733-6994
145 W. Deloney Ave.
www.jhplayhouse.com
Price: Expensive
Season: Early June to late Sept.
Hours: Dinner seatings 5 and 6 PM, show-time 8 PM
Cuisine: Gourmet western
Serving: L, D
Credit Cards: D, MC, V
Reservations: Recommended

Nightly dinner shows are the ticket here, obviously with a western theme. Shows include *Seven Brides for Seven Brothers*, *Oklahoma*, *Paint Your Wagon* and *Cat Ballou*. Tickets are $50 for adults, $36 for children 12 and under. Show only: $25 adults, $18 children. The playhouse, constructed in 1916, is one of the oldest buildings in

Jackson. The Saddle Rock Saloon accepts luncheon show reservations for large groups.

Jedediah's House of Sourdough

307-733-5671
135 E. Broadway Ave.
Price: Inexpensive
Hours: 7 AM–2 PM (breakfast), 11 AM–2 PM (lunch)
Cuisine: Sourdough bakery
Serving: B, L
Credit Cards: AE, D, MC, V
Reservations: No

Jedediah's is everything sourdough, including waffles and wheat cakes for breakfast, buffalo burgers and chicken sandwiches for lunch, carrot cake and brownies for dessert. You can find a heaping helping of sourdough at the Jackson Hole Airport.

Mangy Moose Restaurant and Saloon

307-733-4913
Jackson Hole Mountain Resort, Teton Village
www.mangymoose.net
Price: Moderate
Hours: 11:30 AM–5 PM lunch, 5:30–9:30 PM
Cuisine: Steakhouse, seafood
Serving: L, D
Credit Cards: AE, MC, V
Reservations: Yes

Wines, full bar, salad bar, homemade breads and desserts, and regular live entertainment are the specialties at this long-time Jackson Hole landmark. Though some locals say it's lost its appeal, the Mangy Moose definitely remains a mainstay and is still a favored stop among tourists. The salad bar is excellent and bread is baked fresh daily.

Shades Cafe

307-733-2015
82 S. King St.
Price: Inexpensive

Hours: 7:30 AM–4 PM daily
Cuisine: Eclectic
Serving: B, L
Credit Cards: MC, V
Reservations: No

Jackson's original coffeehouse is a popular breakfast spot and sports a quaint setting in an original log cabin with random, reclaimed furniture. A highlight is deck dining under an old willow tree in the summer.

Sidewinders Sports Grill and Tavern

307-734-5766
945 W. Broadway Ave.
Price: Inexpensive to moderate
Hours: 11:30 AM–2 AM daily
Cuisine: New York pizzeria
Serving: L, D
Credit Cards: AE, D, MC, V
Reservations: No

Sandwiches, pizzas and salads and 28 draft beers are all here for the sports buff. Sidewinders has foosball, an arcade, 39 televisions and a kids menu. Look for the giant American flag.

Silver Dollar Bar & Grill

307-732-3939
50 N. Glenwood St., in Wort Hotel
www.worthotel.com/silverdollar_home.html
Price: Moderate to expensive
Hours: Call for current hours
Cuisine: Regional
Serving: B, L, D
Credit Cards: AE, D, MC, V
Reservations: Recommended

Famed for its buffalo baby-back ribs and 2,032 inlaid 1921 silver dollars, this historic bar survived a 1980s fire and has come back decked in rich memorabilia. Modern adornments include eight televisions featuring NFL and NHL Game Plans, a 60-inch big-screen TV, a nightly happy hour and live entertainment.

Snake River Brewing Company and Restaurant

307-739-2337
265 S. Millward St.
www.snakeriverbrewing.com
Price: Inexpensive
Hours: 11:30 AM–midnight daily
Cuisine: Brew pub
Serving: L, D
Credit Cards: AE, D, MC, V
Reservations: No

Winner of the Small Brewery of the Year honors in 2000 and 2001 and gold medals for its Zonker Stout and OB-1 Certified Organic Ale in 2006, this fun little brew pub serves pasta, sandwiches and salads to complement the beers.

Thai Me Up

307-733-0005
75 E. Pearl Ave.
Price: Inexpensive to moderate
Hours: 11:30 AM–2:30 PM (lunch), 5:30 PM–close (dinner); closing time depends on crowds
Cuisine: Thai
Serving: L, D
Credit Cards: AE, D, MC, V
Reservations: Recommended

This popular restaurant features typical Thai dishes and vegan/vegetarian items that include organic tofu. There is a daily chef's menu and full bar. Ask for a ride in their three-wheeled rickshaw from Bangkok.

Vertical

307-734-2375
3345 W. Village Dr., Teton Village, at the Best Western Inn at Jackson Hole
www.innatjh.com/amenities_vertical.htm
Price: Moderate
Hours: Call for current hours
Cuisine: New American
Serving: B, D
Credit Cards: AE, MC, V
Reservations: Recommended

Seasonal menus and special features such as elk tenderloin and ribs, wild sockeye salmon, duck and island chicken make for a unique dining experience near the ski hill. There are inspired daily specials and vegetarian options.

Wild Sage Restaurant at the Rusty Parrot Lodge

307-733-2000
175 N. Jackson St.
www.rustyparrot.com
Price: Inexpensive to moderate
Hours: Call for current hours
Cuisine: Regional, seafood
Serving: B, D
Credit Cards: AE, D, MC, V
Reservations: Recommended

This distinctive restaurant offers Montana Legend beef, elk loin, organic lamb, halibut cheeks, smoked duck and an extensive wine list. These are just a few tempting reasons why the Wild Sage earned a four-diamond designation from AAA.

Alta, Wyoming

Targhee Steakhouse/Trap Bar & Grille

800-827-8433 or 307-353-2300
3300 E. Ski Hill Rd.
Price: Inexpensive to moderate
Season: Year-round
Hours: Open daily
Cuisine: Steakhouse
Serving: B, L, D
Credit Cards: MC, V
Reservations: Accepted in restaurant

This typical steakhouse is the only restaurant and bar at the base of Grand Targhee Resort. Bands play live music on Mondays, Thursdays and Saturdays at the Trap Bar & Grille.

Driggs, Idaho

Warbirds Cafe

208-354-2550

At Teton Valley airport
www.tetonaviation.com
Price: Moderate to expensive
Season: Year-round (closed for one month in spring after Grand Targhee closes, reopens Mother's Day)
Hours: 7–11 AM breakfast Sat.–Sun., 11 AM–2 PM lunch daily, 5–9 PM dinner Wed.–Sun.
Cuisine: Regional American, International
Serving: B, L, D
Credit Cards: AE, D, MC, V
Reservations: Yes

It isn't often that an airport restaurant has such renown, but folks in Wyoming, Montana and Idaho with private planes will make a trip here just for the breakfast. Morning menu items include crab cakes benedict and smoked trout hash. Lunch is known for such entrée salads as chicken salad with gorgonzola and grapes. Dinner is famous for elk and buffalo entrees as well as fresh fish flown in daily. The menu changes with the seasons and most dishes can be prepared for vegetarians. A full bar, a small but thoughtful wine list and mostly locally produced beers in the bottle or on draft add to the appeal. Special buffets are held on Easter and Mother's Day; live jazz can be heard most Friday nights. There is a free museum of "warbirds" (military planes that have been restored and are operable) on site, hence the name.

Dubois, Wyoming

Cowboy Cafe

307-455-2595
115 E. Ramshorn St.
Price: Inexpensive to moderate
Season: Year-round
Hours: 6:30 AM–9 PM (earlier close in winter)
Cuisine: Regional western
Serving: B, L, D
Credit Cards: AE, D, MC, V
Reservations: No

This often-busy cafe sports the largest menu in town and is known for hearty breakfasts, large portions and ranch-sized desserts. Menu items like steak, shrimp, Cobb salad, trout, BBQ ribs, salmon, beef liver, maple pecan pork chops or smoked chicken make roping in a decision tough. Or, just ask for the rib eye served with the chef's special bourbon sauce. Belly up to the bar for a glass of wine, beer or local microbrew. One thing's for certain: you won't leave hungry.

Peter's Cafe

307-527-5040
129 Sheridan Ave.
Price: Inexpensive
Season: Year-round
Hours: 6:45 AM–6 PM Mon.–Sat.
Cuisine: American cafe
Serving: B, L
Credit Cards: MC, V.
Reservations: No

They pile the subs and sandwiches high with meat here. Breakfast specialties include pancakes, eggs any style, biscuits and gravy.

Rustic Pine Steakhouse

307-455-2772
119 E. Ramshorn St.
www.rusticpinetavern.com
Price: Moderate
Season: Year-round
Hours: 5:30–9:30 PM Tues.–Sat.
Cuisine: American steakhouse
Serving: D
Credit Cards: MC, V
Reservations: No

Traditionally the No. 1 watering hole in Dubois, this historic 1930s restaurant is a classic western tavern known for its excellent food, service and drive-up beverage window. Steaks, chops, burgers, seafood and a full bar lure diners from miles around. The restaurant and bar are filled with western memorabilia and log furniture. Eat downstairs amid music, billiards and darts in the bar, or move upstairs for a cozier, quieter experience on wood tables with checkered tablecloths.

FOOD PURVEYORS IN YELLOWSTONE AND GRAND TETON NATIONAL PARKS

Yellowstone National Park

General stores with limited groceries, drinks and snacks are located at Bridge Bay, Canyon, Fishing Bridge, Grant Village, Lake, Mammoth, Old Faithful and Tower Fall.

Grand Teton National Park

No grocery stores are located within the park boundaries.

FOOD PURVEYORS IN YELLOWSTONE/TETON GATEWAY COMMUNITIES

Bakeries

CODY
Heritage Bakery (307-587-2622; 1526 Wyoming Ave.)
Peter's Cafe and Bakery (307-527-5040; www.peters-cafe.com; 1219 Sheridan Ave.) Cookies, Danish, pies, cinnamon rolls, scones, brownies.
Sweetheart Bakery (307-587-3862; 326 C St.)

DRIGGS
Idalia's Organic Bakery (208-354-5900; 105 E. Johnson Ave. #F)
Pendl's Bakery & Cafe (208-354-5623; www.pendlspastries.com; P.O. Box 784) Austrian pastries.

JACKSON

The Bunnery (307-734-0075, 800-349-0492; www.bunnery.com; 130 Cache Dr.) The hottest place for breakfast in town also has Jackson Hole's best daily assortment of fresh-baked goods. Coffee cakes, muffins, croissants and sandwich breads are made from the Bunnery's trademark "OSM" (oatmeal, sunflower and millet). Take it to go, eat inside and savor an idyllic northwest Wyoming morning on the shaded deck. Open 7 AM–9 PM (summer), 7 AM–3 PM (winter).

Harvest Natural Foods Cafe (307-733-5418; 130 W. Broadway Ave.) Organic ingredients for fresh-baked pastries and bread comes from regional producers. Also serves breakfast and lunch.

Jackson Hole Bakery (307-734-1253; 1160 Alpine Lane)

Wild Flour Bakery (307-734-2455; 1410 Gregory Lane) French baguettes, pies, bread, cookies, pastries, etc.

WEST YELLOWSTONE

Sweetheart Bakery (406-646-7800; 425 Firehole Ave.)

Tubby's Bakery (406-646-9737; 29 Kenyon St.)

Breweries

JACKSON

Snake River Brewing Company
208-739-2337
www.snakeriverbrewing.com
265 S. Millward St.
More than 20 brews, many of them good for gold medals, ranging from the light Indian Paintbrush Pilsner to the dark Zonker Stout. Give the Ned Flanders Brown Ale, Snake River Pale Ale and Snake River Lager a taste as well. The bar features a half-dozen or more of Snake River's beers on tap. Lunch and dinner are served as well in this energetic gathering place.

VICTOR

Grand Teton Brewing Company (208-787-4000; www.grandtetonbrewing.com; Hwy. 33, just east of Victor) Six different beers, including Old Faithful Ale, Teton Ale and Bitch Creek ESB. Try Old Faithful Root Beer or Teton Jack Ginger Ale for a refreshing nonalcoholic brew.

WEST YELLOWSTONE

Wolf Pack Brewing Company (406-646-7225; www.wolfpackbrewing.com; 139 N. Canyon St.) Wolf Pack is known for authentic German lagers, especially its award-winning Wapiti Wheat and Old Snaggletooth Schwarzbier.

Candy and Ice Cream

CODY

Sweet Sisters Candies (307-587-8212; 1362 Sheridan Ave.) Chocolate confections, fudge, truffles, brittles, and sugar-free selections. Formerly Cowtown Candy Co.

GARDINER

Yellowstone Gifts & Sweets (406-848-7011; 108 2nd St. S.) Candy, ice cream, espresso, gifts, art, and jewelry.

Minnie's Old Fashioned Fountain and Candy Store (406-848-7745; US Hwy. 89 north of Gardiner)

JACKSON

Cioccolato (307-734-6400; www.cioccolato express.com; 225 N. Cache Dr.) Exquisite handmade chocolates, truffles, bonbons, Mexican cakes and espresso drinks.

Moo's Gourmet Ice Cream (307-733-1998; 36 E. Broadway Ave.) 32 flavors of organic ice cream, sorbet and dairy products. Belgian truffles.

The Bunnery (307-734-0075, 800-349-0492; www.bunnery.com; 130 N. Cache Dr.)

Yippy I-O Candy (307-739-3920; 84 E.

Broadway Ave.) More than 600 kinds of candy, ranging from chocolate and fudge to jelly beans. Open 10 AM–9 PM.

WEST YELLOWSTONE

Amazen Yellowstone (406-646-4321; 140 Madison Ave.) Shaved ice, ice cream, candy, games and a giant maze.

Rustic Candy Shop (406-646-7538; www .rusticcandyshop.com; 33 N. Canyon St.) Family recipes for taffy, peanut brittle, fudge, fruits, and chocolates.

Coffee Shops

CODY

Beta Coffeehouse (307-587-7707; 1132 12th St.)

Breadboard (307-527-5788; 1725 17th St.)

Cody Coffee Co. and Eatery (307-527-7879; 1702 Sheridan Ave.)

Daylight Donuts (307-527-7658; 1452 Sheridan Ave.)

Rawhide Coffee (307-587-6807; 1155 Sheridan Ave.)

JACKSON

Bagel Jax's (307-733-9148; 145 N. Glenwood St.) Bagels and egg sandwiches.

Betty Rock Coffee House & Cafe (307-733-0747; www.bettyrockcafe.com; 325 W. Pearl Ave.) Coffee cakes, bagels, reading area and artists' work featured.

Hard Drive Cafe (307-733-5282; www .harddrivecafe.biz; 1110 Maple Way) Internet cafe, organic, fair-trade, wraps, panini and sandwiches.

Mountunes Music Espresso & Internet Cafe (307-733-4514; 265 W. Broadway Ave.) Internet.

Pearl Street Bagels (307-739-1218; 245 W. Pearl Ave.) Jackson's most popular stop for coffee and bagels.

Shades Cafe (307-733-2015; 82 S. King St.) Log cabin setting with waffles and drinks named after area landmarks.

WEST YELLOWSTONE

The Book Peddler (406-646-9358; 106 Canyon St.)

Go-Go Expresso (406-646-0820; 302 Firehole Ave.)

Mocha Mommas (406-646-7744; www .freeheelandwheel.com/mocha; 40 Yellowstone Ave.) Italian coffee, homemade cookies and snacks.

Morning Glory Coffee & Tea (406-646-7071; www.morningglory.net; 129 N. Dunraven St.) Coffees from around the world, specialty drinks, baked goods, gifts and collectibles.

Timberline Cafe (406-646-9349; 135 Yellowstone Ave.)

WILSON

Pearl Street Bagels (307-739-1218; 245 W. Pearl St.)

Starbucks (307-733-7473; 3447 N. Pines Way) Coffee cake and pastries.

Farmers Markets

Cody Farmers Market (307-358-0778) Ninth St. by City Park, 4–8 PM Friday, July to mid-October. Open-air market.

Cody Farmers Market (307-754-8225) Albertson's parking lot, 4:30–6 PM Thursday, early July to October.

Dubois Community Food Market (307-455-2182) No. 9 South First St., noon–3 PM Saturday, July to mid-September. Open-air market.

Jackson Farmers Market (307-690-2657; www.jacksonholefarmersmarket.org)

Town Square, 8–11 AM Saturday, July to September. Live music, cooking demonstrations, fresh fruits, vegetables, flowers and baked goods.

Fast Food

CODY

Burger King (307-587-6500; 1910 Mountain View Dr.)

Dairy Queen (307-587-2151; 1701 Eighth St.)

Dominos Pizza (307-587-4781; 1454 Sheridan Ave.)

Dominos Pizza (307-587-4784; 2201 17th
St., Unit 7)

McDonald's (307-527-6423, 2005 17th St.)

Papa Murphy's Take & Bake Pizza (307-
587-6601, 1901 17th St.)

Pizza Hut (307-527-7819; 736 Yellowstone
Ave.)

Pizza On The Run (307-587-8875; 1302
Yellowstone Ave.)

Quiznos (307-587-5746; 2201 17th St.)

Subway (307-527-5052; 1913 17th St.)

Subway–Wal-Mart (307-587-5825; 321
Yellowstone Ave.)

Taco Bell (307-527-6565; 2207 17th St.)

Taco John's (307-527-6424; 1001 Sheridan
Ave.)

Wendy's (307-527-7636; 1456 Sheridan
Ave.)

DRIGGS

Burger King (208-354-3185; 195 N. Main
St.)

Subway (208-354-7827; 131 Valley Center
Dr.)

GARDINER

Subway (406-848-9448; 401 Scott St. W.)

ISLAND PARK

Subway (208-558-7471; 4141 Sawtelle Peak
Rd.)

JACKSON

Billy's Giant Hamburgers (307-733-3279;
55 N. Cache Dr.)

Dairy Queen (307-733-2232; 575 N. Cache
Dr.)

McDonald's (307-733-7444; 1110 W.
Broadway Ave.)

Quiznos Subs (307-733-0201; 1325 S. Hwy.
89)

Subway (307-739-1965; 1357 S. Hwy. 89)

Taco Bell (307-739-9229; 399 W.
Broadway Ave.)

Wendy's (307-733-5636; 525 W. Broadway
Ave.)

WEST YELLOWSTONE

Arby's (406-646-7101; 138 Firehole Ave.)

Dairy Queen (406-646-4106; 40 N.
Canyon St.)

KFC (406-646-9011; 120 Firehole Ave.)

McDonald's (406-646-4592; 100 S.
Canyon St.)

Subway (406-646-4132; 215 Canyon St.)

Grocery Stores

ASHTON

Dave's IGA (208-652-7771; 108 S. US Hwy.
20)

CODY

Albertson's (307-527-7007; 1825 17th St.)

Red Eagle Food Store (307-587-5554; 1543
Depot Dr.)

Red Eagle Food Store (307-587-9331; 221
Yellowstone Ave.)

DRIGGS

Broulim's Supermarkets (208-354-2350;
240 S. Main St.)

DUBOIS

Dubois Super Foods (307-455-2402; 455
Ramshorn St.)

GARDINER

North Entrance Shopping Center (406-
848-7524; 701 Scott St. W.)

JACKSON

Albertson's (307-733-5950; 109 Buffalo
Way)

Creekside Market & Deli (307-733-7926;
545 N. Cache Dr.)

Foodtown (307-733-0450; 970 W.
Broadway Ave.)

Helen's Market & Deli (307-733-9888;
582 E. Broadway Ave.)

Point Store (307-739-1367; 10880 S. US
Hwy. 89)

Smith's Food and Drug (307-733-8908;
1425 S. US Hwy. 89)

VICTOR
Victor Valley Market (208-787-2230; 5 S. Main St.)

WEST YELLOWSTONE
Food Roundup Supermarket (406-646-7501; 107 N. Dunraven St.)
Marketplace (406-646-9600; 22 Madison Ave.)

Health Food Stores
CODY
Mountain High Health Foods (307-587-1700; 1914 17th St.)
Whole Foods Trading Co. (307-587-3213; 1239 Rumsey Ave.)

JACKSON
Harvest Natural Foods (307-733-5418; 130 W. Broadway Ave.) Organic produce and breads.
Jackson Whole Grocer (307-733-0450; 974 W. Broadway Ave.) Organic meats, poultry, fish and produce.
The Herb Store (307-733-0450; 170 E. Deloney Ave.) Culinary and medicinal herbs.

Liquor Stores
CODY
Cooter Brown's (307-587-6261; 1134 13th St.)
Downtowner Liquors (307-587-9481; 1535 Sheridan Ave.)
Eastgate Liquors (307-587-3380; 1801 17th St.)
Rocky Mountain Discount Liquor (307-587-2980; 1820 17th St.)
3 H Bar Liquor (307-587-3661; 1907 Big Horn Dr.)
West Strip Discount Liquors (307-527-5391; 219 Yellowstone Ave.)
Whisky River Discount Liquor (307-587-6461; 544 Yellowstone Ave.)

DRIGGS
The Beverage Shop (208-354-8414; 465 S. Main St.)

GARDINER
North Entrance Shopping Center (406-848-7524; 701 Scott St. W.)

JACKSON
Horse Creek Station (307-733-0810; south of Jackson)
Jackson Whole Grocer (307-733-0450; 974 W. Broadway Ave.)
Liquor Store/Wine Loft (307-733-4466; 115 Buffalo Way)
Plaza Liquors (307-733-8888; 832 W. Broadway Ave.)
Teton Liquors (307-739-1122; 520 S. Hwy. 89)
Virginian Liquor Store (307-733-8741; 750 W. Broadway Ave.)
Wagon Wheel Village Liquor (307-733-8741; 475 Cache St.)

TETON VILLAGE
Mangy Moose Market & Cellars (307-734-0070; 3285 W. McCollister Dr.)
Teton Village Bottle Shop (307-732-2337; 3200 W. McCollister Dr.)

WEST YELLOWSTONE
Montana State Liquor Store (406-646-9600; 22 Madison Ave.)

WILSON
Stagecoach Liquor Store (307-733-4590; 5755 W. Hwy. 22)

Wine Shops
JACKSON
Dornan's Wine Shoppe
307-733-2415, ext. 202
www.dornans.com
At the Southeast Entrance to Grand Teton National Park
Hours: 10 AM–10 PM daily

Before or after a meal at Dornan's pizzeria or restaurant, check out the largest wine selection in northwest Wyoming—up to 1,700 bottles. *Food and Wine* magazine gave the Wine Shoppe one of its "Superior Selection" awards. Make a note of the periodic "Wine Tasting on a Budget" events, which take place every two months or so.

Jackson Hole Wine Company

307-739-9463
www.jhwine.com
200 W. Broadway Ave.
Hours: 10 AM–10 PM daily, noon–10 PM Sun.

Stop by for Friday wine tastings and sample different wines each week. Jackson Hole Wine Company doesn't have the largest selection in the valley, but it might have the most sophisticated and international. Buy a bottle to enjoy at the Koshu Bar in back.

Westside Wine & Spirits

307-733-5038
www.westsidewineandspirits.com
The Aspens on Teton Village Rd., 4 miles south of Teton Village and 4 miles north of Wilson
Hours: 10 AM–9 PM daily

More than 800 bottles are in stock for Teton Village or Wilson visitors who don't want to battle the traffic in Jackson.

6

RECREATION

Surfing. That completes the list of recreation activities that aren't available in the Greater Yellowstone ecosystem—though enterprising youths have learned to ride wave trains on rivers outside the parks by attaching boogie boards to bridges and trees using rope.

If it can be done outdoors, it can be done here, and there's something for every time of year. Hiking, camping, bicycling, climbing and more under glorious summer skies. Fishing, hunting and mountain biking on crisp autumn days. Skiing, snowshoeing and snowmobiling on delicate powder on bright winter days. Even spring, with its unpredictable weather, slushy roads and mucky trails, is a harbinger of brighter days to come, offering some of the best times to fish and *the* best time to ride a road bicycle in Yellowstone.

Be advised that in an effort to put the ecosystem first, rules regarding recreation in Yellowstone and Grand Teton National Parks have evolved. No group of outdoor enthusiasts has been affected more than snowmobilers, whose activities are tightly regulated and could one day be banned altogether. Park newspapers and rangers at visitor centers also will have updated information on closures due to bear activity, fire or warm fishing waters. Even so, there are thousands of square miles of national forest and wilderness beyond the park's borders, opening up a new world to the adventurous.

Here's a closer look at all the Greater Yellowstone ecosystem has to offer for the active and the curious:

BALLOONING

Albuquerque it isn't, but the countryside around Yellowstone and Grand Teton can't be topped for scenic beauty and wildlife viewing in the calm postdawn hours when the sun is just creeping over the eastern horizon. The Wild West Balloon Fest takes place in early August at Cody's Mentock Park and typically features about 20 balloons. Spectators can watch or volunteer to join five-person balloon crews. **Teton Balloon Flights** offers early-morning rides in nine-story balloons on the gentler but still spectacular west side of the Grand Tetons. **Wyoming Balloon Company** offers hour-long rides over the largest private open space in Jackson Hole, bordering on Grand Teton National Park.

Balloon Festivals
Teton Valley Balloon Festival, Jackson, Wyoming, late June.
Wild West Balloon Fest, Cody, Wyoming, early August.

Balloon Tours

Teton Balloon Flights (866-533-6404 P.O. Box 188, Driggs, ID 83422)

Wyoming Balloon Company (307-739-0900; www.wyomingballoon.com; P.O. Box 2578, Jackson, WY 83001) charges $235 adults, $135 children (6–12); includes champagne and hotel shuttles.

Bicycling/Mountain Biking

At first pedal stroke, you'll think Yellowstone and Grand Teton National Parks would be a cycling paradise. Miles of winding roads and spectacular views. A stunning proximity to wildlife. A sensory feast of rushing water, pine-scented air and distant calls of the wild. And it's all true. Here's the rub, especially for road cyclists: The roads are narrow, and they're crowded from Memorial Day to Labor Day. Stories of cyclists getting clipped by the passenger-side rearview mirror of an RV are legend, and many avoid the parks altogether in summer. Mountain bikers can get away from the crowds, but trails are limited. Fat-tire enthusiasts will be happier in Jackson Hole, which fancies itself as Moab without the crowds. Adventure Cycling in Moose has a map detailing at least two-dozen rides, ranging from the relatively flat to hair-raising. Teton Mountain Bike Tours (800-733-0788) offers group rides in and around both parks. Many of Jackson Hole's best rides extend into Idaho. Remember that bicyclists are required to obey all traffic laws that apply to cars, trucks and campers.

Yellowstone National Park

Road Cycling

Locals know the trick to road cycling in Yellowstone: Go in April and early May, after snow melt yet before the roads open to general auto traffic. You'll find that the park is a cyclist's nirvana, with all 300 miles of roads to yourself. Most pavement is rolling with gentle

Cycling is a great way to see the park up close and personal, though summer traffic can make it treacherous at times. National Park Service

climbs, though Dunraven, Craig and Sylvan passes will challenge the fittest. A favored ride is the Hayden Valley, where wildlife abounds in spring. Be prepared for sudden inclement weather regardless of season, and bring bear spray, especially during those off-traffic months. Prime time for road cycling coincides with when bears are hungriest, and they have occasionally chased bicyclists. At all times, it's best to go with at least three other riders. Always pedal single file, wear reflective clothing, strap on a helmet and observe all traffic laws.

Mountain biking

There are five designated mountain-bike trails: Bunsen Peak near Mammoth Hot Springs, Lower Geyser Basin, Lone Star Geyser, Old Faithful and Natural Bridge. In addition, mountain bikers are allowed on the gravel Old Gardiner Road and Blacktail Plateau Drive. Most hiking trails are off-limits to bikes.

Grand Teton National Park

Road Cycling

Grand Teton features 100 miles of paved roads and tremendous views for the thin-tire crowd. There isn't much variation in terrain, and most is relatively flat, so don't expect a great workout. The best ride is Teton Park Road from Jackson Lake Junction to Moose. From there, pedal the winding paved portion of the Moose-Wilson Road through aspen and pine, keeping an eye out for wildlife. It's the one place on pavement where park terrain varies. The 3-mile Jenny Lake Scenic Drive is worth a side trip, and Antelope Flats has limited traffic.

Mountain Biking

If you're on fat tires, continue on the gravel portion of the Moose-Wilson Road for several more miles before the road is paved and widened for the Jackson Hole Ski Area crowd. In some places, roads have comfortable shoulders; in many places, they don't. Mountain bikers have limited options within the park. Trails are off-limits. The 3-mile Two-Ocean Lake Road ride, the 15-mile River Road along the Snake, and the 52 miles on Grassy Lake Road from Flagg Ranch to Ashton are exceptional experiences. For a true muscle-grinder, ride to the summit of Shadow Mountain, so named because the Tetons cast a shadow on it at sunset. Much of the ride is outside the park, but it starts and ends inside the east boundary.

Jackson Hole

Road Cycling

On a clear, calm morning, visitors to Jackson will readily notice a steady stream of cyclists heading west on WY 22 through Wilson, where they begin the arduous 6 percent grade up to Teton Pass. For a breezier ride, go south from Wilson on Fish Creek Road or, if you don't mind the golf-course construction, from Wilson to Teton Village on a newly constructed bike path. Jackson also is in the process of developing a paved trail system.

Mountain Biking

For the fat-tire crowd, Jackson is heaven. It doesn't have Moab's slick-rock, but neither does it have the crowds. Try these muscle-wrenching single-tracks and solitary trails:

Black Canyon Creek: Not for the faint of heart, this 11-miler is either all lactic-burning uphill (3 miles) or hair-raising descent (8 miles), starting near the top of Teton Pass at Old Pass Road and finishing in Wilson. The views of Jackson Hole would be spectacular—if you dared look up long enough from this technical trail.

Cache Creek: This 23-miler starts at the base of Snow King and winds through aspen and pine high into a meadow, where cyclists are rewarded with a sweet descent toward US 191.

Dog Creek: A relatively flat single-track that starts near Hoback Junction and continues through grasses and spruce to the base of Indian Peak. Modest bike-handling skills are required for this one.

Monument Ridge Loop: One of the area's most popular rides, this 21-mile loop features a heady ascent and screaming descent that's all too short. Catch your breath at the fire lookout at the crest. The climb is on a paved and then gravel Forest Service road about 15 miles south of Hoback Junction; the return descent is mostly on single track.

Phillips Canyon: An arduous and technical 14.6-miler mostly on single track with stream crossings and tough turns. For a less-strenuous version, i.e., avoiding the ascent, drive to the Phillips Pass parking lot about halfway up Teton Pass. The trailhead is 1 mile up Trail Creek Road from WY 22 at Wilson.

Other Bicycling in the Area

Given the scenery of Yellowstone, Grand Teton and Jackson Hole, it's not surprising that first-rate bicycling awaits just outside their boundaries. Try these bonus rides:

Road Cycling

Paradise Valley: Just north of Gardiner, East River Road splits to the right from US 89 and continues north until it rejoins the highway at Carter's Bridge just south of Livingston. Traffic is light, the road is relatively flat and deer are everywhere. Views of the Absaroka and Gallatin Mountains are stupendous, and you can soak tired muscles at Chico Hot Springs midway.

Mesa Falls Scenic Byway: This one is more of a muscle-wrencher, but you'll be rewarded with solitude, views of the Tetons and Warm River, and stops at the upper and lower falls of the Henry's Fork of the Snake River. Start in Ashton, Idaho, or near Osborne Bridge on US 20 just south of Last Chance, Idaho. It's 25 miles, so you might consider an out-and-back.

Mountain Biking

Tunnel: Just off the Mesa Falls Scenic Byway northeast of Ashton is an intriguing ride suitable for beginners, at least for a few miles. Start at Warm River Campground just off ID 47 and continue on a gentle ascent on the old Union Pacific railroad grade. The trail follows scenic Warm River to the tunnel, which arrives quickly. After that, it's a designated trail for another 50 miles to the Montana border. It's a bit more challenging because of the gravel, and you're sure to encounter ATVs as you get closer to the spring headwaters of the Henry's Fork of the Snake.

Teton Valley: Lesser known are the Aspen Trail, Mill Creek Trail and Horseshoe Canyon Trails that traverse the gentler but still rugged foothills leading up to the Tetons east of the town of Driggs.

Bicycle Rentals, Repairs and Tours

JACKSON
Cooke City Bike Shack (307-838-2412)
The Edge Sports (307-734-3916; 490 W. Broadway Ave.)
Hoback Sports/Fat Tire Tours (307-733-5335; 520 W. Broadway Ave.) Jackson's first bicycle shop.
Sternberg Bicycles (307-733-7081; 5570 S. US Hwy. 89)
Teton Cycle Works (307-733-4386; 175 N. Glenwood St.)
Teton Mountain Bike Tours (800-733-0788)

MOOSE
Adventure Sports (307-733-3307)

Old Faithful
Xanterra Parks and Resorts (866-439-7375; Old Faithful Inn)

Teton Village
Teton Village Sports (307-733-2181; Crystal Springs Lodge)
Wildernest Sports (307-733-4297; Village Center Building)

WEST YELLOWSTONE
Free Heel and Wheel Bicycles (406-646-7744; www.freeheelandwheel.com; 40 Yellowstone Ave.) Mountain bike rentals, trailers, repairs and bike racks. Specializes in Nordic skiing in winter.
Yellowstone Bicycles (406-646-7815; 132 Madison Ave.) Rentals, repairs and accessories.

WILSON
Wilson Backcountry Sports (307-733-5228; located downtown)

BOATING

Yellowstone and Grand Teton have no shortage of places to enjoy a peaceful afternoon on a lake, whether it's the broad waters of Jackson or Yellowstone or such smaller jewels as Leigh and Jenny. Several lakes feature launches for canoes, kayaks or recreational boats, and some have marinas where rentals are available.

As placid as these lakes appear, there are inherent dangers and caution is advised. Waters are *cold,* and an unexpected dunking far from shore is a surefire path to hypothermia and possibly death, especially in the 41-degree waters of Yellowstone Lake. In 2007, two canoeists flipped and perished on Shoshone Lake. Keep an eye on the horizon for storms that could turn a serene day into a tragedy. *Always stay within 100 yards of shore.*

Permits are required for all boats in Yellowstone and Grand Teton; Yellowstone's boating season is May 1 to November 1. Motorized-boat permits for Yellowstone may be obtained at the Bridge Bay Marina, Grant Village Backcountry Store, Lake Ranger Station, Lewis Lake Campground and South Entrance. Nonmotorized boat permits are available at Bechler Ranger Station, Canyon Backcountry Office, Lewis Lake Ranger Station, Mammoth Backcountry Office, the Northeast Entrance, Old Faithful Backcountry Office and West

Entrance. Fees are $20 annually and $10 for 10 days for motorized vessels, $10 annual and $5 for 10 days for nonmotorized.

Grand Teton permits are available at all ranger stations and visitor centers. Motorized boats are allowed only on Jackson, Jenny and Phelps Lakes; Jenny Lake motors must be 8 horsepower or less. No motorized boats are allowed on the Snake River within park boundaries. A Coast Guard–approved personal flotation device (PFD) is required for each person on board.

Marinas

Yellowstone National Park

Bridge Bay (307-344-7311), which provides access to Yellowstone Lake just south of Lake Village, is open from 8 AM to 8 PM to rent boats and dock space ($12–16). Scenic cruises ($10.50, $6.75 children), guided fishing trips ($66–85/hr), and backcountry shuttles also are available. Rowboats are $8 an hour. Forty-HP outboards are $37 an hour. No reservations are accepted. It is the lake's only marina, given the demise of the spendy Grant Village Marina, which today is unusable.

Grand Teton National Park

Colter Bay (800-628-9988, 307-543-3100; www.gtlc.com) has 9.9-HP motorboat, rowboat and canoe rentals. Jackson Lake Cruises also are an option at Colter Bay's marina, including narrated breakfast and dinner floats. The latter trip is to Elk Island.

Leek's Marina (307-543-2494; www.signalmountainlodge.com) is just north of Colter Bay and is as well-known for its pizzeria as its boating facilities. Overnight docks and gas are available.

One of the perks of staying at Yellowstone Lake is access to the Bridge Bay Marina. National Park Service

Signal Mountain Lodge (307-733-5470, 307-543-2831; www.signalmountainlodge.com) rents deck cruisers, pontoon boats, runabouts, motorboats, canoes and sea kayaks for Jackson Lake from mid-June to early September, Rates range from $12 an hour for the kayaks to $79 for a deck cruiser. Signal Mountain also has Snake River float trips for $51.

Boat Ramps

Lewis Lake has a ramp for motorized and nonmotorized craft at the south tip, just off the road between the South Entrance and West Thumb. This launch provides the only boating access to Shoshone Lake, via a channel that's sometimes too shallow for paddling. Motorized craft are allowed only on Lewis Lake; they are prohibited on Shoshone and in the channel.

Jenny Lake has a boat dock at the southern end of the lake, where the shuttle takes hikers or backpackers across to Inspiration Point.

Tours

Jackson Hole Kayak School (307-733-2471; www.jacksonholekayak.com) teaches kayaking and offers backcountry-kayaking tours. Options range from lessons on Slide Lake to three-day tours on Yellowstone Lake and Shoshone and Lewis Lakes.

O.A.R.S. (800-346-6277, 209-736-4677; www.oars.com) is an international outfit that has day and overnight sea kayaking trips on Jackson and Yellowstone Lakes. One-night trips on Jackson Lake are $240 and two-nighters are $382. Toss in a Snake River float and the price is $406 for two days and $597 for three. The Yellowstone half-day is $65. O.A.R.S. also has a five-day, four-night paddling/hiking combo package for $1,194.

Snake River Kayak and Canoe (800-529-2501, 307-733-9999; www.snakeriverkayak .com) has paddling adventures on Yellowstone Lake that range from three-hour evening trips to overnighters lasting up to eight days. Options include kayaking, canoeing, whitewater rafting, sea kayaking, fishing trips and rentals. Floats on Lewis and Shoshone Lakes and adventures in the Tetons are offered as well.

Boating Outside the Parks

Boaters don't have to look far for lakes with fewer restrictions close to Yellowstone and Grand Teton. **Hebgen Lake** just northwest of West Yellowstone has several marinas and excellent fishing. **Buffalo Bill Reservoir** west of Cody features 800 acres of sun-kissed boating.

CAMPING

Campgrounds in Yellowstone and Grand Teton National Parks fill up quickly in the summer, so reserve the ones you can and get there early for the first-come, first-serve variety. Yellowstone has 12 campgrounds, Grand Teton five. In addition, the U.S. Forest Service has campgrounds available as well as cabins and fire lookouts for rent in the vicinity of the two parks. Jackson Hole also has nice undeveloped campgrounds along the Gros Ventre River near Kelly. All of the gateway communities have RV parks with tent sites.

At the seven Yellowstone campgrounds where generators are allowed, they must be turned off between 8 PM and 8 AM. Reservations at Yellowstone are accepted through

Xanterra Parks & Resorts (307-344-7311) or at any campground registration desk. Future reservations can be made at 866-439-7375 or www.travelyellowstone.com. No overflow camping is allowed. Check-out time is 10 AM, and stays are limited to 14 days from July 1 through Labor Day, then 30 days thereafter. Quiet hours are 10 PM to 6 AM.

It is especially important to keep a clean camp to avoid confrontation with bears. The following items must ALWAYS be kept inside hard-sided vehicles (not tents): water and beverage containers; cooking, eating and drinking utensils; stoves and grills; coolers and ice chests; trash; food; cosmetics and toiletries; pet food and bowls; pails, buckets and washbasins.

Yellowstone National Park

Bridge Bay: 425 sites, $17 per night, handicapped accessible, flush toilets, dump station, generators OK, reservations accepted. Open Memorial Day through mid-September.

Canyon: 250 sites, $17 per night, handicapped accessible, flush toilets, pay showers and laundry nearby, generators OK, reservations accepted. Open early June through early September.

Fishing Bridge RV: 325 sites, $35 per night, flush toilets, showers and laundry nearby, dump station, generators OK, reservations accepted. Open mid-May through late September.

Grant Village: 400 sites, $17 per night, handicapped accessible, flush toilets, showers and laundry nearby, dump station, generators OK, reservations accepted. Open late June through late September.

Madison: 250 sites, $17 per night, handicapped accessible, flush toilets, dump station, generators OK, reservations accepted. Open early May through late October.

Indian Creek: 75 sites, $12 per night, vault toilets, 10 sites for 40-foot pull-through RVs

An aerial view of the RV park at Fishing Bridge just north of Yellowstone Lake. National Park Service

and 35 sites for 30-footers. Open early June through mid-September.

Lewis Lake: 85 sites, $12 per night, vault toilets, a few 40-foot pull-through RV sites.

Mammoth: 85 sites, $14 per night, handicapped accessible, flush toilets, pay showers, generators OK, most sites pull-through for RVs. Open year-round.

Norris: 100 sites, $14 per night, flush toilets, generators OK, two marked 50-foot pull-through RV sites and five 30-footers. Open mid-May through late September.

Pebble Creek: 30 sites, $12 per night, vault toilets, some long pull-throughs. Open early June through late September.

Slough Creek: 29 sites, $12 per night, vault toilets, 14 sites for 30-foot pull-through RVs. Open late May through late October.

Tower Fall: 32 sites, $12 per night, vault toilets, all suitable for 30-foot RVs.

Grand Teton National Park

Grand Teton's five campsites are first-come, first-serve. RVs are welcome at all but Jenny Lake. Reservations are available only for groups of 10 or more. Maximum stay is seven days.

Colter Bay: 350 sites, $12 per night, flush toilet, showers, laundry, dump station, groceries, service station. Cabins $41. Open mid-May through mid-September.

Gros Ventre: 360 sites, $12 per night, flush toilet, dump station. Open early May through mid-October.

Jenny Lake: 49 sites, $12 per night, flush toilet, tents only, groceries. Open late May through late September.

Lizard Creek: 60 sites, $12 per night, flush toilet. Open mid-June through early September.

Signal Mountain: 86 sites, $12 per night, flush toilet, dump station, groceries, service station. Open late May to early October.

Jackson Hole

Atherton Creek (307-739-5400; www.fs.fed.us/r4/btnf/teton) is on the north shore of Lower Slide Lake, at the end of the pavement on Gros Ventre Road about 20 miles northeast of Jackson.

Coal Creek (208-354-2312; www.fs.fed.us/r4/caribou) is just the other side of Teton Pass, still in Wyoming.

Curtis Canyon (307-739-5400; www.fs.fed.us/r4/btnf/teton) is 7 miles northeast of Jackson on a gravel road on the Bridger-Teton National Forest

Crystal Creek (307-739-5400; www.fs.fed.us/r4/btnf/teton) is the highest Forest Service campground along the Gros Ventre River, about 25 miles northeast of Jackson.

Hatchet (307-739-5400; www.fs.fed.us/r4/btnf/teton) is just off US 26/287 about 8 miles east of Moran Junction.

Red Hills (307-739-5400; www.fs.fed.us/r4/btnf/teton) is the next-to-last campground up the Gros Ventre.

Trail Creek (877-444-6777, 518-885-3639; www.reserveusa.com) is on the back side of Teton Pass on the way to Victor, Idaho.

RV Camping near Yellowstone National Park

Gardiner

Rocky Mountain Campground (877-534-6931, 406-848-7251; www.rockymountain

campground.com; 14 Jardine Rd.) sits on a hill, well above the east side of the Yellowstone River, facing the North Entrance. Tent sites are on grass; there are a few RV pull-throughs and two cabins. Rates are always $25 for tents, $29–42 for water and electric, $31–44 for full hookups, $30–45 for one-room cabins and $45–70 for two-room cabins. Rates are highest between June 16 and August 31, lowest from April 15 to May 15. Open April 15–October 31.

Yellowstone RV Park and Camp (406-848-7496; www.ventureswestinc.com/yellowstone rvpark; 121 US Hwy. 89.) is a snug RV campground with 48 sites on a dusty bluff overlooking the Yellowstone, on the north end of town about a mile from the North Entrance. River access is limited because of the steep embankment. Some tent spaces and 30 x 70 RV sites. Rates average about $35. Open year-round.

WEST YELLOWSTONE

Lionshead RV Resort (406-646-7662; www.lionshead.com; 1545 Targhee Pass Hwy.) has 194 spaces in the trees west of town, including 50-amp and 30-amp hookups, camper sites and tent spaces. Call for rates. Open summers only.

Madison Arm Resort (406-646-9328; www.madisonarmresort.com; 5475 Madison Arm Rd.) is 9 miles north of the park's West Entrance, just off US 20/191 at Hebgen Lake. Site features 20- and 30-amp full hookups with a couple of pull-throughs, tent sites on the lake, relatively modern cabins and cottages. Rates are $23 for tent sites and $30–32 for RV spots. Cabins are $120 and cottages $140. A variety of boat rentals are available at the resort's marina. Open mid-May to October 1.

Pony Express RV Park (800-323-9708, 406-646-7644; www.yellowstonevacations.com; 4 FireholeAve.) is a basic RV park that virtually backs up to the park. All sites are pull-through, many with full hookups. Rates from $29. Open April to November, with dry camping (no water) available in winter.

Wagon Wheel RV Campground and Cabins (406-646-7872; www.wagonwheelrv.com; 408 Gibbon Ave.) is an attractive site tucked into the lodgepole pines near the northwest edge of town. Rates $26.95 for tent sites to $37.95 for pull-through full hook-up RV sites and starting at $58 for one-, two- and three-bedroom camping cabins. Open Memorial Day through October. Two cabins open year-round.

Yellowstone Park KOA (800-562-7591; www.yellowstonekoa.com; 3305 Targhee Pass Hwy.) features three types of Kamping Kabins, 50-amp pull-throughs for RVs and tent sites in an isolated area west of town. Rates $28 for tent sites and up to $56 for cabins. Open mid-May to early October. Voted KOA's Franchise of the Year in 1998.

Yellowstone Grizzly RV Park and Cabins (406-646-4466; www.grizzlyrv.com; 210 Electric St.) offers three types of RV sites, tent camping and three styles of cabins. RV sites range from 30-amp to 100 amps in premium 70-foot pull-throughs with full hookups. Tent sites are $25. RVs range from $42.95 to $52.95, with wireless Internet extra except at the premium sites. Cabins start at $59 for no-frills and extend to $95 for a kitchenette and full bath. Expanded in 2006, much of this park backs up to the Gallatin National Forest. Open May 1 through late October.

RV Camping near Grand Teton National Park

Colter Bay RV Park (307-543-2811; www.gtlc.com) has 112 sites, including tent sites. Reservations accepted. RV sites $49 peak season, $32 late season. Open late May to mid-September.

Flagg Ranch Resort (800-443-2311, 307-543-2861; www.flaggranch.com) 100 trailer sites and 75 tent sites, full hookups, shower, laundry, reservations accepted. RV sites $45, tent sites $20. Open late May to early September.

Dubois

Longhorn RV & Motel (307-455-2337; www.duboislonghornrv.com; 5810 US Hwy. 26), once called the Riverside Inn, is 3 miles east of town and operating under new ownership since reopening in the summer of 2007. The 50 new RV sites include 50-amp pull-throughs with full hookups and wireless Internet. Big motor coaches are welcome. Many sites are on the Wind River. The resort has 24 new motel rooms with kitchenettes as well. Open year-round.

Moran

Grand Teton Park RV Resort (800-563-6469, 307-733-1980; www.yellowstonerv.com) 50-amp pull-through RV sites, hot tub, seasonal pool, showers, recreation room, grocery store, playground, rentals. RV sites range from $38.95 for no hookups to $56.95 for 50-amp full hookups. Tent sites $34.95. Camping cabins $67.95 and $74.95. Heated pool and hot tub available Memorial Day through Labor Day. RV resort open year-round, with reduced services.

Jackson

Snake River Park and KOA (800-562-1878, 307-733-7078; www.srpkoa.com; 9705 S. US Hwy. 89) is 13 miles south of Jackson's Town Square, near the renowned whitewater stretch of the Snake River Canyon where the river is joined by Horse Creek. Tent sites are grassy and secluded. Rates range from $34.95 for teepee and $35.95 for tent sites to $52.95 and $54.95 for RV spaces and $65.95 (one room) and $75.95 (two rooms) for cabins. It's extra for 50-amp RV hookups. Rates are lower from mid-April to mid-June and from late August to early October. Open early April to October 1.

Wagon Wheel Village RV Park & Campground (800-562-1878, 307-733-4588; www.wagonwheelvillage.com; 525 N. Cache St.) is a 40-site (32 RV, eight tent) campground that's part of a larger lodging facility. The campground is on the banks of Flat Creek, a short walk from the Town Square. RV rates are $45 along wall, $60 along the creek. Tent sites are $30. The campground has shower and restroom facilities separate from the main village. Open early May through late October, depending on weather.

Tetonia

Teton Mountain View Lodge & RV Park (208-456-2741; www.tetonmountainlodge.com; 510 Egbert Ave.) is a new resort in the valley on the west side of the Tetons. It features pull-through spaces with 20-, 30- and 50-amp full hookups. Wireless Internet is in the office, as well as a TV lounge. There's a hot tub on the premises. Western barbecues and live entertainment are offered on weekends. The lodge also has 25 rooms, most with views of the Tetons. Open year-round.

Victor

Teton Valley Campground (208-787-2847; www.tetonvalleycampground.com; 128 W. Hwy. 31) has full hookup pull-throughs, wireless Internet, a heated pool, showers, laundry and a recreation room. Camping cabins are on the premises. Tent sites are $22, no hookups $24, water/electric $26, full hookup standard $32, full hookup premium $36 and 50-amp service an extra $4 per night.

CLIMBING

Rock Climbing/Mountaineering

Few experiences can match the thrill of standing atop 13,770-foot Grand Teton on a cloudless day, and especially on one of those rare windless days. The world stretches forever in every direction. Combined with the different challenges each peak presents, it's no wonder that climbers from around the globe bring their ropes, ice axes and climbing bolts. More than 4,000 people climb Grand Teton each year, usually in July and early August, and not all are experienced even though it's a technical climb. Novices can get training and go with trained guides. Expect to pay anywhere from $750–1,000.

For less-technical climbs, hikers can reach the summits of South and Middle Teton in a day after spending a night at one of four campsites. Mount Moran's isolation from the others often renders it a forgotten peak, but it has several memorable routes to its 12,605-foot summit. Registration isn't necessary to climb any of the Tetons, but overnight camping requires a backcountry-use permit. As with most climbing, it's best to go early, before afternoon winds and frequent lightning storms arrive. Once mid-August arrives, anything is possible with the weather.

Check with the **Jenny Lake Ranger Station** (307-739-3343) between 8 AM and 6 PM for advice, guidebooks and the availability of campsites. Climbers also have an inexpensive option for lodging before making their assault: The American Alpine Club's **Grand Teton Climbers' Ranch** (307-733-7271) charges $10 per night for bunks in small cabins, cooking facilities and hot showers; bring your own bedding and food. Reservations are recommended, and the ranch is limited to climbers only.

The Jackson Hole area also has two outstanding climbing schools offering instruction and guides for summer and winter adventures:

Exum Mountains Guides (307-733-2297; www.exumguides.com) has an office at the south boat dock at Jenny Lake. The company was founded by Glenn Exum, one of the Grand's early summiteers. Exum guides ascents on all seven of the Teton Range's major peaks.

Jackson Hole Mountain Guides (307-733-4979, 800-239-7642; www.jhmg.com) doesn't have the name or history, but it's also not quite as expensive and it's also top-notch. Jackson Hole Mountain Guides also operates an office in Cody (877-587-0629) for rock climbing along the North Fork of the Shoshone and four- and five-day excursions into Montana's Beartooth Mountains and Wyoming's Wind Rivers.

Core Mountain Sports (877-527-7354, 307-527-7354; www.coremountainsports.com; 1019 15th St.) guides rock climbing on the North Fork of the Shoshone River and ice climbing on the South Fork of the Shoshone. Core also features an indoor climbing wall.

Do-it-yourselfers wanting to pit themselves against lesser challenges have several options in the Jackson area:

Blacktail Butte, a rock face near Moose, is a popular hangout for weekend warriors.

Teton Rock Gym (307-733-0707; 1116 Maple Way) features indoor climbing walls, rental gear and classes.

For gear, try **Moosely Seconds Mountaineering** (307-739-1801) in Moose or **Teton Mountaineering** (800-850-3595, 307-733-3595; www.tetonmtn.com;170 N. Cache Dr.) whether purchasing or renting.

Ice climbing

The Yellowstone ecosystem region also is famed for at least two ice-climbing meccas: the **South Fork of the Shoshone River** west of Cody and **Hyalite Canyon** south of Bozeman. Ice climbers from around the world come to test their mettle on the hundreds of frozen waterfalls along the South Fork. Check codyice.com for updates. Hyalite Canyon isn't as prolific, but the season starts as early as Thanksgiving, and many of the frozen falls rise far above the forest below. Go to montanaice.com or hyalitecanyon.com for information, including updates on a controversial Gallatin National Forest travel plan that could make access more challenging. The plan was to take effect in early 2008, closing a gated road from January 1 through May 15. Climbers fear the plan will effectively reduce the climbing season from five months to about eight weeks.

FISHING

Yellowstone National Park note: A $15 three-day permit is required in Yellowstone National Park for all anglers over 16, and a free permit is necessary for anyone ages 12 to 16. Children under 12 must fish with an adult who has purchased a permit and understands park regulations. Seven-day permits are $20 and a season pass is $35. Permits are available at general stores, visitor centers and ranger stations. Individual state licenses for Wyoming, Montana or Idaho are neither valid nor required to fish within Yellowstone boundaries. Much of the fishing on Yellowstone's 800 miles of rivers is catch-and-release on a fly. Barbless hooks are gentler on the fish's mouth and make them easier to release; they are required everywhere but Yellowstone Lake. Native Yellowstone cutthroat trout (on the Atlantic side), Snake River fine-spotted cutthroat trout (on the Pacific side), grayling and mountain whitefish must be released unharmed. Be sure to check the frequently changing park regulations for limits and sizes on individual streams and lakes before fishing; they're available at all visitor centers. In the summer, rules can change at a day's notice, when low flows and heat have caused die-offs and forced park officials to halt fishing on certain streams.

Grand Teton National Park note: Rules are generally more liberal in Grand Teton. Angling simply requires a Wyoming license. Anglers 14 and under may fish free if accompanied by an adult with a valid Wyoming license. Treble hooks are allowed. Check park regulations for limits and sizes on individual streams and lakes.

If catching a rising rainbow trout on a dry fly or hooking a lunker German brown on a nymph is a passion, then welcome to utopia. The rivers birthed on this high plateau are a veritable who's who, or what's what, of trout fishing: Madison, Gallatin, Firehole, Gibbon, Yellowstone, Clark's Fork of the Yellowstone, Shoshone, Lamar, Lewis, South Fork of the Snake, Henry's Fork, Wind and Gros Ventre. The lake fishing isn't bad, either, though less than one-fourth of the 200 lakes are fishable. In addition, the famed Yellowstone cutthroat trout has taken a beating in Yellowstone Lake from lake trout illegally introduced in the mid-1990s. Lake trout must be kept or killed when caught.

Even here, on some of America's greatest trout waterways, the fish have faced mighty challenges. Rainbow trout populations, especially in the Madison River, have been dramatically tested by whirling disease, though they seem to have pushed through the worst of it. Another threat is the transient New Zealand mud snail, which push native aquatic insects out, providing less food for fish. Both whirling disease and the mud snails are

Lake trout caught in Yellowstone Lake must be kept or killed. They are voracious eaters that threaten native Yellowstone cutthroat populations. National Park Service

brought in from elsewhere, often on unscrubbed waders and boats. Anglers can do their part by cleaning waders and boots with a bleach solution if they've been worn in other waters.

Of more concern of late is drought and higher temperatures. In the summer of 2007, the Yellowstone had its lowest flows since 1930. River temperatures exceeding 80 degrees caused fish die-offs and river closures on the Firehole in the park. Downstream, Montana officials were forced to impose so-called "hoot owl" restrictions, prohibiting fishing between 2 PM and midnight on many rivers to keep fish from becoming overstressed in the low, warm waters.

That said, there are still few places anywhere like the Greater Yellowstone ecosystem for trout fishing, even though less than 200 of the park's 2,650 river miles are fishable. Expect fish to be wilier in heavily pressured areas, especially where the Madison and Firehole are accompanied by roads. For the more adventurous, venturing into the Grand Canyon of the Yellowstone or to the nearly 200 backcountry lakes and creeks is worth the effort for the resulting angling success, solitude and the company of wildlife.

To fish outside the parks, you must purchase the appropriate state license. Hundreds of guides and outfitters are available for half-day, full-day and overnight trips in and out of the park, and fly shops are a dominant species in the parks' gateway communities. Prime times on many of these rivers are the Mother's Day caddis hatch in early May, the world-famous salmon fly hatches in June and the shorter days of autumn, when cooler water and regular hatches reenergize the trout after a lazy summer. The parks open to fishing in June, when many rivers are still running chocolate brown from snowmelt, making them danger-ous to wade and diminishing the odds of catching fish.

Rivers in and around Yellowstone National Park

Bechler River

Never heard of it? Few people who visit Yellowstone have, largely because few people ever visit the remote southwest corner of the park. And for fishermen, it isn't what you catch, but where you are and the effort required in getting there. The Bechler is accessible only from Ashton, Idaho. For as few people as the cutthroats and rainbows here see, they're surprisingly wary. And then there's the rugged terrain and mosquitoes. The rewards are in seeing the spectacular waterfalls and a portion of the park few experience.

Clarks Fork of the Yellowstone

This is another relatively undiscovered treasure with substantial rewards for the trout fisher. The Clarks Fork starts near Cooke City, Montana, and makes a headlong dash through canyons, forest and sage country in Wyoming before turning northeast for a more sedate run through the agricultural lands of Montana and a meeting with the Yellowstone at Laurel. Some of the best dry-fly fishing in the Yellowstone region can be had where the Clarks Fork rushes alongside US 212. The river is awash in caddis, drakes, blue-winged olives, pale morning duns and other dries. The region is dotted with private property, but access isn't difficult to find. Given the stunning Beartooth Highway and Sunlight Basin drives nearby, it's a wonder more visitors don't spend more time in this breathtaking area just outside of Yellowstone.

Firehole River

For dry-fly fishing and the pure Yellowstone experience, nothing tops the Firehole in June and July. Especially on cloudy days, pale morning duns and caddis will flutter above the river and entice trout to the surface. The fish aren't big, but they're feisty. The hatches tend to occur late morning, but get there early because others will stake out prime holes and

Cave Falls on the Bechler River is one of the many falls in the rarely visited southwest corner of Yellowstone.
National Park Service

wait for the water to boil with activity. No doubt you've seen photos of fly anglers casting with geysers, bison and elk in the background. That's the Firehole.

Gallatin River

Tucked in a narrow valley between the more renowned Madison and Yellowstone, the Gallatin is sometimes overlooked, even by residents. It isn't as renowned as its bigger brothers, and truthfully the fishing isn't as prolific, but it merits attention on several counts. One, it's the first river in Montana to be declared navigable, meaning it belongs to the public below the high-water mark even where it goes through private property. Two, this is *the* river that ran through it, at least for much of *A River Runs Through It*. Best of all, the fishing for rainbows and browns is outstanding, especially during the harshest of summer months. While the sun bakes the broad Madison and Yellowstone, the Gallatin's emerald-green waters stay cool in the shade of the canyon and commonly render 20-inch trout.

Gardner River

If you're a dad or mom looking to introduce your child to fishing, take the family to this pretty little stream rushing from the northwest corner of the park to its confluence with the Yellowstone. Just upstream from the North Entrance, before the river tumbles over Osprey Falls, it is fed by Panther, Obsidian and Indian Creeks in a meadow shadowed by Bunsen Peak. All four streams may be fished with worms by children 12 and under. The rainbows and brook trout are small, but the kids won't care. They'll delight at a trout wriggling on their hook, and any quiet fishing stretches are likely to be punctuated by close proximity to elk, moose, beaver and other wildlife.

Henry's Fork of the Snake

Like the Madison, these nutrient-rich waters birthed from an Idaho spring southwest of Yellowstone move even the greatest of fly anglers to genuflect. To get a taste for the mammoth trout that lurk in the Henry's Fork, drive east of Island Park to Big Springs and peer over the bridge railing at the fat rainbows gorging themselves near the river's birthplace. Downstream, the Henry's Fork has two prime angling areas: Box Canyon and the Railroad Ranch. The Box Canyon stretch between Island Park and Last Chance is the briskly moving water where nymph anglers go deep for big fish. Farther downriver, at Railroad Ranch, is the world-renowned dry-fly portion, where rising fish tease the best anglers and shrug off any less-than-perfect presentation. Fishing is still good until the river warms when it arrives at the Snake River Plain below Ashton.

Lamar River/Slough Creek

Intimidated by the Orvis-clad anglers on the Madison and Henry's Fork? Feel crowded by the Firehole? Uncomfortable with the speed of the Shoshone? Then try Slough Creek and, farther downstream, the Lamar River. They're perfect streams for the beginning fly fisher. Both meander through meadows in the Lamar Valley, offering easy access from the road, comfortable back casting and pretty little cutthroat trout. These ravenous fish are even forgiving to rookie dry-fly casters. Oh, and while you're casting, keep an eye out for bison, elk, bears and wolves on the Serengeti of the Yellowstone.

Madison River

"Madison" and "trout fishing" are inextricably linked, like Bogey and Bacall. Famed local angler Charles Brooks once described the Madison as the world's largest chalk stream, a reference to its nutrient-laden calcium bicarbonate. Birthed at the junction of the Firehole and Gibbon, the Madison meanders westerly and leaves the park north of West Yellowstone before turning north after leaving Hebgen Lake. The river is best known for a world-class 40-mile stretch between Quake Lake and Ennis that produces large rainbows and browns, but fishing is exceptional all the way to Three Forks, where it joins with the Gallatin and Jefferson to form the Missouri River. Because the Madison is dam-controlled, it can offer top fishing in May and June when the region's other rivers are blown out.

North Fork of the Shoshone River

It's no longer on the "best-kept secrets" list, but the North Fork remains an extraordinary experience. Where else can an angler find elbow room on a blue-ribbon trout stream that flows alongside a major highway? Apparently most visitors are in such a hurry to get from Cody to the park's East Entrance that they neglect 50 miles of free-flowing river teeming with native browns, rainbows and cutthroats averaging about 16 inches. The best fishing, especially with dry flies, is right after runoff ends in early July and again in the fall. Expect smaller fish in August and early September. Study your maps. This is a dude-ranch corridor and much of the river flows through private land. Unlike more-progressive Montana, Wyoming has no laws guaranteeing access to streams that run through private property.

Yellowstone River

The longest undammed river in the United States (OK, there are five diversion dams for agriculture in eastern Montana, but let's not split hairs), the Yellowstone is one of America's most prolific trout streams. It meanders, cascades and tumbles violently through the park, creating prime habitat for threatened Yellowstone cutthroat population as well as rainbows, German browns and brook trout. Though technically only the cut-throats are native, the other species have reproduced naturally for so long they are de facto wild—and fight like it. Cutthroats averaging about 16 inches tend to inhabit the river above the Upper Falls of the Grand Canyon; below the falls, rainbows, brookies and browns dom-inate. Wading is mandatory in the park, where float craft aren't allowed. As is the case with most rivers, the most resourceful will prevail. Scramble down into the canyon or hike into the remote backcountry above Yellowstone Lake; your rewards will be tranquility and less-wary trout. Once the river leaves the park at Gardiner it broadens and braids, but the fish-ing remains world-class for trout almost all the way to Billings.

Rivers in and around Grand Teton National Park

Gros Ventre

The Gros Ventre is a pretty freestone stream that enters the Snake just north of Jackson. Most of the best fishing for cutthroat and the occasional rainbow is downstream from Kelly to the confluence. The fish range from about 8–15 inches and aren't too fussy, even about dry flies. Though swift, it's suitable for wading and much of the river can be fished from the banks. Floating is not recommended.

Hoback

Only 15 miles long, the Hoback nevertheless will produce and is a solid place for the novice

The Madison River, which is formed by the confluence of the Firehole and Gibbon Rivers just east of West Yellowstone, is one of the world's great trout streams. National Park Service

fly angler to experience success. Most of this meandering little freestone river is easily accessed from US 189/191. Don't let its small stature scare you off. The Hoback has many scrappy cutthroat that'll reach 13 inches, with the occasional larger trout that cruises up from the confluence with the Snake south of Jackson. Toss an attractor dry fly and get ready for action. Be sure to ask permission if you want to bank fish from private property.

South Fork of the Snake

Many learned anglers consider this tailwater fishery below Palisades Dam southwest of Jackson to be the finest for trout in the nation. The water is big, broad and braided, providing excellent habitat for huge fine-spotted cutthroat and brown trout, and a smattering of rainbows. One reason it doesn't receive as much publicity as the Madison and Henry's Fork is that not everyone has access to a raft or driftboat, easily the best way to fish the swift and precarious South Fork of the Snake. The river also isn't famed for its hatches, though they do occur. Exceptional fishing exists right in the heart of Grand Teton National Park on the South Fork, typically referred to simply as "the Snake" until it reaches Palisades. Guides are at the ready to lead you to big cutthroats on the entire 80 miles from Jackson Lake to the reservoir.

Lakes in Yellowstone National Park

Heart Lake

Heart Lake is favored by longtime Yellowstone anglers because it's just far enough off the beaten path to provide some isolation and it offers exceptional fishing for trophy lake trout. Getting to Heart Lake requires an 8-mile hike on the Heart Lake Trail, which starts just north of Lewis Lake off the road between the South Entrance and West Thumb. Despite the remoteness, don't expect to have the lake to yourself. About 40 percent of Yellowstone's backcountry trips have Heart Lake as the destination. A bonus to the hike in is little Heart Lake Geyser Basin.

Lewis Lake

The third largest lake in Yellowstone is also prized for its browns as well as the occasional brook and lake trout. Other readily accessible lakes known for trout and mountain white-fish angling are Trout, Blacktail, Wolf and Heart Lakes.

Shoshone Lake

At 80,000 acres, it's the second largest lake in Yellowstone, and perhaps the favorite of all 200 lakes in the park for angling. Shoshone is famed for its big brown and rainbow trout, with some scrappy cutthroats and decent-sized brook trout as well. It's fishable all summer, but the best time is fall, when the big fish move into the Lewis River channel. The Shoshone can be fished from trails or by boat, with access from Lewis Lake's boat ramp.

Trout Lake

This pretty little lake a short hike from the Lamar Valley is worth noting for its ravenous cutthroats. They'll charge after a dry fly with unabashed fury. Make the trek in summer, when the rivers are low and warm. The hike is about 1 mile and begins about 1 mile southeast of the Pebble Creek Campground, with a marked trailhead. Trout Lake provides some of the earliest fishing in the park.

Yellowstone Lake

To the angler, the Yellowstone can be a big, imposing, 87,000-acre body of water—with good reason. Boaters caught off-guard by an afternoon thunderstorm have paid the ultimate price. Anyone pitched into these frigid waters won't last long. So many fishermen go to the rivers or smaller lakes. The lack of attention has been a bonus for the struggling Yellowstone cutthroat trout, which is starting to make a comeback thanks to strict regulations. Yet in a roundabout way, those cutthroat also provide a reason to fish these pristine waters: the lake trout. Illegally introduced a decade or so ago, these predators are exacting a toll on the native cutthroat. Anglers who catch a lake trout are required to keep or kill it. To catch cutthroat, ply some of the areas closer to the shores in a float tube or boat. You'll be glad you did—Yellowstone cutthroat can be seen rising from the lake depths for dry flies or emergers.

Lakes in Grand Teton National Park

Jackson Lake

You name the trout, the deep and cold waters of Jackson have it. A state-record 50-pound lake trout (mackinaw) was coaxed from these depths. Cutthroat, brook and brown trout also inhabit these rich waters, best accessed by boat except in May when bank anglers have a crack at trophy trout cruising the shores for bait fish. In summer, you'll have to drop line as deep as 200 feet to catch fish. A few coves or inlets can be fished with a fly rod from float tubes. Note that Jackson Lake is closed in October so mackinaw can spawn undisturbed.

Fishing is a popular pastime in Yellowstone Lake. Anglers must release such native fish as cutthroat trout unharmed, but they are required to kill illegally introduced lake trout. National Park Service

Jenny Lake

The most beautiful lake in Wyoming also has its fair share of mackinaws, cutthroats and browns. Fish from a canoe or kayak around the edges, where the fish will lurk for insects, including a renowned flying black ant "hatch" in late June or early July. Try streamers, woolly buggers or other submerged flies. Cutthroats will occasionally rise for a dry. Jenny Lake is an excellent choice in October when Jackson Lake is closed.

Leigh Lake

This remote lake north of Jenny and String Lakes is famed for its views and solitude. Fish it the same as Jenny—with flashy streamers, woolly buggers or other deep wet flies. A canoe will provide the best serenity and provide distance from the surprisingly gnarly mosquitoes that inhabit the shoreline on the channel between String and Leigh Lakes.

FITNESS FACILITIES

For that rainy day, a few of the gateway communities around the parks provide an indoor workout on a Stairmaster, stationary bicycle or weight machines either individually or in classes.

CODY

Fitness Center (307-587-3467; 1310 Sheridan)
Curves For Women (307-587-1900; 1802 14th St.) National chain. Workouts focusing on weight loss for women.

DRIGGS

Curves For Women (208-354-3488; 15 W. Depot St.) National chain. Workouts focusing on weight loss for women.
High Peaks Health and Fitness Inc. (208-354-3128; 50 Ski Hill Rd.) Exercise studio, weight room, cardio. Also features physical therapy.

JACKSON

Bell Fitness (307-754-5878; www.bellfitness.net; High School Rd.) Classes, personal trainers, state-of-the-art equipment, massage, tanning, group classes.

Curves For Women (307-732-2348; 890 S. US Hwy. 89) National chain. Workouts focusing on weight loss for women.

Enclosure Climbing & Fitness Center (307-734-9590; www.enclosureclimbing.com; 670 Deer Lane) Treadmills, bikes, strength training, climbing walls, classes, instruction.

Jackson Hole Athletic Club (307-733-8830; www.jacksonholeathletic.org; 838 W. Broadway Ave.) Free weights, HammerStrength, group classes, personal trainers, day rates.

WEST YELLOWSTONE

Madison Crossing Fitness (406-646-7621; 121 Madison Ave.) Part of indoor retail complex. Day memberships welcome. Bikes, treadmills, steppers, free weights, elliptical equipment.

Salon West Spa & Fitness Center (406-646-7874; 299 US Hwy. 20) Aerobic and weight equipment, racquetball courts, classes. Also a full-service salon for hair, nails, facials, pedicures, massage therapy.

WILSON

Teton Sports Club (307-733-7004; www.tetonsportsclub.com; 4030 W. Lake Creek Dr. Cardio, circuit training, free weights, group classes, sauna, hot tubs.

GLIDER RIDES

DRIGGS

Teton Aviation (800-472-6382, 208-354-3100) offers one-hour glider rides in which clients are towed toward the west face of Grand Teton and cut free to soar back to the Driggs Airport. Cost is $225 per passenger.

JACKSON

Soaring Eagle Glider Flights (800-329-9205) take in the National Elk Refuge, Sleeping Indian, Snow King and Teton Crest in 75- and 45-minute rides. Call for current pricing.

GOLF

Welcome to a golfer's summer paradise. Picture drives rising from the tee to a backdrop of the Grand Tetons or a lush lodgepole forest. Some of the biggest names on the PGA Tour— Tom Weiskopf, Arnold Palmer, Hale Irwin, Robert Trent Jones Jr.—have vacationed in the area and built courses. Some of the most stunning links in America are within 100 miles of the Yellowstone/Teton boundaries. So toss your clubs in the trunk, take a break from wildlife viewing and check out these nearby public and semiprivate courses.

ALTA

Targhee Village Golf Course (307-354-8577; www.targheevillage.com; 530 Perimeter Dr., Alta, WY 83414) is a pretty nine-hole course at the edge of the Targhee National Forest.

Greens fees: $17 daily for nine holes, $25 for 18. Golf carts $6. Tee times recommended on weekends and holidays.

ASHTON

Aspen Acres Golf Course (208-652-3524; 4179 E. 1100 North, Ashton, ID 83420) is a surprisingly challenging 18-hole, par-60 executive course about 6 miles southeast of town in the upper Snake River Valley. Narrow fairways are lined with aspens and other modest-sized trees. No water hazards, but plenty of bunkers. Shaded RV hookups on site. Open May 1–October 15. Greens fees $30 daily.

CODY

Olive Glenn Golf and Country Club (307-587-5551; www.oliveglenngolf.com; 802 Meadow Lane Ave., Cody, WY 82414) is a semiprivate, wonderfully manicured 18-hole championship course in the broad sage country of western Wyoming. Mostly flat with moderate-sized trees lining contoured fairways and well-placed water hazards. Beautiful views of the Absaroka Mountains to the west. Typically ranked among the top five courses in the state by *Golf Digest.* Open April 1–November 1. Greens fees: $65 daily.

DRIGGS

The Links (208-456-2374; www.linksattetonpeaks.com; 400 W. 127th North) is a 6,344-yard, 18-hole course with a Scottish flair located near Grand Targhee Ski Area. Terrific Grand Tetons backdrop from the west side. Greens fees: $49 daily.

DUBOIS

Antelope Hills Golf Course (307-455-2888; mwiener@dtworld.com; 126 Club House Dr., Dubois, WY 82513) is a gentle, mostly flat nine-hole course with wide fairways on the west end of town. Open April–October. Greens fees: $23 daily.

ISLAND PARK

Island Park Village Resort Golf Course (208-558-7550; www.islandparkvillageresort .com; 4153 N. Big Springs Loop Rd., Island Park, ID 83429) is a nine-hole course with a few hills set amid lodgepole pines. Open May 1–October 15. Greens fees: $22 weekends, $20 weekdays.

JACKSON

Jackson Hole Golf & Tennis Club (307-733-3111; www.jhgtc.com; 5000 Spring Gulch Rd., Jackson, WY 83001) is described by *Golf Digest* as the finest course in Wyoming and one of the top 10 in the country. It's hard to argue. Built in 1961 as a Robert Trent Jones Jr. signature course, this exquisite 7,168-yard layout combines challenging championship yardage with a stunning Teton backdrop. A recent $15 million renovation has only added to the ambience. It's semiprivate, so anyone can play, but call for reservations. Greens fees: $155 daily including golf cart, $95 twilight fees.

Teton Pines Golf Club (307-733-1733; www.tetonpines.com; 3450 N. Clubhouse Dr., Jackson, WY 83001) was designed by Arnold Palmer and covers 7,412 yards. *Condé Nast Traveler* rated this relatively flat course 6 miles from town among the top 100 courses in America and the Caribbean. Look for wildlife. Greens fees: $175 daily including golf cart.

Hang Gliding

Jackson

Cowboy Up Hang Gliding (307-413-4164; www.cuhanggliding.com; 3465 N. Pines Way, Suite 104, Wilson, WY 83014) offers two introductory flights in tandem with a flight instructor over Jackson Hole. The "Great" flight ($169) is taken at 2,000–2,500 feet and the "Grand" flight ($249) is at 3,000–4,000. Training is offered for beginners and advanced pilots. Rental equipment available.

Hiking

If you truly want to experience Yellowstone and Grand Teton National Parks, there's no better way than to strap on a backpack, don sturdy hiking shoes, clip bear spray to your belt and head into the backcountry, even if for a short distance. Yellowstone alone has more than 1,100 miles of trails, ranging from easy short hikes through geyser country to more strenuous ambles up Mount Washburn and Avalanche Peak; Grand Teton has 200 miles of trails. It's best to start with the National Park Service's "Day Hikes" and "Backcountry Camping" guides. These will provide the pointers necessary for a successful journey.

Naturally, it's prudent to never forget that you're in wild country, with all the inherent hazards ranging from an encounter with a grizzly sow and her cubs or a temperamental moose to loose rock and unpredictable weather. Always have proper clothing, including rain gear, a hat and jacket. Hike with at least one other person. Insect repellent is a good idea because pockets of Yellowstone and Grand Teton with standing or slow-moving waters are fraught with mosquitoes. Keep vigilant for afternoon thunderstorms and lightning. If you are caught in a lightning storm, get away from ridges and trees, stay off water and, if you're caught with no other alternative, lie flat on low or indented ground until the storm passes. And even though the water here is a pristine as anywhere, to avoid intestinal disorders such as giardia don't drink from a stream or lake without a purifier. If you run out of water and are desperately thirsty, look for places where water is just emerging from a spring or, worst-case scenario, sip from water pouring over rocks.

Yellowstone National Park

No permits are required for day hikes in either park; backcountry permits are required for overnight excursions. To get a Backcountry Use Permit for one of the 300 backcountry campsites, call 307-344-2160. Backcountry campsites may be secured more than 48 hours before the start of a trip for $20; within 48 hours they're free. Maximum stays range from one to three nights. Permits are available at nine ranger stations and/or visitor centers in Yellowstone.

For day hikes, it's advisable to stop at a ranger station near where you plan to go to check on wildlife activity or other important information. Backcountry hikers should always camp at least 200 feet from water sources, use established campsites and ensure campfires are fully out before retiring for the night. Fires are allowed only in established pits. Most sites feature storage poles to keep food away from bears. Avoid detergents and soaps. Bury human waste at least 6 inches deep and at least 300 feet from water sources. Check with the Park Service for fire bans; given the recent spate of hot, dry summers, chances are fires won't be allowed in July, August and even until the first good September soakings.

It's also a good idea to check weather reports; snow has fallen in every month in Yellowstone and Grand Teton, though rarely in July.

Here is a list of day hikes worth checking out in Yellowstone National Park:

CANYON AREA

Cascade Lake: Forests, wildflower-laced meadows and small creeks with a pretty lake at the end. Difficult level: Easy. Trailhead: Cascade Lake Picnic Area, 1.5 miles north of Canyon Junction.

Canyon Rims: Some of the most spectacular vistas in Yellowstone are from the north and south rims of the Grand Canyon of the Yellowstone. On the south rim, visitors will recognize the view from **Artist Point** from numerous paintings and photographs. (Note: The Artist Point parking lot will be closed for renovation at least until 2009.) The more adventurous should take **Uncle Tom's Trail** and its 500-foot descent on 328 metal steps to the Lower Falls. On the north rim, if a little vertigo doesn't bother you, hike the paved switchbacks to the **Brink of the Lower Falls**, where you can peek over the railing at the lip of the thundering 308-foot drop and steam from the hot springs downstream. A more soothing, but no less inspiring view is from **Inspiration Point**, probably the second-most popular tourist stop. **Grandview Point** is another worthwhile stop, as is the half-mile descent to **Red Rock Point**, where the mist from the Lower Falls will provide relief on those rare hot summer days. Difficulty level: Ranges from easy to moderately strenuous. Trailheads are well marked on both rims upon leaving Canyon Junction.

Grebe Lake: Explore the headwaters of the Gibbon River and cast a fly in a lake known for the increasingly rare Arctic grayling, a prized fish that requires exceedingly cold water for survival. Much of the 6-mile roundtrip winds through the charred remnants of the 1988 fire. Difficulty level: Moderately easy. Trailhead: 3.5 miles west of Canyon Junction.

Howard Eaton Trail: This 12-mile one-way hike is part of the 150-mile Howard Eaton Trail, longest in Yellowstone. It connects Canyon and Norris while traversing between a number of small lakes. It's often inaccessible until July because of marshy conditions. Difficulty level: Moderate. Trailhead: Canyon and Norris.

Mary Mountain: Two trailheads lead to this small mountain on the park's Central Plateau, in the heart of the park. Look for bison and elk, especially in the Hayden Valley. Keep an eye out for grizzly-activity signs as well. The entire trail is 21 miles. Difficulty level: Moderate. Trailheads: 4 miles south of Canyon Junction (east trailhead) and Nez Perce Creek turnout south of Madison Junction (west trailhead).

Mount Washburn: If there's one don't-miss hike in this region, it's Mount Washburn, weather permitting. The views of Yellowstone's mountains are terrific and on clear days they extend to the Tetons. Two routes lead to the 10,243-foot summit, both 3 miles. Look for bighorn sheep. Bring a jacket, even if it's warm in the parking lot. Winds howl off the summit, where a fire lookout offers telescopes, water and a break from quick storms. The north trailhead typically has less traffic, but the Dunraven Pass parking area provides a slightly more interesting hike. Go in the morning, before the winds blow and thunderstorms move in. Difficulty level: Moderately strenuous. Trailheads: Dunraven Pass (south) and Chittenden (north), just off the Tower-Canyon Road.

Observation Peak: A challenging 3-mile hike from Cascade Lake to the top of a 9,397-foot mountain that offers views of the Absarokas to the east, Central Plateau to the south, Prospect Peak to the north and Gallatins to the northwest. Difficulty level: Strenuous. Trailhead: Cascade Lake.

Seven Mile Hole: A terrific six- to eight-hour adventure for fit hikers who want to get off the beaten path. This 11-mile jaunt leaves the south rim of the Grand Canyon of the Yellowstone near Inspiration Point, sneaks past Silver Cord Cascade and quickly drops 1,400 feet to the Yellowstone River. It's the only real trail to the bottom of the canyon. Watch for dormant and active hot springs. Though not a secret among diehard fishermen, it's worth strapping a fly rod to your back. There are three campsites at the bottom as well; a Backcountry Use Permit is required. Difficulty level: Strenuous. Trailhead: Glacial Boulder turnout near Inspiration Point.

Madison Area

Harlequin Lake: A brisk 1-miler through charred lodgepoles to a small lake. Don't forget mosquito repellent. Difficulty level: Easy. Trailhead: 1.5 miles west of Madison Campground.

Purple Mountain: Another trail through burned pines, though the views at the end are better than Harlequin and mosquitoes are fewer. The route climbs 1,500 feet and offers a good look at where the Firehole and Gibbon Rivers join forces to become the Madison. Difficulty level: Moderate. Trailhead: One-quarter mile north of Madison Junction.

Two Ribbons: A short, pretty boardwalk trail through regenerated forest that follows the Madison River through lodgepole and sage meadow. Look for bison and elk. Wheelchair accessible. Difficulty level: Easy. Trailhead: 5 miles east of the West Entrance on road to Madison Junction.

Mammoth Area

Beaver Ponds Loop: Get a good overview of the Mammoth area on this 5-mile loop hike through pine and aspen forest, past beaver ponds and into wildflower-rich meadows that belie the stark beauty of the hot springs. Look for elk, pronghorn, beaver, deer and moose. Keep your eyes and ears open for black and grizzly bears. Difficulty level: Moderate. Trailhead: Between Liberty Gap and the stone house at Mammoth Terraces.

Blacktail Deer Creek: A memorable 12.5-mile trail along tumbling Blacktail Deer Creek down more than 1,000 feet to the Yellowstone, where a steel suspension bridge leads you to the Yellowstone River trail. Continue along the Yellowstone on the dusty trail to Gardiner at the North Entrance. Bring a fly rod; you're sure to have some of the Yellowstone's best fishing waters to yourself. Difficulty level: Moderate. Trailhead: 7 miles east of Mammoth.

Bunsen Peak: Another of Yellowstone's accessible hikes to the top of a peak offering panoramic views, in this case of the park's northwest corner. Of all the climbs to a mountaintop, this might be the easiest yet most rewarding. The journey can be as few as 2 miles and as much as 10, depending on how much time and effort you want to exert. Views include Mammoth Village and the Gallatin, Madison and Absaroka Mountain Ranges as well as the Yellowstone River Valley. Difficulty level: Moderate. Trailhead: 5 miles south of Mammoth at entrance to Old Bunsen Peak Road.

Lava Creek: This 3.5-miler follows Lava Creek past Undine Falls to the Gardner River and back to the North Entrance Road. Difficulty level: Moderate. Trailhead: Lava Creek picnic area on Tower-Mammoth Road.

Osprey Falls: A rugged trail into a starkly beautiful area rarely seen by visitors despite its proximity to the Mammoth-Norris Road. You might share the first 3 miles of the Old Bunsen Peak Road with mountain bikers until you reach the actual Osprey Falls Trail. At the rim of Sheepeater Canyon, the trail drops about 700 feet in less than a mile to the 150-foot Osprey Falls on the Gardner River. You're deep in a canyon here, looking up at 500 vertical feet of walls. The spray from the falls will offer a refreshing respite from what's sure to be a toasty hike in summer. Difficulty level: Difficult. Trailhead: 5 miles south of Mammoth, at Old Bunsen Peak Road.

Rescue Creek: Another deceiving hike that starts out moderately difficult on the Blacktail Creek Trail before diverting onto the actual Rescue Creek Trail, which includes a dramatic 1,400-foot drop into the Gardner River Canyon. The 8-mile trail crosses the river and winds up less than a mile from the North Entrance station. Difficulty level: Moderately difficult. Trailhead: 7 miles east of Mammoth.

Sepulcher Mountain: Another mountaintop, another panoramic vista. This hike isn't as well-known as Bunsen Peak, but the 3,400-foot ascent to 9,652 feet provides its share of rewards, especially late-summer wildflowers. This trail takes in the Beaver Ponds and Howard Eaton trails. Check with rangers for bear activity. Difficulty level: Strenuous. Trailhead: The Beaver Ponds trailhead, between Liberty Gap and the stone house at Mammoth Terraces.

Wraith Falls: This is the easiest hike in this part of Yellowstone, excellent for families or anyone wanting a quick break from driving. Minutes after leaving the parking area, after a quick 1-mile jaunt through sage and Douglas fir, you'll be at the falls on Lupine Creek. Difficulty level: Easy. Trailhead: A quarter-mile east of Lava Creek Picnic Area on Mammoth-Tower Road.

NORRIS AREA

Artist Paint Pots: Though not as popular as the Fountain Paint Pots viewing area, this one is worth checking out. The boardwalk and newly cut trail make access easy on a 1-mile roundtrip walk through burned lodgepole pine that brings visitors up close and personal with the two mud pots. Difficulty level: Easy. Trailhead: About 4.4 miles south of Norris.

Cygnet Lakes: Anyone seeking a little solitude will savor the 8-mile roundtrip hike through marsh and burned lodgepole to this tiny lake. The trail isn't maintained and mosquito repellent might be required. Keep an eye out for bears, too. Difficulty level: Easy. Trailhead: 5.5 miles west of Canyon.

Grizzly Lake: Grizzlies? Probably not. Fire history? Definitely. Few hikes in Yellowstone paint a more vivid portrait of conflagrations than this 4-mile round-tripper through spires of burned lodgepole. They're in every direction once you arrive at the rim of the lake—some charred in the historic 1988 blazes but others burned in 1976 as well. The lack of green vegetation opens up vistas of the Gallatin Range. Look for elk, wildflowers and, alas, mosquitoes. Difficulty level: Moderate. Trailhead: One mile south of Beaver Lake on Mammoth-Norris Road.

Ice Lake: Like Grizzly Lake, this short hike (less than a half-mile) features the charred remains of lodgepole burned in 1988; unlike Grizzly, this one ends in a lush green lodgepole forest. It's a great jumping-off point for other hikes in the area. Difficulty level: Easy, with handicapped accessible backcountry campsites. Trailhead: 3.5 miles east of Norris on Norris-Canyon Road.

Monument Geyser Basin: Want geyser viewing without the crowds? Try this modestly rugged hike from the Artist Paint Pots up a steep mile-long trail to these gnarled cones. One cone even has a name: Thermos Bottle Geyser. Nice views, too. Difficulty level: Moderate. Trailhead: Artist Paint Pots, about 4.4 miles south of Norris.

Solfatara Creek: An interesting hike that combines thermal features, lodgepole forest, springs, a creek and even some park power lines. Mostly flat, with a 400-foot gain. Difficulty level: Moderately easy. Trailhead: Norris Campground.

Wolf Lake Cut-Off: This 6-mile roundtrip trail, which follows the Gibbon River for about a mile before veering toward Wolf Lake, features burned lodgepole forest and Little Gibbon Falls. Difficulty level: Moderately easy. Trailhead: Between Canyon and Norris.

OLD FAITHFUL AREA

Black Sand and Biscuit Basin: Two boardwalks lead to several pools and a lake in Old Faithful's busy geothermal areas. Both are less than a mile long. Difficulty level: Easy. Trailheads: Old Faithful.

Fairy Falls/Twin Buttes: Waiting at the terminus of this hike is 197-foot Fairy Falls on Fairy Creek, one of the highest in the park. The creek meanders and drops through a lush forest where elk, bison, coyotes and eagles are known to roam or soar. With several options for access, it's suitable for those wanting a leisurely 5-mile stroll or anyone wanting more exertion on a 7-mile journey. Difficulty level: Easy. Trailhead: Steel Bridge parking area one mile south of Midway Geyser Basin or Fountain Flats parking area.

Fountain Paint Pot: One of Yellowstone's most visited geothermal areas offers close-up views of geysers, hot springs, fumaroles and mud pots on a short loop trail. Difficulty level: Easy. Trailhead: 8 miles north of Old Faithful.

Geyser Hill Loop: Lots of geothermal activity, including Beehive, Castle, Daisy and Firehole geysers. Some geysers in the area, such as Anemone, erupt every few minutes. Beehive shoots higher than Old Faithful and has a cone shaped like a beehive. Castle is shaped like its name and erupts about every 12 hours, shooting spray up to 75 feet. The Morning Glory Pool was once one of the park's most brilliant, though years of tourists tossing coins and other junk from the road have tempered its hues and helped spur algae growth. Be wary of bison and elk in the area. Difficulty level: Easy. Trailhead: Several trails through this area depart from Old Faithful.

Lone Star Geyser: Popular with bicyclists, this trail is a flat 5-miler through lodgepole pine on an old paved road to one of the park's more powerful geysers. Lone Star erupts about every three hours and never disappoints. Difficulty level: Easy. Trailhead: 3.5 miles southeast of Old Faithful at Kepler Cascades parking area.

Mallard Lake: Slip away from the Old Faithful crowds for some solitude amid lodgepole, meadows, rock and burnt forest. For its proximity to Old Faithful, surprisingly few visitors have made the 6.8-mile walk to this little jewel. Difficulty level: Moderate. Trailhead: Old Faithful Lodge cabin area.

Midway Geyser Basin: Another easily accessed trail from the road, this short walk takes in Grand Prismatic Spring and Excelsior Geyser. The latter sends 4,000 gallons of hot water into the Firehole River. The ever-colorful Grand Prismatic Spring is the largest hot spring in the world, producing 6 million gallons of water per day. Difficulty level: Easy. Trailhead: 6 miles north of Old Faithful.

Mystic Falls: For a terrific perspective on Old Faithful, take this 2.4-mile jaunt. Many visitors turn back after reaching the 70-foot falls, but it's worth veering to the right where the trail forks for a climb up a series of quad-testing switchbacks to an overlook. The Upper Geyser Basin fans out below you, with Old Faithful in the background. Difficulty level: Moderate. Trailhead: Biscuit Basin boardwalk.

Observation Point Loop: Another excellent way to get an overview of the Old Faithful area without too much exertion. This 1.1-mile loop trail rises 200 feet above Upper Geyser Basin to an overlook. Keep an eye out for bison and check out the regeneration from the 1988 North Fork fire. Difficulty level: Moderate. Trailhead: Firehole River footbridge behind Old Faithful.

TOWER-ROOSEVELT AREA

Garnet Hill Loop: This dusty 4-mile journey offers a remote Old West vision of the park, with the Yellowstone River thrown in for good measure. The trail traverses sage and pine on the road used for stagecoach cookouts and then follows Elk Creek to the river. The trail starts less than 100 yards from the Tower-Roosevelt junction and goes to the cookout shelter, then beyond to the Yellowstone. Bring a fly rod for some solitary trout angling. Difficulty level: Moderate. Trailhead: About 100 yards north of the Tower-Roosevelt junction on the Northeast Entrance Road.

Hellroaring: This 7.5-mile trail veers west from the Garnet Hill Loop Trail at the Yellowstone River. It crosses the river on a suspension bridge, rises to a sage plateau, then drops down into the scenic Hellroaring Creek drainage. Watch for wildlife and bring a fly rod to fish the pools in the creek. This can be one of the warmest areas of the park, so bring water. Difficulty level: Moderately strenuous. Trailhead: Garnet Loop trailhead at Tower-Roosevelt or Hellroaring parking area 3.5 miles west of Tower Junction.

Lost Lake: This scenic 4-mile walk through a pine forest rises 300 feet from Roosevelt Lodge to a pretty little lake where beaver, black bear and raptors are frequent sights. Continue on to the Petrified Tree. Difficulty level: Moderately strenuous. Trailhead: Behind Roosevelt Lodge.

Slough Creek: A fly angler's favorite, this pretty hike follows a popular creek along an old wagon road into two meadows and Douglas fir forest in the scenic northern range. Cross-country skiers cherish this route in the winter. It's also the only access to private Silver Tip Ranch, which is 11 miles from the trailhead, just across the park's northern boundary. You might even see visitors being hauled to the ranch in a horse-drawn wagon. The first meadow is a relatively breezy 4-mile round-trip; the second meadow is 3 miles beyond the first meadow. This is known grizzly country and the trail starts near a hillside where the once-dominant Slough Creek Pack of wolves had a den readily visible to the public in 2005. Unfortunately for wolf watchers, the Slough Creek Pack lost a turf war in 2006 and hasn't been seen much since. Difficulty level: Moderate to moderately strenuous. Trailhead: Slough Creek Campground.

Specimen Ridge: Technically, this isn't considered a marked trail, but the 1.5-mile walk across a portion of the Lamar Valley to the ridge has tremendous rewards if you're comfortable with going off-road on foot. The ridge gets its name from the more than two-dozen types of trees petrified by volcanic activity in the past 50 million years. Many are trees nowhere to be found naturally in the Northern Rockies, including magnolia, mangrove and distant relatives of California redwoods. Check at the Albright Visitor Center about ranger-led hikes into the area.

Yellowstone River Picnic Area: A rarely used way to see a portion of the Grand Canyon of the Yellowstone, this 3.7-mile roundtrip excursion on the east rim is nevertheless a good one. Views of the river and canyon are exceptional, and it's not uncommon to see eagles, osprey and bighorn sheep. Thermal activity is common here, too. The Overhanging Cliff is part of this trek and you'll also see the Tower store across the canyon. Difficulty level: Moderately strenuous. Trailhead: 1.25 miles northeast of Tower Junction.

West Thumb/Grant Village Area

Duck Lake: This easy 1-miler offers views of Yellowstone and Duck Lakes, as well as remnants of the 1988 fires. Difficulty level: Easy. Trailhead: West Thumb Geyser Basin parking area.

Lewis River Channel/Shoshone Lake/Dogshead Loop: Two choices here, most notably an 11-mile round-trip that takes in Shoshone and Lewis Lakes and the pretty channel connecting the two. For a shorter forested hike, return on the 4-mile Dogshead Trail. This is a great fishing area, for fly anglers and osprey alike. In the fall, big browns and cutthroats from the lakes head into the channel to spawn. Difficulty level: Moderate. Trailhead: 5 miles south of Grant Village.

Riddle Lake: Trek through pretty meadows and marshes to the Continental Divide and a sweet little lake. Whenever you're in willowy marshes, there's a chance to run into an obstinate moose. Because of bear activity, this trail is closed until mid-July. Difficulty level: Moderate. Trailhead: About 5 miles south of Grant Village.

Shoshone Lake/DeLacy Creek: A 6-mile trek to the largest lake in the lower 48 states without road access, through meadows and wildflowers. Lots of wildlife possibilities, including sandhill cranes and moose. Hiking the entire circumference of the lake is 28 miles. Difficulty level: Easy to moderate. Trailhead: 8.8 miles west of West Thumb.

West Thumb Geyser Basin: Lots of hot springs and dormant geysers on Yellowstone Lake's shores. This short walk features handicapped access on trails and boardwalks. Difficulty level: Easy. Trailhead: One-quarter mile east of West Thumb.

Yellowstone Lake Overlook: A popular 2-mile trail with terrific views of the lake, Absaroka Mountains and West Thumb area after a 400-foot elevation gain. Difficulty level: Easy. Trailhead: West Thumb Geyser Basin parking area.

Yellowstone Lake Area

Avalanche Peak: A challenging 5-mile roundtrip climb that's worth the effort once you see stunning views of the lake and mountains. The trail switchbacks up 1,800 feet through forest, whitebark pine and open scree. Grizzlies are common in this area because of whitebark pine. Difficulty level: Strenuous. Trailhead: Across East Entrance Road at the west end of Eleanor Lake, near Sylvan Pass.

Elephant Back Mountain: A 3-miler that climbs 800 feet through lodgepole pine to views of the northwest corner of the lake. Difficulty level: Moderately strenuous. Trailhead: 1 mile south of Fishing Bridge junction.

Natural Bridge: A breezy 3-mile walk on gravel and asphalt to the 51-foot-high Natural Bridge. Difficulty level: Easy. Trailhead: Bridge Bay Marina parking lot near campground entrance.

Pelican Creek: This pretty 1-mile loop hike traverses lodgepole forest on the lakeshore and a small marsh where bison and birds like to hang out. Difficulty level: Easy. Trailhead: One mile east of Fishing Bridge Visitor Center.

Storm Point: For views of the lake and its wildlife, take this 2.3-mile loop. The route goes through forest to a rocky promontory that juts into the lake. Check the Fishing Bridge Visitor Center for possible closure due to grizzly activity. Watch for yellow-bellied marmots. Difficulty level: Easy. Trailhead: At Indian Pond, 3 miles east of Fishing Bridge Visitor Center.

Grand Teton National Park

The same hiking rules for Yellowstone apply to Grand Teton, especially when it comes to safety. It's especially important to keep an eye on those afternoon cumulus clouds. Much of Grand Teton is exposed, so if you hear the crack of thunder it's advisable to consider looking for safe ground away from the park's ridges and lakes. You're more likely to encounter a grizzly in the northern reaches of the park than the south, but the prevalence of black bear still requires hanging food when camping in the backcountry. Some campsites provide special food-storage boxes. Bring water, a jacket and rain gear. For guided private hikes into the backcountry of Grand Teton, Yellowstone and Jackson Hole, contact **Hole Hiking Experience** (866-733-4453; www.holehiking.com).

Cascade Canyon: This is Grand Teton's most popular hiking area, with most visitors taking the Jenny Lake boat ride to the base of the mountains. Nearly everyone hikes the 1.1 miles to 200-foot Hidden Falls. The majority hike another 1.8 miles to Inspiration Point, which features a busy collection of marmots and stirring views of the lake, Jackson Hole and the Gros Ventre Mountains. From there, the more adventurous turn left and continue on another 3.4 miles to Lake Solitude and the rest of the way to Hurricane Pass and views of Schoolroom Glacier, a 19-mile roundtrip. The trail forks right toward Paintbrush Canyon and Leigh Lake, then back to Jenny Lake. Moose are common in the canyon and black bears are frequently spotted. The boat fee is $7.50 adults ($5 children) for a round-trip and $5 for one-way if you want to hike the 2.4 miles through Englemann spruce and lodgepole around the south shore of the park's most cherished lake. Difficulty level: Moderate to strenuous, depending on distance. Trailhead: East boat dock on Jenny Lake.

Chapel of the Configuration: A breezy half-mile round-trip walk to century-old buildings on the Snake River at Menor's Ferry, including a log church built in 1925. Sunday services are conducted here in the summers. Other buildings include Bill Menor's old cabin and store. Self-guiding maps and information are at the trailhead. Difficulty level: Easy. Trailhead: Just inside the South Entrance.

Colter Bay: A delightful 8.8-mile round-trip stroll through lodgepole forest and meadows along streams and past ponds. Several trails branch from the trailhead, all returning to the same place. Look for waterfowl, moose and trumpeter swans in marshy areas. The end is Hermitage Point, which juts into Jackson Lake. Difficulty level: Easy. Trailhead: South end of Colter Bay Visitor Center parking lot.

Cunningham Cabin: Check out an 1890-ish Jackson Hole homestead, which features two cabins with sod roofs. The trail is self-guided and a brochure tells of the Cunningham family's attempt to raise cattle here at the turn of the previous century. They built the first classic split-rail fences for which the region is renowned.

Death Canyon: Take your pick of the brisk 1.8-mile round-trip to the Phelps Lake overlook on a glacial moraine or do the muscle-wrenching trek 8 miles into the wilderness to Static Peak Divide. From the overlook, it's another fairly steep mile down to the lake—remember that you'll have to return this way—and then 2 strenuous miles up into Death Canyon. Here the trail forks at the Death Canyon Patrol Cabin toward Static Peak on steep switchbacks through whitebark pine. It's a challenging up, down and up to the cabin built in the 1930s by the Civilian Conservation Corps for trail maintenance. A half-mile beyond the cabin is another overlook of Death Canyon. Difficulty level: Moderate to very strenuous. Trailhead: 3 miles south of Moose on Moose-Wilson Road

Flagg Ranch: Two quite different hikes leave from the ranch, which sits between Grand Teton and Yellowstone off the John D. Rockefeller Memorial Parkway. The 5-mile Flagg

Canyon stroll offers great views of the Snake River as it carves the canyon before spilling out to the south in Jackson Hole. The 2.3-mile Polecat Creek Loop Trail encompasses lodgepole forests and marshlands resplendent with wildlife, especially waterfowl. Difficulty level: Easy for both. Trailhead: Flagg Ranch.

Granite Canyon: Go for the gusto on this one. Unlike Cascade and Death Canyons, this one doesn't have natural stopping points on the way to the Teton Crest. It's 10 miles along Granite Creek into subalpine meadows at Marion Lake. Two-thirds of the way up, you can backtrack to the south to where the tramway at Jackson Hole Ski Area drops off riders. Or head down Open Canyon to Phelps Lake. Of course, you can always turn around and head back at any point. Difficulty level: Strenuous. Trailhead: One mile north of Granite Canyon Entrance Station on Moose-Wilson Road.

Jackson Lake Lodge: A popular half-mile stroll that ends at a perch overlooking Jackson Lake, Willow Flats and the Tetons in the distance. Interpretive signs are at the top of the hill. Difficulty level: Easy. Trailhead: Jackson Lake Lodge.

Leigh Lake: Two options are available here—a 2-mile round-trip walk to the lake along the channel connecting Leigh to String Lake or a 7.4-mile adventure along Leigh's east shore northward to Bearpaw Lake. On the latter hike, Mount Moran will constantly be in view across the lake. Mosquitoes can be brutal here and bears of both types are known to frequent the area. Difficulty level: Easy for both. Trailhead: 2 miles off Teton Park Road, north of Jenny Lake.

Lupine Meadows: One of the park's most rugged trails leads to Garnet Canyon and Amphitheater Lake. It's 8.2 miles to the canyon and another 1.4 to a series of glacial lakes on switchbacks. No horses allowed. Difficulty level: Strenuous. Trailhead: 2 miles off the Teton Park Road, about a mile south of Jenny Lake.

String Lake: Many visitors miss this one because of its proximity to Jenny Lake, but locals like it for the solitude. It's 3.3 miles around the skinny lake between Jenny and Leigh. This trail also serves as the starting point for the hike up Paintbrush Canyon. A 12.4-mile round-trip journey encircles Holly Lake and returns. Keep going to Lake Solitude and return down Cascade Canyon, an arduous 19.2-mile affair. Difficulty level: Easy to very strenuous. Trailhead: Same as Leigh Lake, about 2 miles off Teton Park Road.

Taggart Lake: A popular choice for those wanting to skip the crowds at Jenny Lake. A 4-mile round-trip rises on glacial moraines to Taggart and then Bradley Lakes, both surrounded by burns from a 1985 fire. Several loop options are available, including along tumbling Beaver Creek. Difficulty level: Moderate. Trailhead: About 4 miles north of Moose on Teton Park Road.

Teton Canyon: Here's a rugged 11-mile round-trip scramble up the back, or west, side of the Tetons. The trail rises to within a half-mile of the summit, where it becomes talus. Go the extra half-mile for splendid views. Difficulty level: Strenuous. Trailhead: Teton Canyon Campground near Grand Targhee Ski Resort.

Teton Crest: The king of all Teton hikes; plan to spend at least four days to cover the entire 40 miles on the west side of the Tetons. Only a portion of the trail actually enters the park, and once you're on the trail, it's moderately challenging compared to the canyon hikes that intersect the route. The southernmost terminus is Teton Village, and the trail goes to Paintbrush Canyon in the north. Most hikers wanting to walk the entire trail start either at Teton Village in the south or Paintbrush Canyon in the north, though there are numerous entry or exit points. Difficulty level: Moderately strenuous. Trailhead: Teton

Village, Granite Creek, Cascade Canyon, Leigh Lake.

Two Ocean Lake: Get an entirely different perspective on the park than from any other trails. While most head up canyons into the Tetons, these wrap around Two Ocean and Emma Matilda Lakes in the northeast corner of the park, just outside the Bridger-Teton Wilderness. The hikes range from 6.4 miles round-trip to a 13-mile journey that encompasses both lakes. The focus here is the lakes, forests and wildflowers, as opposed to mountain views—though Grand View Point between the two lakes offers vistas of Mount Moran and its siblings. Black bears are common here, and grizzlies were frequenting the area in the summer of 2007. Difficulty level: Easy to moderate. Trailhead: About 3 miles north of Moran Junction, off Pacific Creek Road.

Jackson Hole

Snow King: A half-mile trail at the top of Jackson's local ski hill offers panoramic views of Jackson Hole, Tetons and Gros Ventre. It's $10 to take the chairlift to the summit, or you can give your legs a workout by hiking the entire distance. Difficulty level: Easy to strenuous. Trailhead: Snow King Resort.

Cabin Creek: Enjoy Snake River scenery, as well as rafters plying the whitewater, on this trail following a Snake tributary to a low pass that offers great views of the river's drainage. Difficulty level: Moderate. Trailhead: Cabin Creek Campground.

Cache Creek: A pleasant 6-mile stroll on a forested road that follows a gurgling creek of the same name. It has a wilderness feel close to town. Difficulty level: Easy. Trailhead: Off Upper Cache Creek Drive.

Granite Creek Falls: Soak weary muscles in one of two hot springs after this easy 2-mile hike in a lush valley. Granite Falls has a primitive rock-and-sand natural hot springs where it's possible to soak under the warm falls, though most prefer the 104-degree developed pool at Granite Hot Springs up the trail. A small fee is charged. Swimsuits and towels are available for rent. Difficulty level: Easy. Trailhead: Confluence of Granite and Swift Creeks, about 8 miles from US 189 after driving 12 miles east of Hoback Junction.

Putt-Putt: Add a few extra miles to a Cache Creek hike on this breezy stroll just outside of Jackson. Difficulty level: Easy. Trailhead: 2 miles up Cache Creek Trail.

Ski Lake: An excellent 4.6-mile hike near Teton Pass that's suitable for families looking for more than a walk around town. The reward is spectacular views of Jackson Hole and a pretty alpine lake. The elevation gain is modest and evenly spread. Difficulty level: Modest. Trailhead: About halfway up Teton Pass off WY 22, near Phillips Canyon.

Note: The **Teton County Parks and Recreation Department** (307-739-9025; www .tetonwyo.org/parks) offers guided hikes twice a week during the summer for a small fee. Longer overnight hikes also are available. Other guided hikes are offered through **Grand Teton National Park** and **The Hole Hiking Experience** (866-733-4453; www.holehike .com), which leads adventures into Jackson Hole, the park and Teton Valley.

Outside the Parks

Yellowstone, Grand Teton and Jackson Hole are surrounded by thousands of miles of trails through wilderness and national forests. US 191 through the Gallatin Valley of Montana is a hiker's paradise, with trails leading into the Gallatin and Madison Mountains. Ditto for the Paradise Valley north of Gardiner, the Shoshone Valley west of Cody, the Targhee National Forest of Idaho, the Hebgen and Quake Lake areas northwest of West Yellowstone, and the Teton Wilderness east of Moran. Pick up Forest Service maps at any district office.

HORSEBACK RIDING

For anyone who lives east of the Rockies or on the West Coast, no trip to the region is complete without playing cowboy for at least a few hours. A variety of possibilities await you, from a short trail ride on programmed horses to treks on the wilder side through outfitters. Many outfitters also have llamas. The best bet is to choose a guide through the Wyoming (307-527-7453; www.wyoga.org), Montana (406-449-3578; www.moga-montana.org) or Idaho (800-494-3246, 208-342-1919; www.ioga.org) **Outfitters and Guides Association.** Yellowstone has authorized 42 outfitters to guide horse trips and four to guide llamas into the park. Many lodges also offer horseback riding either as part of their all-inclusive deals or for an extra charge. No experience is required. If you're bringing your own horses, be sure to check regulations in both parks. Horses and other stock such as burros, mules and llamas are a tradition and thus welcome in portions of Grand Teton National Park, which has five backcountry stock campsites. Call 307-739-3309 for permit information for Grand Teton National Park and go to www.nps.gov/archive/grte/pubs/brochures/stock.pdf for the park's stock rules. Stock use is also permitted in Yellowstone, though not until July 1 for overnight stays. Call 307-344-2160 for more information on backcountry riding in the park. Advance reservations for backcountry campsites may be made, but permits must be picked up within 48 hours of entry into the park.

In and around Yellowstone National Park

Xanterra Parks and Resorts (307-344-7311; www.nps.gov/yell/planyourvisit/horseride .htm) is the park's concessionaire and offers rides at Mammoth, Tower-Roosevelt and Canyon. Wagon rides and cookouts also are available. Following are a few of the outfitters who offer trail rides suitable for all ages:

BELGRADE

Sunrise Pack Station (406-388-2236; www.sunrisepackstation.com) guides horse and mule pack strings into Yellowstone. Full-day $165, half-day $100. Fishing trips are $185. A wide variety of lengthy overnight pack trips ranging from about $1,400 to $1,800 also are available.

BIG SKY

Canyon Adventures (406-995-4450; www.snowmobilemontana.com) just south of the mountain resort on US 191 offers rides in the Gallatin River Canyon from May to September. One-hour rides are $36, two-hour rides $46. Riding/rafting combinations are also available, featuring float trips on the Gallatin.

Jake's Horses (800-352-5956, 406-995-4630; www.nationalparkreservations.com/yellowstone_activity_horseback.htm) offers one-, two-, three-hour and all-day trail rides and pack trips into Yellowstone. Prices range from $34 to $106. A steak fry dinner ride is $80. Hay rides and winter sleigh rides also are offered.

CODY

Cedar Mountain Trail Rides (307-527-4966) is based at the Cody KOA and the Cody Nite Rodeo grounds.

Big Bear Motel (800-325-7163, 307-587-3117; www.bigbearmotel.com) has hour-long rides for $20.

DRIGGS

Dry Ridge Outfitters (208-354-2284; www.dryridge.com) leads trips into the Tetons and the remote Bechler River region of Yellowstone's southwest corner. Short trail rides, extended day trips and overnighters are available. Trail rides start at $30. Guided pack trips range from $200 to $235 per person per day. Hunting, fishing and trips that include stays in townhouses also are offered.

GARDINER

Flying Pig Adventure Company (866-807-0744, 406-848-7510; www.flyingpig rafting.com) in Gardiner features trail rides that leave from a mountain lodge near Yellowstone's northern border. Two-hour rides are $50, half-day $95 and full-day $155. Overnighters, riding/rafting combinations on the Yellowstone and a one-hour ride followed by a chuck-wagon cookout are also available.

Hell's a Roarin' Outfitters (406-848-7548; www.jardinehorses.com) has one-hour, two-hour, half-day, full-day and longer rides out of Jardine into Yellowstone and the Absaroka-Beartooth Wilderness, about 5 miles on gravel up the hill from Gardiner.

Montana Guide Service (406-848-7265; www.montanaguide.com) has 2.5-hour ($50), half-day ($75) and full-day ($125) trail rides to the Montana ghost towns of Aldridge and Electric.

Montana Whitewater (800-799-4465, 406-848-7398; www.montanawhitewater.com) features "paddle and saddle" riding and rafting combinations on either the Yellowstone or Gallatin Rivers. Options for the Yellowstone are a morning ride and lunch at a local ranch followed by a Yellowstone float or lunch followed by a ride and rafting to close the day. Cost is $89 for adults, $77 for children ages 10–12. The Gallatin trips feature a morning ride up Hellroaring Creek and then rafting in the afternoon. Prices are $119 and $109.

The Thorofare Region of southeast Yellowstone is the wildest part of the park and the least visited by tourists. The Thorofare Ranger Station is the most isolated residence in the Lower 48. National Park Service

LIVINGSTON

Wilderness Pack Trips (406-222-5128; www.wildernesspacktrips.com) offers full-day rides from early June to early July in various locations in the northern part of Yellowstone. Cost is $240 per person. Lengthier pack trips also are available, ranging from just under $2,000 to just under $3,000 per person.

Yellowstone Wilderness Outfitters (406-223-3300; www.yellowstone.ws) has everything from day trips into Yellowstone to overnighters deep into the remote Thorofare country, led by veteran park guides. Trips can be geared toward photography, fishing or wildlife viewing. Half-day in northwest corner of park $110, full-day in northern range $165, full-day in southern part of the park $250.

WEST YELLOWSTONE

Diamond P Ranch (208-558-7077, 406-646-7246; www.yellowstonehorses.com) is located between West Yellowstone and Island Park. Half-day trips guided by Halo "A" Ranch outfitters to near the Continental Divide are $50, and a trail ride featuring a chuckwagon supper is $60. On Thursdays, Fridays and Saturdays a rodeo is included with the trail ride and chuckwagon supper for $76.

Yellowstone Mountain Guides (406-646-7230; www.yellowstone-guides.com) offers an array of rides into Yellowstone, including fishing trips. Deer and elk bow and rifle hunting forays just outside the park's northern boundary also are available. Trail rides start at $60 for two hours, $75–95 for half-day and $135 for full day. Fishing and photography rates start at $135.

In and Around Grand Teton National Park

Grand Teton Lodge Company (307-543-2811; www.gtlc.com) has rides of varying lengths into the park from Jackson Lake Lodge, Colter Bay and Teton Village.

FLAGG RANCH

Teton Wagon Train and Horse Adventures (800-443-2311, 307-543-2861; www.flagg ranch.com) has one-hour, two-hour, half-day and full-day rides on the wooded trails near the ranch between Yellowstone and Grand Teton.

JACKSON

A/OK Corral (307-733-6556; www.horsecreekranch.com) in Hoback Junction has trail rides, pack trips, covered wagon adventures and hunting excursions out of Horse Creek Ranch. Rates start at $35 for a one-hour ride and go to four figures for lengthy pack and hunting trips.

Jackson Country Outfitters (800-434-0368, 307-413-5267; www.jacksoncountryout fitters.com) is just outside of Hoback Junction. Rates start at $30 for one hour to $150 for full-day fishing trips. JCO also offers a "paddle and saddle" package with Dave Hansen Whitewater, which includes a trail ride plus a whitewater and/or scenic float on the Snake. Several options are available.

Mill Iron Ranch (888-808-6390, 307-733-6390; www.millironranch.net) is about 10 miles south of Jackson and features two-, four- and eight-hour rides above the ranch. Full-day and pack trips also are available.

Scott's Jackson Hole Trail Rides (307-733-6992) is in Teton Village.

Spring Creek Ranch (307-733-8833; www.springcreekranch.com) starts its rides on top of Gros Ventre Butte. Included are short trail rides, full-day adventures and breakfast or dinner trips.

Teton Wagon Train and Horse Adventures (888-734-6101, 307-734-6101; www.teton wagontrain.com) features Double H Bars Ranch Conestoga wagon trains rolling into the Targhee National Forest for four days and three nights between the two parks. For those who'd rather ride, gentle horses are available. Adults are $875, children 9–14 are $795 and children 4–8 are $745. Departures are on each Monday from early June until late August.

Togwotee Mountain Lodge (800-543-2847, 307-543-2847; www.togwoteelodge.com) is on the west side of Togwotee Pass, with rides featuring views of the Tetons. Prices range from $30 for a one-hour ride to $225 for a riding/fishing combination package on the Buffalo Fork River.

MOOSE

Gros Ventre River Ranch (307-733-4138; www.grosventreriverranch.com) is a guest ranch that offers commercial trips.

Triangle X Ranch (307-733-2183; www.trianglex.com) prides itself on taking riders off the beaten path on pack trips into wilderness areas east of the two parks from early June to September. Four-night minimum. Cost ranges from $210 to $300 per day per person, depending on the number in the group.

PHOTO SAFARIS

Wyoming Photo Experience (307-413-3777) of Jackson specializes in wilderness photography in Grand Teton National Park led by Wyoming photographer Jim Laybourn. Half- and full-day tours available and include photography tips (www.wyomingphoto experience.com).

RAFTING

Surprisingly, given the rugged contours of the land, whitewater rafting and boating aren't as prolific in the Yellowstone/Teton/Jackson Hole region as they are in neighboring areas. One reason is that floating rivers isn't allowed in Yellowstone, much to the consternation of kayakers who salivate over the canyon stretches of the Yellowstone and Gardner Rivers. The natural ebb and flow of water levels is another.

Nevertheless, plenty of thrills and spills are at hand for those wanting a wild ride, and more sedate boating is even more readily available.

Anyone considering a whitewater float, whether with an outfitter or self-supporting, should understand the rating system for rapids, ranging from Class I scenic floats to Class VI for waterfalls that should only be attempted by expert extremists, if at all. Most of the major whitewater floats around the parks are Class II–III, which provide an adrenalin rush while remaining forgiving in the event of a mishap. Options range from renting your own raft—be sure know what you're doing—to hiring an outfitter to do all the work with the oars. If you're new to the sport, the most exhilarating approach is to be on a "paddle raft," meaning a guide will steer and give commands from the back, but you'll be a part of a six- or eight-person paddling team. For the biggest thrills, and if you have whitewater

experience, rent a one- or two-person inflatable kayak, hard-shell sit-on-top or traditional hard-shell kayak (if you know how to roll upright).

Whitewater Rafting

Clarks Fork of the Yellowstone River: The Clarks Fork is a stunning river as it thunders
through a narrow canyon in Sunlight Basin, not far from the Northeast Entrance to
Yellowstone. It is an experts-only stretch, with water ranging from Class IV to virtually
impassible Box Canyon. More Class IV water is accessible below the canyon. Don't try this
river unless you're an experienced kayaker with a reliable roll.

    Gallatin River: Two words—Mad Mile. That sums up the Gallatin, which carves a beau-
tiful narrow canyon from the northwest corner of Yellowstone for 70 miles until it opens
into the broad Gallatin Valley west of Bozeman. The river moves briskly for most of the
run, but the highlight is the stretch called the Mad Mile, which features the giant boulder
called House Rock at river center near its beginning. For another mile, the river bounces
and jounces through technical Class II–III water. It looks easy when done right, and thousands navigate the stretch with no problem, but a spill at House Rock likely means a long
cold swim and a few bruises. Leading up to this stretch are a few challenging Class III
rapids. If this is more than you want, a calmer Class II float is available downstream. The
Gallatin Canyon is narrow, and water flows can get so low that kayaks are sometimes the
only option in July and August. Half-day rafting trips run about $45 and full-day about
$80. Companies offering Gallatin River whitewater trips include:
Geyser Whitewater (800-914-9031, 406-995-4989; www.raftmontana.com)
Montana Whitewater (800-348-4376, 406-763-4613; www.montanawhitewater.com)
Yellowstone Raft Company (800-348-4376, 406-995-4613; www.yellowstoneraft.com)

    Madison River: The Madison is more renowned for its world-class fishing, but it does
offer a memorable float through Bear Trap Canyon in the Lee Metcalf Wilderness, about 80
miles north of Yellowstone. The notorious Class IV/V Kitchen Sink is about halfway
between the put-in below the Ennis Lake Dam and the take-out at either Warm Springs or
Black's Ford. The Kitchen Sink Rapid is so daunting most floaters avoid this run. The rec-
ommendation here is to hire **Yellowstone Raft Company** (800-348-4376, 406-995-
4613;www.yellowstoneraft.com) to get you through the Kitchen Sink and a significant drop
soon after, then spend the rest of the day fishing. Lack of traffic this deep into the canyon
leaves a lot of big browns and rainbows uncaught. Another stretch for highly skilled
boaters is the 3.5 miles below Quake Lake, where the river turns frothy with Class III to
Class V whitewater before leveling off for 60 miles of prime fishing waters. The river is
extremely difficult to access from US 287 and contains some brawling waters.

    Snake River: About 25 miles south of Jackson, the mighty Snake quickens its pulse in a
headlong rush to get to the Columbia River at Tri-Cities, Washington. For 8 miles, the river
roils and boils in a series of Class III and Class IV drops, most notably Big Kahuna and
Lunch Counter Rapids. The popular journey starts swiftly at West Table Creek Campground
with the soon-to-follow Station Creek Drop, S-Turns and Cutbanks. It mellows in the
middle and then collects its debt with Big Kahuna, Lunch Counter, Rope and Champagne
Rapids. The river puts on its best show of force in June before becoming more sedate in
August. The 3.5-hour trips range from $40 to $85, depending on such amenities as food.
When the trip is over, check with **Float-O-Graphs** (307-733-6453; www.floatographs
.com; 130 W. Broadway Ave.) or **Whitewater Photos and Video** (307-733-7015; www
.snakeriverphotos.com; 140 N. Cache Dr.). They'll have photos or videos of you riding the

big rapids for sale in the shops or online. Do-it-yourselfers who want isolation might consider the challenging Class III Southgate stretch where the river leaves Yellowstone and rushes toward Flagg Ranch. Companies offering Snake River whitewater trips through the canyon south of Jackson include:

Barker-Ewing Whitewater (800-448-4202, 307-733-1000; www.barker-ewing.com)

Dave Hansen Whitewater (800-732-6295, 307-733-6295; www.davehansenwhitewater .com)

Jackson Hole Whitewater (800-700-7238, 307-733-1007; www.jhww.com)

Lewis and Clark Expeditions (800-824-5375, 307-733-4200; www.lewisandclark expeditions.com)

Mad River Boat Trips (800-458-5375, 307-733-6203; www.mad-river.com)

Sands Wild Water (800-358-8184, 307-733-4410; www.sandswhitewater.com)

Snake River Kayak and Canoe School (800-529-2501, 307-733-9999; www.snakeriver kayak.com)

Snake River Park Whitewater (800-563-1878, 307-733-7078; www.srpkoa.com)

Shoshone River: Sun-kissed trips through Red Rock Canyon and Lower Canyon hover between scenic floats and tumultuous whitewater. The rapids are a cushy Class I–II. Guided trips through the dusty canyon are available, but this is an excellent place to try your own hand at entry-level rapids using a rented raft or inflatable kayak. The popular float starts at Demaris Street west of Cody and goes for 7 to 13 miles, ranging from 90 minutes to three hours. Expect to pay anywhere from $25 to $65. For more action with a similar pace, at least until water flows are too low in July, put in on the North Fork of the Shoshone for a half-day float. Expert kayakers will find the highly technical Class IV action between Buffalo Bill Dam and DeMaris Springs a thrill.

Companies offering Shoshone River and North Fork whitewater trips include:

Core Mountain Sports (877-527-7354; www.coremountainsports.com)

Gradient Mountain Sports (307-587-4659; www.gradientmountainsports.com)

Red Canyon River Trips (800-293-0148, 307-587-6988; www.imt.net/~rodeo/raft.html)

River Runners (800-535-7238, 307-527-7238;www.riverrunnersofwyoming.com)

Wyoming River Trips (800-586-6661, 307-587-6661; www.wyomingrivertrips.com)

Yellowstone River: For a mountain-birthed stream that flows undammed (sort of) for 678 miles to the Missouri, the Yellowstone has surprisingly few whitewater stretches. In fact, there are two, both short: the Gardiner town stretch and Yankee Jim Canyon. Both are Class III at best, but their proximity to Yellowstone's North Entrance and easy access from US 89 make it possible to spend a half-day in the park and another half on the river. The Yellowstone narrows at Yankee Jim before spilling into Paradise Valley, serving up three modest Class II-III drops, their difficulty dependent on the season. By midsummer, they're pretty tame. The Gardiner town stretch requires hauling boats about 100 yards down a modestly steep trail from town to where the Gardner River thunders into the Yellowstone. Technically, you're in the park for only a few feet, but it's enough to give the Park Service control over commercial operations on the river. Most trips range from 8 miles in a half-day to 17 miles in a full day, costing from $40–80. Companies offering Yellowstone River whitewater trips include:

Flying Pig Adventure Company (866-807-0744, 406-848-7510; www.flyingpigrafting.com).

Montana Whitewater (800-799-4465, 406-763-4465; www.montanawhitewater.com).

Rendezvous Outfitters Yellowstone Rough Riders (406-848-7967; www.yellowstone roughriders.com)

Wild West Rafting (800-862-0557, 406-848-2252; www.wildwestrafting.com)
Yellowstone Raft Company (800-858-7781, 406-848-7777 www.yellowstoneraft.com)

Scenic Floats

Clarks Fork of the Yellowstone River: Most of this federally designated Wild and Scenic
River is a wild rush, but below Box Canyon the river mellows out for pretty floats offered by
Red Canyon River Trips (800-293-0148, 307-587-6988; www.imt.net/~rodeo/raft.html)
in Cody.

Madison River: Most who ply the scenic waters of the Madison do so in a drift boat and
take a fly rod. Anyone who takes the time to look up from casting to big browns and rainbows will note the splendor of the Madison Range to the east, Tobacco Root Mountains to
the north and Gravelly Range to the west. Plenty of outfitters are at the ready to offer
guided fishing trips. The scenery comes at no extra charge.

Snake River: Few backdrops are as spectacular as the Snake River's as it leaves Jackson
Lake and cuts through the pine and sage country of Jackson Hole. Most floats start at
Deadman's Bar and go to Moose. Some companies go from Moose to Wilson. Flagg Ranch
offers trips on the upper Snake before it enters Jackson Lake. Canoeists wanting an easy
float will appreciate the 5 miles just below the dam. Launch sites are at Oxbow Bend,
Pacific Creek, Deadman's Bar, Schwabacher's Landing and Moose. Look for moose, eagles,
deer and elk. Kick back and enjoy a Class II ride from these companies:
Barker-Ewing Float Trips (800-448-4202, 307-733-1800; www.barker-ewing.com)
Flagg Ranch (800-443-2311, 307-543-2861; www.flagranch.com)
Fort Jackson River Trips (800-735-8430, 307-733-2583)
Mad River Boat Trips (800-458-5375, 307-733-6203; www.mad-river.com)
Signal Mountain Lodge (307-733-5470; www.signalmtnlodge.com)
Solitude Float Trips (888-704-2800, 307-733-2871, www.solitudefloattrips.com)

Yellowstone River: Downstream from Yankee Jim Canyon, the Yellowstone begins a
serpentine journey through one of the most splendid valleys in the country. The northern
Absarokas tower above Paradise Valley to the east and the Gallatins provide a barrier to the
west. The Yellowstone meanders past ranches and large log homes, all the while serving up
some of the world's finest trout fishing. The river is suitable for rafts, kayaks, drift boats
and canoes. Launch sites are at regular intervals off US 89. Eagles, osprey and deer are
common sights. Companies offering scenic floats in Paradise Valley include:
Montana Whitewater (800-799-4465, 406-763-4465; www.montanawhitewater.com)
Rubber Ducky River Rentals (406-222-3746; www.riverservices.com)
Wild West Rafting (800-862-0557, 406-848-2252; www.wildwestrafting.com)
Yellowstone Raft Company (800-858-7781, 406-848-7777; www.yellowstoneraft.com)

RUNNING/BIATHLONS/TRIATHLONS

Joggers will find miles of pleasant and scenic trails, and those wanting a more organized
environment have plenty of events to choose from, ranging from fun runs to marathons.

ASHTON

Mesa Falls Marathon (208-604-1348; www.mesafallsmarathon.com) is a spectacular run
that begins in the Targhee National Forest and ends in Ashton after 26 miles of forest

with views of the Tetons and thundering Upper Mesa Falls. Ranked among the top 50 marathons in the country. Third week in August.

CODY

Summer Tri-Sprint Distance Triathlon (307-587-2550) has a 500-yard pool swim, 13-mile bike ride and 3.1-mile run around Beck Lake Reservoir. Late July.

JACKSON

Exum Guide Rendezvous Mountain Run (307-733-5200; www.snowking.com) is a 7.2-miler up the side of Jackson Hole's Rendezvous Mountain. Late August. The event was canceled in 2007 because the Jackson Hole Mountain Resort tram was shut down. It was scheduled to resume in 2008.

Old Bill's Fun Run for Charity (307-739-1026; www.oldbills.org) features 2K, 5K and 10K competitive and recreational races where creative costuming is part of the gig. The event, sponsored by Jackson's Community Foundation, has raised more than $45 million in 10 years. It starts from the Rendezvous Campus and features live entertainment. Second Saturday in September.

Snow King Runners Hill Climb (307-733-5056) touts itself as one of the most difficult foot races in the West. It starts at the Jackson Town Square and ends atop Snow King Mountain. Late July.

Thanksgiving Day Turkey Trot (307-733-5200; www.snowking.com) is a leisurely 5K run or walk for those who don't mind the late autumn chill. Late November.

VICTOR

Grand Teton Ultras & Trail Marathon (800-827-4433; www.grandtarghee.com) is serving up a standard marathon, 50-mile ultramarathon and 100-miler on a 25-mile loop consisting of single-track and service roads around the Grand Targhee Resort. Labor Day weekend.

WEST YELLOWSTONE

Janet Clarkson Memorial Triathlon (406-646-9328; www.janetstriathlon.com) consists of a 1K swim in the Madison Arm of Hebgen Lake, 7.3-mile bike ride and a 5.2-mile run. Clarkson was an avid area athlete who died of bone cancer at age 37. Proceeds benefit West Yellowstone School's scholarship fund and the American Cancer Society. Mid-June.

Pine Needle Stampede Foot Race (406-646-7744) has been considered one of the most scenic running courses in the country. The event features 10K and 6K runs for adults and kids. Early September.

Summer Biathlon Series (406-646-7097; www.rendezvousskitrails.com) features running and target shooting on 35 miles of gentle rolling terrain. Late July. The series was canceled in 2007 because of Forest Service fire restrictions.

SKATEBOARDING

CODY

The **Cody Skate Park** opened in 2003 in Mentock Park in east Cody. The 8,000-square-foot facility has six bowls with rails, stairs and ledges. It's open daily from 8 AM until dusk and there is no admission charge. Skateboards and in-line skates only.

Jackson

Airspeed Skateparks built the **Jackson Hole Skatepark** (307-734-7267) in 2001 on Gregory Lane. It's free and features a significant vertical bowl. The **Boardroom** (307-733-8327; boardroomjacksonhole.com; 225 Broadway Ave.) offers rentals and has a small half-pipe ramp for skateboarding and BMX riders in its parking lot. No charge for kids as long as a waiver is signed.

Skating

Cody

Cody's indoor rink, **Victor J. Riley Arena** (307-587-1681; 1400 Heart Mountain St.), offers public skating, lessons and hockey time from late October to March.

Jackson

Public indoor figure skating is available year-round at the **Snow King Ice Arena** (307-734-3137; wwwsnowking.com). Schedules are limited and can change, so call the hot line at 307-734-3000 before arriving. Typical hours are noon–1:45 PM Monday–Saturday and 1:15–2:45 PM on Sundays. Admission is $6 adults and $4 children. Season passes were $125 in 2007. Rentals and lessons are available. The rink is home to the Jackson Hole Figure Skating Club, the Jackson Hole Moose Hockey Club and hosts a variety of events on and off the ice. Before bringing a pair of skates on vacation, check first for summer rink closures.

Skiing (Alpine)

Think Utah is known for deep powder? Try a day at Grand Targhee. Though prolonged drought means snow isn't what it once was, it's still possible to ski in powder up to your eyebrows after a storm rolls in and hits a wall against the Tetons. You can't go wrong with the two dramatically different options in Jackson Hole: The swanky Jackson Hole Mountain Resort and the neighborly Snow King Resort. Farther north, Sleeping Giant Ski Area west of Cody was a low-key family resort, but it closed and has no immediate plans for opening. North of Yellowstone, Big Sky and Moonlight Basin share a high-brow destination resort on par with Sun Valley and Aspen. Bridger Bowl near Bozeman is popular among locals and renowned for some colossal snow depths. For the more adventurous, **Hellroaring Ski Adventures** (406-646-4571; www.skihellroaring.com) in West Yellowstone will drop skiers into the backcountry.

Alta

Grand Targhee Ski Resort (800-827-4433, 307-353-2300; www.grandtarghee.com/winter/skiing; 3300 E. Ski Hill Rd.) receives more than 500 inches of snow annually and features more than 3,000 acres of terrain on two mountains. Fred's Mountain has 1,600 acres, 400 of which are groomed. The rest is for powder hounds who savor the 2,000 vertical feet of descent. Peaked Mountain piques the interest of more skilled skiers with 2,419-foot vertical and 1,500 ski-able acres, most of which are served exclusively by snowcat. Rentals and instruction are available. Lift tickets: $59 adults, $38 seniors, $36 children.

BIG SKY

Big Sky Resort (800-548-4486, 406-995-5000; www.bigskyresort.com; 1 Lone Mountain Trail), the vision of former NBC newsman Chet Huntley, has become Montana's poshest ski destination. Towering Lone Mountain receives 400 inches of snow each year. The 85 named runs, including a whopping 6-miler, ensure short lines at the lifts. Vertical drop is 4,350 feet and ski-able terrain is 3,600 acres. The resort recently completed a family-oriented snow-tubing park ($15 adults/$10 children). Ski rentals and instruction available. Lift tickets: $75 adults, $65 half-day; $65 seniors (70-plus); $55 juniors.

Moonlight Basin (888-362-1666, 406-993-6000; www.moonlightbasin.com) provides Big Sky visitors a more affordable option with plenty of elbow room. The resort on Lone Mountain features 4,150 feet of vertical and 1,900 ski-able acres, with a 2.8-mile run. Average snowfall tops 400 inches. Rentals and instruction available. Lift tickets: $51 adults, $39 half-day; juniors (11–17) $39/$29; seniors (70-plus) $46.

BOZEMAN   *MSU students frequent here*

Bridger Bowl (800-223-9609, 406-587-2111; www.bridgerbowl.com; 15795 Bridger Canyon Dr.) is a nonprofit ski area cherished by locals who kept one eye on work and kept one eye on the blue flashing light atop Bozeman's Baxter Hotel, which until 2007 told skiers that Mother Nature has been kind again. Because it's nonprofit, lift tickets are remarkably reasonable for such an outstanding ski area. Bridger is sandwiched between two bowls and features 2,600 ski-able acres with a 1,500 vertical. Average snowfall is 350 inches and most of the runs are geared toward intermediate and advanced skiers, though there's plenty for beginners. Those literally wanting a walk on the wild side hoof it another 400 feet to "The Ridge" for extreme skiing. One run is 3 miles long. Rentals and instruction available. Lift tickets: $41 adults, $33 half-day; seniors $33; children (5–12) $15.

JACKSON

Jackson Hole Mountain Resort (888-333-7766, 307-733-2292; www.jacksonhole.com; 3395 W. Village Dr., Teton Village) is as known for the Bridger Gondola as its snow. Jackson Hole Mountain Resort traverses Rendezvous and Apres Vous Mountains with more than 4,100 feet of vertical and access to more than 3,000 acres of terrain. The mountain receives about 450 inches a year and has snowmaking capability on 160 acres. Rentals and instruction available. Snowboarding is allowed on all runs. Lift tickets: $51–75 adults; $26–39 seniors; $26–39 children.

Snow King Resort (800-522-5464, 307-733-5200; www.snowking.com; 400 E. Snow King Ave.) was Wyoming's first ski area when it opened in 1939 and is known fondly as Jackson's in-town ski hill. With 1,571 feet of vertical on 400 acres, it's surprisingly steep and challenging; 60 percent of the runs are suited for advanced skiers. About one-fourth of the ski-able terrain is open to night skiing. The resort also has a snow-tubing park. Rentals and instruction available. Lift tickets: $35 adults full-day, $23 half-day; juniors $25/$15.

RED LODGE

Red Lodge Mountain Resort (800-444-8977, 406-255-6973; www.redlodgemountain .com) is a family-oriented area at the edge of Montana's Beartooth Mountains. The mountain receives a modest 250 inches of snow on 1,600 acres, with a 2,500-foot vertical. Despite its small size, there's an equal amount of terrain for each skill level. One problem: With the winter closure of the Beartooth Highway, it takes some doing getting here. Snowmaking is possible on nearly one-third of the mountain. Rentals and instruction available. Lift tickets: $44 adults, $33 half-day; seniors $33; juniors (13–18) $38/$31; children $15/$12.

Skiing (Nordic) and Snowshoeing

Welcome to paradise. Imagine hearing the whisper of your skis as you glide across soft powder past snorting bison and steaming geysers in Yellowstone. Or stepping gently into unbroken powder along a river. Nordic (cross-country) skiing and snowshoeing are primary reasons why many locals cherish winter as much as summer in the Greater Yellowstone region. Many of the same trails hikers use in summer are blissfully free of human traffic in winter. Most backcountry trails are marked with orange ribbons. Roads are suitable for Nordic skiing, though you'll share some routes with snowmobiles. Mammoth Hot Springs and Old Faithful hotels rent skiing and snowshoe equipment. When the days turn warm in the spring, a popular pastime is "skate skiing"—sliding on morning or evening ice after a day's melt. Yellowstone offers numerous guided snowcoach and ski/snowshoe tours from Mammoth and Old Faithful.

Most of the Alpine resorts in the area also feature extensive Nordic trails. Separate from those, many of the gateway communities have groomed trails, and the city of Jackson grooms several miles of trails in Cache Creek and Game Creek Canyons as well as on the Snake River Dike. In Yellowstone, shuttles from Xanterra (307-344-7311) are available at Mammoth for excursions going east to Tower or south to Golden Gate. The fee is $14. Anyone venturing into the backcountry should first check with the **Gallatin National Forest Avalanche Center** (406-587-6981; www.mtavalanche.com) in Bozeman or **Backcountry Avalanche Hazard & Weather Forecast** (307-733-2664; www.jgavalanche .org) out of Jackson for updates regarding weather and avalanche-prone areas.

Big Sky

Lone Mountain Ranch (406-995-4644; www.lmranch.com) features 80 kilometers (about 46 miles) of groomed trails for $19 per day for adults, $15 for seniors (60–69). Seniors age 70 and older and kids 12 and under are free. Season passes and rentals are available. Located about two-thirds of the way up the mountain on the right-hand side of the highway.

Cody

North Fork Nordic Trails (800-628-7791, 307-527-7701; www.nordicskiclub.com) are 25 miles of groomed trails between Pahaska Tepee and the defunct Sleeping Giant Ski Area between Cody and Yellowstone's East Entrance, on the Shoshone National Forest. The trails, supported by the Park County Nordic Ski Association, follow the North Fork of the Shoshone River and are suitable for classic and skate skiing. Rentals are available in Pahaska Tepee.

Jackson

Jackson Hole Nordic Center (800-443-6139, 307-739-2629; www.jacksonhole.com/ info/ski.nordic.asp) has 12 miles of mostly flat professionally groomed track and skating lines. Season passes are $99 and a one-day trail pass is $12. Instruction and rentals are available. Guided nature trips are offered as well. Located on Village Road in Teton Village.

Rendezvous Ski Trails (406-646-7097; www.rendezvousskitrails.com) are 35 miles of groomed trails on gently rolling terrain through lodgepole pine forest on wildlife-filled national forest land. Passes are required between November 1 and March 1. In November, passes are $45 for the month, $20 for three days and $8 for a day. After that, thanks to a cooperative effort between the Forest Service, West Yellowstone Chamber of Commerce and Ski Education Foundation, a season-long pass is $25 and a one-day pass $5.

SKIING (HELI-SKIING)

If backcountry adventure is your bag and lift lines aren't, go for the gusto in untracked country with **High Mountain Heli-Skiing** in Teton Village (307-733-4297; www.heliski jackson.com). This outfit accesses some 305,000 acres south of the Jackson Hole Ski Area with helicopters. Each day features six runs spread between the Snake River, Palisades, Hoback, Gros Ventre and Teton Ranges. The six runs of 12,000–15,000 vertical feet each run $850 per person. Expert skiers and snowboarders only.

SLED DOG RIDES

A number of companies offer the chance to be pulled through winter wonderlands by Siberian or Alaskan huskies on the intimate comfort of a sled.

BIG SKY
Spirit of the North Adventures (406-682-7994; www.huskypower.com) runs half-day trips at 9:30 AM and 1 PM daily out of Moonlight Basin at Lone Mountain. Cost is $110 for adults (13 and up) and $80 for children (7–12). Spirit of the North is operated by the parents of Jessie Royer, an Ennis, Montana, native who was the top female Iditarod finisher in 2005. Royer often spends December and January training in Ennis, and if you're lucky you might get a demonstration.

DUBOIS
Continental Divide Dog Sled Adventures (800-531-6874, 307-455-3052; www.dogsled adventures.com) traverses the Targhee, Teton and Shoshone National Forests under the guidance of former Iditarod musher Billy Snodgrass. Full-day, half-day, overnight and extended trips typically are offered from the end of November into April. Half-day tours start at $145 for adults and full-day rides are $249. Overnighters in a yurt start at $640 for one night and range to $1,950 for four days/three nights. Trips are at Grand Targhee Ski Resort, Brooks Lake Lodge and Togwotee Mountain Lodge.

JACKSON
Togwotee Snowmobile Adventures (877-864-9683, 307-733-8800;www.togwoteesnow mobile.com/dog_sled.shtml) features full-day treks for $249 and half-day adventures for $145 for adults, $159 and $95 for children. Snowmobile/sled-dog combination

packages are also available, with one option at $259 and another at $295. The company offers lodging at Togwotee Mountain Lodge east of Yellowstone.

PARADISE VALLEY

Absaroka Dogsled Treks (800-444-8977, 406-222-4645; www.extrememontana.com) operates out of Chico Hot Springs north of Gardiner and runs primarily Siberian huskies on trails in the Gallatin Range from Thanksgiving until the end of March, snow permitting. Full-day Denali treks are $275 and include lunch cooked outdoors. The half-day Yukon adventure is $200 and includes a picnic lunch. Absaroka has a two-hour Tenderfoot ride for $100. Clinics are offered as well.

SNOWCOACHES

All-Yellowstone Sports Sno-Vans of Yellowstone (800-548-9551, 406-646-7656; www .allyellowstone.com) is based in West Yellowstone.

Buffalo Bus Touring Company (800-426-7669, 406-646-9564; www.snowcoachyellow stone.com) is also in West Yellowstone.

Backcountry Adventures (800-924-7669; www.backcountry-adventures.com) of West Yellowstone offers guided snowcoach tours to Old Faithful and rents snowmobiles.

Holiday Inn SunSpree Resort (800-646-7365, 406-646-7365; www.doyellowstone .com) operates out of the Holiday Inn in West Yellowstone.

Goosewing Snowcoach Adventures (888-733-5251) of Jackson Hole specializes in daily snowcoach and snowmobile tours to Old Faithful and also has a snowmobile ride to the Grand Canyon of the Yellowstone (www.yellowstoneexplorer.com/daytours.cfm).

See Yellowstone Snowcoach Tours (800-221-1151, 406-646-9310; www.yellowstone -tours.com) leads trips into Old Faithful and elsewhere out of West Yellowstone. Trips leave from the Three Bear Lodge.

Yellowstone Expeditions (800-728-9333, 406-646-9333; www.yellowstoneexpeditions .biz) offers snowshoe and cross-country skiing adventures as well out of West Yellowstone.

Yellowstone National Park Lodges (877-439-7375, 307-344-7311; www.travelyellow stone.com) is a park concessionaire featuring snowcoach tours that include Mammoth, Old Faithful and Flagg Ranch.

SNOWMOBILING

Few recreational activities have generated as much controversy as snowmobiles, which arrived on the Yellowstone scene in 1963. In the 1990s, as many as 2,000 would enter the park on peak weekends, queuing up 20 or 30 deep at the West Entrance. The numbers were a boon to local economies, especially in West Yellowstone and Cooke City, which were built around the whine of snowmobiles cruising their streets.

By the late 1990s, though, the increasing number of visitors who came for winter solitude and quiet—such as snowshoers, Nordic skiers, wolf watchers and snowcoach riders— grew increasingly disenchanted with the noise, smell and air pollution. Occasionally the air would get worse than in major metropolitan areas. Biologists also feared snowmobiles were causing stress to the park's animals. Wildlife, weary from summer crowds and the struggle during the park's harsh winters, needs a break.

Only quieter, cleaner-running four-stroke snowmobiles like these are allowed in Yellowstone now, and only on guided excursions. Limits have been placed on the machines because of pollution and stress to park animals. National Park Service

In 2000, mindful that some 75,000 snowmobilers were entering Yellowstone over 100-day periods, the Park Service under the Clinton Administration created a furor by announcing it intended to phase out snowmobiling in the Yellowstone. Panicked, the city of West Yellowstone, which contributed about 60 percent of the park's snowmobile traffic, filed a suit against the Park Service. The city argued that new four-stroke sleds were much more fuel efficient and cleaner burning than the old two-stroke variety. Two years later, the Bush Administration split the difference, announcing that snowmobile entries into Yellowstone were not to exceed 1,100 and that only four-stroke engines were allowed. A year later, a federal judge overturned Bush's decision and reverted the policy back to the phase-out.

But the controversy didn't end there. The snowmobile industry and State of Wyoming soon received an injunction from a Wyoming judge. The federal judge responded to the injunction by threatening Park Service officials with contempt if they allowed numbers to return to historic levels. The current maximum number of snowmobiles allowed is exceeded only on the busiest weekends. But the rulings still impact the people of West Yellowstone and Cooke City. The towns began reinventing themselves as perception spread that snowmobiles weren't as welcome. In 2006, Montana Governor Brian Schweitzer, a moderate Democrat, took a ride into the park on a four-stroke snowmobile and pro-claimed the park and West Yellowstone open for winter business. From 2004 to 2007, the limit was 720 commercially guided snowmobiles per day, allowed only from 7 AM to 9 PM. In late September 2007, park officials further upset both sides by announcing that the maximum per day would be reduced to 540, including a cap of 300 at the West Entrance and a requirement for Best Available Technology (BAT) on all machines. Snowmobile backers said the new limits would hurt business in West Yellowstone even though in recent years the average daily use has typically been 250 to 290 sleds. Environmental groups say the limits don't go far enough. Speeds are not to exceed 45 mph and off-road use is pro-hibited. Park roads are groomed as trails, except for the route from Mammoth to the Northeast Entrance, which is plowed all winter.

A limit of 83 snowcoaches was also enacted, with a requirement that they be cleaner and quieter; previously there had been no cap. In Grand Teton and the Rockefeller Park-way area, the proposed cap is 140 snowmobiles per day, though commercial guides wouldn't be required. Final rules were scheduled to be in place for the 2007–08 snow-mobile season.

Meantime, the national forests surrounding the parks are still buzzing with the hum of snowmobiles, including the ever-popular 360-mile Continental Divide Snowmobile Trail from West Yellowstone to Lander, Wyoming. The geographic triangle consisting of Island Park, Flagg Ranch and West Yellowstone is particularly popular, with nearly 600 miles of marked trails and an annual average snowfall of 150 to 170 inches.

And don't think the sport is dead or dying in West Yellowstone: The little town has 13 snowmobile rental businesses, many of which rent all-terrain vehicles (ATVs) in the sum-mer. For information on Wyoming's trails, call 800-225-5596 or go to www.wyotrails.state.wy.us/snow.

As always, snowmobiles must be registered in your home state and a valid driver's license is required for operation in Montana. In Wyoming, nonresidents pay a user fee and a driver's license is required only in the park. In Idaho, a nonresident user certificate is required.

Cody's Cody County Snowmobile Association has 70 miles of groomed trails, though most riders in this neck of the woods like to go to Cooke City and the Beartooth Plateau in Montana. Plenty of rentals are available in Cody.

Cooke City has two service stations with gas and two snowmobile dealerships. The de facto headquarters for snowmobiling in this busy little town at the end of the winter road is the Cooke City Exxon (406-838-2244). Some 100 miles of trails connect with the Beartooth trail system. Go to snowmobilecookecity.com for further information.

Dubois has some 150 miles of groomed trails considered to be some of the prettiest in the world for its powdery snow. The season tends to be longer there, too.

Jackson isn't as sensitive about snowmobile restrictions because of the endless web of trails crisscrossing surrounding national forests. A favorite snowmobile junket is the Granite Hot Springs for a good soak after a day on the trail.

West Yellowstone, which fancies itself as the "Snowmobile Capital of the World," has 13 rental facilities and offers plenty of information at the Chamber of Commerce (406-646-7701; www.westyellowstonechamber.com).

SWIMMING

Generally, the waters of Yellowstone and Grand Teton are either too hot or too cold for a swim, and for the most part soaks are discouraged because of the instability of ground where thermal features and streams converge. It is illegal to swim, bathe or soak in any of Yellowstone's thermal springs or pools. Damage to the environment can occur, and the thermal areas can be a health hazard because of scalding temperatures, waterborne fungi and bacteria, and the levels of acidity. That mostly leaves streams that have been warmed by thermally heated waters, though it's legal to swim in the frigid lakes of Yellowstone and Grand Teton. The only designated swimming area in Grand Teton is at Colter Bay, which includes picnic facilities but no lifeguards.

Primitive

Boiling River Hot Springs is the best and most popular spot in Yellowstone for soaking. The Boiling River emerges from the ground just off the North Entrance Road between Gardiner and Mammoth. It sprints about 100 yards to a churning collision with the chilly Gardner River. The meeting of 140-degree and 60-degree water meshes for a 50-yard stretch on the west bank, where soakers enjoy idyllic pools. Water temperature will depend on the Gardner's depth, so the ideal spot might change each time you visit. The Park Service has placed enough restrictions on Boiling River to eliminate some of the rowdiness, trash and car burglaries that once plagued the area. It's against regulations to move rocks or dig in the river to create pools. Swimsuits are required and the only private changing facilities are the parking-lot outhouses. Summers are busy; you might have the place to yourself on a winter weekday because the chilly quarter-mile walk is a deterrent.

Firehole River Swimming Area is another popular spot where hot runoff warms the river to just the right temperature in a swimming hole downstream. The hole is between modest rapids. A popular method of getting to the calm water is to ride the waves.

Madison Campground Warm Springs is just that—warm. Not hot. A 100-degree spring trickles into the Madison River, where the 50-plus temperatures are better suited for its renowned trout populations. The convergence near the bank makes for temperatures between 80 and 90. It's dandy for a refreshing dip on a warm summer day, but that's about it. You won't find anybody here in the winter.

The Firehole River offers one of the two good swimming holes in Yellowstone. Hot springs combine with the cool waters of the river to form the perfect temperatures for soaking and swimming. National Park Service

Developed

Granite Hot Springs (307-734-7400) is a pretty mineral pool in a forested valley about 35 miles southeast of Jackson, near Hoback Junction. A maintained gravel road follows Granite Creek to the pool, which has changing rooms and a deck for sunning. Water temperatures typically are in the low 90s in the summer and about 110 in winter. Hours are 10 AM–8 PM June–October and 11 AM–5 PM December–March, when you'll have to use cross-country skis or snowmobiles to access the pool. Cost is $6 for adults and $4 for children. Stay at the nearby campground ($15) and hike into the canyon, where 50-foot Granite Falls is the highlight. Granite Creek also features some primitive pools worth checking out.

Teton County/Jackson Recreation Center (307-739-9025; www.tetonyo.org/parks; 155 E. Gill Ave., Jackson) has an indoor lap pool, water slide, hot tub, wading pool and geyser. Fees for use of the gym range from $4 to $6.25 per day, depending on age. A family pass is $20. It includes use of gym and weight facilities.

7

Shopping

Let's be honest. If shopping were high on your list for choosing a vacation destination, you wouldn't be headed for Yellowstone, Grand Teton or Jackson Hole. You come to see the spectacular natural wonders, the wildlife and an intact ecosystem at work. Shopping tends to limit out with souvenir stands where tourists purchase hats, T-shirts and key chains with pictures of bears, geysers and mountains, or cowboy and Indian trinkets. And of course, outdoor stores are in vogue, too, always at the ready to supply hiking boots, flies and river gear.

Still, if there's a shopping itch requiring a scratch, dozens of trendy, upscale shops are waiting in Jackson to provide a fix. Truth be known, for a town of 18,000, Jackson has an extraordinary cadre of art galleries, bookstores and others.

Antiques

There are plenty of surprises awaiting the frontier treasure hunter, if you know where to look.

Cody

Auntie Q Antiques (307-272-1449; 2350 Mountain View Dr.) has a little bit of everything for the home.

Cottage Antiques (307-527-4650; 1327 Rumsey Ave.) features furnishings, art and other home décor.

Old West Antiques (307-587-9014; 1200 Sheridan Ave.) is the place for classic Old West artifacts and antiques, ranging from art to cowboy and Indian lore.

Wild Rose Antiques (307-587-0440; 1526 Beck Ave.) offers lots of antique furnishings and collectibles.

Dubois

Barto Collectibles (307-455-3272; 7026 US Hwy. 26) has antiques, collectibles, home furnishings, jewelry and other western items.

Dancing Bear Antiques (307-455-4095; 302 E. Ramshorn St.) has a wide assortment of knickknacks.

Jackson

Cayuse Western Americana (307-739-1940; www.cayusewa.com; 255 N. Glenwood St.) features regional antique art, especially related to cowboys, Indians, the parks and the Jackson Hole region.

Davies Reid (307-739-1009; 15 E. Deloney Ave.) offers not only antiques but Asian artifacts, exotic jewelry and handmade rugs.

Fighting Bear Antiques (307-733-2669, 866-690-2669; 375 S. Cache St.) specializes in
mission, hickory and Thomas Molesworth furniture.

Galleries West Fine Art (307-733-4525; gallerieswestjacksonhole.com; 260 N. Cache St.)
features antique furnishings as well as art, sculptures and artifacts.

Kismet Rug Gallery (307-739-8984; 140 E. Broadway Ave.) has all types of rugs, including
antiques. Appraisals also offered. If you happen to bring an old rug along for the ride,
they'll consider buying it here.

Rustic Antiques (307-733-6517; www.rusticantiquesfrance.com; P.O. Box 2355, Jackson,
WY 83001) offers, of all things, 18th and 19th century French antiques from Brittany
and Normandy.

Tetonia

Steve Horn Mountain Gallery (208-456-2719; www.stevehorn.com; 112 S. Main St.) is a
unique, out-of-the-way 4,000-square-foot warehouse featuring art, furniture and
other items with a western motif. Views of the Tetons don't hurt the ambience.

West Yellowstone

Flying T Trading Post (406-646-7557; 311 Canyon St.) features a variety of western artifacts, including old dolls, firearms, toys, china, primitive dinnerware, coins and Indian
beads.

Madison Crossing Businesses (406-646-7621; 121 Madison Ave.) is an all-purpose
indoor retail center with a wide variety of home goods, including antiques.

Art Galleries

Jackson alone features more than 30 art galleries, ranging from the expected wildlife art to
contemporary. Before wandering the streets, pick up a guide produced by the Jackson Hole
Gallery Association (jacksonholegalleries.com); they're available at the visitor center or
any gallery. Because of their prolific nature, Jackson's galleries are listed first, followed by
the other gateway communities in alphabetical order.

Jackson

Buffalo Trail Gallery (307-734-6904; www.jacksonholegalleries.com/galleries/buffalo
trail.htm; 98 Center St.) offers impressionistic landscapes, wildlife, figurative, cowboy,
Native American art. Artists in residence are on hand summers.

Caswell Gallery and Sculpture Garden (307-734-2660; www.caswellgallery.com; 145 E.
Broadway Ave.) shows wildlife bronzes by Rip Caswell and an outdoor sculpture garden.
It also exhibits original paintings, pottery, jewelry and steel sculpture. Other artists
include Jim Demetro, Jacques and Mary Regat, Sharles, and Chris Navarro.

Cayuse Western Americana (307-739-1940; www.cayusewa.co; 255 N. Glenwood St.)
includes cowboy, Indian and national park antiques and memorabilia. Also vintage art
and photography, Navajo weavings and pawn jewelry, Plains Indian beadwork, books on
western Americana, cowhand gear and vintage furnishings.

Center Street Gallery (888-733-1115, 307-733-115; www.centerstreetgallery.com; 30
Center St.) is home to original contemporary art, jewelry, sculpture, limited edition

prints and furniture. Featured artists include Marshall Noice, Jean Richardson, Brent Lawrence, Robert Deurloo, Fran Jenkins and Stephen Powell.

Craft Gallery (307-413-4205; www.jacksonholegalleries.com/members.html; 50 King St.) This is a contemporary American craft gallery with an eclectic array of fine art in glass, clay, metal, wood and textiles. It carries a wide-ranging selection of jewelry as well.

DiTommaso Galleries (307-734-9677; www.ditommasogalleries.com; 172 Center St.) has a collection of 19th- and 20th-century art, African art and fine furniture. Top works by renowned artists such as Clyde Aspevig, Michael Coleman, Harry Jackson, and C. M. Russell.

Fighting Bear Antiques (307-733-2669; www.jacksonholegalleries.com/galleries/ fightingbear.htm; 375 Cache St.) Specializing in 19th- and early 20th-century American furniture, this gallery is nationally known for authentic Mission and Thomas Molesworth furniture, early Navajo rugs, Native American beadwork and Western Americana.

Fossil Portal (307-733-1019, 307-733-3613; www.fossilportal.com; 150 E. Broadway Ave.) offers fish fossils from southwestern Wyoming turned into floor tiles, table tops, wall pieces, etc.

Galleries West Fine Art (307-733-4525 north, 307-733-4412 south; www.gallerieswest jacksonhole.com; 260 N. Cache St. and 70 S. Glenwood St.) includes artistic impressions of Jackson Hole represented by custom furniture from New West Designs as well as original paintings, bronzes, wood carvings and pottery. Resident sculptor R. Scott Nickell is frequently on hand.

Hennes Studio and Gallery (888-733-1115; www.joannehennes.com; 5850 N. Larkspur Dr.) presents a variety of Teton paintings in oils, watercolors and limited edition lithographs and giclée prints on canvas by Joanne Hennes. Paintings range from familiar views to high country vistas and wildflowers. Crystal sculptures by Jeff and Karen Ladd are also displayed.

Horizon Fine Art Gallery (307-739-1540; www.horizonfineartgallery.com; 165 N. Center St.) possesses a diverse collection of paintings, sculpture and glass art. Air landscapes, figurative pieces, wildlife and western art. Bronzes and glass works.

Horse of a Different Color (307-734-9603; 60 E. Broadway Ave.) has contemporary American craft and fine art. Features ceramics, metal, hand blown glass, fiber, jewelry, wood and paintings.

Legacy Gallery (800-870-5413; 307-733-2353; www.legacygallery.com; 75 N. Cache St.) specializes in original oil paintings, watercolors and bronze sculptures. Features impressionistic and traditional western works, wildlife and landscapes by noteworthy contemporary and deceased artists.

Lyndsay McCandless Contemporary (307-734-0649; www.imcontemporary.com; 130 S. Jackson St.) is a small-engine repair shop converted to urban-chic space with contemporary art. It's best known for its award-winning contemporary wildlife artists. The collection includes abstraction, realism and social/political commentary. Artist openings, art talks and music events are periodically scheduled.

Meyer-Milagros Gallery (307-733-0905; www.meyermilagrosgallery.com; 155 N. Center St.) is dedicated to promoting national and international contemporary art. It caters to the taste and trends of a sophisticated art market and a discerning worldwide collector base. Clients include private collectors, art consultants, corporate art consultants, architects and interior designers.

Mountain Trails Gallery (307-734-8150; www.mtntrails.net; 155 N. Center St.) offers bronze sculptures and original oil paintings. Bronze artist Vic Payne captures the Old West and Walt Horton touches your heart. The impressionistic paintings of Alan Wolton capture the show along with the stunning realism of Ed Kucera's paintings of the Native American.

Muse Gallery (307-733-0555; www.jhmusegallery.com; 745 W. Broadway Ave.) shows contemporary fine art by regional and national artists: abstract, figurative and landscapes. Also limited-edition designer jewelry and handcrafted furniture.

National Museum of Wildlife Art (307-733-5771; www.wildlifeart.org; 2820 Rungius Rd.) comprises twelve galleries with permanent and changing exhibitions, a children's discovery center, shop and the Rising Sage Cafe. The museum chronicles the history of wildlife in art, ranging from 2500 B.C. stone carvings to works by contemporary masters. Free to locals on Sundays.

Rawson Gallery (307-733-7306; www.jacksonholegalleries.com/galleries/rawson.htm; 50 King St.) has watercolor paintings, prints and cards of the Rocky Mountains, plus western wildlife and cowboy life by Phil Clark, Sheila Langlois and Mary Blain. Sculptures by Anthony Guzzo. Open July 1–October 15.

Shadow Mountain Gallery (307-733-3162; www.topgifts.com; 10 W. Broadway Ave.) features emerging and established artists locally and nationally who paint, sculpt and make prints from realism to impressionism, wildlife, landscapes, western and Indian art.

Trailside Galleries (307-733-3186; www.trailsidegalleries.com; 105 N. Center St.) offers traditional and representational American art.

Trio Fine Art (307-734-4444; www.triofineart.com; 545 N. Cache St.), operated and owned by local painters, includes the work of Kathryn Mapes Turner, September Vhay, Lee Carlman Riddell and Russell Chatham.

Two Grey Hills (307-733-2677; www.fineindianart.com; 110 E. Broadway Ave.) specializes in Navajo weavings; handmade Navajo, Hopi and Zuni jewelry; hand-coiled Pueblo pottery; and southwestern Indian baskets. Also features handwoven Zapotec Indian rugs, Hopi Kachinas, stone sculptures, Zuni fetishes, Navajo dye charts and unique Navajo folk art.

West Lives On Gallery (307-734-2888; www.westliveson.com; 75 N. Glenwood St.) emphasizes the rich heritage of the American West. It features western, wildlife and landscape art in original oils, acrylics, watercolors and bronze. More than 45 regional and local artists are represented.

Wilcox Gallery (307-733-6450; www.wilcoxgallery.com; 1975 N. US Hwy. 89) shows representational and impressionistic wildlife, westerns and landscapes, also such art as oriental scenes, florals, seascapes and bronzes. The gallery is home to the Jackson Hole Art Academy. Five-day painting workshops are offered.

Wild Hands Gallery (307-733-4619; www.wildhands.com; 265 W. Pearl St.) is a whimsical gallery featuring local painters Fred Kingwill, Elli Sorenson and Melissa Brown. Handcrafted furniture by Sticks and David Marsh showcased as pottery, handblown glass, clocks and jewelry.

Wyoming Gallery (307-733-7548; www.jackdennis.com; 50 E. Broadway Ave.) offers landscape, wildlife and sporting art in oil, watercolor, photography and bronze and wood sculpture. The gift gallery features distinctive home furnishings and accessories. Located above Jack Dennis's Outdoor Shop.

Cody

Bison Legacy (307-587-4199; www.bisonlegacy.com; 1191 Sheridan Ave.) specializes in handcrafted bison leather goods and other regional art, all from Wyoming.

Cody Country Art League (307-587-3597; www.codyart.vcn.com; 836 Sheridan Ave.) offers crafts, photos, sculptures, paintings, workshops and specialty shows. Free admission to shows.

Simpson Gallagher Gallery (307-587-4022; www.simpsongallaghergallery.com; 1161 Sheridan Ave.) has an impressive collection of high-end art with a wide array of artists from around the country, including Harry Jackson and Charles Rumsey.

Wyoming Artisans (307-587-7000; 1426 Sheridan Ave.) is an all-Wyoming cooperative featuring carvings, paintings, pottery and jewelry.

Driggs

Blue Fly Gallery (208-456-0900; www.kenmorrisonfineart.com; 535 N. Hwy. 33) shows Idaho-oriented art of varying types.

Teton Arts Council (888-434-8882, 208-354-8882; www.tetonartscouncil.com; 76 N. Main St.) exhibits works by regional artists in the backroom of Dark Horse Books.

Dubois

Antler Workshop & Gallery (307-455-2204; www.antlergallery.com; P.O. Box 824, Dubois, WY 82513) features antler chandeliers, tables, lamps, mirrors and other items.

Horse Creek Gallery (307-455-3345; www.antler-carving.com; 104 E. Ramshorn St.) offers antler carvings by Monte Baker. Adjoining Tukadeka Traders features antique trade beads and Indian trinkets.

Trapline Gallery (307-455-2800; 120 E. Ramshorn St.) carries Indian-crafted beadwork, artwork, jewelry and furs.

Velvet Thorn Gallery (307-455-2500; 12 Stalnaker St.) offers art and sculpture by local and regional artisans.

Gardiner

Yellowstone Gallery and Frameworks (406-848-7306; www.yellowstonegallery.com; 216 W. Park St.) shows wildlife and western art, crafts and gifts that reflect Yellowstone National Park and surrounding habitats. It features authentic, original, handcrafted items and reproductions, and includes watercolors and oil paintings, giclées, limited-edition prints, sculpture, photography, posters, pottery, weavings, basketry, jewelry and woodworks.

Tetonia

Steve Horn Mountain Gallery (208-456-2719; www.stevehorn.com; 112 S. Main St.) is a 4,000-square-foot warehouse featuring western art and many other items.

Bookstores

Cody

Cody Newsstand (307-587-2843; 1121 13th St.) is a traditional store with new books and tons of magazines.

Gentleman Jim's Book Ranch (307-899-0499, 888-446-2396; www.bookranch.com; 1108 14th St., Suite 232) specializes in hard-to-find, out-of-print titles and other used books with a heavy emphasis on the Old West.

LJ's Books (307-527-7449; www.ljsbooks.com; 1042 13th St.) is an independent seller of hard-to-find, out-of-print, used and rare books. Specialties include religion, science, history, children's and literature.

The Thistle (307-587-6635; 1243 Rumsey Ave.) offers books and gifts, many of which are regional.

Driggs

Dark Horse Books (208-354-8882, 888-348-3356; 76 N. Main St.) has a wide-ranging regional collection.

Dubois

Two Ocean Books (307-455-3554; www.cowboybookseller.com; 128 E. Ramshorn St.) is a quaint store with a strong emphasis on regional titles ranging from Old West and mountain-man lore to contemporary hunting and fishing. Also cowboy music and art.

Water Wheel Gifts & Books (307-455-2112; 113 E. Ramshorn St.) has many regional and state titles along with gifts.

Gardiner

Tumbleweed Book Store & Cafe (406-848-2225; 501 Scott St. W.) carries new and used books with an emphasis on the Greater Yellowstone area. Also features sandwiches, snacks, smoothies and fair-trade coffee. Open year-round.

High Country Trading (406-848-7707; 308 Park St.) offers coffee, gifts, souvenirs and western books in the historic Hall's Store building across from the arch. Open year-round.

Jackson

Jackson Hole Book Trader (307-734-6001, 800-722-2710; 980 W. Broadway Ave., Suite F, Powderhorn Mall) features new, used and rare books.

Main Event (307-733-7112; 980 W. Broadway Ave., Powderhorn Mall) is a traditional mall bookstore with new books, video rental, toys, magazines, gift cards and CDs.

Valley Bookstore (307-733-4533; www.valleybook.com; 125 N. Cache St.), the area's largest local bookstore, emphasizes regional titles and frequently has author signings and readings. It features fiction, rare books, magazines and used books. In business for 35 years.

West Yellowstone

The Book Peddler (406-646-9358; www.thebookpeddler.com; 106 Canyon St.) is a bookstore and coffee shop with an Old West atmosphere serving bagels and pastries. Lots of regional books, cards, calendars. A favored local hangout.

Bookworm Books (406-646-9736; 14 Canyon St.) presents new and used books in a unique environment featuring tons of Yellowstone-related antiques and memorabilia, including thousands of Haynes postcards. If it has been written about Yellowstone National Park, it's here.

Clothing

Chic isn't the word in the Yellowstone-Grand Teton region, unless you're in Jackson, where trendier shoppers will enjoy strolling downtown. If you're looking for some western duds to take home, however, you've come to the right place—Jackson or otherwise.

CODY

Coral Ranch Westwear (307-587-4493; 1625 Stampede Ave.) offers western wear for men, women and children.

The Plush Pony (307-587-4677; www.plushpony.net; 1350 Sheridan Ave.) features sophisticated clothing and accessories for women.

Rags to Riches (307-587-7576; 1308 Sheridan Ave.) has trendier clothes for the younger set.

JACKSON

Accentuate (307-734-2487; 60 W. Broadway Ave.) features women's apparel, accessories and jewelry.

Altitude (307-733-4717; 48 E. Broadway Ave.) has velvet, Paige denim, Hudson jeans and other stylish clothing.

Baggit Jackson Hole (307-733-1234; www.baggitjacksonhole.com; 35 W. Broadway Ave.) features western fashions for men and women.

Coldwater Creek (307-734-7771; 10 E. Broadway Ave.) is the nationally renowned women's clothing store that began two decades ago in Sandpoint, Idaho. Coldwater Creek's rapid expansion includes an expansive new outlet downtown.

Ella's Room (307-733-7114; www.ellasroom.com; 180 E. Deloney Ave.) is Jackson's foremost lingerie and sleepwear boutique.

Goodie2shoes (307-733-0233; www.goodie2shoes.com; 81 S. King St.) of course has shoes, but it also offers such accessories as cosmetics, jewelry and purses.

Hide Out Leather Apparel (307-733-2422; 40 Center St.) features high-quality leather clothes for men and women, as well as jewelry and more.

Jackson Hole Clothiers (307-733-7211; www.jhclothiers.com; 45 E. Deloney Ave.) looks western, feels western and is western, with everything necessary to look like a chic cowgirl out for a night on the town.

Jackson Hole Pendleton (307-733-1040; 30 N. Center St.) is an outlet for the biggest name in wool, along with classic men's and women's coats, shirts and jackets. The signature product here is colorful Indian blankets.

Jackson Hole Traders (307-733-1849; 1130 S. US Hwy. 89) is a specialty store offering hand-painted western wear, including fishing and skiing apparel and other goods for the home.

Jolly Jumbuck Leathers (307-733-6562; www.jollyjumbuckleathers.com; 20 W. Broadway Ave.) has been a Jackson staple for three decades, selling leathers, furs, belts, scarves, handbags and other leather goods and accessories.

Leslie (307-733-9558; 60 Center St.) features women's accessories, apparel and jewelry.

Michelle Julene Couture (307-734-1009; 185 W. Broadway Ave.) offers leather, fur, denim and lace for men and women.

Queenie & Co. (307-732-0017; www.queenieandcompany.com; 36 E. Broadway Ave.) offers women's clothing, jewelry and accessories, including footwear and lingerie.

Sun-Urban Clothing (307-733-4514; www.mountunes.com; 265 W. Broadway Ave.) has stylish clothing for men and women, along with accessories, jewelry, gifts and a collection of CDs. Check your e-mail at their Internet cafe.

Terra (307-734-0067; 105 E. Broadway Ave.) features contemporary clothing for men and women.

West Yellowstone

Bargain Depot Outlet (406-646-9047; www.wyellowstone.com/bargaindepot; 22 Canyon St.) has low prices on clothing, souvenirs and travel gear.

Madison Crossing Businesses (406-646-7621; 121 Madison Ave.) is an indoor retail center with everything from women's clothing to a one-hour photo stand. Goods for the home are available, too.

Outdoor Gear

As you might expect, the streets of the gateway communities to Yellowstone, Grand Teton and in Jackson Hole are lined with shops selling fishing gear, bicycles, boats—anything and everything to assist a vacationer yearning for a variety of experiences in the great outdoors.

Cody

North Fork Anglers (307-527-7274; www.northforkanglers.com; 1438 Sheridan Ave.) is Cody's bestknown fly-fishing shop, with instruction on casting and tying, guide service, stream reports and all things fly fishing.

Sierra Trading Post (307-578-5802, 800-713-4534; www.sierratradingpost.com; 1402 Eighth St.), the nationally known outlet store, has a spacious facility in Cody if you missed the one in Cheyenne . . . or Boise . . . or Reno. Much of Sierra's outdoor clothing is 35–70 percent off because it buys closeouts and overstocks from around the world.

Sunlight Sports (307-587-9517; www.sunlightsports.com; 1131 Sheridan Ave.) is Cody's largest and most popular store for general outdoor-gear needs. Sunlight has gear for everything from camping and fishing to skiing and snowshoeing. Rentals also are available for winter sports.

Wyoming Outdoor Industries (307-527-6449, 800-725-6853; www.wyomingoutdoors .com; 1231 13th St.), based out of Half Moon Lake Resort, has rugged gear oriented to hard-core backpackers, climbers, packstring leaders and other backcountry enthusiasts. But it also features an Orvis store.

Driggs

Yostmark Mountain Equipment (208-354-2828; www.yostmark.com; 285 E. Little Ave.) specializes in backcountry trips and Nordic skiing, as well as all the equipment necessary for such adventures. Rentals are available for cross-country skiing, hiking and backpacking. Yostmark opened an expansive new store in the fall of 2007. The former address was 12 E. Little.

Dubois

Wind River Gear (307-455-3468; 19 N. First St.) features backpacking gear and back-country clothing.

Whiskey Mountain Tackle (307-455-2587; 1428 Warm Springs Dr.) takes care of your fishing needs for the Wind River or assortment of lakes in the mountains.

Gardiner

E.L.K. (406-848-7655; www.elkinc.com; 224 Park St.) is, as the name implies, a hardware store for hunters looking to bag that big bull elk or mule deer buck in the Absaroka or Gallatin Ranges.

Flying Pig Camp Store (866-807-0744, 406-848-7510; www.flyingpigrafting.com) has outdoor gear as well as horseback riding, rafting trips on the Yellowstone, cabins, guided fishing trips, safaris and hikes.

Jackson

The Edge Sports (307-734-3916; 490 W. Broadway) offers sales, rentals and repairs of skiing gear and apparel.

High Country Flies (307-733-7210, 866-733-7210; www.highcountryflies.com; 185 N. Center St.) focuses on regional fly fishing, including instruction, recipes, apparel and equipment.

Hoback Sports (307-733-5335, 307-734-2118 in winter; www.hobacksports.com; 520 W. Broadway Ave.) offers a winter base at Snow King Resort. All the usual brands are available, with sales, demo rentals and repairs. Cycling and hiking gear are offered as well.

Jack Dennis Outdoor Shop (307-733-3270, 307-733-6838, 800-570-3270; www.jack dennis.com; 50 E. Broadway Ave.) has outlets downtown and in Teton Village serving every outdoor need, whether it's climbing and skiing or hunting and fishing. Jack Dennis has three ski shops, a fly shop, guided fishing trips and professional fly-angling instruction. In winter, there are snowboard and ski rentals. Check out the wildlife art gallery as well.

Jackson Hole Sports (307-739-2687; Bridger Center Teton Village) is at the base of the Bridger Gondola at the Jackson Hole Ski Area. Look for sales, service and rentals in this full-service mountainside shop.

Leisure Sports (307-733-3040; www.leisuresportsadventure.com; 1075 S. US Hwy. 89) rents anything you need to get the most out of your outdoor experience, including the SUV to get you there. Also available is equipment for hunting, fishing, floating and camping. Three types of snowmobiles are offered, and trailers if you need a way to get them to the trailhead.

Orvis Jackson Hole (307-733-5407; www.orvis.com; 485 W. Broadway Ave.) is another high-end fly-angling shop offering high-quality rods, reels, flies and other equipment.

Pawn Shop & Sporting Goods Inc. (307-733-5152; 560 W. Broadway Ave.) is the place to get used gear for a wide variety of outdoor pursuits.

Pepi Stiegler Sports (307-733-4505; 3395 W. McCollister Dr., Teton Village) has one advantage over the other ski-oriented shops in the valley—the ability to ski in and ski out. The shop is at the base of Jackson Hole Ski Area, in the Pepi Stiegler Sports Plaza. Snowboard sales, rental and service are available.

Rendezvous River Sports (307-733-2471; www.jacksonholekayak.com; 945 W. Broadway Ave.) has everything a river runner needs to ply the rapids of the Snake River Canyon or the calmer waters upstream. Guides, instruction and tours are available.

Skinny Skis (307-733-6094, 888-733-7205; www.skinnyskis.com; 65 W. Deloney Ave.) deals in all kinds of skiing, whether your interests are alpine or roller-skiing. Clothing and supplies are offered as well. Rent everything from ski gear and in-line skates to tents and ice axes. Nordic skiing gear is available, including free guides to Jackson Hole's best cross-country skiing.

Sports Authority (307-733-4449; www.sportsauthority.com; 485 W. Broadway Ave.), once known as Gart Sports, is a Denver-based chain that sells the standard outdoor gear for every adventure, whether it's backcountry hikes or a leisurely float down the Snake.

Teton Mountaineering (307-733-3595; www.tetonmountaineering.com; 170 N. Cache St.) runs the gamut from climbing equipment and maps to yoga and Pilates classes. Lots of rentals are available for excursions into the mountains. This is also the place where outdoor folks post used items they have for sale.

Teton Village Sports (307-733-2181; www.tetonvillagesports.com; Teton Village) has sold and rented ski gear and apparel at the base of Jackson Hole Ski Area for 12 years. Summer outdoor apparel for hiking, biking and fishing is also available, as well as a large assortment of bicycles—including cruisers.

Westbank Anglers (307-733-6483, 800-922-3474; www.westbank.com; 3670 Teton Village Rd.) is the best known fly fishing shop in Jackson Hole. Westbank offers the top brand names in fly fishing as well as expertise for landing a big cutthroat from the Snake River. For off-season thrills, Westbank books trips to the Bahamas, Mexico, New Zealand and other high-end fly fishing destinations. Instruction and guide service available.

Wildernest Sports (307-733-4297; www.wildernestsports.com; Mountainside Mall, Teton Village), located next to the aerial tram at Teton Village, is the largest ski rental shop in the region. Sales, rentals and repairs are available, as well as a large demo selection.

MOOSE

Moosely Seconds Mountaineering (307-739-1801) at Dornan's focuses on such mountain climbing gear as boots, clothing and camping paraphernalia. Boot rentals available.

VICTOR

Victor Outdoor Seconds (208-787-2887; 8 Main St.), just over the hill from Jackson, is a cluttered store with some remarkably high quality used gear sold on consignment. The discerning shopper can find extraordinary deals on outdoor gear—mostly winter sports, though it's possible to find just about anything.

WEST YELLOWSTONE

Arrick's Fly Shop (406-646-7290; www.arricks.com; 37 Canyon St.) has all your fly fishing needs, including instruction in fly tying, guiding and the latest information on stream conditions and hatches.

Bud Lilly's Trout Shop (800-854-9559, 406-646-7801; www.budlillys.com; 39 Madison Ave.) was begun by the famed fly fisherman more than 50 years ago, and he can still be found tossing a fly on the Madison near his home in Three Forks. Anglers throughout the world consider this a must-stop for gear, advice and the possibility of rubbing shoulders with a legend before heading to the Madison, Firehole or Henry's Fork. Bud Lilly's also has permits to guide on neighboring national forests as well as in Yellowstone.

Eagle's Tackle Shop (406-646-7290; www.eagles-store.com; 3 Canyon St.) began in 1908 as an all-purpose business for early pioneers and is now on the National Register of Historic Places. The general store sells Chevron gas, snacks, books and souvenirs as well as an assortment of fishing tackle geared toward area lakes and streams. Flies are available, but the spin and bait angler is taken care of here, too. The shop is named after the first licensed Yellowstone fishing guide, S. P. Eagle, a renowned fly fisherman.

Jacklin's Fly Shop (406-646-7336; www.jacklinsflyshop.com; 105 Yellowstone Ave.) is the creation of yet another area fishing legend, Bob Jacklin, who caught a 10-pound, 30-inch brown trout on the Madison River in 2006. It sells all the usual fly apparel, has fishing reports and offers instruction in casting and tying.

Madison River Outfitters (406-646-9644; www.flyfishingyellowstone.com; 117 Canyon St.) focuses on fishing in and around the park but is also a full-service camping store with tents, sleeping bags, cooking gear and all the essentials. Guides, instruction and stream reports are available.

Yellowstone Rental and Sports (406-646-9377, 888-646-9377; 1630 Targhee Pass Hwy.) is about 8 miles west of West Yellowstone on US 20. It has a wide variety of rental gear for just about any outdoor need.

WILSON

Wilson Backcountry Sports (307-733-5228; www.jak-biz.com/wilsonsports; 1230 Ida Dr.) is yet another Jackson Hole sporting goods store catering to all things skiing. Rent bikes in summer and get the inside dope on what's happening in the backcountry.

PHOTO GALLERIES

The areas around Yellowstone and Grand Teton National Parks have enticed photographers ever since the days of Harry Jackson and Ansel Adams, and now the inspirational qualities have made the region an appealing place for creative sorts to live. Not surprisingly, many of the galleries in the area feature photos of the breathtaking scenery.

JACKSON

Brookover-Muench Gallery (307-732-3988; www.brookover-muench.com; 125 N. Cache St.) offers examples of nature's dramatic landscapes from two of the more renowned photographers in the country, especially the American West.

Images of Nature (307-733-9752; www.mangelsen.com; 170 N. Cache St.) features the work of renowned nature photographer Thomas D. Mangelsen, a wildlife biologist who spends more than nine months a year in the field documenting the wild lands and creatures. Mangelsen works in cinematography and still photography. His work is offered in 16 Images of Nature galleries across the country.

Light Reflections (307-733-4016, 800-346-5223; www.lightreflections.com; 35 E. Deloney Ave.) shows landscapes, still lifes and desert abstractions in the American West from Fredric Joy, noted outdoor photographer.

Oswald Gallery (307-734-8100; www.oswaldgallery.com; 165 N. Center St.) presents vintage and contemporary photographs and art from the 19th and 20th centuries, as well as the world's finest contemporary photographers. The expansive inventory includes vast array of images of the American West.

Wild by Nature Gallery (307-733-8877, 888-494-5329; www.wildbynaturegallery.com; 95 W. Deloney Ave.) carries wildlife and landscape images by local photographer Henry H. Holdsworth, who is nationally recognized for his work in publications such as *National Geographic, Birder's World* and *National Wildlife*. Photos are available as limited-edition prints, note cards and books.

Wild Exposures Gallery (307-739-1777; www.wildexposuresgallery.com; 60 E. Broadway Ave.) exhibits panoramic outdoor works from internationally renowned local photographers Jeff Hogan, Scott McKinley and Andrew Weller.

SOUVENIRS

No listing required here—every time you turn around in and around the parks, regardless of town size, you'll run into a shop selling T-shirts, hats, key chains, sweatshirts, bumper stickers and anything else that'll let your friends know you were in Yellowstone, Grand Teton or Jackson Hole.

In Yellowstone National Park, you'll find gift shops run by Xanterra Parks & Resorts at nearly every junction, notably Canyon, Grant, Lake Lodge, Mammoth and Roosevelt. If you forget or run out of cash, you can shop online at www.travelyellowstone.com/shop. **Yellowstone General Stores** offer not only souvenirs but all the other tourist necessities, whether it's a snack or toothpaste or gasoline. **The Old Faithful Inn Gift Shop** has a larger assortment of gifts, with an especially impressive array of regional artwork.

In Grand Teton National Park, gifts and souvenirs are available at Colter Bay, Flagg Ranch, Jenny Lake Lodge, the Jenny Lake area, Moose and Signal Mountain. A great place to get souvenirs is the **Jackson Hole and Greater Yellowstone Visitor Center** at the National Elk Refuge, one of the finest visitor centers anywhere.

There isn't much shopping anymore at Mormon Row—just solitude and spectacular views of the Tetons.

8

Practical Information

Here you'll find everything else you might need to know about Yellowstone, Grand Teton and Jackson Hole—information on emergency services, federal offices, chambers of commerce, health and safety tips, weather reports, valuable Internet sites, road services and more.

AMBULANCE, FIRE AND POLICE

For emergencies dial 911. Remember that much of the Greater Yellowstone ecosystem is remote and populations are scattered; help isn't always close at hand, even with a cell or satellite phone. Following are listings for emergencies:

Yellowstone National Park
Emergency services: Dial 911 for fire, medical or ranger assistance, accidents or injuries. Park rangers are available at 307-344-7381. Emergency medical technicians and park medics are on duty 24 hours a day, year-round.

Grand Teton National Park
Emergency services: Dial 911 for fire, medical or ranger assistance, accidents or injuries.

Gateway Communities

CODY
Ambulance: 307-527-7501
Fire: 307-527-8550
Sheriff: 307-527-8700
Search & Rescue: 307-527-8740

COOKE CITY
Ambulance: 911
Fire: 406-838-2244
Sheriff: 406-222-2050

GARDINER
Ambulance: 911
Fire (volunteer): 911
Sheriff: 406-222-2050

The colorful Grand Canyon of the Yellowstone is one of the most photographed sites in the world.

National Park Service

ISLAND PARK
Ambulance: 307-624-7332
Fire: 208-558-0230
Fish & Game: 208-558-7202
Sheriff: 208-624-4482

JACKSON
Ambulance: 307-733-4742
Crimestoppers: 307-733-5148
Fire: 307-733-4732
Police: 307-733-1430
Search & Rescue: 307-733-7131

WEST YELLOWSTONE
Fire: 406-646-7600
Police: 406-646-7600
Search & Rescue (Gallatin County): 406-582-2100

State Police
Idaho (Idaho Falls): 208-525-7377
Montana (Butte): 406-494-3233
Wyoming: 800-442-9090

AREA CODE, ZIP CODES, CITY HALLS AND LOCAL GOVERNMENTS

Town or Park	Telephone	Zip Code
Ashton, Idaho	208-652-3987	83420
Cody, Wyoming	307-527-7511	82414
Cooke City, Montana	406-838-2495	59020
Driggs, Idaho	208-354-2362	83422
Dubois, Wyoming	307-455-2345	82513
Gardiner, Montana	406-848-7971	59030
Island Park, Idaho	208-558-7867	83429
Jackson, Wyoming	307-734-3993	83001
Mammoth, Wyoming	307-344-7381	82190
Moose, Wyoming	307-739-3399	83012
Moran, Wyoming	307-543-2847	83013
Teton Village, Wyoming	307-734-3993	83025
West Yellowstone, Montana	406-646-7795	59758
Yellowstone N.P.	307-344-7381	82190

BANKS

Yellowstone National Park: ATMs are at Old Faithful Inn, Old Faithful Snow Lodge, Lake Yellowstone Hotel, Mammoth Hot Springs Hotel, Grant Village, Canyon Lodge and general stores.

Grand Teton National Park: ATMs are at Jackson Lake Lodge and Colter Bay Village (summers only).

Firefighters hose down buildings in Gardiner's business district during the 1988 fires. National Park Service

Idaho

ASHTON
Bank of Ashton (208-652-3599; 600 Main St.)
Key Bank (208-652-7401; 24 S. 5th St.)

DRIGGS
Bank of Commerce (208-354-8633; 65 E. Wallace Ave.)
First Bank of the Tetons (208-354-7500; 189 N. Main St.)
Key Bank (208-354-2355; 15 N. Main St.)

ISLAND PARK
Bank of Idaho (208-558-0226; 4128 Lodge Pole Dr.)

REXBURG
Bank of Commerce (208-356-8080; 184 E. 2nd N.)
Beehive Federal Credit Union (208-356-3955; 65 S. Center St.)
Beehive Federal Credit Union (208-359-5453; 1087 Erikson Dr.)
Citizens Community Bank (208-356-5377; 220 N. 2nd E. #6)
East Idaho Credit Union (208-356-0191; 60 S. 2nd W.)
Key Bank (208-356-5454; 110 E. Main St.)
U.S. Bank (208-356-3641; 77 E. Main St.)
Washington Federal Savings (208-356-3648; 80 N. 2nd E.)
Wells Fargo (208-356-4415; 39 E. Main St.)
Zions Bank (208-356-7688; 149 W. Main St.)

Rigby
U.S. Bank (208-745-8181; 183 S. State St.)
Westmark Credit Union (208-745-0446; 567 Rigby Lake Dr.)
Wells Fargo (208-745-6659; 127 N. State St.)
Zions Bank (208-745-0019; 219 E. Main St.)

Ririe
Bank of Commerce (208-538-5566; 386 Main St.)

St. Anthony
Bank of Idaho (208-624-4900; 135 N. Bridge St.)
East Idaho Credit Union (208-624-4352; 99 N. Bridge St.)
Key Bank (208-624-3478; 30 W. Main St.)
Wells Fargo (208-624-3412; 30 W. Main St.)

Victor
Bank of Jackson Hole (208-787-8200; 11 W. Center St.)
First Bank of the Tetons (208-787-7601)

Montana
Belgrade
First Interstate Bank (406-388-0917; 6999 Jackrabbit Lane) In Albertson's grocery store.
First Security Bank (406-388-3700; 511 W. Main St.)
Stockman Bank (406-388-5025; 6345 Jackrabbit Lane)
Valley Bank of Belgrade (406-388-4283; 98 N. Broadway St.)
Valley Bank of Belgrade (406-388-9550; 205 W. Madison Ave.) In Lee & Dad's grocery store.

Big Sky
Big Sky Western Bank (406-995-7566; West Fork) Auto branch.
First Security Bank (406-993-3350; 78 Meadow Dr.)

Bozeman
American Bank (406-586-7968; 2825 W. Main St.)
American Bank (406-587-1234; 501 E. Main St.)
American Federal Savings Bank (406-586-0251; 606 N. 7th Ave.)
Bank of Bozeman (406-587-5626; 2610 W. Main St.)
Big Sky Western Bank (406-582-1010; 106 E. Babcock)
Big Sky Western Bank (406-587-2922; 4150 Valley Commons Dr.)
First Interstate Bank (406-556-4900; 202 W. Main St.)
First Interstate Bank (406-556-1058; 2023 Burke St.)
First Interstate Bank (406-586-0757; 1404 S. 6th Ave.)
First Interstate Bank (406-582-0458; 1809 S. Tracy Ave.)
First National Bank of Montana (406-587-2227; 1336 Stoneridge Dr.)
First Security Bank (406-585-3900; 208 E. Main St.)
First Security Bank (406-585-3800; 642 E. Cottonwood St.)
First Security Bank (406-585-3930; 912 N. 7th Ave.) In County Market grocery store.
First Security Bank (406-585-3801; 670 S. 19th Ave.)

First Security Bank ATM (406-585-1269; 15795 Bridger Canyon Dr.)
Heritage Bank (406-582-9188; 1460 N. 19th Ave.)
Mountain West Bank (406-587-5600; 1960 N. 19th Ave.)
Rocky Mountain Bank (406-556-7600; 2901 W. Main St.)
Rocky Mountain Credit Union (406-586-1505; 8645 Huffine Lane)
Sky Federal Credit Union (406-587-1750; 777 E. Main St. #102)
State Farm Bank (406-587-8287; 1805 W. Dickerson St.)
Sterling Savings Bank (406-586-2309; 5 W. Mendenhall St.)
Stockman Bank (406-556-4100; 1815 S. 19th Ave.)
U.S. Bank (406-585-5222; 104 E. Main St.)
Wells Fargo (406-586-3381; 211 W. Main St.)
Wells Fargo (406-586-3839; 1400 N. 19th Ave.)

EMIGRANT
Bank of the Rockies (406-333-9009; 307 Story Rd.)

ENNIS
First Madison Valley Bank (406-682-4215; 132 E. Main St.)
Valley Bank Ennis (406-682-3124; 118 E. William St.)

FOUR CORNERS
Big Sky Western Bank (406-582-1500; 7730 Shedhorn Dr.)
First National Bank of Montana (406-582-9944; 20 Avalanche Dr.)

GALLATIN GATEWAY
Big Sky Western Bank (406-995-2321; 47995 Gallatin Rd./US Hwy. 191)

GARDINER
First Interstate Bank (406-848-7474, US Hwy. 89)

LIVINGSTON
American Bank (406-222-2265; 120 N. 2nd St.)
Bank of the Rockies (406-222-9010; 1203 W. Park St.)
First Interstate Bank (406-222-2950; 207 W. Calendar St.)
Sky Federal Credit Union (406-222-1750; 111 N. B St.)
Sterling Savings Bank (406-222-1981; 123 S. Main St.)
Wells Fargo (406-222-3648; 323 W. Park St.)

RED LODGE
Avanta Federal Credit Union (406-651-2328; 821 S. Hauser Ave.)
Bank of Red Lodge (406-446-3208; 401 S. Broadway)
First Interstate Bank (406-446-1422; 602 N. Broadway)
Wells Fargo (406-446-1620; 1 S. Broadway)

WEST YELLOWSTONE
First Interstate Bank (406-646-7646; 106 S. Electric St.)
First Security Bank (406-646-7646; 23 Dunraven St.)
Yellowstone Basin Bank (406-646-4000; 216 Grizzly Ave.)

Wyoming

ALPINE

Bank of Alpine (307-654-0703)
Bank of Jackson Hole (307-654-0700; 140 US Hwy. 89)
First National Bank (307-654-3629; 79 US Hwy. 89)

CODY

Big Horn Federal Savings Bank (307-587-5521; 1701 Stampede Ave.)
U.S. Bank (307-527-9621; 1132 Beck Ave.)
Community First National Bank (307-587-2243; 1130 Sheridan Ave.)
First National Bank & Trust (307-587-3800; 1507 8th St.)
Pinnacle Bank (307-527-9690; 627 Yellowstone Ave.)
Pinnacle Bank (307-527-7186; 1702 17th St.)
State Farm Bank (307-527-7176; 1808 Sheridan Ave.)
Shoshone First Bank (307-587-4237; 1401 Sheridan Ave.)
Shoshone First Bank (307-587-2424; 1825 17th St.) In Albertson's grocery store.
Sunlight Federal Credit Union (307-587-9690; 1601 S. Park Dr.)

JACKSON

Bank of Jackson Hole (307-733-8064; 975 W. Broadway Ave.)
Bank of Jackson Hole (307-733-0708; 10 E. Pearl St.)
Bank of Jackson Hole (307-732-7676; 1425 S. US Hwy. 89)
Bank of the West (307-733-4884; 160 W. Pearl St.)
Community First National Bank (307-732-8800; 160 W. Pearl St.)
First Bank of the Tetons (307-733-7000; 130 W. Broadway Ave.)
First Interstate Bank (307-734-7373; 842 W. Broadway Ave.)
First Interstate Bank (307-732-7883; 120 E. Broadway Ave.)
First Interstate Bank (307-732-0194; 105 Buffalo Way) In Albertson's grocery store.
Jackson State Bank & Trust (307-733-3737; 112 Center St.)
Jackson State Bank & Trust (307-733-3737; 50 Buffalo Way)
Jackson State Bank & Trust (307-733-3737; Teton Village Rd., The Aspens)
Meridian Federal Credit Union (307-734-8034; 120 N. Center St.)
Wells Fargo (307-734-7598; 235 E. Broadway Ave.)

TETON VILLAGE

Bank of Jackson Hole (307-733-8064; 3285 W. Village Dr.)
Jackson State Bank & Trust (307-733-3737; 3300 W. Village Dr.)

WILSON

Bank of Jackson Hole (307-733-8064; 3525 Moose Wilson Rd.)
Bank of Jackson Hole (307-733-8066; 5650 W. Hwy. 22)
First Bank of the Tetons (307-733-9111; 1260 N. West St.)
Rocky Mountain Bank (307-732-2265; 4050 Lake Creek Dr. N.)

Bibliography

A guidebook more or less covers the basic tenets of journalism: The Whos, Whats, Whens, Wheres, Whys and Hows. Here are a few books that'll provide insights and help you further explore the people, histories and natural works that make Yellowstone, Grand Teton and Jackson Hole so extraordinary:

Autobiographies, Biographies and Reminiscences

Burt, Nathaniel. *Jackson Hole Journal*. Norman, Okla.: University of Oklahoma Press, 1983. 221 pp., $9.95.

Cahill, Tim. *Lost in My Own Backyard: A Walk in Yellowstone Park*. New York: Crown Journeys, 2004. 144 pp., $16.95.

Ferguson, Gary. *Hawks Rest: A Season in the Remote Heart of Yellowstone*. Washington, D.C.: National Geographic, 2003. 288 pp., $15.

Hoaglund, Bill. *Ring of Fire: Writers of the Yellowstone Region*. Missoula, Mont.: Rocky Mountain Press. 204 pp., $9.95.

Krakell, Dean. *Downriver: A Yellowstone Journey*. San Francisco: Sierra Club Books, 1987. 250 pp.

Mattes, Merrill J. *Colter's Hell & Jackson Hole, the Fur Trappers' Exploration of the Yellowstone and Grand Teton Region*. Yellowstone Library and Museum Assn., 1962. 87 pp.

Murie, Margaret E. *Wapiti Wilderness*. Boulder, Colo.: University of Colorado Press, 1985. 302 pp., $24.95.

Nelson, Fern K. *This Was Jackson's Hole*. Moose, Wyo.: High Plains Press, 1994. 384 pp., $15.95.

Potts, Merlin K. *Campfire Tales of Jackson Hole*. Moose, Wyo.: Grand Teton Natural History, 1995. 96 pp., $4.95.

Stewart, Donald C. *My Yellowstone Years: The Life of a Park Ranger*. Manchester, Mich.: Wilderness Adventure Books, 1989. 309 pp., $12.95.

Thompson, Edith M., and William Leigh Thompson. *Beaver Dick: The Honor and the Heartbreak*. Laramie, Wyo.: Jelm Mountain Press, 1982.

Turner, Jack. *Teewinot: Climbing and Contemplating the Teton Range*. New York: St. Martin's Griffin, 2001. 272 pp., $15.95.

——. *Teewinot: A Year in the Teton Range*. New York: Thomas Dunne Books, 2000. 240 pp., $15.95.

Whittlesey, Lee. *Death in Yellowstone: Death and Foolhardiness in the First National Park*. Boulder, Colo.: Roberts Rinehart Publishers, 1995. 240 pp., $16.95.

——. *Lost in the Yellowstone: Truman Evert's Thirty Seven Days of Peril*. Salt Lake City: University of Utah Press, 2002. 65 pp., $14.95.

Children's Books

Compton, Carrie L. *A to Z: Yellowstone Park (Illustrated)*. New York: Graphic Arts Center Publishing Company, 2004. 80 pp., $5.95.

Craighead, Shirley A. *Bugling Elk and Sleeping Grizzlies*. Guilford, Conn.: Falcon Press, 2004. 48 pp., $9.95.

Halvorsen, Lisa. *Letters Home from Our National Parks: Yellowstone*. Blackbirch Press, 2000. 32 pp., $3.95.

Lauber, P. *Summer of Fire: Yellowstone 1988*. Scholastic, 1991. 64 pp.

Swinburne, Stephen. *Once A Wolf: How Biologists Fought to Bring Back the Gray Wolf.* Boston and New York: Houghton Mifflin, 2001. 48 pp., $6.95.

Wilkinson, Todd. *Yellowstone Wildlife: A Watcher's Guide.* Charlottesville, Va.: Northwood Press, 1992. 96 pp.

Exploration

Adler, Warren. *Jackson Hole: Uneasy Eden.* Moose, Wyo.: Homestead Publishing, 1997. 223 pp., $15.95.

Bach, Orville J. *Exploring the Yellowstone Backcountry.* San Francisco: Sierra Club Books, 1998. 276 pp., $9.95.

Butler, Susan Springer. *Scenic Driving Yellowstone and Grand Teton National Parks.* Guilford, Conn.: Falcon Press, 1995. 262 pp., $16.95.

Carrighar, Sally. *One Day at Teton Marsh.* Lincoln, Neb.: University of Nebraska Press, 1979. 258 pp.

Clark, Tim W. *The Natural World of Jackson Hole: An Ecological Primer.* Moose, Wyo.: Grand Teton Natural History, 1999. 88 pp., $16.95.

Craighead, Charlie. *Portrait of Jackson Hole and the Tetons.* Helena, Mont.: Farcountry Press, 2007. 119 pp., $24.95.

Craighead Jr., Frank C. *For Everything There is a Season: The Sequence of Natural Events in the Grand Teton-Yellowstone Area.* Guilford, Conn.: Falcon Press, 2001. 228 pp., $9.95.

Daugherty, John. *A Place Called Jackson Hole.* Moose, Wyo.,: Grand Teton Natural History, 2002. 403 pp., $19.95.

An aerial view of Yellowstone's Grand Prismatic Spring, one of the largest hot springs in the world. National Park

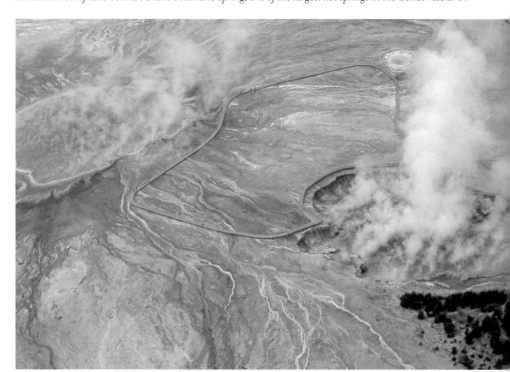

Ferguson, Gary. *Walking Down the Wild: A Journey Through the Yellowstone Rockies.* Guilford, Conn.: Falcon Press, 1997. 208 pp., $12.

Henry, Jeff. *Yellowstone Winter Guide.* Boulder, Colo.: Roberts Rinehart Publishers, 1998. 128 pp., $13.95.

Holdsworth, Henry. *Grand Teton Impressions.* Moose, Wyo.,: Farcountry Press, 2002. 80 pp., $9.95.

Lange, Joseph K. *Photographer's Guide to Yellowstone and the Tetons.* Mechanicsburg, Pa.: Stackpole Books, 2000. 122 pp., $18.95.

Meyer, Judith L. *The Spirit of Yellowstone.* Boulder, Colo.: Roberts Rinehart Publishers, 2003. 128 pp., $19.95.

Murphy, Tom. *Silence & Solitude: Yellowstone's Winter Wilderness.* Helena, Mont.: Riverbend Publishing, 2001. 128 pp., $29.95.

Pflughoft, Fred. *Grand Teton Wild and Beautiful.* Helena, Mont.: Farcountry Press, 2000. 120 pp., $29.95.

———. *Yellowstone Impressions.* Helena, Mont.: Farcountry Press, 2003. 80 pp., $9.95.

Reese, Rick. *Greater Yellowstone: The National Park and Adjacent Wildlands.* Helena, Mont.: Two Bears Press, 1991. 103 pp.

Rubenstein, Paul, Lee H. Whittlesey, and Mike Stevens. *The Guide to Yellowstone Waterfalls and Their Discovery.* Englewood, Colo.: Westcliffe Publishers, 2000. 295 pp., $24.95.

Saylor, David J. *Jackson Hole, Wyoming: In the Shadow of the Tetons.* Norman, Okla.: University of Oklahoma Press, 1971. 268 pp., $17.95.

Schmidt, Jeremy. *Yellowstone Grand Teton Road Guide: The Essential Guide for Motorists.* Jackson, Wyo.: Free Wheeling Travel Guides, 1998.

Schullery, Paul. *Searching for Yellowstone: Ecology and Wonder in the Last Wilderness.* Boston and New York: Houghton Mifflin, 1997. 338 pp., $24.95.

Shaw, Richard J. *Wildflowers of Yellowstone and Grand Teton National Parks.* Salt Lake City: Wheelright Press, 1976.

Tawney, Robin. *Family Fun in Yellowstone.* Guilford, Conn.: Falcon Press, 1998. 176 pp., $11.95.

Turner, Jack. *Jackson Hole: On a Grand Scale (The Great Ski Resorts of America).* Missoula, Mont.: Mountain Press, 2002. 180 pp., $29.95.

Wieneke, Connie. *Jackson Hole: Crossroads to the West.* Helena, Mont.: Farcountry Press, 2001.

Geology

Bauer, Clyde Max. *Yellowstone: Its Underworld.* Whitefish, Mont.: Kessinger Publishing, 2004. 136 pp., $20.95.

Bryan, T. Scott. *The Geysers of Yellowstone.* Boulder, Colo.: University of Colorado Press, 1995. 463 pp., $23.95.

Foley, Duncan. *Yellowstone's Geysers: The Story Behind the Scenery.* Las Vegas, Nev.: KC Publications, 2006. 48 pp., $9.95.

Fritz, William J. *Roadside Geology of the Yellowstone Country.* Missoula, Mont.: Mountain Press Publishing Company, 1985. 150 pp., $12.

Good, J. M. M., and Kenneth L. Pierce. *Interpreting the Landscape: Recent and Ongoing Geology of Grand Teton and Yellowstone National Parks.* Moose, Wyo.: Grand Teton Natural History, 1997. 58 pp., $12.95.

Love, J. D., Kenneth L. Pierce, and John C. Reed Jr. *Creation of the Teton Landscape: The*

Geologic Story of Grand Teton National Park. Moose, Wyo.: Grand Teton Natural History, 2003.

Schmidt, Jeremy, and Thomas Schmidt. *Grand Teton: Citadels of Stone.* Oakland, Calif.: Thunder Bay Press, 2002. 130 pp.

Schreier, Carl. *Yellowstone's Geysers, Hot Springs and Fumaroles.* Moose, Wyo.: Homestead Publications, 1987. 128 pp., $13.95.

Smith, Robert B., and Lee J. Siegel. *Windows into the Earth: The Geologic Story of Yellowstone and Grand Teton National Parks.* New York: Oxford University Press USA, 2000. 254 pp., $29.95.

History

Barringer, Mark Daniel. *Selling Yellowstone: Capitalism and the Construction of Nature.* Lawrence, Kan.: University of Kansas Press, 2002. 248 pp., $29.95.

Barker, Rocky. *Scorched Earth: How the Yellowstone Fires Changed America.* Washington, D.C.: Island Press, 2005. 288 pp., $24.95.

Bartlett, Richard A. *Yellowstone: A Wilderness Besieged.* Tucson, Ariz.: University of Arizona Press, 1989. 437 pp., $19.95.

Betts, Robert B. *Along the Ramparts of the Tetons: The Saga of Jackson Hole, Wyoming.* Boulder, Colo.: University of Colorado Press, 1978. 249 pp., $25.95.

Chase, Alston. *Playing God in Yellowstone: The Destruction of America's First National Park.* Fort Washington, Pa.: Harvest Books, 1987. 480 pp., $23.

Diem, Kenneth Lee. *Scalawags, Renegades, Discharged Soldiers, and Predestined Stinkers? A History of Northern Jackson Hole and Yellowstone's Influence.* Moose, Wyo.: Grand Teton Natural History, 1999. 198 pp., $14.95.

Ehrlich, Gretel. *Yellowstone: Land of Fire and Ice.* Oakland, Calif.: Thunder Bay Press, 2002. 130 pp.

Haines, Aubrey L. *The Yellowstone Story: A History of Our First National Park.* Boulder, Colo.: University of Colorado Press, 1996. 385 pp., $22.50.

——. *Yellowstone Place Names: Mirrors of History.* Boulder, Colo.: University of Colorado Press, 1996. 318 pp., $39.95.

Hayden, Elizabeth Wied, and Cynthia Nielsen. *Origins, A Guide to the Place Names of Grand Teton National Park and the Surrounding Area.* Moose, Wyo.: Grand Teton Natural History, 1988. 44 pp.

Huidekoper, Virginia. *The Early Days of Jackson Hole.* Moose, Wyo.: Grand Teton Natural History, 1996. 132 pp., $26.95.

Huyler, John S. *And That's the Way It Was in Jackson's Hole.* Jackson, Wyo.: Jackson Hole Historical Society and Museum, 2000. 239 pp., $9.95.

Janetski, Joel. *Indians in Yellowstone National Park.* Salt Lake City: University of Utah Press, 2002. 145 pp., $15.95.

Langford, Nathaniel Pitt. *The Discovery of Yellowstone Park; Journals of the Washburn Expedition to the Yellowstone and Firehole Rivers in the Year 1870.* Lincoln, Neb.: University of Nebraska Press, 1972. 147 pp., $16.95.

Lauber, P. *Summer of Fire: Yellowstone 1988.* Scholastic, 1991. 64 pp.

Loendorf, Lawrence L., and Nancy Medaris Stone. *Mountain Spirit: The Sheep Eater Indians of Yellowstone.* Salt Lake City: University of Utah Press, 2006. 256 pp., $19.95.

Magoc, Chris J. *Yellowstone: The Creation and Selling of an American Landscape (1870–1903).* Albuquerque: University of New Mexico Press, 1999. 266 pp., $5.95.

Lake Yellowstone Hotel employees show off a long stringer of trout caught in 1901. National Park Service

Moulton, Candy. *Legacy of the Tetons: Homesteading in Jackson Hole.* Cheyenne, Wyo.: La Frontera Publishing, 2007. 192 pp., $18.95.

Nabokov, Peter, and Lawrence L. Loendorf. *Restoring a Presence: American Indians and Yellowstone National Park.* Norman, Okla.: University of Oklahoma Press, 2004. 381 pp., $39.95.

Righter, Robert J. *Crucible for Conservation: The Creation of Grand Teton National Park.* Boulder, Colo.: University of Colorado Press, 1882. 192 pp., $7.95.

Schullery, Paul, and Lee Whittlesey. *Myth and History in the Creation of Yellowstone National Park.* Lincoln, Neb.: University of Nebraska Press, 2003. 125 pp., $22.

Wallace, David Rains. *Yellowstone: A Natural and Human History.* Washington, D.C.: National Park Service, 2001. 127 pp., $17.95.

Whittlesey, Lee H. *Yellowstone Album: A Photographic Celebration of the First National Park.* Boulder, Colo.: Roberts Rinehart Publishers, 2000. 208 pp., $19.95.

———. *Yellowstone Place Names.* Wonderland Publishing Company, 2006. 290 pp., $39.95.

Wingate, George Wood. *Through the Yellowstone Park on Horseback.* Moscow, Idaho: University of Idaho Press, 1999. 250 pp., $9.95.

Wuerthner, George. *Yellowstone: A Visitor's Companion.* Mechanicsburg, Pa.: Stackpole Books, 1992. 240 pp., $15.95.

———. *Yellowstone and the Fires of Change.* Salt Lake City: Haggis House Publications, 1988. 64 pp., $5.95.

Recreation

Boating

Nelson, Don. *Paddling Yellowstone and Grand Teton National Parks.* Guilford, Conn.: Falcon Press, 1999. 128 pp., $10.95.

Climbing

Jackson, Reynold G., and Leigh N. Ortenburger. *A Climber's Guide to the Teton Range.* Seattle: Mountaineers Books, 1996. 415 pp., $35.

Rossiter, Richard. *Teton Classics: 50 Selected Climbs in Grand Teton National Park.* Guilford, Conn.: Falcon Press, 1994. 136 pp., $15.

Fishing

Charlton, Robert E. *Yellowstone Fishing Guide.* Ketchum, Idaho: Lost River Press, 1995. 61 pp., $5.95.

Juracek, John. *Yellowstone: Portraits of a Fly-Fishing Landscape.* Boulder, Colo.: Pruett Publishing Company, 2002. 64 pp., $14.95.

Mathew, Craig, and Clayton Molinero. *The Yellowstone Fly-Fishing Guide.* Guilford, Conn.: Lyons Press, 1997. 176 pp., $16.95.

Parks, Richard. *Fishing Yellowstone National Park: An Angler's Complete Guide.* Guilford, Conn.: Lyons Press, 2007. 160 pp., $17.95.

Hiking

Anderson, Roger and Carol. *Ranger's Guide to Yellowstone Day Hikes.* Helena, Mont.: Farcountry Press, 2000. 152 pp., $11.95.

Duffy, Katy. *Teton Trails: A Guide to the Trails of Grand Teton National Park.* Moose, Wyo.: Grand Teton Natural History, 1995. 164 pp., $6.95.

Marschall, Mark C. *Yellowstone Trails: A Hiking Guide.* Yellowstone National Park: The Yellowstone Association, 1999.

Nystrom, Andrew Dean. *Top Trails Yellowstone and Grand Teton National Parks: Must-Do Hikes for Everyone.* Berkeley, Calif.: Wilderness Press, 2005. 351 pp., $16.95.

Schneider, Bill. *Best Easy Day Hikes Grand Tetons.* Guilford, Conn.: Falcon Press, 2003. 112 pp., $7.95.

——. *Best Easy Day Hikes Yellowstone.* Guilford, Conn.: Falcon Press, 2005. 80 pp., $7.95.

——. *Day Hikes Around Yellowstone National Park.* San Francisco: Day Hikes Books, 2005. 184 pp., $12.95.

——. *Hiking Yellowstone National Park.* Guilford, Conn.: Falcon Press, 2003. 368 pp., $16.95.

——. *Hiking Grand Teton National Park.* Guilford, Conn.: Falcon Press, 2005. 200 pp., $14.95.

Stone, Robert. *Day Hikes in Grand Teton National Park.* San Francisco: Day Hikes Books, 2004. 160 pp., $11.95.

——. *Day Hikes in Grand Teton National Park and Jackson Hole.* San Francisco: Day Hikes Books, 2000. 96 pp., $7.95.

Woods, Rebecca. *Jackson Hole Hikes: A Guide to Grand Teton National Park, Jedediah Smith, Teton and Gros Ventre Wilderness and Surrounding National Forest Land.* Mukilteo, Wash.: Alpen Books, 1999. $16.95.

Mountain Biking

Prax, Brian, and Mark Schultheis. *The Book: Guide to Mountain Biking in the Jackson Hole Area.* Jackson, Wyo.: Prax Photography and Productions, 2001. 94 pp., $16.95.

Travsky, Amber. *Mountain Biking Jackson Hole.* Guilford, Conn.: Falcon Press, 2001. 144 pp., $10.95.

Skiing

Dumais, Richard. *50 Ski Tours in Jackson Hole and Yellowstone.* 1991.

Olsen, Ken, Marchant, Dena, Scharosch, Steve, and Hazel Scharosch. *Cross-Country Skiing Yellowstone Country.* Guilford, Conn.: Globe Pequot Press, 1994. 164 pp.

Viola, Bob. *Jackson Hole Ski Guide.* Guilford, Conn.: Falcon Press, 1998. 128 pp.

Watters, Ron. *Winter Tales and Trails: Skiing, Snowshoeing and Snowboarding in Idaho, the Grand Tetons and Yellowstone National Park.* Pocatello, Idaho: Great Rift Press, 1997. 350 pp., $19.95.

Wildlife

General

Biel, Alice Wondrak. *Do (Not) Feed the Bears: The Fitful History of Wildlife and Tourists in Yellowstone.* Lawrence, Kan.: University of Kansas Press, 2006. 186 pp., $15.95.

Harry, Bryan. *Wildlife of Yellowstone and Grand Teton National Parks.* Salt Lake City: Wheelright Lithographing Co., 1964. 56 pp., $10.75.

Holdsworth, Henry. *Born Wild in Yellowstone and Grand Teton National Parks.* Helena, Mont.: Farcountry Press, 2003. 80 pp., $9.95.

———. *Yellowstone and Grand Teton Wildlife Portfolio.* Helena, Mont.: Farcountry Press, 2001. 120 pp., $24.95.

Smith, Bruce, Eric Cole, and David Dobkin. *Imperfect Pasture: A Century of Change at the National Elk Refuge in Jackson Hole, Wyoming.* Moose, Wyo.: Grand Teton Natural History, 2004. 151 pp., $14.95.

Varley, John D., and Paul Schullery. *Yellowstone Fishes: Ecology, History, and Angling in the Park.* Mechanicsburg, Pa.: Stackpole Books, 1998. 160 pp., $19.95.

Bears

Craighead, Frank J. *Track of the Grizzly.* San Francisco: Sierra Club Books, 1982. 272 pp., $19.95.

Lapinski, Mike. *Grizzlies and Grizzled Old Men: A Tribute to Those Who Fought to Save the Great Bear.* Guilford, Conn.: Falcon Press, 2006. 200 pp., $14.95.

McMillion, Scott. *Mark of the Grizzly: True Stories of Recent Bear Attacks and the Hard Lessons Learned.* Guilford, Conn.: Falcon Press, 1998. 272 pp., $14.95.

Peacock, Doug and Andrea. *The Essential Grizzly: The Mingled Fates of Men and Bears.* Guilford, Conn.: Lyons Press, 2006. 264 pp., $22.95.

Schullery, Paul. *Yellowstone Bear Tales.* Boulder, Colo.: Roberts Rinehart Publishers, 2001. 224 pp., $14.95.

Birds

McEneaney, Terry. *Birds of Yellowstone.* Boulder, Colo.: Roberts Rinehart Publishers, 1988. 171 pp., $19.95.

Raynes, Bert. *Birds of Grand Teton: And the Surrounding Area.* Moose, Wyo.: Grand Teton Natural History, 1989. 90 pp., $7.95.

Raynes, Bert, and Darwin Wile. *Finding the Birds of Jackson Hole.* Jackson, Wyo.: Darwin Wile, 1994. 161 pp., $11.95.

Tiekela, Stan. *Birds of Yellowstone and Tetons Field Guide.* Cambridge, Minn.: Adventure Publications, 2007. 148 pp., $9.95.

Bison

Franke, Mary Ann. *To Save the Wild Bison: On the Edge in Yellowstone.* Norman, Okla.: University of Oklahoma Press, 2005. 328 pp., $29.95.

Mountain Lions

Mangelsen, Thomas D. *Spirit of the Rockies: Mountain Lions of Jackson Hole.* Jackson, Wyo.: Thomas D. Mangelsen, Inc, 2000.

Wolves

Dutcher, Jim, Cherullo, Helen, and James Manfull. *Living With Wolves.* Seattle: Mountaineers Books, 2005. 172 pp., $34.95.

Halfpenny, James. *Yellowstone Wolves in the Wild.* Helena, Mont.: Riverbend Publishing, 2003. 104 pp., $19.95.

McIntyre, Rick. *War Against the Wolf: America's Campaign to Exterminate the Wolf.* Osceola, Wis.: Voyageur Press, 1995. 495 pp., $19.95.

McNamee, Thomas. *Return of the Wolf to Yellowstone.* New York: Owl Books, 1998. 325 pp., $19.95.

Phillips, Michael K., and Douglas W. Smith. *The Wolves of Yellowstone.* Osceola, Wis.: Voyageur Press, 1996. 125 pp., $19.95.

Smith, Douglas W., and Gary Ferguson. *Decade of the Wolf.* Guilford, Conn.: Lyons Press, 2005. 256 pp., $23.95.

CHAMBERS OF COMMERCE

ASHTON

Ashton Chamber of Commerce: 208-652-7711; www.ashtonidaho.com; 714 Main St., Ashton, ID 83420.

BIG SKY

Big Sky Chamber of Commerce: 800-943-4111; www.bigskychamber.com; allison@bigskychamber.com; P.O. Box 160100, 3091 Pine Dr., Big Sky, MT 59716.

BOZEMAN

Bozeman Chamber of Commerce: 800-228-4224; www.bozemanchamber.com; info@bozemanchamber.com; 2000 Commerce Way, Bozeman, MT 59715.

CODY

Cody Country Chamber of Commerce: 307-587-2297; www.codychamber.org; info@codychamber.org; 836 Sheridan Ave., Cody, WY 82414.

Park County Travel Council: 307-587-2297; fax 307-527-6228; www.yellowstonecountry.org; pctc2@codychamber.org; P.O. Box 2454, Cody, WY 92414.

Cooke City
Cooke City Chamber of Commerce: 406-838-2495; www.cookecitychamber.org; info@cookecitychamber.org; 230 W. Main St., Cooke City, MT 59020.

Gardiner
Gardiner Chamber of Commerce: 406-848-7971; fax 406-848-2446; www.gardinerchamber.com; info@gardinerchamber.com; 222 W. Park St., Gardiner, MT 59030.

Idaho Falls
Idaho Falls Chamber of Commerce: 208-523-1010; www.idahofallschamber.com; info@idahofallschamber.com; 630 W Broadway St., Idaho Falls, ID 83402.

Island Park
Island Park Chamber of Commerce: 208-558-7755; www.islandparkchamber.org; ipchamber@yahoo.com; P.O. Box 83, Island Park, ID 83429.

Jackson
Jackson Hole Chamber of Commerce: 307-733-3316; www.jacksonholechamber.com; info@jacksonholechamber.com; 532 N. Cache St., Jackson, WY 83001.

Livingston
Livingston Chamber of Commerce: 406-222-0850; www.livingston-chamber.com; info@livingston-chamber.com; 303 E. Park St., Livingston, MT 59047.

West Yellowstone
West Yellowstone Chamber of Commerce: 406-646-7701; fax 406-646-9691; www.westyellowstonechamber.com; visitorservices@westyellowstonechamber.com; 30 Yellowstone Ave., P.O. Box 458, West Yellowstone, MT 59758.

CLIMATE AND WEATHER REPORTS

The old axiom about weather changing every five minutes never rang truer than in the Greater Yellowstone ecosystem, where 7,500-foot-plus elevations mean it can snow in July and undulating terrain is the perfect recipe for lightning storms. Warm and sunny summer mornings can turn to rain, sleet or even snow by afternoon. Average summer highs are in the upper 70s with lows in the mid-40s. Winter highs are in the 30s, lows below 10. Subzero weather is not uncommon. Warm jackets and rain gear are a must even in July if you're planning to leave your car, lodging or campsite. Remember: You can always remove layers of clothing; you can't add what you don't have. If you're caught in lightning, get away from water or beaches and leave ridges, exposed spots and isolated trees. If you can't, lie flat on the ground, preferably in a low-lying ravine.

The varied topography also means weather could be dramatically different from Jackson Hole to Yellowstone. The sun can be shining in one area and a downpour occurring in another. Along with cold-weather gear, be sure to bring sunscreen and/or a hat. Don't let the cool temperatures fool you: It doesn't take long to burn under the intense sun at such high elevations.

For information in Yellowstone, go to www.yellowstone-natl-park.com/weather.htm or www.yellowstoneparknet.com/report_center/weather_forecast.php?zc=82190 for reports

Two bald eaglets await a feeding in their nest near Fishing Bridge in Yellowstone. National Park Service

and forecasts. For Grand Teton and Jackson Hole, go to www.jacksonholewy.net/
report_center/weather_forecast.php?zc=83001.

The National Weather Service number in Billings, Montana, is 406-652-0851; for
Jackson Hole it's 406-329-4840 out of Missoula, Montana. For winter adventurers, check
the Backcountry Avalanche Hazard & Weather Forecast (307-733-2664; www.jhavalanche
.org) or the Gallatin National Forest Avalanche Center (406-587-6981; www.mtavalanche
.com) in Bozeman for potentially dangerous snow conditions.

ENVIRONMENT

Protecting Yellowstone, Grand Teton and Jackson Hole for future generations is an ongoing
struggle against overdevelopment and other threats. Following are a few environmentally
oriented organizations with a variety of missions:

Buffalo Field Campaign (406-646-0070; www.wildrockies.org/buffalo) has hunkered
down in West Yellowstone, hub of the controversy involving the many bison that wander
from the park. They're often seen protesting or handing out leaflets, especially during a
bison hunt. In some ways, this passionate group is a throwback to the tree-hugging sit-
in days of antilogging in the Pacific Northwest.

Grand Teton National Park Foundation (307-732-0629; www.gtnpf.org) in Moose is a
nonprofit outfit that raises money from private entities to help with a variety of projects

in the park. It is partially supported by the profits from Grand Teton Bottled Water.

Grand Teton Natural History Association (307-739-3606; www.grandtetonpark.org) is based in Moose and is the park's equivalent of the Yellowstone Association. Its emphasis is education and it is supported through classes and book sales.

Greater Yellowstone Coalition (406-586-1593; www.greateryellowstone.org) keeps an eye on all things Yellowstone and the park's periphery from its headquarters in Bozeman. It is a nonprofit organization.

Yellowstone Association (307-344-2289; www.yellowstoneassociation.org) emphasizes education and understanding of the park's goals. It offers classes through the Yellowstone Association Institute and sells books at a variety of places, including the old buffalo ranch in Lamar Valley.

Yellowstone Park Foundation (406-586-6303; www.ypf.org) in Bozeman helps finance infrastructure improvements within the park by tapping businesses and private individuals. This is where your money goes if you use a Yellowstone National Park Visa. Like the Greater Yellowstone Coalition, it's nonprofit.

FEES

Yellowstone and Grand Teton National Parks

Private, noncommercial automobiles: $25 (seven days, good for Yellowstone and Grand Teton).

Individual motorcycle: $20 (seven days, both parks).

Single entry (foot, bike, ski, etc.): $12 (seven days, both parks).

Yellowstone–Grand Teton Pass: $50 (valid for one year from month of purchase).

America the Beautiful Pass: $80 (valid for one year from month of purchase to all national parks and federal recreation lands).

Senior Pass: $10 (for U.S. citizens 62 and older).

Access Pass: Free for U.S. citizens and permanent residents who are legally blind or disabled; documentation required.

Note: All current valid passes are accepted until expired, including the National Parks Pass, Golden Eagle Pass, Golden Age Passport and Golden Access Passport.

FEDERAL GOVERNMENT

Bureau of Land Management

Idaho (Boise): 208-373-4000

Montana (Billings): 406-896-5000

Wyoming (Cheyenne): 307-775-6256

U.S. Forest Service

Bighorn National Forest (Sheridan, Wyoming): 307-674-2600

Medicine Wheel/Paintrock (Patrick): 307-548-6541

Powder River (Buffalo): 307-684-7806

Powder River (Worland): 307-347-5105

Tongue: 307-674-2600

Caribou-Targhee National Forest (Idaho Falls, Idaho): 208-524-7500
    Ashton: 208-652-7442
    Dubois: 208-374-5422
    Island Park: 208-558-7301
    Montpelier: 208-847-0375
    Palisades (Idaho Falls): 208-523-1412
    Soda Springs: 208-547-4356
    Teton Basin (Driggs): 208-354-2312
    Westside (Pocatello): 208-236-7500
Custer National Forest (Billings, Montana): 406-657-6200
    Ashland: 406-784-2344
    Beartooth (Red Lodge): 406-2103
    Sioux (Camp Crook, S.D.): 605-797-4432
Gallatin National Forest (Bozeman, Montana): 406-587-6701
    Big Timber: 406-932-5155
    Cooke City: 406-838-2388
    Gardiner: 406-848-7375
    Hebgen Lake (West Yellowstone): 406-823-6961
    Livingston: 406-222-1892
Shoshone National Forest (Cody, Wyoming): 307-578-1200
    North Zone Districts (Cody): 307-527-6921
    Washakie: 307-332-5460
    Wind River: 307-455-2466
Bridger-Teton National Forest (Jackson, Wyoming): 307-739-5500
    Big Piney: 307-276-3375
    Buffalo (Moran): 307-543-2386
    Greys River (Afton): 307-886-5300
    Kemmerer: 307-877-4415
    Pinedale: 307-367-4326

Other Federal Lands

Big Hole National Battlefield (406-689-3155; Wisdom, Montana) Scene of a key battle between the U.S. Cavalry and the Nez Perce Indians in the summer of 1877, when they zig-zagged from Oregon to Idaho, Montana and Wyoming in a futile attempt to escape to Canada.

Bighorn Canyon National Recreation Area (406-666-2412; Billings, Montana) The Bighorn River below Yellowtail Dam might be the best all-round trout fishery in Montana.

Glacier National Park (406-888-7800; St. Mary's, Montana) Towering mountains, grizzly bears, wolves and glaciers receding amid warming climates.

Grant-Kohrs Ranch National Historic Site (406-846-3388; Deer Lodge, Montana) One of the more famous cattle ranches in a state renowned for ranching.

Little Bighorn Battlefield National Monument (406-638-2621; Crow Agency, Montana) Custer's Last Stand was made here on what is now the Crow Reservation. Newer exhibits now feature the famed battle from the perspective of the Sioux and Northern Cheyenne.

Virginia City National Historic Landmark (406-843-5247; Virginia City, Montana) This small town in the mountains northwest of Yellowstone clings to its gold-rush past. It was once the largest city between Minneapolis and San Francisco. Raucous frontier entertainment is a specialty here.

Fuel

All of the park's gateway communities have gas stations, most available 24 hours thanks to credit cards. Stations are located in Yellowstone National Park at Canyon Village, Fishing Bridge, Grant Village, Mammoth Hot Springs, Old Faithful and Tower Junction. Though the road between Mammoth and the Northeast Entrance is open all winter, the pumps at Tower are covered. Gas is available in Cooke City all year, however.

Gasoline in the communities surrounding the park tends to be at about the national average, or slightly higher. Expect to pay about 15 percent more at Yellowstone National Park pumps. Diesel is readily available. If you're into biofuels, West Yellowstone and Belgrade offer places to fill-er-up.

Guided Tours

Both national parks have a plethora of ranger-led activities, mostly in the summer but also during the other three seasons. Check the monthly *Teewinot* newspaper in Grand Teton and *Yellowstone Today,* at Web sites or at park entrances for updated program information. For an extensive list of tour operators in the gateway communities of Jackson Hole, Cody, West Yellowstone, Gardiner and Big Sky, go to: www.yellowstonenationalpark.com/tours.htm#Big%20Sky or www.yellowstoneparknet.com/guides_tours/guides_tours.php.

In an effort to be even greener, Yellowstone has evolved to using biofuels in its trucks. National Park Service

Ranger-led tours (www.nps.gov/yell/planyourvisit/rangerprog.htm) are available year-round in Yellowstone National Park (www.nps.gov/yel /planyourvisit/rangerprog.htm) and Grand Teton National Park (307-739-3399).

Auto/Bus Tours

Callowishus Park Touring Company (307-733-9521; www.callowishus.com) offers van tours of Grand Teton out of Jackson.

Cody Trolley Tours (307-527-7043; www.codytrolleytours.com) operate daily from early June through late September and offer 22-mile tours of Cody and the surrounding area. Stops include historic sites, viewpoints and other attractions. $18 adults, $16 seniors 65 and older, $8 youths (5–17). A trolley tour Buffalo Bill Historical Center combination package is $28. Tours start at the Irma Hotel.

Grand Teton Adventure Company (307-734-4454/800-700-1558; www.grandteton adventures.com) has vans that take visitors through Grand Teton from Jackson.

Grayline Bus (800-443-6133; www.graylinejh.com) of Jackson Hole offers narrated tours of Yellowstone and Grand Teton Parks, as well as private tours in smaller vehicles.

Karst Stage (800-287-4759, 406-388-229; www.karststage.com) of Belgrade, Montana, takes passengers from Bozeman's airport, Gallatin Field, to the park at West Yellowstone and Gardiner.

Jackson Hole Adventure (800-392-3165, 307-654-7849; www.jacksonholeadventure.com) is another Jackson business offering van tours.

Journey Taxi and Transportation (307-690-0887; www.journeytaxi.com) can get you from here to there in a variety of ways.

Powder River Tours (800-442-3682, 307-527-3677) of Cody features day tours of Grand Teton National Park.

Wyoming Photo Experience (307-413-3777; www.wyomingphotoexperience.com) offers tours geared toward those who want to bring their cameras.

Yellowstone Alpen Guides (800-858-3502, 406-646-9591) has been operating out of West Yellowstone for 20 years and offers snowcoach tours to Old Faithful, wildlife viewing/photography and other family-oriented activities (www.yellowstoneguides.com).

Yellowstone and Grand Teton Custom Tours (307-734-8387; www.ygtcustomparktours.com) is geared toward park visitors who arrive in groups and want to see the area from the comfort of vehicles. Tours include single- and multiday, and guides can be hired for your own personal vehicle.

Xanterra Parks and Resorts (307-344-7311, www.travelyellowstone.com), the park's concessionaire, has full-day bus tours and has reintroduced the famed old yellow touring coaches, which went back into business in the summer of 2007.

Wildlife Safaris

Upstream Anglers and Outdoor Adventures (800-642-8979) allows visitors to see wolves, bears, elk and other wildlife year-round in Yellowstone, Grand Teton and Jackson Hole from the comfort of 4x4 SUVs (www.upstreamanglers.com).

Teton Science Schools Wildlife Expeditions (888-945-3567) motto is "Connecting People to Nature Through Education." Expeditions range from four hours to four days in both parks, and trips can be tailored toward such interests as photography (www .wildlifeexpeditions.org).

HANDICAPPED SERVICES

Yellowstone National Park: Major tourist sites such as Old Faithful, Mammoth Hot Springs, Canyon, Grant Village, Madison and Norris are deemed handicapped accessible by the National Park Service. The Visitors Guide to Accessible Features in Yellowstone National Park is available through the Park Accessibility Coordinator at P.O. Box 168, Yellowstone National Park, WY 82190. Phone: 307-344-2017. It is also free online and available at all park entrances. Information for the hearing impaired is available through TDD at 307-344-2386.

    Grand Teton National Park: Visitor centers and some campsites, restrooms and trails are handicapped accessible, especially in the Jenny Lake area. Easy Access pamphlets at visitor centers show park features accessible to the disabled, senior citizens and small children. TDD: 307-739-3400.

    An outfit called **Access Tours** (307-733-6664) gives tours in both parks for the disabled.

HEALTH AND SAFETY

Hospitals

Yellowstone National Park: Mammoth Hot Springs Clinic (weekdays, year-round): 307-344-7965; Old Faithful Clinic (early May to mid-October): 307-545-7325; Lake Hospital (summer): 307-242-7241.

Grand Teton National Park: Grand Teton Medical Clinic (mid-May through mid-October) at Jackson Lake Lodge: 307-543-2514 (10 AM–5 PM) and 307-733-8002 (after hours).

Cody: West Park Hospital, 707 Sheridan Ave., 307-527-7501.

Jackson: St. John's Medical Center, 635 E. Broadway St., 307-733-3636.

West Yellowstone: Yellowstone Family Medical Clinic, 236 Yellowstone Ave., 406-646-0200.

Health Issues

Altitude Sickness: If you're coming from near sea level, it's possible that spending time in the thin air of higher elevations in Grand Teton and the Beartooth Plateau could bring on altitude sickness. Symptoms include shortness of breath, headaches, disorientation, nausea and nosebleeds. The best antidote is to move to a lower elevation until the symptoms disappear.

    Giardia: When they say don't drink the lake/stream water, they mean it. Even in the pristine waters of Yellowstone and Grand Teton, these protozoa live, thanks to their spreading by humans and animals through waste. Always purify drinking water by boiling, using special tablets or bringing water purifiers. Giardia won't ruin your vacation because it takes weeks to appear, but when it does, the intestinal pain is unforgettable.

    Hantavirus: Another rare disease, but not one to mess around with. Hantavirus is spread by rodents, mostly deer mice and voles, via their droppings. A handful of residents in Wyoming and Montana have been killed by the disease while cleaning out old buildings infested with rodent waste. Avoid contact with mouse, rat or vole droppings, and make a quick check of rustic cabins. It's extremely unlikely that you'll contract hantavirus, even if you do come in contact with rodent feces, but better safe than sorry.

Hypothermia: This is the greatest health threat in the parks, far more than bears, lightning or any sickness. Even on the warmest days of summer, the right combination of wind, cold and wet can quickly drop your body temperature to dangerous levels to where even death is possible. It isn't limited to flipping a kayak or canoe in 41-degree Lake Yellowstone, either, though that's an almost certain recipe for disaster. A soaking from a sudden storm can turn the trick as well. It begins with uncontrollable shivering, followed by disorientation, unconsciousness and death. The way to avoid it is to dress for all occasions, avoiding cotton and denim if you plan to venture far from your car or room. Always bring a waterproof raincoat, windbreaker or shell. Dress in layers. Wool and polypropylene are terrific because they insulate, retain heat and dry quickly. In a worst-case scenario, where a hiking partner is showing signs of hypothermia, strip them of their wet clothes and wrap yourself around them, preferably skin to skin, so you're transferring your body heat.

Sun: Don't let the moderate days, cool nights and even the presence of snow fool you. Altitudes in Yellowstone and Jackson Hole are well over 5,000 feet, and the air is dry. It doesn't take much to get a severe burn, even on hazy days. Use sunscreen of at least 30 SPF and wear a hat when venturing into the backcountry.

Ticks: This tiny spiderlike creature devastated human populations in parts of Montana at the turn of the previous century by transmitting Rocky Mountain spotted fever. Though the fever is rare, it's still possible to acquire it. Also rare, but of slightly greater concern, is Lyme disease, which was identified in the East but has since moved west. And there are other diseases spread by the tick. Covering as much skin as possible when walking through brushy areas is the best way to avoid them. After a day in the woods, spend some extra time in the shower checking yourself carefully, especially your hair. If you find one, use tweezers to "unscrew" them. Make sure you get the head and don't leave the tongs. Neosporin or

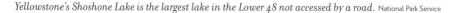

Yellowstone's Shoshone Lake is the largest lake in the Lower 48 not accessed by a road. National Park Service

the natural oil tea tree applied to the bite will reduce swelling. Keep a close eye on any bites. The ramifications can last a lifetime, perhaps even be deadly.

West Nile Virus: This disease is on the rise in the Northern Rockies, where several cases are reported each summer. They're caused by mosquito bites. Chances are you'll get bites from mosquitoes that don't carry the virus, but it only takes one. If you plan to hike in mosquito-prone areas, especially around standing or slow-moving water, use insect repellents with DEET. If you prefer to avoid chemicals, splash yourself with citronella.

INTERNET SITES

Some Web sites that could come in handy as you're planning your Yellowstone/Teton vacation:

www.nps.gov/yell: Yellowstone's official Web site.

www.nps.gov/grte: Grand Teton's official Web site.

www.jacksonholetraveler.com: Everything you need to know about Jackson and Jackson Hole.

www.jacksonholeresort.com: The Jackson Hole Central Reservations site for lodging, trips and other adventures in the area.

www.travelyellowstone.com: The park's concessionaire site focuses on lodging, dining, tours and other business activities.

www.yellowstoneassociation.org: The what, when and where of the organization's classes, membership information, book sales, etc.

www.yellowstone.net/newspaper: All things Yellowstone.

www.yellowstoneparknet.com: A close look not only at what's happening in the park but especially what's available in the gateway communities.

www.yellowstonereservations.com: A good way to book a room and other things to do in and around the park.

www.grandtetonpark.org: The Grand Teton Natural History Association's Web site.

www.reserveusa.com: For making reservations at a number of Forest Service campgrounds, cabins and lookouts.

www.nationalelkrefuge.fws.gov: Official site for the National Elk Refuge.

www.wyomingbnb-ranchrec.com: A quick way to find lodging out of the ordinary, especially bed and breakfasts as well as guest cabins and ranches.

www.gf.state.wy.us: Wyoming's Fish and Game Department site.

www.wyoga.org: Web site for the Wyoming Outfitters and Guides Association, which will help with horse packing, fishing and other backcountry adventures.

www.wyomingdra.com: The place to start when looking to stay at one of the state's many dude ranches.

MEDIA

Magazines and Newspapers

Billings Gazette (406-657-1200; www.billingsgazette.com; P.O. Box 36300, Billings, MT 59107-3600) Regional daily covers most of eastern Montana and northern Wyoming, with a reporter assigned to Yellowstone. Part of Lee Enterprises chain that includes Casper Star-Tribune.

Bozeman Daily Chronicle (406-587-4491; www.bozemandailychronicle.com; 2820 W. College St., Bozeman, MT 58718) Part of the Pioneer Newspapers chain from Seattle, the *Chronicle* circulates every morning to West Yellowstone and Gardiner, and in 2007 staged a coup when Yellowstone National Park made it the only paper to be sold in the park.

Casper Star-Tribune (307-266-0500; www.trib.com; 170 Star Lane, Casper, WY 82601) Statewide daily has reporter based in Jackson and emphasizes natural resources issues surrounding Grand Teton and Yellowstone.

Cody Enterprise (307-587-2231; www.codyenterprise.com; 3101 Big Horn Ave., Cody, WY 82414) Twice-weekly paper founded in 1899 by Buffalo Bill Cody covers northwest Wyoming.

Idaho Falls Post Register (208-522-1800; www.postregister.com; 333 Northgate Mile, Idaho Falls, ID 83401) Regional morning newspaper covers most of southeast Idaho on the western flanks of Yellowstone and Grand Teton, and into western Montana and Wyoming.

Jackson Hole News & Guide (307-733-2047; www.jacksonholenews.com; 1225 Maple Way, Jackson, WY 83002) The Jackson Hole area's primary news source.

Livingston Enterprise (406-222-2000; www.livingstonenterprise.com; 401 S. Main St., Livingston, MT 59047) Afternoon paper prints Monday through Friday and covers the Paradise Valley from Livingston south to Mammoth Hot Springs.

Montana Quarterly (406-587-4491; www.montanaquarterly.com; 2820 W. College St., Bozeman, MT 59718) New magazine's coverage includes Yellowstone.

Planet Jackson Hole (307-732-0299; www.planetjh.com; 567 W. Broadway Ave., Jackson, WY 83001) Free weekly and independent paper concentrates on news, entertainment and the arts in Jackson Hole and park regions.

West Yellowstone News (406-646-9719; www.westyellowstonenews.com; 309 Canyon St., West Yellowstone, MT 59798) Weekly newspaper owned by Big Sky Publishing in Bozeman concentrates heavily on park issues.

Radio Stations

IDAHO

KBYI-FM 100.1 (208-496-2907), Rexburg; Brigham Young University–Idaho public radio sponsored by LDS Church.

KBYR-FM 95.3 (208-496-2907), Rexburg; BYU-Idaho inspirational sponsored by LDS Church.

KBLI-AM 1620 (208-785-1400), Blackfoot; Spanish radio.

KCHQ-FM 102.1 (208-354-4102), Driggs.

KID-AM 590 (208-524-5900), Idaho Falls; news and talk.

KID-FM 96.1 (208-524-5900), Idaho Falls; country.

KFTZ-FM 103.3 (208-785-1400), Idaho Falls; top 40.

KLCE-FM 97.3 (208-785-1400), Blackfoot; adult contemporary.

KLLP-FM 98.5 (208-233-1133), Chubbuck; adult contemporary.

KMGI-FM 102.5 (208-233-2121), Pocatello; classic rock.

KOUU-AM 1290 (208-234-1290), Pocatello; country.

KPKY-FM 94.9 (208-233-1133), Pocatello; oldies.

KPLV-FM 105.5 (208-785-1400), Idaho Falls; '80s rock.

KRTK-AM 1490 (208-237-9500), Chubbuck; religious.

KRXK-AM 1230 (208-356-3651), Chubbuck; sports.

KSEI-AM 930 (208-233-2121), Pocatello; sports with strong signal reaching into Montana, Wyoming and the parks.

KUPI-FM 99.1 (208-522-1101), Idaho Falls; country.

KWIK-AM 1240 (208-233-1133), Pocatello; news and talk.

KZBQ-FM 93.7 (208-234-1290), Pocatello; country.

KZNI-AM 1260 (208-785-1400), Idaho Falls; sports.

KZNR-AM 690 (208-785-1400), Blackfoot; talk.

Idaho Public Radio (208-282-2857, kisu.org), Public Radio International programming and Idaho issues are on KISU-FM in Pocatello (91.1).

Montana

KBBB-FM 103.7 (406-248-7827), Billings; adult contemporary.

KBLG-AM 910 (406-652-8400), Billings; news and talk.

KBOZ-AM 1090 (406-587-9999), Bozeman; news, talk and sports.

KBOZ-FM 99.9 (406-587-9999), Bozeman; country.

KBUL-AM 970 (406-248-7827), Billings; news and talk.

KBZM-FM 104.7 (406-993-4545), Big Sky; classic hits.

KCMM-FM 99.1 (406-388-4281), Belgrade; Christian contemporary.

KEZY-FM 92.9 (406-535-0704), West Yellowstone; classic rock.

KGHL-AM 790 (406-238-1000), Billings; country.

KGHL-FM 98.5 (406-238-1000), Billings; country.

KGVW-AM 640 (406-388-4281), Belgrade; religious.

KISN-FM 96.7 (406-586-2343), Belgrade; top 40.

KKBR-FM 97.1 (406-248-7827), Billings; oldies.

KLMT-FM 89.3 (800-541-5647), Billings; Christian contemporary.

KMMS-AM 1450 (406-586-2343), Bozeman; local and national talk.

KMMS-FM 95.1 (406-586-2343), Bozeman; adult album alternative.

KMXE-FM 99.3 (406-446-1199), Red Lodge; classic rock.

KMZK-AM 1240 (406-245-3121), Billings; Christian contemporary.

KNDZ-FM 105.1 (406-259-3490), Billings; adult album alternative.

KOBB-AM 1230 (406-587-9999), Bozeman; nostalgia and oldies.

KOBB-FM 93.7 (406-587-9999), Bozeman; oldies.

KOZB-FM 97.5 (406-587-9999), Livingston; alternative.

KPRK-AM 1340 (406-222-2841), Livingston; classic hits.

KRKX-FM 94.1 (406-652-8400), Billings; classic rock.

KRZN-FM 96.3 (406-652-8400), Billings; alternative.

KXLB-FM 100.7 (406-586-2343), Bozeman; country.

KWYS-AM 920 (406-646-7361), West Yellowstone; oldies, local news and Wolverine high school sports.

KYYA-FM 93.3 (406-652-8400), Billings; adult contemporary.

KZMY-FM 103.5 (406-586-2343), Bozeman; adult contemporary.

KZRV-FM 107.5 (406-238-1000), Billings; smooth jazz.

Yellowstone Public Radio (406-657-4192, www.yellowstonepublicradio.org), NPR programming and regional issues affecting Montana east of the Continental Divide and northern Wyoming. Also available in the Yellowstone-Teton region in Big Sky (95.5), Big Timber (90.5), Bozeman (102.1/106.7), Cody (88.5), Emigrant (91.1), Greybull (99.1), Livingston (88.5), Red Lodge (89.1), Sheridan (88.1) and Yellowstone National Park (104.9).

WYOMING

KSGT-AM 1340 (307-733-4500), Jackson; country music with local news, weather, sports, ag reports, ABC News and Paul Harvey.

KJAX-FM 93.3 (307-733-4500), Jackson; country music.

KMTN-FM 96.9 (307-733-4500), Jackson; wide range of contemporary music from blues and jazz to hard rock and reggae, with local personalities, concert information, contests, etc.

KODI-AM 1480 (307-587-5000), Cody; talk.

KPOW-AM 1260 (307-754-5183), Powell; country.

KPIN-FM 101.1 (307-367-2000), Pinedale; country.

KROE-AM 930 (307-672-7421), Sheridan; oldies.

KTAG-FM 97.9 (307-587-5000), Cody; adult contemporary.

KTWO-AM 1030 (307-265-1984), Casper; 50,000-watt news and talk can be heard throughout the region.

KYTI-FM 93.7 (307-672-7421), Sheridan; country.

KZJH-FM 95.3 (307-733-4500; www.jacksonholeradio.com), Jackson; on-air morning personality, '80s music, CBS News, local flavor.

KZMQ-AM 1140/KZMQ-FM 100.3 (307-587-5000), Greybull; country.

KZWY-FM 94.9 (307-672-7421), Sheridan; classic rock.

Wyoming Public Radio (307-766-4240, uwadmnweb.uwyo.edu/WPR), NPR programming and Wyoming issues, based in Laramie with stations in the national parks region in Alta/Driggs (91.3), Cody (90.1), Dubois (91.3), Jackson (90.3), Pinedale (90.9), Sheridan (91.3) and Thermopolis (91.3).

Television Stations

IDAHO

KIDK TV Channel 3 (208-522-5100), Idaho Falls, CBS.

KPVI TV Channel 6 (208-529-0540), Pocatello, NBC.

KIFI TV Channel 8 (208-233-8888), Idaho Falls, ABC.

KISU TV Channel 10 (208-282-2857), Pocatello, PBS affiliate from Idaho State University.

KPIF TV Channel 15 (208-237-5743), Pocatello, CW.

KUNP TV Channel 24, Pocatello, Telefutura.

K26EW TV Channel 26, Idaho Falls, TBN.

KFXP TV Channel 31 (208-232-3141), Pocatello, FOX.

MONTANA

KTVQ TV Channel 2 (406-252-5611), Billings, CBS.

KSVI TV Channel 6 (406-652-4743), Billings, ABC.

KULR TV Channel 8 (406-656-8000), Billings, NBC.

KBZK TV Channel 7 (406-586-3280), Bozeman, CBS.

KHMT TV Channel 4 (406-652-7366), Billings, FOX

KWBM TV Channel 31 (406-652-7457), Billings, CW.

KUSM TV Channel 9 (406-994-3437; www.montana.edu), Bozeman, PBS affiliate based at Montana State University campuses in Billings and Bozeman.

The Lamar Valley in the northern range is often called the "Serengeti of Yellowstone." It's a prime place for viewing such wildlife as wolves, bears, bison and elk. National Park Service

KJWY TV Channel 2 (307-733-2066), Jackson, NBC.

KBEO TV Channel 11 (847-674-0864; www.kbeo.net), Jackson, America One affiliate takes feed from KBIF in Idaho Falls/Pocatello.

K13FX TV Channel 13, Jackson, ABC affiliate takes feed from KIFI in Idaho Falls.

K50BL TV Channel 50, Jackson, PBS.

K56BT TV Channel 56, Jackson, ABC affiliate with feed from KTWO in Casper.

MULTIMEDIA

Customized guides to Yellowstone are available with podcasts that can be downloaded free from **iTunes** or at www.gov/yell. "Inside Yellowstone" features rangers talking about the park, a map and history.

PETS

Yellowstone National Park: Pets are allowed in Yellowstone, with restrictions. They must be caged, crated, kept in a vehicle or on a leash no longer than 6 feet. They must be kept within 100 feet of roadways, camping areas or parking areas. Pets may not be left unattended, even if tied up. They can be with you in cabins, but not hotels.

    Grand Teton National Park: Pets are allowed but must be restrained at all times and are not permitted on hiking trails, inside visitor centers or in other facilities.

POSTAL SERVICE

Yellowstone National Park: The main post office is at Mammoth Hot Springs. Summer facilities are at Old Faithful, Lake Village, Canyon Village and Grant Village.

Grand Teton National Park: Moose, Moran and Kelly.

Post Offices in Gateway Communities

Ashton, ID: 208-652-3976, 500 Fremont St.

Cody, WY: 307-527-7161, 1301 Stampede Ave.

Cooke City, MT: 406-838-2210, 209 US Hwy. 212.

Driggs, ID: 208-354-2330, 70 S. Main St.

Dubois, WY: 307-455-2735, 804 Ramshorn St.

Gardiner, MT: 406-848-7579, 707 Scott St. West.

Island Park, ID: 208-558-7476, 3978 US Hwy. 20.

Jackson, WY: 307-739-1740, 220 W. Pearl St.

Jackson, WY: 307-733-3650, 1070 Maple Way.

Kelly, WY: 307-733-8884, 4486 Lower Gros Ventre Rd.

Macks Inn, ID: 208-558-7070, 4110 S. Big Springs Loop.

Moran, WY: 307-543-2527, 1 Central St.

Tetonia, ID: 208-456-2211, 115 S. Main St.

Teton Village, WY: 307-734-9599, 3230 McCollister Dr.

Victor, ID: 208-787-2233, 92 S. Main St.

Wapiti, WY: 307-527-7434, 3189 North Fork Hwy. (west of Cody).

West Yellowstone, MT: 406-646-7704, 209 Grizzly Ave.

REAL ESTATE

So you've spent a week or two in the Greater Yellowstone ecosystem and you're ready to pull up stakes and live the good life? The good life it is, but it won't come cheaply. The area has been discovered. Even the subprime mortgage fiasco hasn't been felt in the Northern Rockies like it has elsewhere. Now, if you're from California or some of the pricier areas on the East Coast, chances are you won't blink at the cost of land and housing surrounding the parks, except perhaps for the million-dollar trophy homes. It is here, at the Big Sky playground for the über-rich called the Yellowstone Club, that the most expensive home in world history is under construction. For a mere $155 million, this 53,000-square-foot stone and wood starter home on 160 acres—complete with a private ski slope, heated driveways and 8,000-bottle wine cellar—can be yours.

It doesn't get much better downstream: The median home price in Jackson was $1.2 million in the summer of 2007, double what it had been four years earlier. Montana's Paradise Valley isn't terribly far behind. In Bozeman, considered the best "micropolitan" city in the nation by BizJournal.com, it's about $270,000. West Yellowstone? $340,000 and climbing. And the prices in those towns have caused a spillover, dramatically raising real estate values in once-middle-of-nowhere venues like Idaho's Teton Valley, Montana's Madison Valley and Wyoming's Wind River Valley as the hub communities move beyond the reach of even the upper middle class.

Check a newspaper in each community for listings and realtors.

ROAD SERVICES

A broken-down vehicle doesn't have to ruin your vacation. Repair services are available in Yellowstone at Canyon Village, Fishing Bridge, Grand Village and Tower Junction. Mechanics are also at the ready in all the gateway communities.

Road Closures

Only the road between Mammoth and Cooke City remains plowed and open all year, largely because it's the only way out for residents, snowmobilers and wolf watchers in Cooke City and Silver Gate; US 212 isn't plowed in winter east of Cooke City. The remainder of Yellowstone's roads close in early November and reopen usually by late April or early May, depending on weather conditions and plowing progress. As noted earlier, April is the ideal time for road bicycling in Yellowstone, before the roads open to auto traffic. Dunraven Pass is usually the last to be plowed. Road construction is always an issue in Yellowstone in the summer as crews work to rebuild old, weather-beaten asphalt. Check the park's newspapers for updates or call 307-344-7381 before your trip.

The three primary US highways that go north-south through Grand Teton—26, 89 and 191—as well as US 26/287 east to the Wind River Valley are plowed and remain open all year. The paved highway north to Yellowstone is plowed to Flagg Ranch. The Moose–Wilson Road is closed in winter; it's plowed from WY 22 to Teton Village.

Road Reports

Idaho: 511 or 888-432-7623; http://itd.idaho.gov/highways.
Montana: 511 or 800-226-7623; www.mdt.mt.gov/travinfo.
Wyoming: 511 or 888-996-7623; www.wyoroad.com/info.

Speed Limits

Most roads in the parks are posted at 45 mph and strictly enforced, though the speeds are reduced in congested areas. The only exception in Yellowstone is US 191 in the northwest corner, where the standard speed limit of 70 mph on the highway is reduced to 55. The same highway in Grand Teton is 55 mph.

John D. Rockefeller Jr. Memorial Parkway

The 8-mile highway connecting Yellowstone and Grand Teton is named for the wealthy philanthropist who made Grand Teton and other national parks possible. Congress dedicated 24,000 acres in his name in 1972, including the highway. The Rockefeller Parkway actually extends from the southern border of Grand Teton to West Thumb in Yellowstone. Speed limit is 55 mph.

TOURIST INFORMATION

Idaho (208-334-2470, 800-635-7820; www.visitid.org)
Montana (406-841-2870, 800-VISIT-MT; www.visitmt.com)
Wyoming (307-777-7777, 800-225-5996; www.wyomingtourism.org)

VISITOR CENTERS

Yellowstone National Park

Canyon (307-242-2550) traditionally features natural history and geology exhibits, with book sales in the lobby. In May 2007, the Canyon Visitor Education Center opened two floors of interactive exhibits about Yellowstone's supervolcano. Open Memorial Day weekend to early October.

Fishing Bridge (307-242-2450) is famous for its "parkitecture" as the prototype for national park buildings. It offers animal and geological exhibits and has books for sale. Open Memorial Day weekend to late September.

Grant Village (307-242-2650) sheds insight on Yellowstone's fire history, most notably the massive 1988 blazes that burned one-third of the park. A film called *Ten Years after the Fire* is a highlight. Open late Memorial Day weekend to late September.

Madison Information Station (307-344-2821) has information and a bookstore. Included is a junior ranger station with programs for children ages 5–12. Open early June to late September.

Mammoth Albright Visitor Center (307-344-2263) is the park's headquarters, named after the first superintendent, Horace Albright. This old stone building features a theater and animal exhibits. Open year-round.

Norris Geyser Basin Museum (307-344-2812) has a bookstore and exhibits about thermal features. Open Memorial Day weekend to late September.

Norris Museum of the National Park Ranger shows the evolution of the park ranger. Watch a video and hobnob with former rangers who volunteer here. Open Memorial Day weekend to late September.

Old Faithful (307-545-2750) features books, maps, videos and the clock forecasting its namesake geyser's next eruption. It was relocated temporarily to the Old Faithful Lodge in 2007 for construction. Open late April to early November, then mid-December until March.

Grand Teton National Park

Colter Bay (307-739-3594) opens from 8 AM to 7 PM during peak time from early May to early September and from 8 AM to 5 PM in late spring and early fall. It features the Indian Arts Museum. Demonstrations, tours and crafts are exhibited much of the summer.

Flagg Ranch (307-543-2372) is open from 9 AM to 5:30 PM from June to August and has irregular hours from mid-December to mid-March. It is between the two parks, along the John D. Rockefeller Memorial Parkway, 16 miles north of Colter Bay.

Moose (307-739-3399) is open from 8 AM to 7 PM in the summer and from 8 AM to 5 PM spring, fall and winter. It's at the south end and serves as park headquarters. The only day it closes is Christmas. The new Grand Teton Discovery & Visitor Center opened across the street from the original visitor center in mid-August 2007. It features exhibits, a relief map of the park and a close look at the area's endangered species.

Jenny Lake (307-739-3343) stays open from 8 AM to 7 PM all summer, then 8 AM TO 5 PM in September. It's 8 miles north of Moose at the junction of Teton Park Road and also is the location of a ranger station.

WORSHIP SERVICES

Visitors of all Christian denominations will find churches representing their faiths in all of the gateway communities surrounding Yellowstone and Grand Teton. Protestant and Catholic churches are common. Especially prolific, because of the area's proximity to Utah, is the Church of Jesus Christ of Latter-day Saints (Mormon). Eastern Idaho and northern Wyoming are heavily Mormon, with chapels in each little community. Jackson has 26 churches covering a broad spectrum, including a Jewish community church, Jehovah's Witness, Friends/Quaker, Christian Science and Charismatic. The closest mosques are in Salt Lake City, Boise and Laramie.

Yellowstone National Park

Yellowstone Park Chapel (307-344-7430) offers interdenominational Christian services at Mammoth in conjunction with the Gardiner Community Church, 318 Main St. From Memorial Day through Labor Day, services are at 9 AM in Gardiner and 10:30 AM at the Yellowstone Park Chapel. In winter, the park chapel services are at 9 AM and the Gardiner services at 11:15 AM.

Grand Teton National Park

Chapel of the Transfiguration (307-733-2603) has Episcopal Holy Communion at 8 and 10 AM each Sunday from Memorial Day through the last Sunday in September.

Chapel of Sacred Heart (307-733-2516) offers Catholic mass at 5:30 PM Saturdays and 8 and 9:30 AM Sundays from June through August.

Church of Jesus Christ of Latter-Day Saints (307-733-6337) has services at Jackson Lake Lodge.

Miscellany: Interdenominational services are conducted at park campgrounds. Check a visitor center for updated information.

IF TIME IS SHORT

If at all possible, don't let time be short. You need at least a week to get a sense of what Yellowstone, Grand Teton and Jackson Hole are all about. That said, if you're just passing through, it's possible to experience the major attractions in a day or two.

One Day in Yellowstone

It's virtually impossible to take in both parks in one day without stopping. Traffic slows to a crawl at busy junctions and frequent wildlife jams. If you have a day in Yellowstone, do the Grand Loop—plus a jaunt into the Lamar Valley, time permitting. If you're coming from the south, stop for a peek at Lewis Falls and then move on to Old Faithful for the obligatory eruption and breakfast at the lodge. Head east to Yellowstone Lake and stop for a tour of the historic Lake Hotel. Continue northward through the Hayden Valley and look for wildlife jams. Make a point of stopping at the Grand Canyon of the Yellowstone; you can't go wrong on either rim of the canyon. Have lunch at Canyon Village and take a gander at Tower Falls before moving on to Tower Junction. It's worth a stop at Roosevelt Lodge to get an Old West flavor. Check your time here. If you're moving along, head northeast toward Lamar Valley and keep an eye out for the yellow Nissan Xterra driven by "The Wolf Man," aka Rick McIntyre, who tracks wolves. Look for bison, elk, coyotes, beaver and perhaps even bears and wolves. Turn around at the Yellowstone Institute and return to Tower. Drive to Mammoth for a brisk walk among the travertine terraces before having dinner. Close the day with the drive to Norris and back to Old Faithful, stopping at Roaring Mountain and Geyser Basin if you've still got enough daylight.

One day in Grand Teton/Jackson Hole

Start with breakfast at the Bunnery in Jackson and a tour of the faux Old West shops near Jackson's fabled Town Square. Hit the Jackson Hole and Greater Yellowstone Visitor Center at the Elk Refuge, then head north along the base of the Tetons. Take in the boat ride at Jenny Lake and hike to Hidden Falls or Inspiration Point. Upon returning to the highway, go north for a stop at Jackson Lake Lodge. Walk up the stops to the lobby and the famed picture window framing the Tetons behind Jackson Lake, then watch the moose in Willow Flats while having lunch. Continue north for a stop at Colter Bay and then Moran Junction. Snap a few photos of the famous shot at Oxbow Bend. Turn around and return south, taking the Teton Road.

Must-Sees in Yellowstone

Boiling River
Fountain Paintpot
Geyser Basin
Grand Canyon of the Yellowstone
Hayden Valley
Lake Hotel
Lamar Valley
Lewis Falls
Madison River
Mammoth Hot Springs
Old Faithful and Old Faithful Inn
Petrified Tree
Roaring Mountain
Steamboat Geyser
Tower Falls
Undine Falls
Yellowstone Association Institute
Yellowstone Lake

Must-Sees in Grand Teton

Chapel of the Transfiguration
Colter Bay Village
Cunningham Cabin
Hidden Falls
Jackson Lake Lodge
Jenny Lake
Jenny Lake Lodge
Oxbow Bend
Snake River Overlook

Must-Sees in Jackson Hole

Jackson
Jackson Hole/Greater Yellowstone Visitor Center
Jackson National Fish Hatchery
National Elk Refuge
National Museum of Wildlife Art
Snow King Mountain
Teton Village

Trumpeter swans, one of the rarest of native North American birds, have found refuge on the waters of Yellowstone, the Tetons and Henry's Fork of the Snake River.

Index

U

V